A-LEVEL
AND AS-LEVEL

SOCIOLOGY

Stephen R. Harris

LONGMAN A AND AS-LEVEL REVISE GUIDES

Series editors:
Geoff Black and Stuart Wall

Titles available:
Accounting
Art and Design
Biology*
Business Studies
Chemistry*
Computer Science
Economics*
English
French
Government and politics
Geography*
German
Law
Mathematics*
Modern History
Physics*
Psychology
Sociology*
*New editions

Addison Wesley Longman Ltd.
Edinburgh Gate, Harlow,
Essex CM20 2JE, England
and Associated Companies throughout the world.

© Longman Group Limited 1991
© This edition Addison Wesley Longman Limited 1996

First Published 1991
Second Edition 1996

ISBN 0582 27691-8

British Library Cataloguing in Publication Data
A catalogue record for this title available from the British Library

Set in 10/12 pt Century Old Style by 33

Produced by Longman Singapore Publishers Pte
Printed in Singapore

CONTENTS

EDITOR'S PREFACE

Longman A-level Revise Guides, written by experienced examiners and teachers, aim to give you the best possible foundation for success in your course. Each book in the series encourages thorough study and a full understanding of the concepts involved, and is designed as a subject companion and study aid to be used throughout the course.

Many candidates at A-level fail to achieve the grades which their ability deserves, owing to such problems as the lack of a structured revision strategy, or unsound examination technique. This series aims to remedy such deficiencies, by encouraging a realistic and disciplined approach in preparing for and taking exams.

The largely self-contained nature of the chapters gives the book a flexibility which you can use to your advantage. After starting with the background to the A, AS-level and Scottish Higher Courses and details of the syllabus coverage, you can read all other chapters selectively, in any order appropriate to the stage you have reached in your course.

Geoff Black and Stuart Wall

ACKNOWLEDGEMENTS

I am indebted to the following examination boards for permission to reproduce their questions. The answers given are not the only possible answers and are entirely my own responsibility.

Associated Examining Board
University of London Examinations and Assessment Council
Welsh Joint Education Committee
University of Cambridge Local Examinations Syndicate
University of Oxford Delegacy of Local Examinations
Northern Examinations and Assessment Board
Scottish Examination Board

My thanks go to Geoff Black and Stuart Wall for their encouragement, Alan Ducklin, Hal Westergaard, Suzanne Collinson and Jim Cooper for their critical comments, Patrick Toal for teaching me word processing in ten minutes and the students and ex-students from Redbridge College who allowed me to use their answers.

I also wish to thank Melanie, Sarah, Lily and Prudence for tolerating my neglecting of them during the writing of this book.

1

THE SYLLABUSES AND EXAMINATIONS

STUDYING SOCIOLOGY

TOPICS AND SYLLABUSES

METHODS OF ASSESSMENT

NAMES AND ADDRESSES OF THE EXAM BOARDS

GETTING STARTED

Who is this book for?

This Revise Guide is intended to be a useful tool for students taking an examination course in Sociology at A-level or AS-level. It also covers aspects of the Scottish Certificate of Education higher grade in Modern Studies. The book offers a systematic review of the major sociological issues covered by the various syllabuses, gives guidance on how to study sociology for examinations and provides a large number of real examination questions. These questions have outline answers or full model answers provided by the author or an answer written by an A-level student accompanied by an examiner's comments and mark.

How should this book be used?

It is intended that the book should be useful throughout your course.

- **In the beginning**

  The Table of Contents indicates the major areas of sociology which are studied. Each chapter identifies the major issues to be considered for a particular topic. This should guide you in your reading from other sources.

- **In the middle**

  Studying sociology is not just a question of memorising lots of facts and theories. It also involves learning how to apply your knowledge to sociological problems and how to evaluate sociological evidence. You should attempt to respond to the questions in outline form or to give a complete answer. Your answers can then be compared with the examiners' suggestions. If you are not satisfied, you can then refer to the appropriate material in this book, in a textbook or in your own notes.

- **At the end**

  This book has been written very much with examination success in mind. There are suggestions on study skills, including revision. The summaries of sociological approaches and studies in each chapter can help you compile revision notes, and there are over 90 questions to choose from for practice and to assess your progress. You can see what the examiners are looking for in answer to questions, by reading either the outline answers or the full model answers. You can also see how other actual students have attempted past questions, and what an examiner thinks are the strengths and weaknesses of those answers.

STUDYING SOCIOLOGY

ESSENTIAL PRINCIPLES

Sociology has become increasingly popular as an A-level subject, even during a period marked by a fall in the numbers of 16 to 18-year-olds in the population. Many candidates are adults returning to study who find it both interesting and useful as a preparation for higher education or for various kinds of professional training and qualifications. This good news for teachers and Examination Boards is matched by the good news for students, namely that the quality of examination answers is improving and so too are the grades awarded to candidates.

In 1998 all three Boards will offer A/S-level and coursework options.

The division of sociology into distinct topics is a fairly arbitrary exercise, so I have been guided by the various syllabuses in producing separate chapters. The chapters are not intended to erect barriers between the topics, as some issues are discussed in more than one chapter. There are themes which run through all the topics, such as theoretical and methodological issues and the various forms of inequality (including class and gender).

TOPICS AND SYLLABUSES

This book covers some or all of the knowledge and skills necessary to study the following syllabuses for 1997 and after 1998.

- **A-LEVEL**
  AEB
  Interboard
  NEAB
- **AS-LEVEL**
  AEB
  Interboard
  NEAB

- **SCOTTISH CERTIFICATE OF EDUCATION HIGHER GRADE**
  Modern Studies

Topic	Chapter number	AEB A	AEB A/S	INTER A	INTER A/S	NEAB A	SCOT H
Social class	3	✓	✓	✓	✓	✓	✓
Race & ethnicity	4	✓	✓	✓	✓	✓	✓
Gender	5	✓	✓	✓	✓	✓	✓
Age	6	✓	✓	✓	✓	0	0
Power & politics	7	✓	0	✓	0	✓	✓
World sociology & development	8	✓	✓	✓	✓	✓	0
Locality, community & urbanisation	9	✓	✓	✓	✓	✓	0
Family	10	✓	0	✓	✓	✓	✓
Education	11	✓	0	✓	0	✓	0
Work	12	✓	0	✓	0	✓	✓
Organisations	13	✓	0	✓	0	✓	0
Professions	14	✓	0	✓	0	✓	0
Religion	15	✓	0	✓	0	✓	0
Mass media	16	✓	✓	✓	✓	✓	✓
Poverty & welfare	17	✓	✓	✓	✓	✓	✓
Health	18	✓	✓	✓	✓	✓	✓
Deviance	19	✓	✓	✓	0	✓	✓
Suicide & official statistics	20	✓	✓	✓	0	✓	0
Methods	21	✓	✓	✓	✓	✓	0
Sociological theories	22	✓	✓	✓	✓	✓	0
The nature of sociology	23	✓	✓	✓	✓	✓	0

Table 1.1 Examination syllabuses by topic and chapter (1997)

Topic	Chapter number	AEB A	AEB A/S	INTER A	INTER A/S	NEAB A	NEAB A/S	SCOT H
Social class	3	✓	✓	✓	✓	✓	✓	✓
Race & ethnicity	4	✓	✓	✓	✓	✓	✓	✓
Gender	5	✓	✓	✓	✓	✓	✓	✓
Age	6	✓	✓	✓	✓	✓	✓	
Power & politics	7	✓		✓	✓	✓	✓	✓
World sociology & development	8	✓		✓	✓	✓	✓	
Locality, community & urbanisation	9	✓		✓	✓	✓	✓	✓
Family	10	✓	✓	✓	✓	✓	✓	
Education	11	✓	✓	✓	✓	✓	✓	✓
Work	12	✓	✓	✓	✓	✓	✓	
Organisations	13	✓						
Professions	14	✓		✓	✓			
Religion	15	✓		✓	✓	✓	✓	
Mass media	16	✓		✓	✓	✓	✓	✓
Poverty & welfare	17	✓		✓	✓	✓	✓	✓
Health	18	✓		✓	✓	✓	✓	✓
Deviance	19	✓		✓	✓	✓	✓	✓
Suicide & official statistics	20	✓	✓	✓	✓	✓	✓	
Methods	21	✓	✓	✓	✓	✓	✓	
Sociological theories	22	✓	✓	✓	✓	✓	✓	
The nature of sociology	23	✓	✓	✓	✓	✓		

Table 1.2 Examination syllabuses by topic and chapter (1998 and after)

Tables 1.1 (1997) and 1.2 (1998 and after) show which syllabuses offer which topics and tell you the chapter number where that topic is covered in this book.

Method of assessment	AEB A	AEB A/S	INTER A	INTER A/S	NEAB A	SCOT H
Essay	✓	✓	✓	✓	✓	✓
Data response and/or structured question	✓	✓	✓	✓	✓	✓
Design research				option	✓	
Coursework	option (25%)			option (20%)		

Table 1.3 Examination syllabuses by methods of assessment (1997)

Method of assessment	AEB A	AEB A/S	INTER A	INTER A/S	NEAB A	NEAB A/S	SCOT H
Essay	✓		✓	✓	✓	✓	✓
Data response	✓	✓	✓	✓	✓	✓	✓
Design research			option	✓			
Coursework	option (20%)		option (20%)		option (16.66%)		
Modular syllabus available	✓		✓		✓		

Table 1.4 Examination syllabuses by methods of assessment (1998 and after) NB: The options available are now quite complex. Study the syllabuses very carefully and seek advice on which to choose.

METHODS OF ASSESSMENT

The methods of assessment also vary. Boards have different aims and objectives for the syllabuses and use different types of question. Table 1.3 analyses the examination syllabuses according to their methods of assessment.

TYPES OF QUESTION

Essays

These are required for all the examinations, although their domination of examinations is now challenged by other methods of assessment.

Structured questions

Here a whole question is broken down into a series of components which test different abilities, e.g. knowledge, application and evaluation. Usually the mark for each component is provided and this indicates the suitable length of an answer.

Stimulus questions and data-response questions

Here candidates are presented with a stimulus in the form of a written passage, graph, table or even a map or cartoon. There then follows a series of questions. In *stimulus* questions the data presented is intended to suggest possible responses whereas in a *data-response* question detailed reference to the material is required, e.g. interpretation of statistics.

Coursework

This is currently available for only two of the syllabuses. In 1998 coursework will be available for all three A-level syllabuses. In both of the current cases a single piece of independent research is required. It may be initially marked by your teacher and then moderated by the Board.

MARKING SCHEMES AND OBJECTIVES

The Examination Boards are becoming increasingly open about the methods of assessment used by their examiners. Some have made sample marking schemes available, particularly where new syllabuses are being introduced. For more information, write to the Board or ask your teacher.

The abilities which are rewarded and their relative importance is useful information. In general the list is likely to include:

- **Knowledge** of studies and theories.
- **Understanding** of data.
- **Interpretation** of data.
- **Application** of concepts and theories to actual problems.
- **Analysis** of sociological issues and personal experience.
- **Evaluation** of theories, methods and arguments.

All A-levels must include a subject core approved by SCAA. This is a Government body which supervises both syllabuses and examination procedures. The sociology core specifies skills as well as knowledge. Candidates taking A-levels are also assessed on the quality of language used. The way in which this is done should be indicated in syllabuses and/or mark schemes which are available from the examination boards. Since 1991 the AEB syllabus has involved the examination of three skill areas. These are:

	marks on data-response question	marks on essay
1 Knowledge and understanding.	5	9
2 Interpretation and application.	10	9
3 Evaluation.	10	9
	Total 25	Up to total of 25

This should make it clear that you cannot do well just by learning prepared descriptions of studies. You must answer the set question; this will enable you to gain marks for each of the skills. Questions frequently instruct you to 'Assess' or 'Evaluate' or 'Critically examine', indicating the need for evaluation. Data-response questions which ask you to refer to items are testing interpretation and evaluation as well as knowledge.

Knowledge and understanding

You should show that you know and understand sociological concepts, studies, methods, theories and the main arguments of sociological debates. You can demonstrate understanding by presenting evidence and arguments in a logical and coherent way. You do not need to know studies in minute detail. Particularly for the data-response questions you need a broad understanding of major issues.

Interpretation and application

These skills are concerned with how effectively you can use knowledge to answer a set question. Interpretation on data-response questions usually involves using data in the form of text, tables or graphs to answer a question. Calculations are rare and usually very simple. Interpretation and application on the essay paper might involve choosing an appropriate study (maybe from a different topic) and using it to answer the question.

You will often have the opportunity to apply sociological theories or your knowledge of methods to a specific topic area. You may also apply current affairs and personal experience as long as they are used to make a sociological point. The *Religion* chapter (15) shows how classical sociological theories can be examined in the light of recent events.

Evaluation

This is being critical. Evaluation may take the form of a specific critical point or a more general evaluative framework in an answer. Often you can use alternative theories or approaches to criticise a particular explanation. For example, use feminist approaches to criticise functionalist views on the family.

Criticism can be positive as well as negative. You should get into the habit of considering the strengths and weaknesses of methods, studies and theories.

Weak evaluation often takes the form of listing alternatives. This should be improved by linking arguments. Good evaluative words include: *however, whereas, on the other hand, this can be challenged by*, etc.

The basis of criticism can be:

- **Empirical** (factual, based on evidence).
- **Methodological** (the way data was gathered and interpreted).
- **Theoretical** (challenging assumptions of, say, consensus or conflict approaches).
- **Ideological** (where disagreement is based on value).

Incidentally, to gain maximum marks you need *not* achieve perfection or be as competent as the Chief Examiner. The AEB standard is based on the best that could be achieved by an 18-year-old student who has studied the subject for two years. Therefore, full marks *are* attainable for part or whole questions.

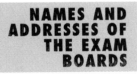
NAMES AND ADDRESSES OF THE EXAM BOARDS

Associated Examining Board (AEB)
Stag Hill House
Guildford
Surrey GU2 5XJ

University of Cambridge Local Examinations Syndicate (UCLES)
Syndicate Buildings
1 Hills Road
Cambridge CB1 2EU

Northern Examinations and Assessment Board (NEAB)
Devas St
Manchester M15 6EX

University of London Examinations and Assessment Council (ULEAC)
Stewart House
32 Russell Square
London WC1B 5DN

Northern Ireland Council for Curriculum, Examinations and Assessment
(NICCEA)
Beechill House
42 Beechill Road
Belfast BT8 4RS

Oxford and Cambridge Schools Examination Board (OCSEB)
Purbeck House
Purbeck Road
Cambridge CB2 2PU

Oxford Delegacy of Local Examinations (ODLE)
Ewert Place
Summertown
Oxford OX2 7BZ

Scottish Examination Board (SEB)
Ironmills Road
Dalkeith
Midlothian EH22 1LE

Welsh Joint Education Committee (WJEC)
245 Western Avenue
Cardiff CF5 2YX

CHAPTER 2

STUDY, EXAMINATION AND ASSESSMENT TECHNIQUES

GETTING STARTED

Doing well in a sociology course involves a great deal more than learning an enormous number of facts and theories. The key abilities which distinguish good students from weaker students are application and evaluation. Your *knowledge* of concepts, theories and studies must be *applied* to meet the demands of questions, whether in class discussion, homework or examination. *Evaluation* of the evidence, methods and theories is the skill most highly regarded by examiners. Therefore during your course, as well as attempting to acquire a comprehensive knowledge of sociological issues, you must practise these skills of application and evaluation in order to obtain a good pass.

This chapter will provide what is often commonsense advice about the whole study process, from the beginning of the course to the last ten minutes of your final examination. My excuse for repeating some things you may already know is that teachers and examiners continually encounter students who make the same sorts of errors in organising their work and sitting the exam, and thus do not realise their full potential.

AN INTRODUCTION TO SOCIOLOGY

DEVELOPING SKILLS

REVISING

THE EXAMINATION

COURSEWORK

AN INTRODUCTION TO SOCIOLOGY

ESSENTIAL PRINCIPLES

Place six sociologists in a room and they will probably give you twelve explanations of what is going on. Disagreement between sociologists is the basis of most questions and can provide a framework for answers.

The reasons for disagreement do not just depend on the whims of the individual sociologist but can be seen as more systematic. Differences in perspectives, approaches, methods and theories can be identified.

- **Perspectives** are the different ways sociologists perceive the social world.
- **Approaches** are the different ways sociologists choose to define problems in sociology, decide what to study, and how.
- **Methods** are the different ways of gathering and interpreting information.
- **Theories** are explanations; e.g. why it is that certain patterns of behaviour are observed.

Perspectives

The conventional division of perspectives distinguishes a number of 'types'.

- **ACTION perspectives**
  These see the construction of the social world as being the result of a process whereby individuals attribute meaning to behaviour and situations. Society is therefore seen as being made by individuals. Theories associated with these perspectives include Social Action theory, symbolic interactionism and ethnomethodology.
- **STRUCTURALIST perspectives**
  These see the social world as existing independently of individuals whose behaviour is constrained by external social forces. Society is seen as making the individual. Structuralist perspectives are sub-divided into:
  - CONSENSUS perspectives, which see societies as harmonious with order based on shared values. The dominant theory here is structural-functionalism.
  - CONFLICT perspectives, which see conflict as normal, and order being imposed by the strong on the weak. Theories associated with conflict perspectives include Marxism, Weberian theories and feminism.
- **POST-MODERNISM** rejects the existence of single grand explanations.

Approaches

These are different ways of defining sociological problems and of deciding what should be studied, and how. The major distinction is between positivist and interpretive approaches.

- **POSITIVIST approaches** involve the search for *cause and effect* laws, using methods similar to those employed in the natural sciences.
- **INTERPRETIVE approaches** involve the search for the *subjective meanings* which people give to behaviour. These are also referred to as **phenomenological** approaches.

There are real, but not inevitable, links between perspectives, theories, approaches and methods. Structuralists tend to adopt a positivist approach and those who have an action perspective tend to adopt an interpretive approach. However, although this makes answering questions more straightforward, it is an oversimplification as sociologists do not necessarily see themselves as belonging to distinctive schools which limit their interests or research. These rather difficult issues are discussed in the later chapters dealing with *Suicide, Sociological theories, Methods*, and *The nature of sociology*.

There are also approaches and methods associated with feminism.

DEVELOPING SKILLS

Learning to *organise* your thoughts so that you provide informed, coherent and critical sociological arguments requires practice. In class you should take every opportunity to ask questions and to take part in discussions. Try to *use* sociological concepts and terminology wherever relevant, and to answer the *specific* question put to you rather than to display all your knowledge on the subject in a rambling account.

Reading can be guided by the topic or issue you are covering in class, and also by previous examination questions. These can help you identify what the examiners see as important *aspects* of the various topic areas. You can then undertake further reading on these aspects to give a well-rounded view. Examination essays usually contain less than 1,000 words, so it is not necessary to be able to write in detail about a single study, however important or interesting. Many answers on the class structure of modern Britain suffer from epic accounts of the 'Luton Studies' at the expense of competing and often more recent and relevant material.

A useful aid in organising your thoughts might be a *summary chart* on a particular topic or issue. On one or two sides of A4 paper you might write briefly on the following:

- Key terms and definitions.
- Major theoretical arguments and viewpoints.
- Major empirical studies and findings.

You might then look at past questions set on that topic and use your summary material as a basis for writing *outline answers* to those questions. This will help you see how important it is to emphasise different aspects of your knowledge when faced with different questions.

It is also useful to practise writing *full answers* under examination conditions, i.e. without notes and giving yourself the same time as in the exam itself. You can always review your work later, this time with your notes and book open.

Text books

There are some excellent *textbooks* available for A-level Sociology. Your teacher will usually indicate which texts to use, since some are better suited to particular syllabuses than others. However, do try to use various texts on a particular topic in order to get a broader view, rather than slavishly to follow a single book. The following textbooks are widely used:

- *Human Societies*, G. Hurd *et al.* (RKP).
- *Introductory Sociology* (2nd edition), Bilton *et al.* (Macmillan).
- *Sociology: Themes and Perspectives* (4th edition), M. Haralambos with M. Holbourn (HarperCollins).
- *Sociology* (2nd edition), A. Giddens (Polity Press).
- *A New Introduction to Sociology* (3rd edition), M. O'Donnell (Nelson).
- *Sociology for A-level. A skills-based approach*, T. Lawson (Collins Educational).
- *An Introduction to Sociology. Feminist Perspectives*, P. Abbott and C. Wallace (Routledge).

Topic books

As well as textbooks which try to cover the whole syllabus there are several series of *topic books* which cover particular areas of the syllabus. These are particularly useful where there are gaps in textbooks or where the topic book is considerably more modern than the textbook. However, the most popular textbooks have all been revised and updated since their original publication. An example of a series of topic books is:

- *Sociology in Focus* (Longman). Separate titles cover Crime, Education, Methodology, Religion, Gender, Media, Work and Unemployment, Suicide, Knowledge.

Reading lists

Examination boards provide *reading lists* which may give you guidance on useful sources. The addresses of the Boards are listed on pp. 5–6 of this book. Do, however, remember that the reading lists are suggestions for teachers as well as students, so that you should consult your teacher about the value and degree of difficulty of any particular book. There may well be some original works included in the list which you would not be expected to read in their entirety.

Readers

There are also *readers*, which contain *extracts* from significant original works. These may provide a useful source of relevant quotations. Often they contain an introduction from the editor, reviewing a series of contributions, which provides a helpful overview of a broad range of material.

Examples of readers include:

- *New Introductory Reader in Sociology* (2nd edition), M. O'Donnell (Nelson).
- *An Introduction to Sociology: A Reader*, edited by R. Bocock, P. Hamilton, K. Thompson, A. Watson (Polity Press).
- *Perspectives on Society*, edited by R. Meighan, I. Shelton and T. Marks (Nelson).

A number of *journals* provide a convenient way of reading around a topic and of getting advice for tackling sociological problems.

- *Sociology Review.* This is aimed at A-level students of sociology and politics. It is very readable and contains both new material and simplified accounts of older debates.
- *The Social Science Teacher.* Although primarily directed at the teacher, this also contains good reviews of the research on particular topics and shows how sociology can be taught to, and thus learned by, students.
- *Society Today.* This is a supplement for sociology students found in *New Statesman and Society* (previously *New Society*).
- *Social Trends.* This is published annually by the Central Statistical Office and is available in most town reference libraries. It gives a detailed breakdown of patterns of household wealth, income and expenditure, together with demographic, housing and social trends.

Serious newspapers often publish useful tables or provide accounts of government survey data, thereby updating textbook material on sizes of households, illegitimacy, crime, employment, incomes, etc. Do cut out any such data and file it under a suitable topic heading for later use.

- The 1991 census is available as a CD Rom.

REVISING

In order to revise effectively and efficiently you must be familiar with your syllabus and with past papers. Choosing how much of the syllabus to revise, and in what depth, is a crucial activity. The syllabus may help by indicating that there is a *minimum number of topics* which can be studied and yet still provide you with sufficient questions for examination purposes.

For instance, the AEB syllabus states that candidates must study:

1 Theory and methods for both papers.
2 At least *two* from the *paper one* topics; i.e. family, education, stratification, work and leisure and culture and identity.
3 At least *three* from the *paper two* topics; i.e. deviance, development, mass media, community, organisations, power and politics, religion and health, welfare and poverty.

Restricting your revision to just the minimum is, of course, a dangerous strategy. At best you will have no choice and so will be unable to avoid a difficult or unusual question. At worst you may find that an unpredictable interpretation of the syllabus by the examiners means that you cannot complete the necessary number of questions. One strategy might be to learn the minimum *plus one* topic for each paper fairly thoroughly, and to learn one more topic for each paper in a more superficial manner, for insurance. There are, however, no hard-and-fast rules. The more able the student, the fewer the number of topics which need be prepared, since revised material can usually be adapted to meet the needs of a range of possible questions. One way to test if you *have* covered sufficient topics is to see if you could answer the appropriate number of questions on the recent exam papers without difficulty. Remember that questions often benefit from the insights you have gained from *more than one* topic area of the syllabus; gender and class, for example, are issues which provide a basis for discussing aspects of many topic areas.

Having chosen your topics for revision, it may be worth returning to our idea of *summary charts.* You could distil the essence from the major approaches and studies you have encountered, and record the key points on a side of A4 paper, say, or on cards. Having the key points listed in this way will be a useful 'memory jogger' to the more detailed expositions in your notes.

You might try organising your notes within a 'perspective framework'. This involves identifying the theories and/or approaches which have been applied to a topic, citing examples of research, and indicating various critiques and criticisms as appropriate.

For example, explaining inequalities in health might follow this plan:

1 Positivist studies.
2 Criticism.
3 Interactionist studies.
4 Criticism.
5 Marxist studies.
6 Criticism, including other conflict theories.
7 Functionalist studies.
8 Criticism.

This kind of structure works well with questions that ask 'How have sociological approaches to the study of ... changed?' or 'Critically examine sociological explanations of ...'

It is less appropriate for questions which ask you to 'Compare and contrast ...' or 'Examine the similarities and differences between ...' These questions benefit from a *point-by-point* comparison.

This would be true of the following question: 'Compare and contrast the approaches of Marx and Weber to the role of religions in society.' A first sentence might begin: 'Marxists see religious belief as shaped by the economic substructure, whereas Weber saw religious belief influencing the economic organisation of society.' Explain this and then go on and discuss their different views on religion and social change.

> Revision should be an *active* process.

Above all, your revision should be an *active* process. Use the concepts and evidence you have learned to answer questions. Do not just memorise chunks of material without considering how to apply it.

THE EXAMINATION

1 Read the rubric, i.e. the set of instructions at the start of the exam paper. This should be familiar to you, but do make sure you answer the right questions and from the appropriate sections.

2 Choose your questions carefully. Read through all the questions before making your selection. Students often fail to 'recognise' questions they could actually answer because they have scanned too quickly through the exam paper.

3 The order in which you attempt the questions is unimportant, as long as your answers are clearly numbered. Some students prefer to start with a straightforward question and not necessarily with the one they could do best in order to complete the first question on schedule. Whatever tactic you adopt, a good start to the exam will give you confidence for the rest of the paper.

4 Calculate the right amount of time to spend on each question and part of a question, and stick closely to your schedule. This depends on the mark allocation. On most papers essay questions carry equal marks. It is bad practice to spend disproportionate amounts of time on different questions, just because you know more about some topics. Once you have written a competent response it gets increasingly difficult to accumulate more marks, whereas the first few marks are relatively easy to acquire. So do make a reasonable attempt at *every* question you need to answer. To miss a question altogether is to throw marks away!

5 Write a *plan* for your answer. You can list the points you wish to make, and then sort them into an appropriate order. Make sure, of course, that your plan answers the question actually set, and not one you wish had been set! Having a plan will help to keep your answer coherent and tightly structured, and will help to stop you from lapsing into irrelevant waffle.

6 Pay close attention to the terms and phrases which are used by the examiners.

Argue	Use theories and evidence to make a case.
Account for	Explain rather than describe a social phenomenon. Answer the question 'why?'
Analyse	Show that you understand a complicated issue by breaking it down into simpler component parts. Identify and explain any relationships which exist between these component parts.
Assess	Examine the strengths and weaknesses of an argument. When assessing a sociological approach the majority of the marks are for criticism rather than for description and illustration.
Compare	Identify similarities. Criticism from the same source is a similarity.
Contrast	Identify differences. Usually paired with 'compare'. Do not write *separate* accounts of two approaches and leave the comparison implicit.
Criticise	Offer arguments for and against. Usually the emphasis is on the limitations of an explanation. This term is often added to another term, such as 'critically examine' or 'critically analyse'.

Discuss	Present at least two views on an issue. Discussion involves criticism.
Evaluate	The same as 'assess'. You must offer a judgement based on evidence.
Examine	Like 'analyse' in that an in-depth view is required of something, say the relationship between two variables.
Explain	To identify the reasons for something or to clarify a situation.
Illustrate	Cite relevant sociological examples.
Outline	Provide a brief description of the essential points. At A-level, this is likely to be combined with another instruction.

GETTING HIGH MARKS

Relevance

Answers must be explicitly relevant to the question. Examiners' reports identify common errors and these include writing everything you know about the topic, answering last year's question or answering the question you would have liked. Examiners are sometimes unable to decide *which* question has been attempted, where the answers have not been numbered accurately or at all. Competent answers should not need to be identified by numbers!

Organisation

Produce a logical and coherent argument. If a question asks you to 'Critically assess the interactionist approach to deviance' then you should not begin with an epic account of positivist approaches. Rather, start with the interactionist view and then use other approaches to criticise it. Some recent questions on suicide have asked about the significance of 'coroners' decisions'. This is a warning *not* to run through the whole of Durkheim's *Suicide* but instead to begin with the studies that treat suicide verdicts as problematic. Careful planning is the key to well-organised and balanced answers.

Content

Introductions, if used at all, should be brief. They should indicate how you intend to interpret the question and to organise your answer. For essay-type answers you can organise your main points in separate paragraphs. A conclusion can review your findings in the light of the original question. On occasions the Chief Examiners have amended mark schemes to deal with a novel interpretation that they had not anticipated. Even though the questions should be clear and unambiguous, so that you know what is required, remember that in sociology there is never a 'right answer'. There is, however, a 'right approach'. The main body of an answer should include:

- Theoretical and methodological issues.
- Evidence from research studies.
- Criticism.

You will often benefit from using comparative material, from linking material with other topics, and from introducing broader debates on theoretical and methodological issues.

> Remember women.

Answers which ignore the existence of women, e.g. on deviance or work, may irritate some examiners. Much pre-feminist sociology is guilty of this omission.

Style, grammar, punctuation, spelling and clarity of writing are not usually assessed separately. (SCE and NEAB do warn students that such deficiencies can be penalised.) However, all contribute to the clarity of your responses and to the force of your arguments, and in this sense are positively rewarded.

All A-levels are now assessed for 'quality of language'. The AEB indicates the standards required in their mark scheme.

Conclusions, like introductions, should be brief. There is no point in repeating material without good reason. If you are asked to evaluate or assess arguments, then a conclusion based on the evidence you have presented is necessary. Conclusions should certainly not contradict the rest of the answer. If you have written a powerful critique of Marxist approaches to education, with little positive comment, do not undermine your answer by giving a balanced conclusion. I have read powerful feminist indictments of family life followed by functionalist-sounding conclusions about the beneficial effects of the family on all concerned. Such contradictions suggest that you do not realise the implications of what you have written.

COURSEWORK   This section refers to formal coursework which is assessed and contributes to the final examination mark.

It is the success of coursework at GCSE which has encouraged its development at higher levels. Although it remains an option for AEB students it should be an attractive one as it provides the opportunity to *do* sociology rather than just to read about it. This should enliven the whole course and allow students to gain a substantial proportion of the final marks before the traditional examinations. This means that work can be spread more evenly throughout the year and other kinds of abilities can be tested and rewarded. Students must, however, learn to manage their time and to work independently.

There are certain key questions which need considering before starting coursework. The answers can usually be found by consulting your teachers and by referring to the syllabus, and to any coursework guidance notes that accompany it. The mark scheme is also very useful.

1   What marks are available for coursework?
2   How are these marks allocated to the assessment of different abilities? For example, is the emphasis on knowledge, evaluation, presentation, etc.?
3   What subjects may be chosen and do they need teacher and/or Board approval?
4   What methods may be chosen and do they need approval?
5   What is the timetable for selection, planning, gaining approval and completion? Teachers will have a deadline for submitting their marks to the Board.
6   Is there a required or recommended format for the presentation of work?

The answers to most of these questions can be found in the syllabuses and regulations of the Examination board concerned. Your research must, of course, employ an accepted method and be on an obviously sociological topic. Here is some further information on the respective Boards.

- Up to 1997 AEB A-level allocates 25% of total marks to coursework; Interboard allocates 20%. In 1998 AEB and Interboard will allocate 20% and NEAB 16.66%.
- Teachers mark the coursework, which is then checked and moderated by the Boards.
- AEB requires only teacher approval of a proposed project; London requires approval by the Examination Board.
- A normal proposal will include:
  a) the working title
  b) the area of investigation
  c) research methods and sources of data.
- Both AEB and London suggest a 5,000-word maximum for a project.
- In terms of presentation there are a number of requirements.
  - The AEB suggests:
    1 Rationale: reason for choosing subject, hypothesis, aims, etc.
    2 Context: theoretical context of study.
    3 Methodology: statement of methodology and critical assessment.
    4 Content: the research evidence and arguments.
    5 Evaluation: evaluation of evidence and conclusions.
    6 Sources: list.
  - Interboard requires:
    1 A title page.
    2 Table of contents.
    3 Abstract.
    4 Rationale.
    5 Division of work into appropriate sections including evaluation.
    6 A bibliography.
    7 A research diary as an appendix containing a critical record of the research process.
- Teachers can provide guidance, supervision and advice. The actual study must be your own independent work.

The above material summarises the respective syllabuses and mark schemes, but you should of course obtain your own copy, where appropriate. NEAB (1998) requires a similar structure. In all cases methodology is a central concern.

CHAPTER

3

SOCIAL CLASS

MARX

WEBER

THE FUNCTIONALIST THEORIES

SOCIAL MOBILITY

THEORETICAL AND EMPIRICAL STUDIES

GETTING STARTED

Stratification refers to the division of society into layers. These layers are distinguished by unequal rewards and life chances. Most sociologists see stratification as involving a classification not only of the groups, but also of the relationships which exist between them.

Class is the kind of stratification found in industrial (capitalist) societies. Other forms of stratification found in pre-industrial societies include **caste** and the **feudal system**.

The issue of social inequality is immensely important to sociologists and crops up throughout sociology. It is, of course, often seen as a social problem as well as a sociological one. This chapter is called *Social class* rather than *Social inequality* in order to restrict our discussion to this particular form of inequality. Other forms of inequality, such as gender, ethnicity and age, are discussed elsewhere.

Since 'inequality' as a concept is at the heart of much of our discussion, it is worth noting that it can be used in at least three contexts:

1　The unequal distribution of opportunities to reach rewarded positions (sometimes called life chances).
2　The unequal distribution of socially valued rewards as between those positions.
3　The subjective feelings of superiority and inferiority, and feelings of class consciousness.

Class is a major variable in considering topics such as health and education. Topics such as poverty, the distribution of power, work, professions and development are frequently analysed as forms of inequality, and of course Marxists reduce the explanation of all social phenomena to a discussion of economic inequality.

The main themes of questions set on this topic are:

1　**Critical evaluation and comparison of major theories of inequality offered by Marx, Weber and the functionalists.**
2　**Analysis of changes in the class structure and in class consciousness in modern industrial societies.**
3　**Critical evaluation of major studies of social mobility.**

ESSENTIAL PRINCIPLES

There are a number of major theories which seek to explain social inequality.

MARX

Economic production is the foundation upon which other social institutions and ideas are built. Classes, which exist in all pre-communist societies, are defined in terms of their relationship to the means of production. The *Ruling Class* own the means of production and dominate and exploit the subject class. The *Subject Class*, who do not own the means of production, are forced to sell their labour to the employers in order to live. They are not paid the full value of their work. This 'Surplus Value' provides profit and rent, and allows the accumulation of capital. In capitalist society the two classes are:

- The **Bourgeoisie** who own the means of production, such as factories and railways. This ownership can either be directly, as sole proprietors, partners or shareholders, or indirectly, e.g. as bankers.
- The **Proletariat** who are the class of wage labourers working in factories and generally living in towns.

CRITICS OF MARX

Theoretical criticism comes from Weber and his followers and from his functionalists (see below). In addition, some modern Marxists now question certain aspects of his work in the light of subsequent developments. *Empirical criticism* comes from analysing the class structure of modern industrial societies (see below).

Critics challenge the following aspects of Marx's analysis and predictions:

1 Class is based on ownership of the means of production.
2 There are only two significant classes.
3 The relationship between classes is based on exploitation and oppression.
4 The working class (Proletariat) is subjugated by both physical and ideological control.
5 Economic laws will lead to the development of class conflict. Marx predicts:

- **Monopolisation** of capital.
- **Homogenisation** of the working class.
- **Pauperisation** of the working class.
- **Polarisation** of the two classes.

6 Class conflict will lead to revolution, the triumph of the working class and the development of a classless society.

Criticisms of Marx

1 Class is not the only form of inequality. People are ranked by caste, status, political power, age, race and gender.
2 Ownership is not the only way to define class. There are significant differences in wages between people at the top and bottom of the occupational ladder, and it is difficult to see them as the same class.
3 Ownership of the means of production is spread fairly widely in modern industrial societies. Some industries are still publicly owned, e.g. British Rail, despite the Government's privatisation policy. Privatisation has increased the number of share-holders who are owners of businesses.
   Individuals' savings and pension contributions are invested in shares, which means that individuals may be owners of a business yet have little control over it.
4 There are more than two classes. There are middle classes and divisions in the working class.
5 The working class is getting richer, not poorer.
6 Communism in practice has not borne out Marx's predictions. There were no communist revolutions in capitalist countries. Russia, China and Cuba were agricultural economies when they had revolutions. The Russian army brought communism to Eastern Europe, not a proletarian revolution.
   Inequalities existed in communist societies.
   Communism in Eastern Europe and the old USSR collapsed after 1989.

WEBER

Social inequality is based on differences in *power* held by groups, not just on differences in class.

The sources of power are:

- **Class.**
- **Status.**
- **Party.**

Class

This is an objective economic category, so people are in a class whether they are conscious of it or not. A class is a group who share the same economic causes as determinants of their life chances, i.e. the opportunities to acquire goods and services. There are three kinds of classes:

- **Property classes** who own more or less wealth (compare this with Marx).
- **Commercial classes** whose market situation varies. This 'market situation' refers to the price they can command for their labour, which in turn depends on their skills, on any control they can exercise over entry, and on other sources of bargaining power (compare this with the functionalist explanation below and refer to Chapter 14 on the *Professions*).
- **Social classes** are groups within which mobility is typical and easy.

Status

This is a subjective category based on honour or prestige, which could be influenced by occupation or birth. Status groups share the same lifestyle, they consume the same goods and may have a common education. They may or may not be conscious of their group identity.

Party

This refers to a group who are organised with the objective of gaining power. A party may represent all, or part, of a class or status group. Examples include Trade Unions, Professional Associations, Bureaucratic Organisations and Political parties.

CRITICS OF WEBER

The value of Weber's work, according to A. Giddens, is that it 'provides what is missing in Marx'. Thus both negative and positive criticisms are to be found in the debate with Marx and with modern Marxists. We might consider the following points on the class structure of modern industrial societies:

1   Class does not depend solely on ownership.
2   There are more than two classes.
3   There are middle classes and working classes. (This is a favourite source of questions.) The middle classes are growing.
4   Social change is not necessarily economically determined. (See Chapter 15 on *Religion* and Chapter 8 on *World sociology and development*.)
5   Class consciousness may or may not develop.

The empirical studies later in this chapter will throw further light on these points.

THE FUNCTIONALIST THEORIES

The dominant writers here are Parsons and Davis and Moore. These theories offer a critical view of the conflict explanations of inequality provided by followers of both Marx and Weber. Inequality is explained in terms of its *functions* and is, in effect, justified. Parsons claims that stratification systems are based on common values and thus *integrate* rather than divide societies. The ranking of individuals is based on a consensual view of the importance of positions. Thus winners, as well as losers, see inequality as legitimate, since the rules of the game are 'fair'. Power is granted to those in important positions in order to help them organise others, and this interdependence of workers is seen as a further encouragement to social integration. Because goals are shared, and because inequality helps to achieve these goals, everyone benefits (compare with Marx). Davis and Moore identify the functions of stratification as *role allocation and performance* rather than integration.

Here inequality ensures that the most important positions in society are conscientiously filled by the most able individuals.

CRITICS OF FUNCTIONALIST THEORIES

Conflict theories reject the whole idea that inequality can be based on consensual values and thereby benefits all members of society. Specific criticisms of Davis and Moore come from both Tumin and Buckley. Tumin questions the following propositions which are made by the functionalists (this also serves as a useful checklist of Davis and Moore's work):

1   Some positions are functionally more important than others.
2   Only a few have the natural talents required to develop the skills needed to perform these tasks.
3   Developing talents into skills through training requires sacrifices, such as loss of earnings.
4   Motivation to make these sacrifices comes from an unequal share of rewards in the future.
5   Unequal rewards lead to differences in prestige, which are generally accepted and are the basis of a stratified society.

Buckley offers some important logical criticisms. He claims that Davis and Moore try (and probably fail) to explain *differentiation* rather than stratification. Differentiation refers to the attaching of unequal rewards to particular *positions* at one moment in time. Stratification refers to the unequal *opportunities* individuals and groups have to reach the highly rewarded positions, and is seen as more or less permanent. Class, race and gender inequality prevent the most able from achieving the most important positions. Thus stratification may be seen as dysfunctional, as it wastes talent, reduces motivation and causes conflict.

THE REGISTRAR-GENERAL'S CLASSIFICATION

This has been used since 1911 for official statistics and is frequently used by sociologists, as it is generally accepted despite the criticisms below. It was updated for the 1991 census.

The grading was based on the status of the job; now it is based on skills and qualifications.

The Department of Employment uses the new Standard Occupational Classification, which has nine categories of jobs and deals more effectively with women's jobs.

Table 3.1 Social class based on occupation 1991: Registrar-General's classification

I	Professional, etc.
II	Managerial and Technical
III (N)	Skilled non-manual
III (M)	Skilled manual
IV	Partly skilled
V	Unskilled

Alternative schemes have been devised because some sociologists find them more useful. A popular one was used in the Oxford mobility studies. It is based on differences in pay and working conditions.

Table 3.2 Marshall's (1988) simplification of Goldthorpe (1983)

Service class	1	Higher prof., admin. and owners.
	2	Lower prof., admin. and managers.
Intermediate class	3	Routine clerical, sales and service.
	4	Owners of small firms, self-employed.
	5	Lower technicians and foremen.
Working class	6	Skilled manual.
	7	Semi-skilled and unskilled manual.

The numbers in each group have changed because of changes in the occupational structure. Generally there has been a consistent increase in non-manual compared with manual jobs, and in particular a growth in professional occupations.

CRITICAL VIEWS OF CLASSIFICATIONS BASED ON OCCUPATION

Sociologists have pointed out problems with using occupation as a measure of class. Some of these problems apply to particular classifications and some to the whole idea of jobs indicating class.

1   Marxists point out the absence of the rich, i.e. owners of the means of production.
2   The poor and unemployed are excluded.
3   Women often appear to be in higher-class occupations than men. However, 'women's jobs' are frequently in the lower levels of each grouping. Women often earn less than men in the same groups or in groups below them. Also their promotion prospects may be worse, particularly in clerical work.
    These criticisms also apply to ethnic minority workers.
4   The division between manual and non-manual jobs which has been used to distinguish the middle class from the working class is not very useful when it is applied to women, as many personal service jobs are low-paid, low-status and low-skilled, yet are still defined as non-manual.
5   Wives and children are classified by male head of family. This may be inappropriate in cross-class families, particularly where women have higher-status jobs than men.
6   It has been argued that all women are proletarianised (i.e. exploited like the working class) by their experience within the family.
7   The ranking of occupations may be based on status, and there may be disagreement about the relative positions of jobs. A particular job could, of course, change its ranking over a period of time.
8   In some schemes the ranking depends on judging the skills used in a job. There are problems of evaluating skills, e.g. skills are judged according to who has them. In particular, women's skilled jobs are ranked lower than men's precisely because it is women who do the jobs. The idea of ranking jobs is almost inevitably subjective, whether it is done by the Registrar-General's staff or by a survey of public opinion (this is done for the Hall Jones scale).
9   Self-assigned class may explain behaviour, such as voting, better than the position in an occupational scale.

Positive points

1   Occupation is a good predictor of life expectancy, infant mortality and many other indicators of health.
2   Parents' occupation predicts educational achievement of children, particularly where both parents' class is considered.

Does it matter if the classifications are inadequate?

The validity and reliability of sociological studies and government statistics are threatened if the occupational groupings are unsuitable.

Social mobility studies measure movement up and down the classifications; therefore we must be confident which occupations are higher-status.

SOCIAL MOBILITY

Social mobility refers to the movement up or down the class structure by individuals or groups. Sociologists are most interested in *cross-class mobility*. *Intra-generational mobility* describes the movement within an individual's working life. *Inter-generational mobility* compares the occupations of fathers and sons. *Stratum mobility* is the movement of a whole occupational group within the occupational ranking.

The main sociological issues include:

1   The causes of the observed mobility rates. These include changes in the occupational structure, educational reforms which provide increased opportunity, and differential fertility rates between classes.
2   The effects or importance of social mobility. An open society (with high mobility rates) ensures that the best get to the top and reduces class conflict. According to Giddens, low rates of mobility encourage the development of class consciousness and are a feature of a *structurated* society.
3   The difficulties of classifying occupations and assessing the extent of mobility.

THEORETICAL AND EMPIRICAL STUDIES

CHANGES IN THE CLASS STRUCTURE

The following issues need examination. Consider whether changes have occurred and, if so, their causes and consequences.

1 Embourgeoisement.
2 A fragmented working class.
3 The underclass.
3 Proletarianisation.
5 A fragmented middle class.
6 A classless society.

THE WORKING CLASSES

Marx anticipated an impoverished and increasingly homogenised working class who would become class conscious and ultimately revolutionary. The studies below, including those by most of the modern Marxists, accept the decline of the traditional working class.

Rose 1968

In a study of working-class conservative voting, Rose found that only 25% of *manual* workers had all five characteristics of his 'ideal type'. These characteristics of the 'ideal' working-class type included being a manual worker, a trade-union member, a tenant, having a minimum education, and being a self-assigned member of the working class.

Lockwood 1966

Lockwood identified three groups within the working class, their differing values being based on residential and occupational communities. He identified: *Proletarian Traditionalism*, e.g. miners; *Deferential Traditionalism*, e.g. farm workers; and the *Privatised working class*, e.g. car workers. Many subsequent studies have reinforced this division between the traditional and the 'new' working class.

Goldthorpe, Lockwood *et al.* 1968

In one of three books based on a study of both manual and non-manual factory workers in Luton in the early 1960s, the authors tested and refuted the then fashionable *Embourgeoisement* thesis, which suggested that affluent workers had become middle class (see Outline Answer to Question 5, Chapter 7). They argued for the continued existence of a gap between manual and non-manual workers. Nevertheless, they did suggest the emergence of a new working class, with instrumental attitudes to work derived from a privatised family life.

Penn 1985

Supports the Goldthorpe *et al.* study by seeing a continued divide between manual and non-manual workers, and thereby a divided working class. However, rather than a 'new' working class he identifies a privileged group of skilled craft workers whose rare skills and organisation maintain high rewards. (The fate of print workers after the Wapping move perhaps challenges this view.)

Hill 1976

Hill found that the allegedly new instrumental attitudes to work existed in a traditional working-class community of dockers.

Parkin 1968

Parkin identified three value systems in modern Britain: a *dominant* value system supporting middle- and upper-class interests influencing increasing numbers of the working class through education and the media. A *subordinate* value system found in sheltered working-class communities. A *radical* value system found among left-inclined middle-class workers.

Rex 1970

Rex used a Weberian approach to identify an ethnically differentiated 'underclass', one which was separate from the white proletariat. He also sees the possibility of an ethnic consciousness cutting across class boundaries (see Chapter 4 on *Race*).

Feminist studies (see also Chapter 5 on *Gender*)

Women are seen as particularly disadvantaged in the labour market. Whether or not this demonstrates a division within the working class depends on the extent to which the writer is influenced by orthodox Marxist views. The same applies to studies of racial disadvantage. The concept of a *reserve army of labour* as applied to women, immigrants and minorities accepts their disadvantage but still locates them *within* a unitary working class.

THE MIDDLE CLASSES

These studies are concerned first with establishing the *existence* of a distinct middle class separated from manual workers by rewards and consciousness, and second with identifying *differences* within the middle classes.

Roberts *et al.* 1972

This study distinguished five groups within the middle classes based on the *image* the group had of the place of the middle class in society. Roberts called these images of society:

- The middle mass.
- The compressed middle class.
- The finely graded occupational ladder.
- The proletarian middle class.
- The new radicals.

Goldthorpe 1978

Goldthorpe suggested that the British middle class was becoming increasingly large and fragmented, and that beneath it there remained the remnants of a traditional working class. By examining the origins of parents, and the likely life chances of children, he identified four major groups within the middle class:

- The *old* middle classes, which were recruited from the higher-class parents.
- The *new* middle classes, which were recruited from the lower-class parents.
- The *established* middle classes, which have children whose future is secure.
- The *marginal* middle classes, which have children whose future is insecure.

Thus clerks could be described as new and marginal, the service class as new and established, small proprietors as old and marginal, and professionals as old and established.

Lockwood 1958 (updated 1989; see *Work*, Chapter 12)

Although Lockwood's 'Blackcoated worker' is the earliest study mentioned here, it has been left to the end, as it provides the best link with the modern Marxist studies which follow. Lockwood tested the Marxist hypothesis that clerks were in fact 'falsely conscious' proletarians. He used the Weberian distinction between class and status to show that the clerk remained a superior worker in terms of *market situation, work situation* and *status.* (See Tutor Answer to Question 3 below). He did, however, predict a diminishing of these advantages and he accepted that clerks were not part of a traditional middle class but, rather, part of a new instrumentally collectivist one. (This idea should remind you of the Luton Studies.)

MODERN MARXISTS

These writers attempt to deal with the various criticisms already mentioned and with the changes in modern industrial societies, such as rising incomes for all classes, the growth of non-manual work at the expense of manufacturing, the institutionalisation of class conflict and its diminishing effects.

Mills 1951

Although his work contains both Marxist and Weberian influences, it extended the concept of alienation from the factory to the office and suggested the increasingly popular hypothesis of 'proletarianisation' of the middle classes. His work is not restricted to routine office workers but also covers managers, professionals and salesmen.

Carchedi 1975

Carchedi adds the *feminisation of office work* to the usual list of factors encouraging proletarianisation of clerical workers.

Braverman 1976

Braverman offers a variation from traditional Marxism by accepting that changes take place in the composition of classes as the methods of production change. His writing (which is further discussed in Chapter 12 on *Work*) emphasises the effects of routinisation, bureaucratisation, fragmentation, and the deskilling of work on the composition of classes.

Westergaard and Resler 1976

Those two authors conducted an empirical study of class in modern Britain which used a Marxist perspective. They argued that too many discussions of class ignore the overwhelming importance of *wealth*. Thus they deal only with divisions *within* the working class and fail to consider the crucial division between the *bourgeoisie* and the rest.

Althusser 1972 and Bowles and Gintis 1976

These studies explain the lack of class consciousness among the working class by discussing the development of *ideological controls*. Both studies identify the importance of *schooling* in this process. Althusser adds the *media* to the list of *ideological state apparatuses* which substitute for overt oppression.

Marcuse 1968

Marcuse attempted to deal with the problems which affluence presents to those Marxists who predict impoverishment. He saw the rich working class enslaved by 'chains of gold'. He thought that they were forced to work in order to pursue 'false needs' created by advertising.

Wright 1989

Wright produced a classification of occupations influenced by:

- Marx – note the significance of **ownership**.
- Weber – note the significance of differences in **power**.

OWNER-EMPLOYER	Employer
	Petty-Bourgeois
MIDDLE CLASS	Expert Manager
	Non-Expert Manager
	Non-Manager Expert
WORKING CLASS	Skilled Worker
	Routine Worker

Power is assessed by the degree of control the occupation has in the workplace. Wright measures power by looking at control over:

- **Investment** decisions, e.g. can open or close a factory.
- **Machinery** used in production, e.g. can speed up the assembly line.
- **Labour**, e.g. can manage, hire and fire workers.

As in other Marxist accounts, the differences within the working class between manual and non-manual workers is not seen as being as significant as the division between capitalists and workers.

However, the power held by managers means that they have *contradictory class locations* sharing the characteristics of both workers and owners. They differ from the working class in terms of

- **Wealth** (they may have shares in companies).
- **Working conditions**.
- **Life chances**, e.g. health, education and social mobility.

SOCIAL MOBILITY

Miller

In a study of Britain in the 1940s and 1950s, Miller showed high rates of upward mobility for manual workers and high rates of downward mobility for non-manual workers.

His 1960 comparative study suggested similar rates of mobility in modern industrial societies, including communist ones. Lipsett and Bendix suggested something similar in the 1940s, although subsequent studies have questioned this view.

Glass

In a major study conducted in 1949, Glass found high levels of short-range mobility. He suggested the existence of a *buffer zone* preventing access to the top positions, but a strong possibility of movement up or down for both skilled manual workers and non-manual workers.

Goldthorpe 1972 and 1980

The Oxford mobility study was interested in the effects of post-war economic growth and education reform on mobility. It found a more open society than Glass, e.g. only 25% of the top class had fathers from this class. However, the life chances of those at the top remained much better than they were for those at the bottom. The major cause of increased mobility was identified as being the expansion of the service class, owing to technological change, rather than to any increased open competition in order to get to the top.

Goldthorpe and Payne 1986

This update on the earlier study found that the previous trends had continued, except that the opportunities for manual workers' *sons* had improved. Downward movement was also reduced, but the arrival of high levels of unemployment had increased the risk of moving down for manual workers themselves.

Criticisms of the empirical studies on social mobility

Evaluation of the major studies is a popular question. Some criticisms are specific to a particular study, others are more general, involving methodological or even ideological concerns.

The positive value of the mobility studies is that they allow us to test hypotheses, such as *Embourgeoisement, Proletarianisation, Structuration, Elite theories* and the success or otherwise of *educational reforms.*

Problems of *measurement* of mobility include:

1   Comparing the father's final position with a possibly temporary one for the son.
2   Relying on possibly unreliable records for fathers' occupations.
3   The ranking of jobs may change.
4   The studies are not strictly comparable, as different categories are often used. For example, Glass used the Registrar-General's classification (which in any case has been updated), whereas Goldthorpe used his own scheme.
5   Studying only two generations conceals the possibility of the sons of downwardly mobile fathers *returning* to their original class. This is illustrated by Jackson and Marsden's finding that working-class boys in grammar schools often had mothers with middle-class origins.
6   The classification of women is problematic, and they were excluded from both the Glass and the Goldthorpe studies. Heath found that women are more often downwardly mobile and are excluded from both skilled manual work and top jobs.
7   Studies tend to neglect both the Bourgeoisie and the unemployed.
8   Mobility studies consider only individual access to jobs, and ignore the fact that the class structure may remain unchanged.

The *Goldthorpe* studies have been specifically criticised:

1   His Service class is so large that it encourages the view of increased mobility.
2   Giddens claims that it ignores the small exclusive elite recruited from the public schools.
3   Heath used Goldthorpe's data to support the view that there was 'closure' at the top.
4   The Marxists Westergaard and Resler point out that it neglects any consideration of wealth.

EXAMINATION QUESTIONS

1   'Social stratification is beneficial for societies, ensuring that the most important positions are conscientiously filled by the most qualified people.' What arguments would you use (a) to support and (b) to criticise this contention?

(NEAB)

2   'We are all middle class now.' Are we?

(UCLES)

3   Have white-collar workers been 'proletarianised'?

(UODLE)

4   Outline the major studies of social mobility in Britain and examine criticisms of them.

(AEB)

5   'The Marxian assumption of two basic antagonistic classes is, in certain important respects, sociologically unsatisfactory' (Anderson and Sharrock eds *Applied Sociological Perspectives*). Critically examine this view.

(AEB)

6   **ITEM A**

How would you like to be referred to as a member of Britain's underclass? No, I wouldn't either. The term has unpleasant connotations. It means that there is a group of people whose position in society is so low they are not even members of the very lowest social class, but have dropped below the entire social structure. The concept lends itself to a
5   political philosophy of blaming the victim. Even more than other simplistic labels which inevitably distort, the underclass is particularly vague and difficult to define. Moreover, the term has been taken over by the rightwing American writer Charles Murray. He has used it to attack the culture of dependency and by extension, those who are dependent on state benefits. There are many policy analysts who refuse to accept
10   that there is such a phenomenon as an underclass at all. This is unfortunate because it means they don't address the fact that there are groups of people who are not merely poor but who are prevented from participating fully in society. Such people have had their links cut with legitimate stable employment, not as a temporary phenomenon but as a condition of existence that has been handed down in some families through two
15   or even three generations.

(Adapted from *The Guardian, Encounters with the Underclass*,
M. PHILLIPS (13 March 1992)

ITEM B

If racial discrimination results in black people being restricted to those occupations which are characterised by low pay, poor job security and few promotion prospects, then status disadvantages are translated into class disadvantages and we can talk of a black underclass. Marxists are reluctant to talk of an underclass. In line with their stress on
5   the primacy of class and the division between capital and labour, they locate ethnic minorities in the working class. Some, indeed, go as far as to argue that the minorities are essentially members of the working class. Westergaard and Resler for example see racial discrimination as merely increasing the impact of otherwise common disadvantages.

(Adapted from *Sociology Review Vol. 1 No. 3 Is there a British underclass?*
A. PILKINGTON (February 1992)

ITEM C

Social class is generally regarded by sociologists as being based upon the differential rewards which are available to people through paid employment in the labour market or through the holding of property. There is considerable inequality in the rewards available to different occupations. Social classes are usually defined, for purposes of
5   research, as groupings of occupations which obtain roughly similar levels of reward from the labour market. Occupations thus provide a useful index or measure of social class. Individuals living by themselves present relatively few problems for the sociologists seeking to allocate them a social class position. Their current or former occupation is the usual basis of the classification system used. The problems arise
10   when, as is very common, two adults live together and both are in paid work. If they are involved in occupations located in different social classes, does it make sense to assign them to different classes or should one person's position be used to classify them

both? Similarly, if one partner is not in paid work, can the other partner's position be used to classify them both?

(From *Sociology Review Vol. 1 No. 3 Theories of Social Class and Gender*
N. BONNEY (February 1992))

a) What do sociologists mean by 'blaming the victim' (ITEM A line 5)? (*1 mark*)
b) Suggest **two** other useful indices or 'measures of social class', apart from those mentioned in ITEM C. (*2 marks*)
c) How useful are occupational classifications in analysing social class in modern societies? Refer to ITEM C in your answer. (*7 marks*)
d) With reference to the ITEMS and elsewhere, evaluate two sociological explanations of the distribution of income and wealth in modern British society. (*8 marks*)
e) With reference to the ITEMS and other sociological sources, assess the usefulness of the concept of the underclass in describing the class position of ethnic minorities.

(*7 marks*)
(AEB)

ANSWERS TO EXAMINATION QUESTIONS

OUTLINE ANSWERS

Question 1

This has been a very popular question for a long time, so examiners now expect increasingly sophisticated answers. A summary of Davis and Moore followed by Tumin's critique and nothing more will not score high marks, however detailed it is.

You are asked to *evaluate* the functionalist theory of stratification. The quotation suggests Davis and Moore's emphasis on role allocation rather than Parsons' contention that the main function is integration. Both should be outlined for the first part of the answer.

Criticism should not be restricted to Tumin, but could also include Buckley. Perhaps more importantly it could include modern Marxist and modern Weberian criticism which challenges the view that stratification is based on value consensus. Westergaard and Resler offer a Marxist critique and Parkin can be used to develop Weberian ideas on closure.

Remember to relate this material directly to the question.

Question 2

This question requires more than just a run-through of the 1960s' 'embourgeoisement' debate. You should use both Marxist and Weberian theories and studies to discuss some or all of the following issues:

- Whether there is a middle class at all or just two classes.
- Whether the lower (or even higher) levels of non-manual workers are being proletarianised.
- Whether there are divisions within the middle class.
- Whether the boundaries between the middle and working classes are being blurred by embourgeoisement.

Question 4

This is a straightforward question. At least two studies must be considered. Glass and Goldthorpe are the most likely, but others will be rewarded. You are asked to 'examine' criticisms, which means look at them in some detail, but the best answers will *assess* the criticisms as well. You should include positive evaluation of the studies as well as pointing out their shortcomings. At the time of writing, feminist criticism has become as popular as the more traditional consideration of methodological issues. Here is a suggested outline plan:

- The main findings of the Glass study.
- The Goldthorpe study, showing how it confirms some aspects of Glass but also suggests different patterns of mobility.

- The methodological problems involved in doing mobility studies.
- The Marxist criticisms denying the significance of an 'open society'.
- The feminist criticism concerning the invisibility of women in such studies.

Question 6

a) Seeing the cause of inequality or disadvantage as the 'victim's' bad or inadequate values and behaviour.
   (Or other reasonable account. Keep it brief for one mark.)
b) Any two indicators, e.g. status, income, housing, class, etc.
c) Use the references in the Item to provide evidence of strengths and weaknesses of occupational classifications as an indicator of class, e.g. predicting rewards; cross-class locations of partners, unemployment of one partner.
   These points and outside knowledge should produce a balanced argument with explicit evaluation and a conclusion. There is a list of critical points earlier in this chapter. The strengths of the classifications lie in their predictive power, i.e. their ability to demonstrate that occupation corresponds with income, health, educational success, etc.
d) Choose *two* explanations. You could choose Marxist, functionalist, or Weberian theories.
   There are references in the items to Weberian and New Right versions of the underclass and to Marxist theory. These, and outside knowledge, should be applied to the question and used to support evaluative points.
e) This requires an evaluation of one or perhaps more than one version of the concept of an underclass. You should focus on both theoretical (e.g. the debate with Marxists) and empirical (the distribution of minorities in the occupational structure) criticisms. There is a lot of useful argument and evidence in the Tutor's Answer in the *Race* chapter (4) and the summary of the different views on the underclass in that chapter.

Questions (c), (d) and (e) should occupy most of your time, and a good answer is likely to be between one and two sides of the examination book (i.e. A4 with margins either side).

TUTOR ANSWER

Question 3

Have white-collar workers been 'proletarianised'?

The essence of this question is the dispute between some modern Marxists and critics of Marx concerning the current position and future of the middle classes.

Marx himself saw capitalist society, like all other kinds of pre-communist society, as being divided into two basic antagonistic classes. These classes were defined in terms of the ownership of the means of production. The ruling class of owners he called the Bourgeoisie, and the subject class of wage labourers, the Proletariat. The proletariat were largely factory workers.

Weber rejected both Marx's definition of class and his view of only two classes. Weber saw inequality as based on party and status as well as on class. Weberian writers identify three kinds of classes: first property classes, who own more or less wealth; second commercial classes, distinguished by their market situation; and third social classes, who are defined as a group within which mobility is likely. Weber observed and predicted the growth of the middle classes prompted by bureaucratisation.

Subsequent critics of Marx have argued for the continued existence, expansion and fragmentation of the middle classes. They also point out the failure of Marx's prediction that class conflict would intensify. The diminishing of apparent conflict is explained by the decomposition of capital, the institutionalisation of conflict through voting and collective bargaining, and the rising of incomes for all classes. Thus it seems that class consciousness is diminishing, not increasing.

This last point is picked up by C. W. Mills, who was among the first to argue that it was little more than false consciousness that separated the alleged middle class from the rest of the working class. In *White Collar* he suggested that office workers had become proletarianised because of changes in their work situation and in their relationship with their employers. Routine clerical workers had become as alienated as factory workers as their jobs became routinised, fragmented and deskilled because of bureaucratisation. Unlike others who argue for proletarianisation, Mills also looks at higher levels of the middle classes, such as salesmen and managers, who are forced to present an alienated self to others, and professionals who have lost their autonomy to the large corporations which now employ them or pay their fees.

In 1958 Lockwood, in *The Blackcoated Worker*, tested the Marxist hypothesis that clerks were falsely conscious proletarians. He used the Weberian concepts of class and status to compare clerks with manual workers. Class was measured by the workers' market and work situations. Despite a narrowing of wage differences, the clerk still enjoyed the advantages of job security, pensions and other disguised forms of pay. Although working conditions in factories had improved, clerks still had a superior working environment and worked more closely with managers and employers. All these factors helped to perpetuate the superior status of the clerk. Though Lockwood still saw the clerk as a superior worker, he did not see him as part of the traditional middle class but as forming a new instrumentally collectivist middle class. This view is echoed 20 years later by Goldthorpe, writing about the British middle class. He describes clerks as part of an intermediate class comprising both the 'new' and 'marginal' middle class, as well as skilled manual workers. These are distinguished from the 'old' and 'established' middle classes who are part of the Service class.

Lockwood did, however, predict the *diminishing* of the advantages experienced by clerks compared to manual workers. It is this decline which has been documented by modern Marxists in trying to argue for the proletarianisation thesis.

In separate studies, Bowles and Gintis and Braverman comment on the importance of the fragmentation and deskilling of office work. Both studies see the continuation of the capitalist relations of production, with office workers being controlled and exploited by the owners.

Carchedi describes similar developments in Italy. The differences in pay, conditions, status and consciousness between office and factory workers have become blurred, and office workers have become increasingly collectivist and unionised. He also sees the feminisation of office work encouraging the proletarianisation of clerical workers as their pay and status declines.

From a more traditional Marxist view, Westergaard and Resler see the issue of proletarianisation of white-collar workers as unimportant, since such workers were always part of the working class. Differences in rewards enjoyed by various ranks of employees are seen as insignificant compared with the gap between the owners of the means of production and the workers.

In conclusion, it is worth considering the implications for the debate above of certain developments in the 1980s, such as high unemployment and changes in the distribution of post-tax income. These may have widened, rather than narrowed, the gap between manual and non-manual workers.

STUDENT'S ANSWER WITH EXAMINER COMMENTS

Question 5

'The Marxian assumption of two basic antagonistic classes is, in certain important respects, sociologically unsatisfactory.' Critically examine this view.

> 66 Yes, Weber is a suitable critic. 99

> 66 Defines the two classes and mentions hostility. 99

> 66 Yes, Weber did. Should explain commercial classes and develop beyond the supply and demand for labour. Social change is not a central issue. 99

It would be too simplistic to dismiss the Marxist argument of there being two basic antagonistic classes in society. Weber himself did not totally reject the argument but instead highlighted different aspects of the explanation.

Marx saw society as having two classes: the Bourgeoisie and the Proletariat. The main factor dividing the classes is that the Bourgeoisie own the means of production and the Proletariat do not. This was evidently the cause of inequality within society which caused hostility between the two classes.

Weber claimed there were a multitude of classes. He saw classes formed from those with different labour skills. However, he did agree with Marx that economic relations were of importance but that ownership was not the prime determinant of class. Other classes - for example, commercial classes - existed. Marx suggested that only when the infrastructure altered did the rest of society - i.e. norms, values, education system, etc. - also change. The infrastructure was therefore the main reason for social change. Weber rejected this, claiming that ideas could contribute to social change. He also claimed that the supply and demand for labour influenced class, not just ownership.

> Weak explanation of life chances.

Weber identified three main sources of power: class, status and party. He argued that certain people were more likely to be placed in more powerful positions simply because they had more access to greater life chances. For example children born into powerful families received better education. Life chances depended on the occupation of the family.

> Functionalism should be related to class not power.

Functionalists dismiss this Weberian argument and conclude that life chances depend on natural talents. The functionalists reject the Marxist view that ownership of the means of production is the source of power. They claim that those who are most able to make use of power for the good of society are given power. They also see inequality as functional for society. They believe it exists because it is beneficial and necessary for the survival of the whole society.

> Relevant but not expressed clearly.

Marx would disagree that inequality in power is justified by value consensus. Instead he would argue that it is based on false consciousness. The proletariat are unaware of the fact that they are being manipulated and exploited. Marx suggested that only when the proletariat realise their exploitation will there be a revolution. This will involve the working class becoming a class for themselves, not just a class in themselves.

> Relevant comparative views on revolution.

Functionalists do not anticipate a working-class revolution. Neither does Weber see revolution as inevitable, but he does not dismiss the possibility. Marx believes that only after the revolution will there be a classless society, and this will be the final stage of economic change.

> Legitimising inequality conceals antagonism. Integration point is good.

Marxists believe that the ruling class legitimise their power by transmitting ideology to the working class. These ideologies are channelled through the education system, the media and religion. The ruling class make people believe that those who are in positions of power deserve to be there. Functionalists support the argument that the working class accept inequality as being in the interests of all. They think that stratification can integrate society rather than creating hostility between them, as suggested by Marxists.

> Not adding much.

Even though the Marxist explanation is criticised by functionalists and Weberians, there still remain similarities between the explanations. Weber seems to develop Marxist ideas of class further and adds the question of how people actually gain power. While Marx relates power solely to ownership of the means of production, Weber rejects this and sees inequality also dependent on the supply and demand of labour. The more a skill is in demand, the more the person who possesses it will be rewarded.

Overall comments

Overall this answer would be worthy of a D grade pass, but not a good grade. The question has been understood and the issues of two classes and antagonism have been addressed.

There is a wealth of material written by modern Marxists and the followers of Weber which could have been used to support the arguments, such as the debates about the fragmentation of the class structure and the proletarianisation of office work. Dahrendorf has explicitly discussed the issues in the quotation dealing with antagonism as well as the more obvious consideration of two classes. Good answers always go beyond the juxtaposition of theories.

A Review Sheet for this chapter may be found on p. 253.

GETTING STARTED

Most sociological studies of race tend to adopt a conflict approach. Race relations are seen either in terms of socially structured inequality or as a social problem.

Some syllabuses treat race and ethnicity as a discrete topic; others treat it as a form of inequality which exists in many aspects of social life, and thus it is considered in different parts of the syllabus. There is generally more interest in ethnic disadvantage than in simple diversity of experience. Diversity is examined in the *Family* chapter (10).

The main themes of questions set on this topic are:

1 **Describing and explaining ethnic disadvantage in the fields of: housing, employment and education.**
2 **Examining racism as a cause and effect of inequality.**
3 **Examining the relationship between ethnicity and class by evaluating Marxist and Weberian theories.**
4 **Examining the causes and effects of media representation of ethnic minorities.**
5 **Comparing the experience of ethnic minorities with other disadvantaged groups such as women.**

Definitions
- *Race* refers to real or perceived biological differences which are given a social meaning, e.g. skin colour.
- *Ethnicity* refers to a distinctive cultural identity accepted by the group themselves and/or attributed to them by others.
- *Racism* usually refers to a hostile attitude towards, or prejudice against, an ethnic group. Marxists use the term to describe practices and social institutions as well as the ideology of inferiority.
- *Racial discrimination* is behaviour which treats those in ethnic minorities worse than others.
- *Related topics* include all those where there is evidence of disadvantage, such as work, education, media, health and deviance. Race and ethnicity are central issues in the study of development and stratification. Discussions of immigration need to include a consideration of race, and vice versa.

Remember to emphasise the diversity of experience *between* different ethnic groups as well as the differences *within* a single group based on age, gender and class. Many questions benefit from using a comparative approach in the study of ethnic differences.

ESSENTIAL PRINCIPLES

Despite the differences between the following perspectives, they all tend to see the sociology of race as being concerned with conflict and social problems.

MARXIST APPROACHES

Marxists begin with the assumption that there are only *two* classes, and these are based on the ownership of the means of production. The whole working class is exploited by the ruling class, and any apparent differences such as race and ethnicity are objectively irrelevant.

Racism is seen as the ideology of inferiority and is part of the superstructure of capitalist society. Racist ideas, practices and institutions enhance the control of the ruling class over the workers. The effects of racism include:

1   Legitimising slavery, colonialism and continued deprivation in capitalist society.
2   Dividing the working class, thereby helping prevent the development of class consciousness. The segregation of the labour market allows further exploitation.
3   Providing scapegoats for the inevitable tensions and frustrations of capitalism. Unemployment, poverty, crime and bad housing can be blamed on a visible and vulnerable group.

CRITICS

Weberians and others reject the view that there are only two classes based solely on ownership. Ethnic minorities are seen as having a distinct position in the class structure. Other critics see the possibility of racism existing independently of economic exploitation.

THE UNDERCLASS

This is based on a Weberian analysis of inequality, where class exists alongside divisions based on status and party. Racial inequality stems from competition for scarce resources and from the differing ability of groups to exclude others from the rewards available in the labour and other markets. An *underclass* is not just the bottom of a class gradient, but is beneath and indeed distinct from the rest of the working class. An underclass could comprise one or more of the following: racial or ethnic minorities, immigrants or temporary migrant workers.

The poverty and powerlessness of the underclass is maintained by racial discrimination in the labour and other markets, by exclusion from working-class organisations and by barriers to upward mobility due to the slowing down of changes in the occupation structure. (This last point can perhaps be criticised on the basis of a predicted shortage of skilled labour in the 1990s.)

Racism is seen not as the cause of the development of the underclass, but as the basis for the allocation of workers to something like a secondary labour market. (See also the Tutor Answer to Question 2 below and the consideration of dual labour market theory in Chapter 5 on *Gender.*)

(On pp. 31–3 this view of the underclass is compared and contrasted with the New Right view.)

CRITICS

Some critics reject the existence of an ethnically distinct underclass on empirical grounds, pointing out the spread of minorities throughout the occupational structure. Or, whilst accepting the low class and status of minorities, some offer a different explanation of exploitation, such as Marxism, or racism based on other criteria.

INTERACTIONIST APPROACHES

Both Marxists and those supporting the underclass theory see racial disadvantage as part of a wider pattern of socially structured inequality. *Interactionists* are mainly concerned with the social construction of racism and with the variety of social meanings attributed to groups which have objective or perceived biological or cultural differences.

Slavery in the USA was facilitated by the distinct skin colour of slaves, but Nazi Germany was able to pursue persecution using bureaucratic means such as identity papers. Apartheid combines both methods of segregation. Interactionists are interested in the role of the media and education in perpetuating racist meanings and in the relationship between the police and offenders. Writers like S. Hall and Pryce provide a Marxist explanation of the negotiation of reality between blacks and the institutions of the dominant white society, such as the media and police.

Some sociologists lean towards social psychology as a basis for explaining racism, using concepts like prejudice. The psychologist Adorno saw racism as explicable in terms of the individual's 'authoritarian personality'. Others see it as being learned, not from direct contact with the object of prejudice but from other prejudiced people.

CRITICS

Some interactionists ignore the systematic nature of racism and its relationship with the class structure. The source of social meanings, such as colonialism, is not always considered.

FUNCTIONALIST APPROACHES

Functionalism tends to offer the most optimistic view of race relations. Immigration is seen as a temporary threat to social order which will be overcome by integration. This integration is aided by the immigrants' acceptance of the dominant values (consider Herberg's claim that religion integrates immigrant Americans) and the tolerance of the host society. (See Chapter 15 on *Religion*.)

CRITICS

Parsons offered this functionalist view in the 1960s, when the move towards political rights for blacks was very apparent. The persistence of class inequality now makes him seem unduly optimistic, like his English follower Patterson, who thought that immigration, and not colour, was the source of temporary disharmony. Economic and political gains by minorities are also explicable in Marxist and Weberian terms, where conflict rather than consensus would be emphasised.

THEORETICAL AND EMPIRICAL STUDIES

MARXIST APPROACHES

Westergaard and Resler

These authors think that academics and politicians are misguidedly preoccupied with race, when the real inequality is based on class exploitation. They see Britain as having a unitary working class, which is not divided by ethnicity or race.

Castles and Kosack

As Marxists, they see a single working class. But they see one that is significantly divided, so that in all Western European societies there is a group of workers distinguished by race, nationality or other characteristics, who tend to do the worst-paid and dirtiest jobs. They use the concept of a reserve army of labour to explain the class position of migrant workers in Europe. These tend to be denied citizenship rights, to experience discrimination and to be confined to low-paid, insecure work. When not required they can be sent home and thus unemployment can be exported. This explanation of exploitation can easily be linked to the sociology of development.

Miles

Miles has criticised the two views above. He argues that there is a distinct *racialised fraction* at each level of the working class where the minority worker is at a disadvantage. The divisions within the working class predate new commonwealth immigration and immigrants were recruited into various levels, not excluded from them.

WEBERIAN APPROACHES

Glasgow

Glasgow used the concept of an underclass to describe the position of blacks in American society. Unlike subsequent groups of immigrants who did not share the history of slavery, black Americans had not experienced much upward mobility. The racial nature of poverty and unemployment in the USA persists. More recent political struggles, the emergence of a substantial black middle class and the growth of Spanish-speaking ethnic minorities have all weakened the view that blacks form a distinct underclass.

Rex and Moore and Rex and Tomlinson

These authors introduced the concept of an underclass to describe the position of blacks and Asians in British society. Their studies of Birmingham describe minorities as experiencing disadvantage because of discrimination. They see these groups as having a worse market situation in the markets for education and housing as well as labour. They are seen as having low status, because of old colonial attitudes reinforced by contemporary racism. Finally, looking at the slow development of ethnically based political groups, they note the exclusion of minorities from working-class organisations such as the Labour Party and the trades unions. Their work is particularly useful in documenting and explaining changes in the patterns of housing of ethnic minorities.

STUDIES OF RACIAL DISCRIMINATION

Daniel

Daniel pioneered the study of racial discrimination in Britain and his work has been followed up by a variety of surveys and experiments by the PEP (Political and Economic Planning) and PSI (Policy Studies Institute). Daniel studied discrimination in employment, housing and the provision of services such as banking. He used a variety of methods to produce both objective data (the amount of discrimination) and subjective data (the victims' experience of discrimination and the discriminator's reasons for doing it).

The Swan Report

The Swan Report and separate studies by Driver, Eggleston and Wright, and Coard, among others, have described and explained differential educational achievement and the role of the 'hidden curriculum'. It is worth noting that the findings on this subject are often contradictory and subject to change. Also the performance of different minorities varies, and class and gender are also relevant variables (see Outline Answer to Question 4 below and Chapter 11 on *Education*).

Hartman and Husband

These authors suggested that the media did *not* form or change attitudes but did provide a 'framework for thinking' about race relations by consistently portraying issues in terms of conflict. The hostile portrayal of minorities was the result of the existing culture and the news value of 'bad news'. The Commission for Racial Equality (CRE) backed up this view in 1984 showing how minorities were presented as a threat or a problem.

Goldsmith's Media Research Group linked racism with the fabricated 'loony left' press reports preceding the 1987 election (see Chapter 16 on the *Mass Media*).

'INSIDER' STUDIES

Some studies try to describe race relations from the viewpoint of ethnic minority members.

Pryce

Pryce studied the St Paul's district of Bristol before the riots. His participant observations revealed a community under considerable strain. The responses to this pressure varied from commitment to religion to 'hustling'.

Chevanne and Reeves

This study also provides participant observers' experience of racism, but more unusually it describes the feelings of a Jamaican nurse towards the white community she has entered.

Cashmore

Cashmore has described and explained the growth of the Rastafarian movement in Britain.

Dhaya

Dhaya has written about the diversity existing within the Pakistani community in Britain and how their experiences here have led to a more unifying culture. Both family life and housing are discussed.

THE UNDERCLASS: A SUMMARY

This summary attempts to examine critically the use, by sociologists and others, of the concept of an *underclass*. The two major applications of the term underclass for A-level sociology are:

1   A theory of *stratification* emphasising *structural* inequality.
2   A view on *poverty* emphasising *cultural* difference.

The concept of an underclass can be applied to *class*, *gender* and *ethnic* groups. Westergaard (1992) referred to these two views as:

1   The **outcast** version.
2   The **moral turpitude** version.

Structuralist views

The **outcast** version sees the underclass as the victims of economic restructuring. Whereas the majority of the population improved living standards during the 1980s, the underclass were relatively or even absolutely worse off. The *secondary labour market* is characterised by unemployment, job insecurity and low pay. Women and ethnic minorities are more likely to compete in the secondary labour market and be *peripheral* rather than *core* workers.

- Rex and Tomlinson (1979) used the term to describe the existence of an ethnically distinct group clearly disadvantaged compared to the white working class. Inequality is explained using the Weberian concepts of *class*, *status* and *party*. These are sources of power which are less available to certain groups. Earlier work (Rex and Moore 1967) emphasised the existence of separate housing classes, but this view was broadened to describe the disadvantage of ethnic minorities in Handsworth (Birmingham) in terms of their market situation for jobs and education as well as housing.
- Giddens (1973) also predicted a split between the working class and underclass based on the dual labour market theory. He saw the mainstream working class protecting their relatively privileged position (in terms of pay, promotion and security) in the primary labour market. The underclass confined to the secondary labour market with little opportunity to be upwardly mobile would resort to 'hostile outbursts'. This underclass was quite a large group, not just the welfare-dependent, who would not have been a large number at that time.
- Frank Field MP sees welfare dependence as the result, not the cause, of inequality. He blames the Government for unemployment, unequal distribution of income and inadequate welfare provision. These may undermine morality and encourage family breakdown and crime.

Cultural views

The **moral turpitude** version, like some versions of the culture of poverty, suggests that the poor are to blame for their poverty, and may even claim that they are poor by choice. The culture is passed on to children, who are influenced by neighbourhood, corrupting role models like relatively successful criminals, and welfare provision which creates dependence. The underclass is characterised by the unwillingness of the young to work, criminality and broken families. They are seen as a threat to the rest of us.

Murray (1984 and 1990), from the American *New Right*, wrote that the underclass, largely found in black inner-city areas, were defined not by their poverty but by 'their deplorable behaviour in response to that condition'. He described family breakdown, welfare dependence, criminality and 'young, healthy low-income males who *choose* [emphasis added] not to take jobs'. British versions from politicians, the media or sociologists tend to emphasise ethnicity less, but share the views on welfare dependence.

Similarities between the two versions

1   Both see the existence of a separate class trapped below the working class.
2   Both see the divisions within the rest of society diminishing.
3   Both see the gap between the underclass and the majority widening as a result of economic restructuring causing rising unemployment and the replacement of permanent full-time jobs with casual part-time work. The left blames Tory policies on employment and welfare.
4   Both see the possibility of crime and violent protest, particularly within the inner city and particularly involving ethnic minorities. (S. Hall, J. Young and R. Dahrendorf, all

from the left, fear the threat to social order.)

5   Both see the solution in the diminishing importance of class. The left sees the welfare state as contributing towards classlessness. The right sees the free market as contributing towards classlessness.

Criticism of both versions

1   Marxists see the major division being between the ruling class and whole working class, and the solution lying in the fall of capitalism.

2   Many manual and even non-manual workers have gained little in the 1980s and are not leaving the underclass behind.

3   The division of the working population into core and periphery or primary and secondary labour markets has been predicted and written about rather than demonstrated.

4   Whatever measure of poverty is used, about 40% of the poor are pensioners who have moved into poverty because of inadequate occupational pensions and are reliant on benefits. This refutes the cultural explanations and also the views which emphasise criminality and the unwillingness to work.

5   It is not only the old who move in and out of poverty; this refutes the cultural views and questions the existence of a separate and relatively permanent underclass.

EXAMINATION QUESTIONS

1   How have sociologists helped us to understand the experiences of different ethnic minorities in any ONE society?

(AEB)

2   'The theory of an underclass offers an inadequate explanation of the social position of ethnic minorities in Britain.' Discuss.

(AEB)

3   'Racism is the only reason for the disadvantage experienced by ethnic minorities.' Assess the sociological arguments for and against this view.

(AEB)

4   Describe and account for different educational achievement between any TWO ethnic groups in any ONE society.

(UCLES)

5   Study the following material and answer the questions below.

ITEM A
Adapted from *Black Like Me* by John Howard Griffin (1960)

This began as a scientific research study of the Negro in the Deep South of the USA, with careful compilation of data for analysis. But I filed the data away, and here publish the journal of my own experience living as a Negro.

How else except by living as a Negro could a white man hope to learn the truth? Though we lived side by side throughout the south, communication between the two races had simply ceased to exist. The Southern Negro will not tell the white man the truth. He long ago learned that if he speaks a truth unpleasing to the white, the white will make life miserable for him.

The only way I could see to bridge the gap between us was to become a Negro. I decided I would do this.

With my decision to become a Negro I realised that I, a specialist in race relations, really knew nothing of the Negro's problem.

After artificially darkening my skin to look like a Negro, I searched for an opening, a way to enter the world of the Negro. My greatest preoccupation was that moment of transition when I would 'pass over'. Where and how would I do it? To get from the white world to the Negro is a complex matter.

ITEM B
Adapted from *Racial Disadvantage in Britain* by David J. Smith (1977)

The importance of the question how many acts of discrimination actually take place can be seen in relation to the work of the Race Relations Board. The Board's report for 1973 states that during that year a total of 150 complaints were received relating to recruitment to employment; decisions that discrimination had occurred were made in 16% of all employment cases – perhaps 20 or 30 cases.

However, tests using actors from different ethnic groups applying for jobs suggest a much higher figure. The tests show that Asians and West Indians will face about 6,000 cases a year of discrimination against job applicants in the non-skilled field alone. This is quite enough to show that the cases of discrimination that come before the Board are only a tiny fraction of all the acts of discrimination that occur.

a) Drawing upon examples from ITEM A, assess the strengths and the limitations of covert participant observation in the study of race relations.   (*8 marks*)

b) Drawing upon examples from ITEM A and ITEM B, discuss how both qualitative and quantitative research methods could be used to complement each other in the study of race relations.   (*8 marks*)

c) What explanations have sociologists offered for the extent of racial discrimination at work suggested by Smith's research? (See ITEM B.)   (*9 marks*)

(AEB, AS-level)

ANSWERS TO EXAMINATION QUESTIONS

OUTLINE ANSWERS

Question 3

The question requires an examination of racism and the competing explanations of disadvantage. An answer could be organised around *areas of inequality* (like housing, education and employment) or around the various *perspectives* of inequality and the way in which they deal with racism.

Different definitions of the concept of racism must be considered. Whereas some writers define it as involving attitude rather than behaviour, Hall sees racism as encompassing ideology, practice and institutions, all of which he links together within a Marxist framework.

a) Marxist views share common assumptions about the use of racism in maintaining ruling-class hegemony. Racism is not seen as the prime cause of ethnic disadvantage. Class inequality explains exploitation. Racism is seen as false consciousness and divides the working class.

b) The neo-Marxist views of Hall and Pryce attribute rather more importance to racism and extend the meaning of the term. Racism supports the continuation of colonial oppression, both at home and abroad.

c) Underclass theories see racism as only one of a variety of factors which maintain the poor market situation of ethnic minorities. Occupational closure strategies and the absence of political power are other contributory factors.

d) The role of education and the media in creating and maintaining or even challenging racism can be discussed.

Question 4

Do note the requirements of the question. You must identify clearly which *two* groups you wish to consider and refer to others only in order to make critical or comparative points.

Reference to the differential performance of class and gender groups must be tied directly to the question. For example, to explain the poor performance of a group which is disproportionately found in the working class or to point out the internal diversity within an ethnic group.

If a broad category such as 'Asian' is chosen, an awareness of internal diversity is essential.

a) Point out the difficulties of assessing differential achievement. These are because of the contradictory nature of the studies, the changing performances recorded in the last 20 years, the changing social position of minorities, the problem of isolating other variables (such as class), and the diversity of performance within groups. (See Chapter 11, *Education*.)

b) Apply the conventional explanations of differential achievement to your two groups. This could include *out-of-school factors*, such as material and cultural deprivation (then consider criticism), and *in-school factors*. The latter could include a consideration of labelling, the curriculum, the racism of teachers and pupils, the quality of schools and the difficulty of attracting and retaining teachers in inner-city areas.

c) You might refer to Marxist notions of reproduction in order to examine both the curriculum (including the hidden curriculum) and performance of pupils.

Remember that your studies should be up to date. Generally, the performance of all minorities has improved, native-born children do better than immigrants and recent studies in London and Bradford show some ethnic minorities doing better than white (particularly working-class) children.

Question 5

The marks are divided roughly equally on this question, so equal time should be spent on each part. Read the whole question carefully and decide in which part you want to make particular points. The question is about methods as much as race, and the answers should reflect this.

a) Drawing on examples from Item A, assess the strengths and limitations of covert participant observation (PO) in the study of race relations.

   Methods can be evaluated in three ways, looking at:

   i) *Theoretical issues*: does participation produce greater validity as the researcher can share the experience of his subjects? Alternatively, are less subjective and more scientific methods more valid? Mention 'my own experience'.

   ii) *Practical issues*: covert research is one way of gaining access to subjects ('communication … had … ceased'), although Liebow made a virtue of being different. Daniel and others have subsequently used deception in experiments to uncover racial discrimination. The problems of PO include gaining access, moving freely if undercover, taking notes, etc. Research is not repeatable and therefore unreliable. Williams found that the responses to questions were influenced by the race of the interviewers. (See Chapter 21, *Methods*.)

   iii) *Ethical issues*: the researcher is involved in deceiving his subjects and may find himself involved in shameful or illegal activities. Pryce was involved with deviants as well as with church-goers in St Paul's. The justification lies in the importance of the subject and the illegal nature of racial discrimination itself.

b) Drawing upon examples from Item A and Item B, discuss how both qualitative and quantitative research methods could be used to complement each other in the study of race relations.

   The essence of this part is to understand the advantages of complementary methods which produce different kinds of data and which can be used to complete, or cross-check, findings.

   Participant observation is a qualitative research method which provides insights into the subjective experience of living as a 'Negro in the Deep South'. It permits an in-depth study of a small social group. This method is often associated with interpretive sociology.

   The experimental testing of racial discrimination using *quantitative* research methods allows an objective picture of the overall extent of the problem, provided the data is representative. It does not provide us with explanations of discrimination, nor does it describe the feelings of victims. Daniel's study used complementary methods. Quantitative data is often more influential in shaping social policy but qualitative data may provoke a greater public reaction.

c) What explanations have sociologists offered for the extent of racial discrimination at work suggested by Smith's research?

   The problem here is in compressing a whole essay into one-third of an answer. The response must be carefully planned to ensure at least two explanations are clearly examined and evaluated.

   i) Varieties of Marxist explanation and criticism.
   ii) The underclass theory and critics.
   iii) Daniel's empirical research, where actual discriminators give reasons and rationalisations for their behaviour.

Other appropriate explanations could include functionalist or dual labour market.

TUTOR ANSWER

Question 2

'The theory of an underclass offers an inadequate explanation of the social position of ethnic minorities in Britain. Discuss.

The concept of an underclass has developed from the critical view of Marx's theory of class offered by Weber and those influenced by his analysis of industrial society. Class and other forms of inequality are seen as the result of the struggle in the market place for scarce resources and the tendency of groups to gain advantages by excluding others. This emphasis on 'closure' is repeated by Halsey when describing class in Britain and is developed at some length by Rex and Tomlinson in their study of ethnic minorities in Birmingham. The actual term 'underclass' was used earlier in the USA (in the same context) by Glasgow when describing the social position of black Americans who, unlike the Birmingham ethnic minorities, were not relatively recent immigrants.

The inequality experienced by non-whites in Birmingham was identified as occurring in all the three dimensions of inequality distinguished by Weber. These minorities were disadvantaged in the markets for education, housing, and particularly labour. In addition to class inequality, Rex and Tomlinson also looked at the low status resulting from colonial history and contemporary racism, and the disadvantages in 'party' terms because of their exclusion from trades unions and political parties. Since the publication of this work there has been a gradual increase in the number of black and Asian politicians and trades union leaders.

Unlike the Marxist idea of a two-class society, an underclass is identified as consisting largely of non-white immigrants and their descendants. It is seen as being beneath, and clearly distinct from, the white working class. Their poverty and powerlessness is maintained by racial discrimination in the three markets and by exclusion from working-class organisations. Unlike previous immigrants, their upward mobility is further limited by immigration control.

Marxist critics persist in their view of a more or less unitary working class, as argued by Westergaard and Resler, who play down the importance of race. Castles and Kosack see the least rewarded members of the working class being the reserve army of migrant labour found throughout Europe. Unlike the women or the black and Asian British workers who allegedly form a reserve army of labour here, European migrant workers frequently lack citizenship or even residence rights. Miles offers an alternative Marxist critique of the underclass theory, emphasising not so much the exclusion of immigrant workers but their deliberate recruitment into a society where racism already existed because of colonial history. Thus there is, he claims, a racialised fraction of relatively disadvantaged workers at all levels of the working class, and not a single, ethnically distinct, underclass.

Apart from the Marxist view there are other critical views which still acknowledge racial inequality but deny the existence of an underclass. Some more or less optimistic research on educational achievement and upward mobility indicates the mistake of seeing ethnic minorities as a homogeneous group. There are differences between and within ethnic groups in patterns of employment. Ethnic minorities are not even predominantly found in the lower working class, let alone in an underclass. Neither, despite the persistence of discrimination, are they segregated from the white workforce.

The more ethnographic studies of S. Hall and Pryce, though both influenced by Marx, put more emphasis on racism as a cause of racial disadvantage. Hall sees racism as both ideology and practice and the result of the continuation of the colonial relationship between Britain and Jamaica which affects the black British. Pryce sees the behaviour of blacks in Bristol as also being influenced by colonial attitudes towards them. Their responses to racism vary, from deviance to Pentecostal religion.

Dhaya concentrates on the internal relationships between Pakistani communities in this country and their continued relationship with Pakistan. He thus offers an explanation of their social position where inequality and disadvantage are *not* identified as major influences. The Rushdie affair perhaps reminds us that Islam may have more influence on attitudes and behaviour than does race relations.

In conclusion, it could be argued that the underclass theory fails to offer an adequate explanation of the social position of ethnic minorities in Britain for two basic reasons: *either* it has not been demonstrated that the class position of ethnic minorities is unambiguously beneath that of the native white working class; *or*, even if such inequality has been demonstrated, there are competing explanations for it.

STUDENT'S ANSWER WITH EXAMINER COMMENTS

Question 1

'How have sociologists helped us to understand the experiences of different ethnic minorities in any ONE society?'

> Identifies 3 suitable areas of experience and 2 minorities.

> Appropriate evidence introduces gender.

> Relevant evidence.

> Marxist point is not clear.

> Good distinction between ethnic groups.

> Challenges conventional view. Gender differences again.

> Marxists confused with conventional deprivation material. Good point about prejudice.

> Variety of evidence.

Since immigration began, sociologists have been focusing their attention upon the experiences ethnic minorities face in their host society. Most sociologists have concentrated their research upon ethnic minorities in the education system, housing and employment. This is where the essay will begin highlighting the experiences of predominantly black and Asian immigrants in England.

A study carried out by Rose looked at the occupational distribution of male immigrants in London. He found the occupational distribution was fairly widespread with no overwhelming concentration in a particular job. Rose did discover a high proportion of black workers in transport and engineering work. He found that in the West Midlands the pattern for male immigrants showed little differences between groups but concentration for all of them in particular occupations. Black females were found in nursing as well as engineering and Indian women in clerical and professional jobs. Both black and Pakistani women were underrepresented in white-collar work. Rose concluded all ethnic groups were underrepresented in desirable jobs. This implies discrimination against minorities in the field of employment.

A study by Daniel used three actors: a Hungarian, a white Englishman and a West Indian. A controlled study gave each similar qualifications and then had them apply for the same jobs in housing, mortgage and insurance. In each case the West Indian was least successful. This phenomenon was demonstrated again in a television programme, 'Black and White', in 1988.

A Home Office report also showed higher levels of unemployment and lower wages among West Indians and Asians. This confirms a Marxist view that changes in the infrastructure causing unemployment are reflected by changes in the superstructure.

Research suggests that black children do worse in education than white or Asian children. The CRE in 1985 claimed that black children were four times more likely to be suspended than white or Asian children. The report blamed insensitive teachers. Black children tended to be stereotyped as less hard-working but better at sport than white or Asian children – who were perceived as more academic and hard-working. These stereotypes were transmitted to the children and thus affected their performance.

Driver challenged the view that black children do worse than others. He studied 2,300 school leavers and found the examination results of black children were better than those of white children. He also found that while white boys did better than white girls, black girls did better than black boys. He concluded that while black children did worse in primary school and the early stage of secondary school, they subsequently improved.

Marxists see the lack of educational achievement as a class problem. They see underachievement linked to deprivation both social and economic. However, Asian children do as well as white children despite deprivation. It has been found that racial prejudice does not have identical effects on every minority group. White attitudes towards different groups vary.

Sociologists also examined ethnic minorities' experience in the housing market. The 1983 Home Office report found that West Indian and Asian immigrants were forced to pay higher rents for run-down accommodation. West Indians had moved from private to council housing. This suggests they had problems in obtaining mortgages. In a study of housing in Newcastle it was found that Asians were more likely to live in privately owned accommodation than council housing. This suggested both their preference for ownership and a way of avoiding discrimination. The housing was often run-down and overcrowded.

> " Hints of possible Marxist vs. Weberian debate. "

In Rex and Moore's study of Sparkbrook they found immigrants were concentrated in the poorest and most dilapidated properties. They were then seen as responsible for the decay of the area. Marxists have criticised Rex and Moore for seeing the housing market as independent of the wider class structure.

As can be seen, there are different ethnic minorities with different experiences but they all experience discrimination.

Overall comments

Overall a competent Grade D/C answer. Its strengths lie in the use of sociological research to support arguments and in an awareness of the diversity of experience between and within particular ethnic groups.

The most apparent weakness is the absence of any theoretical context for the evidence. The debate about the existence of an 'underclass' could be brought in.

A Review Sheet for this chapter may be found on p. 253.

GENDER

GETTING STARTED

Sociological interest in gender is relatively recent. Gender issues were for a long time either ignored altogether or submerged in the sociology of the family. The emphasis was formerly on *difference* rather than on *inequality*, with the rather optimistic suggestion often being advanced of a progressive convergence in roles. The rise of women's movements since 1970 has had a major influence on sociology, and the sociology of gender can be largely seen as the sociology of women.

The main themes of questions set on this topic are:

1 **Women in the labour market.**
2 **The domestic labour debate.**
3 **Sex, gender and sexuality.**

Answering a question based on any one of these themes usually requires reference to the other two areas. Although most textbooks and examination syllabuses have separate sections dealing with gender, the issue of gender inequality now runs through all of sociology. Other topics where gender must be considered include education, media, health, crime, and, of course, the family.

Definitions

- *Sex* refers to the biological differences between male and female.
- *Gender* refers to the socially defined differences between men and women.
- *Sexuality* refers to desires, needs and behaviour which are seen as specifically sexual in nature.
- *Patriarchy* is the power relationship by which men dominate women.
- *Patriarchal ideology* is the set of beliefs which support male domination.

WOMEN AT WORK

ESSENTIAL PRINCIPLES

The main concerns are:

- women's earnings. ■ patterns of employment.
- relationships between home and work.

In general, women are concentrated in low-paid, low-status work. They may be segregated into particular kinds of work which is seen as feminine or located in the lower ranks of those occupations shared with men. Women are frequently found in part-time work.

The main explanations of gender inequality in the labour market include the following.

1 Functionalist

Gender roles are assumed to 'fit' the needs of individuals, the family and the social system. These roles are influenced by biology, are learned through socialisation and emphasise that the woman's primary responsibility is the home.

Critics see such approaches as avoiding a proper consideration of inequalities in the distribution of labour and power, with the consequent exploitation of women in work and at home.

2 Feminist

Emphasis is placed here on the importance of the housewife-mother role in maintaining male advantage in the labour market. Housework is unpaid and housewives are seen as economically inactive. Feminists, in contrast, see it as real productive work. Women's occupations are often extensions of their domestic roles (cooking, caring, cleaning, etc.), and are low-paid and low-status occupations. The primacy given to the housewife-mother role often interferes with women's careers; for instance, women may end up as low-paid home-workers, in an attempt to combine economic activity with the housewife-mother role. (See Tutor Answer to Question 2 below.)

Critics argue that women are not exploited at home, or that the cause of any exploitation which might exist is capitalism and not men.

3 Marxist

Marxism was the inspiration for many feminists (but today it is the modern Marxists who are often influenced by feminism). Women's confinement to the home is to ensure the reproduction of labour power for capitalism. Women are a *reserve army of labour*, available for low-paid insecure work when required but not seen as having a right to work. This view is reinforced by higher rates of female unemployment and by their concentration in part-time work (See Tutor Answer to Question 2 below.)

Critics see this view as underestimating the particular disadvantages of women, and failing to explain gender inequality in socialist societies.

4 A gendered labour market

Women do different jobs from men. They are concentrated in clerical, caring, cooking and cleaning occupations. Some jobs are seen as being more suitable for women. Schools may still encourage this view, and despite the law, discrimination continues. If women do different jobs from men, and if women's employment has risen while men's unemployment has risen, then it is difficult to see women as a reserve army of labour.

5 Dual labour market theory

The labour market is divided into two sectors. The *primary sector* comprises secure, better-paid jobs with career prospects. The *secondary sector* comprises insecure, low-paid jobs with few opportunities. Access to the primary sector depends on having and displaying those characteristics preferred by employers who may see women as worse trained, less experienced and less reliable. Like the Marxist approach, this explanation can be applied to ethnic minorities and to immigrant labour.

Critics see this theory as avoiding the issue of class exploitation and denying the special position of women.

Alternative explanations explain female inequality using concepts like *caste* and *underclass* to emphasise their lack of mobility.

THE DOMESTIC LABOUR DEBATE

Currently the debate over the significance of housework has become rather one-sided. Feminists have successfully challenged the traditional views that housework is naturally a woman's responsibility and that there is a tendency towards more equal conjugal roles. (Both these views are argued from the functionalist perspective in Chapter 10 on *The family*.) Feminists see women as being exploited by men in the home. Marxists explain the development of housework by linking it to the development of the factory system in the early days of capitalism (see Student's Answer to Question 1 below).

GENDER, SEX AND SEXUALITY

Most sociologists reject natural or biological explanations of gender roles and of women's position in society. Functionalists see gender roles, which are learned through socialisation, as fitting the needs of the social system. Feminists see gender roles as unequal, as well as different, and as being imposed on women by men. Marxists also see gender in terms of socially structured inequality, but only as a part of the more important class division of society.

Apparent differences in masculine and feminine sexuality are seen by feminists and Marxists as ideological rather than natural. Interactionists, while agreeing that sexuality is largely a social construction, would emphasise the way in which behaviour follows negotiation, rather than being determined by structural influences. The wider significance of differences in sexuality is the way they are used to control and oppress women. Rape, fear of rape, and the use of hostile language can all be seen as limiting the freedom of women and encouraging them to seek the protection of marriage. The role of the media is seen as increasingly important, reinforcing the images of femininity and masculinity which develop in the home and school.

You will be rewarded for considering masculinity and homosexuality as part of the debate on sex and gender.

> " The sociology of gender is not exclusively about women. "

THEORETICAL AND EMPIRICAL STUDIES

HOUSEWORK

Bernard

'In truth being a housewife makes you sick.' Bernard distinguished 'his' marriage from 'her' marriage. Married men are more successful in their careers, better paid, healthier and live longer. This is an effect rather than a cause of getting married. The 'duties of a wife' enhance a husband's life. Married women are less healthy and less content with marriage than men. They initiate divorce more often. Single women are the cream of the crop. Single men are the bottom of the barrel. (You can also use this study in Health questions.)

Delphy

Housework is productive domestic labour, e.g. food is processed and clothes are cleaned. Delphy presents a Marxist analysis where men own the means of production (the house, washing machine and oven) and exploit women. There is no symmetrical family. Men own and control the family resources and consume more than their fair share. Men and women control the personal spending of women, who are expected to make sacrifices. Women support their husband's work without pay, e.g. as farm labourers, secretaries and hostesses. They provide unpaid health care for children, men, the old and the disabled. Women are pushed into marriage by economic and ideological pressures. Divorce is no escape, since the responsibility for home and children remains.

Oakley

Housework is seen by many as an exclusively feminine activity, regardless of time or class. It is a woman's main responsibility, and women are mainly involved in undertaking it. This includes housewives, daughters, grandparents and servants. Oakley's 40 subjects described their housework in the language of the alienated assembly-line worker. They saw it as monotonous and fragmented and lacking in pay, pension, sick pay or holidays. It is not contractual nor is it observed by adults. Labour-saving devices fail in practice to free women from domestic labour, as standards and expectations rise. Average hours rose from 70 in 1950, to 77 in 1971. The fact that housework is not seen as real work is both the cause and effect of women's low status. The beneficiaries of domestic labour are men, and those employers who have a fit and suitably motivated workforce.

In 1987 Oakley looked again at family life and concluded that the family itself was not the cause of women's problems, but rather a symptom of those problems and a location in which those problems were expressed. The male–female relationship was based on family life and on the class relations of domestic production located in the home. The dual cause of the problems were gender oppression by men and class oppression in a capitalist society. 'The main function of marriage is to keep men and women apart.' This is achieved through women's responsibility for housework and childcare, and paid employment for both men and women outside the home. The family is the *location* for differential gender role socialisation.

Boulton

Boulton noted that men thought that the division of domestic labour had become more equal and should become even more equal. However, empirical research contradicted these views. Only 9 of 50 subjects helped 'extensively' in the home. Men enjoyed and participated in childcare but not that which involved the routine messy stuff. It also seemed as if men were advocating an equal division of labour only after office hours.

Graham

H. Graham (1991) argued that women's experience of housework was influenced by class and ethnicity. She also distinguished the attitudes of women to paid domestic labour from housework in their own homes. (See Chapter 10, *The family*.)

Morris

Morris (1995) had found that wives of men who became unemployed did not necessarily seek paid employment. If wives did get jobs, the men did not take over housework in any significant way. The man was still seen by both partners as the breadwinner, even though he was unemployed. Wives becoming unemployed had no effect on the domestic division of labour.

Wheelock

J. Wheelock (1990) presented evidence which rejected the commonly held view that male unemployment does not alter the domestic division of labour. She argued that the domestic division of labour was influenced by the joint effects of male unemployment and women's working hours. Wives in full-time paid work spent less time on housework and their husbands did more. Often the attitudes in these families lagged behind their actual behaviour in moving towards a more egalitarian division of labour.

WOMEN AT WORK

Structuralist views

Structuralist arguments see women's disadvantaged position in the labour market not as resulting from individual cases of discrimination, but as being embedded in socially structured inequality.

Barron and Norris applied the dual labour market theory to women in the UK. They explained how women, like other disadvantaged groups, can be largely excluded from the *primary sector* of the labour market.

Braverman in the USA and Bland in Britain applied the Marxist concept of a *reserve army of labour* to women. Carchedi, an Italian Marxist, argued that the feminisation of office work was a significant factor in the proletarianisation of white-collar work. Feminisation can be seen as both cause and effect of the low pay and status of a job.

Home and family life

This is seen as a major handicap for women in the labour market by many feminist writers. These arguments are not necessarily alternatives to those above, but could be contributory to women's exclusion from good (or, indeed, any) work.

Oakley has described how the primacy of the housewife-mother role impinges on all other aspects of women's lives. Paid work may be the extension of this housewife-mother role. Apart from caring and cleaning, Bennet has added secretarial work, which is described as the business equivalent of housework.

Land has shown how the inadequacy of proper childcare facilities limits women's choices of work. The projected labour shortage of the 1990s is likely to encourage the expansion of day care for children. In earlier work, she has shown the crucial role women played in maintaining poor families and in keeping families above the poverty line, thus exposing the myth that women worked for 'pin money'.

Klein has produced a study on the causes and effects of more married women working in Britain. Huws has developed previous studies on home-workers to include those using new technology. The same experience of alienation was noted.

Education and the labour market

The links between education and the labour market are discussed in Chapter 11 on *Education*. Sharpe, and more recently Griffin, have shown how schooling lowers girls' ambitions.

Other occupations

Finally, it may be worth considering those women's occupations which are not usually considered to be real work. These include housework, care for the disabled and dependants at home, prostitution and other forms of crime.

GENDER, SEX AND SEXUALITY

Morgan suggested the following possible relationships between sex and gender:

1   Sex determines gender. Biological differences explain behaviour and the social meaning we give to it.
2   Sex sets rigid limits within which minor cultural variations might exist.
3   Sex has a minimal influence, but culture produces a wide variety of gender behaviour and meanings attached to it.

We could, for example, assess the relative importance of gender, race, age and class in different cultures.

Biological determinism

Biological determinism is rejected by sociologists but is supported by other disciplines.

Tiger and Fox argue that natural selection has encouraged hormonal differences which can explain gender differences in instincts, emotions and behaviour. They claim 'nature intended mother and child to be together'.

Wilson advocated the development of sociobiology, where contemporary behaviour is explained by reference to primitive animal instincts. He cites aggression, maternal instincts and male dominance as examples. This approach is echoed by the zoologist Desmond Morris, who has popularised the reduction of social behaviour to simple animal behaviour.

Bowlby wrote a *psychological* account of the ill effects of maternal deprivation on children. This has subsequently been misused as an ideological argument to keep women at home.

Functionalist views and critics

Functionalist sociologists argue that the alleged universality of gender roles is explained in terms of their *usefulness*, rather than biology. The sexual division of labour is seen as functional for both individuals and society.

Murdock emphasises the importance of motherhood and claims that the mother role and the family are universal.

Parsons emphasises the importance of the functions of the family, particularly as regards the stabilisation of the adult personality and socialisation of children. The expressive female role is compared with the instrumental male role, and they are seen as complementary.

The view that gender is largely socially defined is supported by evidence of cultural and historical variation. Therefore comparative and historical studies are important.

Mead was able to identify considerable variation in sex and gender roles in simple societies, including the reversal of traditional roles and the virtual absence of role differentiation.

Oakley, using Murdock's secondary data, refuted his claim that gender roles were universal. The kibbutz was cited as an example of successful child rearing outside the family. She accepted that sexuality, reproduction and maternal care are influenced by biology, but reminded us of their cultural variations. Norms of sexual behaviour vary (even the incest taboo) and fertility and pregnancy have been medicalised and are socially controlled.

Sexuality

Rowbotham gives a Marxist–feminist history of sexuality. Sexuality is part of the *superstructure* which is produced by the economic *substructure* and helps to maintain it. In the seventeenth century, women were seen as sexually insatiable and thus threatening. In the nineteenth century, early capitalism saw a distinction between the brutish sexuality of working-class life and the pure non-sexual bourgeois ideal of women. The sexual liberation of the twentieth century has seen sex used to sell goods and as a commodity itself. This history is a description of norms rather than of actual behaviour.

De Beauvoir and later McRobbie condemn romantic love as a myth to enslave women.

McIntosh notes the acceptance of the male need to casual sex and compares it with the surprise expressed that women can be prostitutes.

Millett sees prostitution as an extreme model of all male–female relations.

Smart notes that women are seen as victims and potential victims of sex crimes and that this controls their movements. Women, and their male 'protectors', ensure that they take precautions against rape. In other cultures women may be seen as sexual aggressors and men also take precautions to avoid sexual attack. (Men in prison avoid homosexual rape.)

McRobbie sees the development of a feminine youth culture based at home, rather than on the streets, as a result of this confinement, though in later work she sees shopping for clothes as part of a feminine youth culture.

Gillespie writes about women shouting sexual insults at men in West African cities where single women have been freed from their subordinate position in extended families.

Lees has described how sexual insults from boys and girls about girls controls girls' behaviour. Girls can deny they are sexually available and reject labels such as slag, slut, slapper, dog, bitch, cow, etc. They do not, however, reject the right of boys and other girls to judge their reputations. Escape from this language comes with a regular boyfriend or separation from boys. The latter course makes girls vulnerable to other insults, such as 'tight bitch' and frigid. The effects of this social control can be seen in a girl's behaviour, clothes, friendships with boys and girls, and social life.

Masculinity

Early feminist sociology protested that women had been neglected in traditional sociological research. They tended to be ignored altogether or perhaps treated as a special case. Masculine behaviour was seen as the norm and feminine behaviour as a variation which needed explanation. Even talking about feminist sociology, where women research women's issues from a woman's point of view, suggests that it is a special approach different from 'normal' sociology. We do not talk about 'masculinist' sociology – it is just sociology.

The study of men and masculinity is very underdeveloped. Masculinity may disadvantage men just as femininity disadvantages women. Certainly studying masculinity helps us to understand how men may oppress women. Men's aggression, sexuality and even violence are used to dominate women (and other men).

Masculinity has been used to explain the development of crime. Young men learn about being 'sharp' and 'hard' in sub-cultures (see sub-cultural theories of deviance, Chapter 19). This masculine behaviour limits the activities of girls as well as boys. Friendship between the sexes is discouraged and feminine behaviour in boys is the subject of ridicule.

Men learn not to show emotion or weakness. This may make it difficult for them to develop relationships with families and may lead them to deny ill health and thus put off getting treatment. Women are more generally willing to discuss their bodies and seek medical help.

Calling a woman a 'slag' indicates disapproval of female sexuality. Male sexuality is celebrated and is a way of demonstrating manhood. Disapproval is reserved for real or imagined homosexuality. The supposed association of homosexuality with femininity is used by some men to insult both women and homosexual men.

EXAMINATION QUESTIONS

1 'The issue of housework is of major interest to feminists, especially its historical development and functions for society.' Explain and discuss.

(AEB)

2 Evaluate TWO different sociological explanations for the continued existence of gender inequality.

(ULSEB)

3 Why do women take different jobs from men?

(UODLE)

4 In what ways does women's paid employment affect domestic labour and power relationships within the family?

(AEB)

5 'Certain biological drives may be innate but gender roles and the ways in which men and women express their sexuality are socially constructed and social controlled.' Discuss.

(AEB)

ANSWERS TO EXAMINATION QUESTIONS

OUTLINE ANSWERS

Question 3

Competing explanations of not just differences, but also inequalities, in the labour market must be evaluated. Evaluation involves positive as well as negative criticism. You might question the notion of choice suggested by the use of the word 'take' in the question.

a) ■ Feminists discuss the effects of patriarchy on occupational choice and employment patterns.

■ The predominance of the housewife-mother role disadvantages women in the paid labour market.

■ Housework itself can be seen as a woman's job.

■ Sexism in the family, school, media and workplace can be discussed.

b) Marxists focus on the reproduction of labour power by the family. They see women as part of a reserve army of labour.

c) The dual labour market theory offers a critical alternative to Marxist and feminist views.

d) Functionalist writers concentrate on difference rather than inequality, but do not really focus on paid labour. They do, however, offer an alternative view on socialisation to the previous accounts.

Question 4

This question links gender difference and inequality in the labour market with the sociology of the family. The domestic division of labour and power is discussed in the family chapter. You should examine the effect of the type and levels of women's employment on family roles. Discuss both the division of labour (housework) and power (decisions, violence, etc.).

a) Functionalists see family roles as complementary and functional and do not often address the question. Goode, however, does discuss the influence of women's paid employment on role-bargaining within the family.

b) Marxists see the family as part of the superstructure of capitalist society. The existing relations of production influence the domestic division of labour and power. Early Marxist writing suggested that paid employment would lead to more gender equality and encourage class consciousness in women.

c) Feminists are more concerned with reversing the argument and with looking at the effect of the domestic role on the workplace. Paid employment does not necessarily change domestic responsibility, even in dual-career families. Neither does male unemployment.

d) Discussion of the roles of grandparents and children, distinguishing boys and girls, will be rewarded. For instance, Griffin saw paid work as freeing daughters of school-leaving age from housework.

Question 5

This is a variation on more straightforward 'nature versus culture' questions, as sexuality is specifically mentioned. You must also consider the social control of girls and women.

a) The biological determinist case comes from disciplines outside sociology.
b) The functionalist explanations tend to take some gender differences, like maternal care, for granted. Others are seen as complementary and functional rather than as exploitative. Social control is, of course, easily explicable in functionalist terms.
c) Comparative studies contradict the idea of innate differences. Mead, and later Oakley, used cross-cultural material to demonstrate the social construction of gender roles and sexuality. Rowbotham gives a historical account of changes in the norms of women's sexuality.
d) The social control of sexuality is examined in studies of rape (the Smarts), feminine youth culture (McRobbie), and language (Lees). You can refer to the sociology of deviance and note how male sex crime controls women and how sexual misdemeanours lead to girls and women receiving custodial sentences.
e) References to masculine roles and sexuality, including homosexuality, are asked for and will be rewarded.

TUTOR ANSWER

Question 2

Evaluate TWO different sociological explanations for the continued existence of gender inequality.

- The explanations should be sociological, not biological, psychological, or common-sense.
- The evaluation should include both positive and negative criticism. Functionalism, which deals with differences rather than inequality, should not be chosen.
- Marxism and feminism can be compared and contrasted with some subtlety.

Marxist explanations of gender inequality developed from the work of Engels on the family. He traces the historical development of gender inequality as the mode of production changes. Both the ideology and the institutions which support gender inequality are seen as part of the superstructure reproducing the existing relations of production. Modern Marxist explanations focus on capitalism itself (and not on a patriarchal society) as the source of inequality. This inequality will be resolved by a communist revolution rather than by the separate liberation of women.

Women, apart from those in the ruling class, have always worked, although the rewards and recognition gained are frequently less than for men. Following the early capitalist period when women and children did work in factories, there has been a long period of partial exclusion from paid labour. Women have become part of a reserve army of labour; available for work if required, but not seen as entitled to employment. This reserve army of labour depresses wages and disciplines the workforce, whilst ensuring that labour is available for expansion. Braverman sees women as sharing this disadvantage with others, such as the migrant workers described by Castles and Kosack. It is sexist ideology and social norms which confine women to the home; this view is shared by the feminist writers below. Carchedi observes that the feminisation of occupations such as office work can depress pay and encourage proletarianisation.

The Marxist view of women's domestic role is their part in the reproduction of labour power. This involves both physical and ideological reproduction. Children are reared and subordinated at no cost to employers, and men are returned daily to the workplace, refreshed by their wife's attention and motivated to work to support their dependants. Feminist accounts observe similar processes except, as Ansley notes, that men may take out the frustration of alienating work by ill-treating wives and children.

Parsons, from a functionalist viewpoint, approves of the soothing and supportive role played by wives. More generally, Marxist accounts have been criticised by feminists for disregarding the special disadvantages experienced by women as compared with other groups within the working class. As with some ethnic minorities, the social meaning given to biological differences prevents social mobility. The major disadvantage for women is the pre-eminence of their housewife-mother role. This both commits them to unpaid domestic labour and inhibits their opportunities in the paid labour market.

Studies of women in communist society by Lane and others suggest that although women have more success in the job market, they remain disadvantaged compared with men. Class exploitation appears not to completely explain gender inequality. However, the Marxist view does allow us to recognise the privileged position of women in the Bourgeoisie and suggests that class inequality is more significant than gender.

This last point is, of course, rejected by feminists. Here patriarchy, not capitalism, is the primary cause of inequality. Oakley and Delphy have borrowed Marxist concepts, like exploitation, subordination and false consciousness, to explain male dominance rather than Bourgeois control.

Sexism and the social construction of sexuality are seen as contributing to the social control of women. Fear of rape and abusive language are seen by Smart and Lees respectively as controlling the movement and behaviour of women.

Critics of the feminist view come from orthodox Marxists. They feel that the gender divisions within societies lack the significance of class inequality, but do contribute to a false consciousness and to the division of the working class.

Weberians, like Parkin, see feminists as underestimating the significance of the husband's occupations on women's lives.

Functionalists concentrate on gender difference rather than inequality. The close relationship between Marxist and feminist approaches must be acknowledged. Modern feminism is largely borrowed from Engels and modern Marxists have been influenced by the contribution of feminism, particularly in analysing the family. Rowbotham sees patriarchy and capitalism as inseparable.

STUDENT'S ANSWER WITH EXAMINER COMMENTS

Question 1

'The issue of housework is of major interest to feminists, especially its historical development and functions for society.' Explain and discuss.

> Housework can be described as labour within a household for the maintenance of its occupants and upkeep of the home and would include such tasks as cleaning, cooking and childcare. It is seen very much as a female activity and Oakley estimates that 76% of employed women and 93% of non-employed women are responsible for the housework in their families. These high percentages are not surprising in view of the prevalent assumption in society that housework is women's work. It can be argued that because women do bear a greater load in the division of labour within the home this has a detrimental effect on their status in society, notably within the labour market.
>
> Historically, women have played an important part in production and although the advent of industrialisation did mean that some women were excluded from production, when the home and workplace became separated and they became primarily housewives, this was certainly not always the case. Women and, indeed, children worked alongside men in the mines and factories in the early stages of industrialisation. As Harris argued, industrialisation did not immediately lead to a differentiation of domestic and factory labour based on gender. As technology increased there was less need for labour, and partly as a result of this and partly from changing values both women and children were excluded from the workplace in many fields. In the early twentieth century it was even a measure of wealth if the wife could stay at home while her husband supported her.
>
> Functionalists such as Talcott Parsons would argue that the family has become a more specialised institution and these developments are a good thing because they enable the family to perform its central responsibilities

66 Description not necessary. Last sentence successfully shows effects of housework on areas outside family. **99**

66 Reasonable history; 'changing values' could be seen as ideology. **99**

> **Needs tying into question; insert 'see housework as a family role rather than domestic labour'.**

such as maintenance of members more efficiently. Functionalists tend to see women as a gender group playing an expressive role within the family. Feminists would criticise this approach, arguing that functionalists do not discuss how the roles women play can adversely affect them.

Ansley, a Marxist—feminist, suggested in her study that the housewife-mother acts as a buffer between the capitalist system and her exploited husband-worker. So the husband takes on a dominant role and his wife a submissive role where she has to cook and clean for her husband, who takes out his frustrations at being exploited on his wife. Evidence in support of this view can be seen in the Dobash and Dobash study that found one of the three main reasons for wife-beating is the husband's dissatisfaction with the housework. Housework is then a means of control that enables men to be dominant.

> **Relevant studies.**

It would seem that research conducted by Willmott and Young on the symmetrical family would be evidence against the unequal division of labour. However, they used very loose criteria for male participation in domestic tasks and the very fact that men are seen as 'helping their wives' shows where the responsibility for housework lies in the end in the eyes of the researchers.

> **Better linked to functionalist studies, para. 3.**

Rapaport and Rapaport, in *Dual Career Families Re-examined*, noted that husbands were tolerant of their wives' careers only as long as they did not interfere with their own needs. This again emphasises what society, and especially men, see as being primarily important in the role women play. Oakley states that as long as work is seen as being only paid labour, then housework will be dismissed as being merely part of the feminine role. This will maintain the low status of women in society.

> **O.K.**

Marxist—feminists would argue that the low perception of women and maintenance of ideologies which place women in the home make women suitable for the reserve army of labour needed by the capitalist system. So a woman can adopt the role of a housewife if she is not needed in the labour market.

> **Good. Deals with outside family again.**

> **Functional for whom?**

> **Total hours, not pay, I presume.**

Women are also functional for society in that they provide unpaid care for the young, sick and elderly and in their role being supportive of their husbands. Delphy showed they also act as unpaid secretaries and hostesses. From a series of studies conducted during the 1960s and 1970s in the USA Hartman concluded that the average working wife will have a combined domestic and paid labour total that will be much higher than her husband's. This trend will persist as long as wives and mothers are subject to ideology from sources such as the media, which promote the idea of good housewives. Although women have made some progress into traditionally male spheres of employment this has sadly not been matched by equal sharing of domestic labour by men.

> **Avoid 'sadly'.**

Overall comments

Overall a sound answer, worth a C grade. For an A or B grade response, theoretical issues need to be further developed. For example, Delphy's view that men appropriate women's labour could be compared with Ansley's view that the wives help in the exploitation of workers by the ruling class by keeping their husbands quiet. Good selection of studies and a relevant answer.

A Review Sheet for this chapter may be found on p. 253.

AGE

GETTING STARTED

Although the concepts of age and generation may be studied as topics in their own right, at A-level they tend to be integrated into the study of other topic areas. Age is frequently seen as a form of social differentiation and inequality, rather like class, ethnicity and gender.

This chapter concentrates on three stages in people's lives: childhood, youth and old age. The study of young or middle-aged adults, as distinct age groups, seems to have been neglected. Perhaps being 'adult' is seen as normal, whereas the other age groups are seen as problems in some way. We do study adults without commenting on their ages in many roles such as wives, parents, workers, voters, politicians and policemen.

A major theme throughout the chapter is to challenge many widely held assumptions about the influence of age on people's lives. Because ageing is seen as a natural process, we tend to take certain characteristics of various age groups for granted. Children are seen as innocent and helpless. Youth is associated with deviance. The old are seen as dependent.

It has been customary, when studying population, to divide a society into three main age groups:

- The dependent young.
- The adult workforce.
- The dependent old.

The main themes of questions set on this topic are:

1 **The social construction of age.**
2 **Changes in childhood.**
3 **Youth as a social problem and ordinary youth.**
4 **The dependent old.**

Definitions

- *Childhood* is not biologically defined. It is the early stage of social life. Not all societies define childhood in the same way and some hardly recognise it at all.
- *Youth* is a stage in life between childhood and adulthood. It may not be recognised but it is often seen as a social problem.
- *Youth culture* is a way of life common to all youth which develops as a response to the particular circumstances of their lives.
- *Youth sub-cultures* are groups of youth who have distinctive attitudes and patterns of behaviour. Often they are identified by dress. Sub-cultures may be based on class, ethnicity or gender.
- *Old age* tends to be defined in terms of retirement from work and dependence.
- *Maturation* is the process of biological and perhaps psychological development.

A checklist

When studying age groups you could compare their experience of:

1 The family.
2 Education.
3 Work or unemployment.
4 Leisure and spending.
5 Portrayal in the media.
6 The law and deviance.

CHILDHOOD

ESSENTIAL PRINCIPLES

CHILDHOOD AS A SOCIAL CONSTRUCT

Age, like race and gender, is generally seen by sociologists as a social construct. There are biological characteristics which distinguish age groups, but the meaning given to them is socially defined. This means that ideas about age vary from time to time and from place to place. P. Aires (1962) is notable for suggesting that childhood is a relatively new social construction. He argued that childhood did not exist in Europe during the Middle Ages. His history has been criticised, but the idea that childhood is not a biological and psychological stage but socially defined is still widely accepted.

The recent history of childhood would need to consider:

- The effects of the control of child labour.
- The introduction of the age of sexual consent to deal with prostitution.
- The introduction and extension of compulsory education.
- The development of psychological ideas about childrearing from Freud and others.

The meaning of childhood and appropriate roles for children is not just historically specific but also varies between class and ethnic groups at a particular time. The extent to which gender influences their experiences also varies from time to time, place to place and between classes, e.g. middle-class boys were educated before girls and middle-class children before the working class. Parsons argued that the modern American family differentiated far less between the gender roles of children than more traditional societies.

CHILDREN IN THE FAMILY

The role of children in the family is historically and culturally specific, i.e. it has varied from time to time and place to place.

1 The normative view, i.e. what the role *should* be, has changed from pre-industrial and early industrial Britain. Children were seen as an *economic asset*, as both present and future *producers*. As such they contributed to family income and provided an insurance for their parents' future at a time when there were no old age pensions. Arguably, this role continues. The Low Pay Unit estimates that two million children under the age of 16 are currently working, and a recent survey showed that about 50% of Year 11 students were doing part-time work.

2 In modern industrial society children have become the *centre of family life*. Functional-ists, particularly Parsons, identify the socialisation of children as one of the remaining essential functions of the family. *The Symmetrical Family* suggested more equality not only between husband and wife but also between parent and child. The census in 1991 indicated that 80% of children still lived in two-parent families, although one in twelve lived in a stepfamily and the number of children living in one-parent families had doubled since 1970.

3 Gittins describes children as a form of *conspicuous consumption*. They are a luxury and we talk of being able to afford to have (more) children. Children are a major aspect of the family as a unit of consumption, demanding the goods and services provided by modern capitalism. Leonard says children are seen as being there to be enjoyed by adults.

4 Marxists see the role of the modern family as the physical and ideological reproduction of *labour power*. The raising of children is seen as a major family activity, with children fed, clothed and taught to be obedient at no cost to employers.

THE NEW SOCIOLOGY OF CHILDREN

Modern approaches suggest that children should not be dismissed as the passive recipients of socialisation but considered as active agents constructing their own lives. For many sociologists they were, like women, studied only within the context of the family or as an influence on the leisure activities of adults.

Children and control

Kitzinger (1990) argued that we should be concerned not just with the *abuse* by parents and others of their power over children, but also with the very existence and maintenance of that power. Hood-Williams (1990) has developed a similar view. Ideas which were previously used by feminists to describe the subordinated position of women have now been applied to children. He talks of the family in terms of 'age patriarchy', seeing similarities between the social control of the lives of children who are required to be obedient and are restricted in the way they dress and in matters such as where and when they are allowed to go out. For example, children are controlled in order to protect them from attack, just like women. In 1971, 81% of seven- and eight-year-olds went unaccompanied to school, whereas by 1993 only 9% went in this way (Policy Studies Institute). Although 95% of parents rate abduction and assault of children as their greatest fear, most abductions are by estranged parents, not strangers.

Children at school

The view of the child as passive and in need of protection can be found in education, where parents are encouraged by the New Right to exercise choice, because parents know best, not teachers. Children's choice is not considered important from this perspective.

Children have also been used by politicians as a weapon to attack 'trendy' teachers. The Black Papers were published in the 1970s by right-wing critics of progressive education. The view of children in these papers was a traditional one:

> Children are not naturally good. They need firm, tactful discipline from parents and teachers with clear standards. Too much freedom for children breeds selfishness, vandalism and personal unhappiness.
>
> (Cox and Boyson, 1975, cited by S. Wagg, *Sociology Review*, Vol. 1, No. 4)

Media and children

Similarly, there is a debate over the effects of the mass media, which emphasises the need to protect children from corruption. The right worries about sex on TV, whereas feminists are concerned with gender stereotypes. The adverse influence of violence is increasingly seen as a problem for children as well as youth.

Children have also been the subject of media coverage, often as victims of crime or abuse, and rarely as offenders. We still prefer to see our children in an idealised way as innocents.

Studying children

The new sociology of childhood recommends that ethnographic methods, which allow children to speak for themselves, will help to change not only the study of childhood but the way we perceive childhood. This is similar to Oakley's argument about feminist methodology letting women speak for themselves.

Child abuse

The rise in child abuse statistics could be the result of one or more of the following:

1   More actual incidents caused by *individual problems*.
2   More actual incidents caused by more *social problems*.
3   More cases *reported*.
4   *Changing definitions* of child abuse so that some kinds of behaviour are no longer tolerated.

Child abuse became a *social problem* in the 1960s. This does not mean that children were treated any better before this. What happened was that certain severe cases of child injury were publicly recognised as 'baby battering', first in the USA and then in Britain. Previously people were unwilling to accept that such violence occurred within families. This was followed by a change in public opinion so that people became less tolerant of ill-treatment of children. Indeed, the social definition of what is regarded as abuse or neglect has also changed as society has begun to expect improvements in the general treatment of children. Later, during the 1980s, attention was focused on sexual abuse of children, and there were *moral panics* where sexual abuse was perceived to be an organised community activity rather than an individual form of deviance. The image of the child abuser changed from the evil stranger to the evil or sick family member, usually the father or stepfather.

Critical thoughts:

1   There may be more actual abuse of children while at the same time we are becoming less tolerant of it.
2   There has not been the same public concern about child poverty as about the more sensational cases of abuse.
3   It may be that poverty, stress, alcohol and drug abuse are linked in a complex way or that families with these problems are more likely to come to the attention of social workers than apparently respectable families. This is similar to the labelling theories of crime (see Chapter 19).

YOUTH

Sociological studies of youth have tended to concentrate on rather small sections of the whole age group. In the 1960s and 1970s there was an emphasis on exotic and exciting groups of deviants such as Teds, Mods, Rockers, Hippies, Skinheads and Punks. The mass media shared this interest and there was a succession of what sociologists call moral panics where youth was seen as presenting a major social problem. Both the media and sociologists were interested in the *styles* adopted by these youth sub-cultures.

In the 1980s sociologists shifted their attention to the problem of youth unemployment. This was often seen by the adult world as a problem presented by the young unemployed to the rest of society rather than as a problem experienced by the unemployed themselves.

In the 1990s there is more emphasis on the lives of ordinary young people, i.e. neither the unemployed nor the deviant, particularly those neglected in previous studies, such as girls.

ORDINARY YOUTH

There seems to have been an overemphasis on a small section of youth. The studies of deviants ignored the majority of conforming young people. Studies concentrated on white, working-class, urban youth and thus paid little attention to ethnic minorities, girls or rural dwellers.

Most young people are 'ordinary'.

The existence of a youth culture depends on the idea that young people have different attitudes and values from the older generation. However, many studies show that the more exotic sub-cultures are exceptional, and most young people are little different in their concerns from their parents.

C. Griffin wrote about 'Typical Girls' who wanted to be homemakers. This confirmed the earlier work of S. Sharpe, who said that the major concerns of schoolgirls were 'Love, marriage, children, jobs and careers. More or less in that order.' However, Fuller's study of West Indian girls showed that they were also determined to find work which would ensure their later independence from men.

Sharpe reminded us that most young people live with their parents and get on with them.

Typical boys seem more concerned with their future role as the breadwinner than with seeking to establish a distinctive form of lifestyle.

Girls

Although Margaret Mead wrote about girls growing up in Samoa in the 1920s, modern sociologists tended to dismiss them as either not participating in youth culture or perhaps as 'hangers-on' to male groups. Incidentally, Mead's work was seen as interesting because of her description of the sexual freedom available for Samoan girls compared to American girls of that period. However, a later study suggested that the Samoan girls had misled Mead about the extent of their sexual experiences.

Modern feminist writers began to write about girls in the 1980s. Initially they described little more than a 'bedroom culture' influenced by romantic magazines, where one or two girls became fans of media stars.

ETHNIC MINORITIES

Asian youth

Asian parents in this country are often seen as exercising rather strict control over their children and young people. However, where young people are the children of first-generation immigrants they may be more independent because of their involvement in the wider society, e.g. through speaking English as a first language and being in school. To some extent Bhangra music, which is Punjabi in origin, has had a unifying effect on Asian youth who come from a variety of national and religious backgrounds.

Afro/Caribbean youth

S. Hall's study of the moral panic about mugging in the 1970s shows how the media, without substantial evidence, presented black youth as criminal.

Racial disadvantage may have led to the development of a variety of Afro/Caribbean youth sub-cultures which have been imported from the Caribbean. Some young people may adopt, or at least admire, the 'hustler' lifestyles of Rude Boys or Yardies. Racial prejudice may be countered by a desire to live separately from the dominant white culture and adopting the religious beliefs and lifestyle of the Rasta. Rastafarians identify with their African roots and their distinctive style is shown in language, hair, clothes, music and the smoking of ganja.

Gender and ethnicity

In *Just Like a Girl* S. Sharpe compared the life of Asian, West Indian and white girls in Ealing and showed that gender and ethnicity act together in shaping the experience of the young.

Remember that 'ordinary youth' are more common than members of more visible and exotic groups, although they may adopt some of the styles of the sub-cultures.

A SINGLE YOUTH CULTURE?

Some sociologists argued that youth shared a common culture based on age, whatever their class or other characteristics. This culture was often seen as a rebellious one in opposition to the adult world.

The reasons suggested for the development of an age-based culture include the following:

1 *Biological* changes associated with puberty, which are seen as influencing behaviour. Youth is neither childhood nor maturity.
2 *Psychological* developments which require children to prepare themselves for a life separate from parents.
3 The *affluent society* of the 1950s and 1960s which produced a new youth market for goods such as clothes and records. Youth earned adult wages but, being without adult financial responsibilities, had large disposable incomes.
4 The *social* position of youth between childhood and adulthood. This period has been extended as full-time education has postponed the time of entering the adult world of work, as has unemployment.

Following violent student unrest in Europe and the USA during the late 1960s, Marxist writers saw students as potential leaders of revolution. There appeared to be a youth culture based on opposition to the war in Vietnam and in favour of freedom from traditional rules, e.g. a permissive attitude to sexuality and drug use. There were characteristic styles in student music and clothes. We must consider, however, whether radical students were ever more than just one more youth sub-culture, especially when students themselves represented only a small minority of the whole age group.

YOUTH SUB-CULTURES

It has been argued that rather than a single youth culture including *all* of an age group, there are a variety of youth sub-cultures which coexist at any one time. These are not just the sensational or threatening ones which are described in the mass media but also include the lifestyles of so-called 'ordinary kids'.

These sub-cultures may be influenced by the family background of the youths. Teds, Mods, Rockers and Skinheads have all been associated with working-class culture. In the USA delinquent gangs were described as exaggerating working-class concerns with masculinity and toughness rather than rebelling against the adult world. The same view might be applied to football hooligans in this country. Young CND members were found to have come from middle-class homes where parents shared their views. The Hippies are generally seen as being a middle-class youth sub-culture.

> Youth in ethnic minorities.

> Reasons for an age-based culture.

> Youth sub-cultures.

YOUTH UNEMPLOYMENT

The high rate of youth unemployment has been a major concern of governments. For example, in the UK in 1992 some 18.7% of males aged 16–19 were unemployed compared to 11.5% for all males. For females, some 13.8% aged 16–19 were unemployed compared to 7.2% for all females.

REASONS FOR THE HIGH RATE OF YOUTH UNEMPLOYMENT

1   *The increased number of school leavers.* The bulge in the birth rate in the 1960s would explain increased competition for jobs from the late 1970s onwards. However, the peak of the demographic upturn for school leavers in 1979 did not coincide with the highest levels of youth unemployment in 1982 and 1983.

2   *The increased number of married women seeking employment.* This also provided additional competition for school leavers.

> Why youth unemployment is high.

3   *High wages.* These were blamed by both economists and politicians, with high wages for job starters taking away any cost advantage in employing school leavers.

4   *New recruits.* These are more vulnerable to unemployment. First, employers respond to falling demand by not employing new staff rather than getting rid of existing workers. Second, there is a tradition of 'last in first out' which is favoured by unions and by employers as a means of minimising redundancy payments.

5   *Extra competition from subsidised labour.* Competition from other youth on training schemes in effect means a new supply of cheap workers lacking normal employment rights. This suggests that some employers may readily accept high labour turnover. Muncie (1984) argued that the Youth Opportunities Programme (YOP) actually encouraged the disappearance of permanent jobs for other young people.

6   *The absence of appropriate skills.* Skill shortage amongst young people has become a political and educational issue. Clarke and Willis (1984) see this as an attempt to blame unemployment on the unemployed themselves and on schools and colleges.

THE EFFECTS OF YOUTH UNEMPLOYMENT

The impact of unemployment on young people and their experience of alternatives to work, such as training schemes, has been widely documented. Youth cannot be regarded as a uniform group and any experience of young people will in turn be influenced by class, race and gender.

1   Griffin (1985) suggested that girls were more likely to spend their time at home and to find it more difficult to enter the hidden economy than boys. The result of this was their being more likely to be involved in housework and perhaps to see pregnancy as an escape from unpaid domestic labour.

2   Troyna and Smith (1983) have shown the increased likelihood of unemployment amongst ethnic minority youth.

3   Wallace (1986) found that long periods of unemployment lowered the job aspirations of some young people who became willing to settle for any job. Boys retained their desire to be 'breadwinners' and girls to be 'homemakers'.

> Consequences of youth unemployment.

4   C. Horton (1986) carried out interviews with young people and found that whilst they had a positive attitude to work and realistic aspirations they tended to regard the YTS as providing cheap labour rather than real jobs or useful training. Similar Government research suggested that the young were ill-informed about training schemes and that the problem lay more with the publicity than with the training itself.

5   Youth unemployment prevents the transition to adulthood marked by full-time work in 'real jobs'. The unemployed young and those still in school or training schemes are excluded from a consumerist society because of their 'wagelessness'.

6   The virtual disappearance of the youth labour market. Very few 16-year-old school leavers go directly into work. This was normal in the 1960s.

7   The growth of 16-plus education in schools, VIth Form Colleges and FE Colleges.

8   The growth of a new industry providing training in competition with Colleges.

OLD AGE

CAUSES OF AN AGEING POPULATION

An ageing population means that the average age of the population rises, so that the proportion of old people in the total population rises. By the year 2021, nearly one in five of the population will be over 65 – compared to only one in ten in 1951. The following factors have played a part in this trend.

1   *Lower birth rates*
    Birth rates have generally fallen this century although there have been baby booms. This means a reduction in the number and proportion of young people.

2   *Longer life expectancy*
    More people survive to old age than was previously the case and the old now tend to live longer. Even during this century, 25 years has been added to life expectancy because of improvements in living standards and to a lesser extent in health care.

3   *Immigration control*
    Immigrants tend to be young and of child-bearing age, and there is a tendency for some immigrants to have larger families in the first generation. However, compared to the 1950s and 1960s there is now virtually no immigration to the UK and this has taken away one of the factors producing a younger population. It is also the young who are most likely to emigrate.

> Why the population is ageing.

THE CONSEQUENCES OF AN AGEING POPULATION: THE SOCIAL POSITION OF OLD PEOPLE

Remember: the old are *not* a homogeneous group. They differ in terms of class, gender, ethnicity, health and other characteristics, including *age* itself! Class, gender and ethnicity also influence access to resources such as housing, cars, health and general care. In other words, the social position of the old is not fixed, it can vary over time and between societies.

Income

There are 'two nations' of the elderly:

1   Those dependent on state pensions and benefits, which in the UK in 1993 were the lowest in the EC as a % of average wages.

2   Those with private pensions or savings. Usually this sub-group of the elderly have earned substantial amounts throughout their lives. These are less likely to be women, even though two-thirds of the elderly are women. Women live longer, but retire earlier, with correspondingly smaller occupational pensions even where they have access to these. In fact women dominate part-time employment and so have little access to occupational pensions.

Housing and care

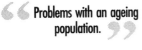

> Problems with an ageing population.

In 1986 only 3% of the elderly were in residential care. During the 1980s there was a shift from state to private provision, which includes profit-making and charitable provision. A DOE study indicated that those elderly living in their own homes wished to stay there. The cost of supporting elderly claimants in residential care has risen from £10m in 1979 to £1,390m in 1990. The estimate for the end of 1992 was as high as £2,000m. Old people's homes have been criticised in recent times for lack of privacy and even the physical abuse of residents. There has been a shift in government policy to encourage community care, frequently by unpaid informal carers. As many as 4m old people are cared for in this way, usually by a lone and ageing child.

Health

The old are often perceived as being unhealthy. They certainly do consume a large and growing proportion of NHS spending. However, other age groups also cost more in terms of health care and it is doctors who spend on the patient's behalf. Perhaps they overdiagnose illness and overprescribe for treatments!

Retirement is often seen as a cause of ill health, although the linkage is two-way since it is more likely that the sick have to retire early. Retired old people in the USA are healthier than workers, but perhaps they are richer. Men leaving work may be more likely than women to lose their self-esteem and friends, which may affect their health.

Dependency

Retirement, whether customary or compulsory, may make the old dependent on the working population. This has been seen as a major problem related to an ageing population. However, there has been a tendency to reduce the working population in many ways, such as raising the legal and customary school leaving age, reducing working hours, increasing holidays and lowering retirement ages. So we cannot blame the shrinking working population and its having to support a growing number of old people on the old themselves. This shrinkage of the working population is in part a defensive measure on the part of governments to reduce the problem of unemployment. There are also substantial numbers of potential workers who are unemployed. Different government policies could bring these workers back into the active labour force.

The proportion of old people working is still falling, despite the fact that the old live longer and are probably more fit for work than in the past. Politicians, judges, doctors, artists and business leaders work when they are old, and there is certainly scope for other groups of elderly to work provided the demand for labour is sufficient and tax incentives exist.

Family life

The old may seem to be a burden on the young who care for them but the old may help the young by providing financial help for children and baby-sitting for grandchildren.

BAD NEWS	THE GOOD NEWS
M. Barron compared the old with racial minorities and women:	An optimistic view:
1 Biological difference is given a social meaning.	1 The old are becoming richer, healthier, better educated and more powerful.
2 They are negatively stereotyped.	2 Age discrimination in the USA is illegal.
3 They experience prejudice, discrimination and even violent abuse.	3 The media image is improving. (Think of examples in TV and film.)
4 They have low self-esteem.	

A COMPARISON BETWEEN THE OLD IN SIMPLE SOCIETIES AND MODERN BRITAIN

In simple, pre-industrial societies:

- The old have *high status*.
- They are the heads of family and kin groups.
- Their knowledge and skills do not become obsolete as technological change is slow.
- Knowledge comes from memory, tradition and wisdom.
- The old continue to contribute to valued activities.

In modern industrial societies, such as Britain:

- The old may have *low status*.
- The old tend not to head the family.
- Families are usually nuclear and kin live in separate households. The old frequently live alone, with their partners, with only one of their children or in institutions.
- The knowledge and skills of the old, and everyone else, become quickly outdated.
- Knowledge and skills come mainly from education and training rather than experience.
- There tends to be a formal, and often compulsory, retirement age which may force dependency onto the old. The Civil Service introduced compulsory retirement at 60 in 1859 because the workers' 'bodily and mental vigour began to decline'.

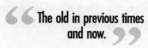
" The old in previous times and now. "

(Critically review this rather stereotyped comparison in the light of the rest of this section on the old. It may be of interest to learn that in some Eskimo cultures the old were expected to wander from the tribe to die rather than be a burden on their kin.)

The beginning of this chapter suggested that age could be seen as a form of *stratification*. In Britain we tend to deal with various social problems associated with age such as child abuse, youth unemployment and retirement. We do not, however, tend to challenge the idea that it is acceptable that age should be a source of inequality.

> and I have attacked this modern variant of the class system root and branch. It will not be possible for very much longer to propose this or that amelioration for the old, or the young, without taking up arms against the ageist society that industrialisation has produced. It was born in Britain and has spread everywhere, our most successful export. (extract from M. Young, 'Slaves of Time', *New Statesman & Society*, 12 July 1991)

As we have seen, the state tells us when we have to begin school, when we will be tested at school and when we can leave. There are laws defining when we can have sexual intercourse, marry, vote, drive, retire and many other activities.

EXAMINATION QUESTIONS

The best opportunity to use sociological theories and studies of age is usually in the *Family* questions. An example follows below.

There have also been a variety of other questions in which you can use the material presented in this chapter. For example, questions on:

- Primary socialisation.
- Parental responsibility for bringing up children.
- Functions in the family.
- Power relations in the family.

The concept of the sociology of youth is often useful in questions on deviance such as those mentioning youth sub-cultures and moral panics. Youth is also a relevant issue in questions on education, training and (un)employment.

The concept of old age is often applicable to questions on the definition of health or health inequalities, poverty and the Welfare State and the loss of community.

Question 1

Consider the following items and then answer the questions set.

ITEM A

Couples marrying in:

1888	1928	1958	1988
99.95% 0.05%	95.7% 4.3%	83% 17%	63% 37%

Duration of average marriage

| 28.8 years | 35.3 years | 34.1 years | 30.5 years |

Marriages ending in death ☐   Marriages ending in divorce ▨

Growing life expectancy has led to longer marriages, but in recent years, growing divorce rates have been reversing this trend.

Marriage rate
per 1,000 population

| 14.7 | 15.4 | 15.3 | 13.7 |
| 1888 | 1928 | 1958 | 1989 |

Divorce rate
per 1,000 married couples

| 0.07 | 0.5 | 1.9 | 12.7 |
| 1888 | 1928 | 1958 | 1989 |

(Adapted from the *Observer Magazine*, June 1991)

ITEM B

One of the major changes in family life over the last century or so has been in the relationships between parents and children. The way that society has perceived childhood has altered, as the economic circumstances of families have changed. The emergence of a distinctive 'teenage' period, which has become longer and longer, is a more recent occurrence, sustained and developed by youth unemployment. Similarly, as people have experienced greater life expectancy, the role of old people has also undergone significant changes. In particular, many of the elderly have been side-lined by the development of modern computer technology, so that they are no longer the source of wisdom.

ITEM C

Resisting the pressure on people to become parents at any cost was the reason the British Organisation of Non-Parents was formed in 1983. The media constantly portray perfect mothers and babies, and depict childless adults as miserable and unfulfilled. No wonder people have children for all the wrong reasons without thinking it through. People often have the worst possible motives for parenthood, in Bennett's opinion. 'Maybe there is a maternal instinct, but I don't think it exists in everyone. Many people have children to keep a bad relationship together, to persuade their partner to marry them, to prove they are real women or men or to "keep trying until they get a boy". What's more we have no right to count on our children for automatic care when we reach the other end of the age spectrum. One woman told us how foolish it was for couples to stay childless because everyone has to think ahead. "Who's going to look after the elderly?" she asked me. I didn't say anything, but I do remember thinking, "Probably not their children."'
(Items adapted from *Modern Lovers: Childless by Choice*,
Helen Chappell, *The Guardian*, May 1990)

(a) With reference to ITEM A, suggest one factor which may make for longer-lasting marriages and one factor which may make for shorter marriages.   (*2 marks*)

(b) Describe the changes in the marriage *rate* and the divorce *rate*, as shown in ITEM A.   (*2 marks*)

(c) The changes shown in ITEM A have led to an increase in 'serial monogamy'. What do sociologists mean by 'serial monogamy'?   (*2 marks*)

(d) Assess sociological contributions to an understanding of the changing 'relations between parents and children' (ITEM B).   (*9 marks*)

(e) ITEMS B and C suggest that the position of the elderly in the family and society has changed. To what extent have sociologists supported this view? *(10 marks)*
(AEB)

ANSWERS TO EXAMINATION QUESTIONS

STUDENT'S ANSWER WITH EXAMINER COMMENTS

a) With reference to ITEM A, suggest one factor which may make for longer-lasting marriages and one factor which may make for shorter marriages.

> One factor which may make for longer-lasting marriages is growing life expectancy within the population. A rising divorce rate may make for shorter marriages.

b) Describe the changes in the marriage *rate* and the divorce *rate*, as shown in ITEM A.

> The marriage rate has remained fairly constant with a slight rise between 1928 and 1958 and a fall again more recently.
> However, the divorce rate has increased greatly.

c) The changes shown in ITEM A have led to an increase in 'serial monogamy'. What do sociologists mean by 'serial monogamy'?

> People are married to one partner at a time but over the course of their lives they are divorced and remarried to different people.

d) Assess sociological contributions to an understanding of the 'changing relations between parents and children'.

> Over the years the relations between parents and children have changed greatly. Over the past century the length of childhood/youth has greatly increased (see ITEM B) due to growing life expectancy, youth unemployment and greater access to education.
>   Not so long ago children used to work and be economically independent and also independent in emotional terms. These days it is more common for children to be dependent wholly on parents for a much longer period. Youth may now last into the early twenties.
>   Also these days children are more at the forefront of family life, whereas in the past they were not recognised so much in their own right. Childhood was seen as a short transitional period of socialisation before adulthood was reached. This period has now been increased to childhood, youth and early adulthood. Thus relations between parents and children have extended in terms of childhood dependency and parental responsibility.
>   Functionalist contributions to an understanding of these changes follow the line of thought that the changes fit the needs of society. The relationship of care—dependency between parents and children has arisen because it best suits the requirements of our society in terms of socialisation and stabilisation. This, however, can be criticised, as there are still some parts of the world where such relationships between parents and children do not exist.

> Also, Marxists have looked at these changes as changes in the
> superstructure supporting ruling-class domination. They have said that the
> economic sub-structure influences families, and so the parents and
> children are falsely conscious in their relations with each other. Thus with
> changes in the economic situation, and hence changes to the requirements
> of the ruling class, relations between parents and children have changed
> accordingly to meet these requirements.
>
> Feminists have explained the changes in a similar manner to the
> Marxists. But instead of conforming to ruling-class ideology, the
> relationships have conformed to a patriarchal ideology. Thus, changes in
> the attitudes, ideas and needs of men/patriarchal controllers alter the
> relationships between parents and children. However, the subordination of
> women has not changed and so they are still subject to exploitation.
>
> Both Marxist and feminist ideas can be criticised, as in many ways the
> changing relationships have had a positive effect on family and social life.

Comments on part d)

- The candidate should use all the available information in all three items above. This was not always the case.
- The position of ageing parents could be discussed: 'no longer a source of wisdom' (Item B), perhaps being dependent on their children for care, but probably not (Item C).
- The emergence of a 'distinctive teenage period' could be discussed in terms of normative views and the social construction of childhood.
- Application of family theories is potentially useful but is generalised rather than focusing on the set question.
- The changes in Item A could be used to discuss one-parent families and step-parents.
- The instruction to 'Assess sociological contributions' does require some explicit evaluation of theories and/or studies.

e) Items B and C suggest that the position of the elderly in the family and society has changed. To what extent have sociologists supported this view?

> The view that the position of the elderly in the family and in society has
> changed is supported by the functionalists, who defend these changes by
> saying they fit the needs of society. Society has positively evolved and the
> position of the elderly has changed with the evolution of the functional
> nuclear family. In the past the elderly were more integrated as they were
> part of the extended family. This has changed because the nuclear family is
> the most functional unit.
>
> Marxists too have supported the view that the position of the elderly
> has changed, but their view is that it has changed because ruling-class
> ideology requires it. This is also true of feminists who see patriarchy
> rather than ruling-class ideology as the root of change.
>
> It is generally true that age is a social construction. There are biological
> changes involved in ageing but the meaning given to these changes
> depends on the society concerned.

Comments on part e)

Again items not used. The candidate has tried to apply previously learned and understood perspectives on the family to answer questions on age and understood perspectives on the family to answer questions on age groups without really focusing on the issues in the question actually set. Broad generalisations used too frequently here.

Overall comments

The candidate has demonstrated knowledge and understanding of potentially relevant arguments and evidence.

However, this knowledge has not been effectively applied to the questions set.

Nevertheless, a grade B answer.

A Review Sheet for this chapter may be found on pp. 253–4.

POWER AND POLITICS

VOTING BEHAVIOUR

THEORIES OF POWER

THEORETICAL AND EMPIRICAL STUDIES

GETTING STARTED

Politics is about power relationships of all kinds, from the family to international relations. In this chapter we concentrate on the macro level of the whole society, which generally coincides with the nation state. The issue of power is also discussed in *particular contexts* in the chapters on *The family, Work, Organisations, Deviance* and *World sociology and development*. The major debates in this chapter tend to be about the competing claims of consensus and conflict perspectives to explain power relationships, political institutions, political attitudes and political behaviour.

The main themes of questions set on this topic are:

1 **Evaluating sociological theories of the nature and distribution of power.**
2 **Evaluating sociological theories of the role of the state.**
3 **Examining the arguments about the existence of a ruling class.**
4 **Examining explanations of voting behaviour and other forms of political behaviour.**

Definitions

■ *Power* is the ability to achieve your will against the will of others.

■ *Authority* is legitimate power.

■ *Ideology* is a set of ideas, based on values, which serve particular interests.

■ *Hegemony* is domination based on the consent of those who accept the ideology of the powerful.

■ *The ruling class* is a Marxist term describing those who have political power because they own the means of production.

■ *Elites* are groups whose power or influence is based on factors other than ownership. The concept, though generally found in conflict theories, is used to criticise Marxists.

■ *Parties* are organisations which seek to govern in order to achieve their common aims.

■ *Pressure groups* are organisations which seek to influence government decisions, but not actually to govern.

Related topics include *stratification* and the *mass media*, as well as the topics mentioned above.

VOTING BEHAVIOUR

ESSENTIAL PRINCIPLES

Class and voting

The key issue in the study of voting behaviour has remained the relationship between class and party allegiance, the traditional assumption about British voting being that the middle classes voted Conservative and the working classes voted Labour. Sociological concern focused on the so-called 'deviant' voters who were seen as explaining Conservative electoral success, despite there being a majority of working-class people in the country. In fact as changes in the occupational structure have led to a decline in the number of manual workers, the left has become rather more successful. This is illustrated by Britain in the 1960s and 1970s, Germany in the 1970s, and France in the 1980s. Despite the Conservative Party's success in winning elections in Britain it has actually lost votes, while the number of office workers has increased.

However, the link between class and voting has become so tenuous that the concept of deviant voting is no longer useful, and the debate has now broadened to consider a variety of explanations of voting behaviour. The failure of the Labour Party in the last three elections and concern for its future prospects have led to new analyses, and to the revival of old theories such as embourgeoisement.

The new explanations of voting behaviour which still see class as significant point out that:

a) Changes in the occupational structure have led to the shrinking of the traditional working class.
b) The fragmentation of the working and middle classes has led to new groups developing within these classes.
c) All classes have become increasingly affluent.

Other correlates

The dissolving of class loyalties, particularly since 1974, has led some writers to suggest that the other divisions in society have become more significant in predicting voting. Some of these divisions are still more apparent in other societies. They include:

a) Cultural divisions such as nationality, language, religion, language and ethnicity; e.g. Scottish and Welsh nationalism.
b) Geographical divisions based on region or housing in urban, suburban or rural areas; e.g. the North–South divide in England.
c) Generation and gender.

Issues

Class de-alignment and partisan de-alignment have led some sociologists to adopt a more 'social action'-based approach to voting. Instead of seeking structural correlates which are seen as causes of behaviour, they emphasise individual reasons for choice of party. The voter is now seen as a more-or-less rational consumer who considers political issues in terms of individual costs and benefits. This suggests a continued volatility in voting behaviour and in electoral outcomes.

Marxist views

There are three main explanations here of the demise of the Labour Party. First, the working class is fragmented by changes in production, such as the decline of manufacturing. Second, there are non-class divisions emerging based on gender, ethnicity, region, education and consumption. Third, ideological control has been extended, so that the political agenda is set to the disadvantage of the Labour Party.

THEORIES OF POWER

The three major theories of power are:

■ The Pluralist model.
■ The Elitist model.
■ The Marxist model.

As well as the debates between these theories there are differences of opinion within each model. The three models can provide a framework for answering questions on the nature and distribution of power, the role of the state and the existence of a ruling class. More detailed discussions about political organisations, such as parties and pressure groups, can also be seen as part of the discussion of pluralism.

THE PLURALIST MODEL

Pluralism is a consensus theory which analyses the nature and distribution of power in liberal democracies and generally approves of what it finds. Pluralism suggests that groups compete for power and rewards but accept the rules of the game and the result.

Classical pluralism

This sees power as diffuse, rather than concentrated. Power is dispersed between a variety of interest groups who compete for influence over the government. No single group dominates and the balance between groups is maintained by the government, which is seen as a neutral arbiter of competing claims. This is the pluralist view of the state. The political system which processes the various decisions is seen as legitimate, as are the decisions which are made through it. Interest groups may object to specific decisions, but they accept the rules under which they were made.

Elite pluralism

This has emerged as the result of criticism of the traditional model. The absence of effective interest groups representing the weaker citizens is compensated for by the protection they are given by governments keen to gain their votes.

The restricted access of individuals and groups to the decision-making process is identified as a problem but one minimised by the diversity of policy-making communities, competition between the influential and the independence of government from any single group interest.

Criticism is found in the alternative models below. The failure of pluralism to deal with the issues of agenda-setting and ideological legitimation has been pointed out by conflict theories. The pluralist model seems more appropriate to the USA, which has weak political institutions constrained by checks and balances (including federalism and the separation of power) than to the UK, which has strong party government.

THE ELITIST MODEL

Classical elite theory

This developed as a critical response to Marx. It questioned both his explanation of the concentration of power and his optimism about a post-revolutionary society which would be free of an oppressive state. (See also the Tutor Answer to Question 1 below.)

The power elite

This was a description of the domination of the weak system of government in the USA by three distinct, but interrelated, elites. Mills was influenced by Marx and Weber rather than by classical elite theory in his criticism of the pluralist analysis of post-war USA. His work lacks the pessimism of theories which see elite rule as inevitable.

Fragmented elitism

This, as with elite pluralism above, has emerged as a compromise to criticism. Elites are fragmented in that they lack some of the characteristics previously thought essential to establish the existence of elite rule. Membership may be closed to the masses, and power exercised in the interests of elites, but they lack the cohesion of a pure elite. Instead, different elite groups form temporary coalitions to achieve particular aims.

Criticism comes in a theoretical form from Marxists, who see the state only as an instrument of power and not as the source of power. Pluralists offer more empirical criticism, showing how decisions are not always made by the few in their own interests.

THE MARXIST MODEL

Marx saw the state as part of the superstructure of exploitative societies. The power of the ruling class derived from ownership, and the role of the state was to maintain the existing relations of production.

The modern Marxists are concerned with three main issues. First, with the autonomy of the state from the ruling class. Second, with the increasing importance of the state in maintaining ideological control over the masses. Third, with whether modern capitalism inevitably produces a liberal democratic system.

Criticism has not been confined to the internal Marxist debates but also comes from a variety of external sources. The underlying theory of class has been challenged by Weber and modern Weberians. Pluralists have presented evidence of decisions being both influenced by, and made in, the interests of the working class. Elite theorists have pointed to the continued concentration of power in socialist states. (See also the Tutor Answer to Question 1 below.)

The New Right and the role of the state

Supporters of free-market economics follow Hayek and advocate the minimum of state interference in the lives of citizens, particularly in the field of economics. There should be no government economic planning and no use of the Welfare State to redistribute income. The state should be restricted to providing what the market cannot provide, such as defence. Privatisation is a natural policy for a government sharing these views. The aim of minimising state activity is not just economic efficiency but also increased freedom of choice for the individual.

CLASS AND VOTING

Rose (1968) argued that there was not a homogeneous working class. The more an individual conformed to an 'ideal type' as defined by five characteristics (manual worker, trade union member, tenant, minimum education, and self-assigned working class), the more likely they were to vote Labour.

> **Note dates and relate them to election results.**

Goldthorpe (1978) makes a similar observation about divisions in the British middle class.

Goldthorpe *et al.* (1969) rejected the embourgeoisement thesis as an explanation of Conservative electoral success in the 1950s. There has, however, been a revival of interest in the effects of affluence on voting in the 1980s.

Parkin (1971) predicted a decline in working-class support for the Labour Party as the isolation of traditional working-class communities from the 'dominant value system' diminished. He rejected the view that working-class Conservatives should ever have been considered as 'deviant voters', as the prevailing social values were conservative. The real deviants were middle-class radicals.

Butler and Kavanagh (1982) noted how the correlation between class and voting, which had been the conventional wisdom since Butler and Stokes' analysis of elections up to 1966, was rapidly breaking down. This was shown by both the working and middle classes abandoning their traditional patterns of support.

Rose and McCallister (1983) showed the declining correlation between parents' and children's voting, suggesting that socialisation within the family no longer produced party loyalty.

Curtice (1987) reconsidered Abrams' 1960 question 'Must Labour lose?' He re-examined the possibility of embourgeoisement contributing to three successive defeats for Labour. The affluence of the 1980s was manifested through increased home-ownership and the popularity of the privatisation share issues. However, he cites Heath *et al.* (1985), who argued that buyers of council houses, though much more likely to vote Conservative than tenants, were *not* more likely to have switched their vote from Labour to Conservative between 1979 and 1983. Curtice concludes that the working class is shrinking (from one-half to one-third of the electorate between 1964 and 1983 according to the Goldthorpe scale), so that even if Labour had retained its popularity within the working class it would still have been defeated. However, the Conservative vote is also shrinking, and the future now depends on voters' calculations of personal gain. He also sees the polarisation between North and South operating to the detriment of the Labour Party.

POLITICAL ISSUES AND VOTING

Himmelweit (1981) identified individual attitudes (which may or may not be influenced by class, education or family) as the main explanation for voting. The voter is seen as a consumer of the parties' policies and promises. This will account for the volatility of voting and suggests an increased importance for the marketing of policies. P. Whiteley (1983) reinforces this view of the well-informed, rational choice replacing loyalty and prejudice.

Sarlvik and Crewe (1983) introduced the concepts of *class de-alignment* (referring to the severing of links between class and voting) and *partisan de-alignment* (referring to the decline of loyalty to the two main parties in terms of membership, support of policy and voting). They claimed that tossing a coin was as good a predictor of voting as class. The best predictor had become the voters' opinions on issues. The success of the Alliance parties (in gaining votes, not seats) was seen as continuing a trend towards the support for minor parties.

Crewe (1987) remarked that issue voting had been less significant than the individual's optimism about the economic future. The Labour Party was perceived as more competent to deal with three of the four most salient issues.

See *Mass Media* chapter.

Dunleavy and Husbands (1985) adopt a more structural approach to the political attitudes of voters. They echo the work of Parkin in seeing the media as setting political agendas and identifying issues. They also see increased divisions between those who are involved as both consumer and worker in the *public sector* and those who are primarily involved in the *private sector*. This division, rather than class itself, is seen as influencing political attitudes and behaviour.

STUDIES OF POWER

Weber defined 'power' as the ability to achieve your will against the will of others. 'Authority' was power accepted as being legitimate. He identified three sources of legitimacy, and thus three ideal types of authority.

a)   *Charismatic authority*, which rested on affection and personal devotion to the leader, and not to his position.
b)   *Traditional authority*, which rested on habit and the acceptance of the social order.
c)   *Rational-legal authority*, which depends on the idea that laws can be enacted and changed by an accepted procedure. Obedience is not to individuals, but to bureaucratic rules.

Parsons introduced a new concept of power which is based on functionalist theory and is less popular among pluralists than Dahl's version of Weber's ideas. Power is derived from the authority given to leaders by subjects to achieve consensual goals. There is thus a variable, not a fixed, sum of power and, like money, more can be created. The functions of the political system include goal attainment as well as integration and social control.

Parsons provides a functionalist approach to power which is distinct from most pluralist approaches.

Giddens criticised Parsons on the following grounds:

a)   Power is used to oppress and to exploit and gives access to scarce resources. Thus it does not appear to be an unlimited resource applied to consensual goal attainment.
b)   Parsons assumes, but does not demonstrate, the existence of consensual goals. Apparently consensual goals may be imposed by the ideology of the powerful.
c)   Unlike Weber, Parsons does not consider the sources of legitimacy.
d)   If power is exercised covertly, it cannot depend on the authority granted by the ruled.

Dahl supported the pluralist case by showing how decisions were not made by an unrepresentative minority in New Haven. He also provided a test for the existence of a ruling elite which involved satisfying the following conditions:

a)   They must be a cohesive group.
b)   Their aims must be against the interests of the majority.
c)   Their preferences must prevail.

Bachrach and Baratz criticised Dahl for considering only the first face of power, i.e. decision-making, but not the second face which is agenda-setting (or deciding what the issues that need decisions will be).

Lukes adds a third face, which considers who benefits from the exercise of power. Like the Marxists, this view assumes that objective class interests can be identified, even if the group concerned does not recognise them. The role of a dominant ideology is crucial here.

Miliband wrote a Marxist analysis of the role of the British state. He sees it as the instrument of the ruling class. This relationship is demonstrated by:

a) recruitment being restricted to the ruling class, or to able and indoctrinated outsiders.
b) the ruling class having the resources to win in an allegedly pluralist society.
c) the state supporting capitalism to ensure its survival. Economic growth is equated with the national interest. The state relies on the ruling class to generate revenue.

Poulantzas offers a structuralist theory of the state similar to that of Althusser. He also points out the increased autonomy of the state from the ruling class, as compared, say, with feudal society. This relative autonomy serves the interests of the whole ruling class by arbitrating between sectional interests and by granting concessions to the working class to maintain ruling-class hegemony.

EXAMINATION QUESTIONS

1   Compare and contrast elite and Marxist theories of the nature and distribution of political power.
(AEB)

2   Critically examine the evidence for the assertion that Britain has a ruling class.
(AEB)

3   Compare and contrast pluralist and Marxist explanations of the role of the state in industrial society.
(AEB)

4   Examine sociological explanations of the successes of the Conservative Party in the General Elections since 1975.
(AEB)

5   Do the social and political trends of the last ten years (i.e. 1979 to 1988) suggest that the embourgeoisement thesis was rejected prematurely?
(UODLE)

6   Discuss the view that institutions such as the mass media maintain the political status quo by spreading the ideas of the dominant class to the rest of society.
(AEB)

ANSWERS TO EXAMINATION QUESTIONS

OUTLINE ANSWERS

Question 3

This question requires a consideration of both similarities and differences, although the emphasis is likely to be on contrasts.

Diversity within each approach should be emphasised, e.g. the distinction between pluralism and elite pluralism and the debate between instrumental and structuralist theories of the state. The theories of the state should be discussed within the broader context of theories of power.

If you wish to deal with the theories in sequence, rather than to make a point-by-point comparison, then the similarities and differences must be made explicit. The straightforward juxtaposition of alternatives without bringing out comparisons would probably produce no better than a D grade answer.

Points of comparison could include:

■ Consensus or conflict theory.

■ The nature and distribution of power.

■ How power is exercised: by consensual goals or class interests.

■ The state as a neutral arbiter (pluralism), as an instrument of class domination (Miliband), or as an arbiter between sectional ruling-class interests (Poulantzas).

- The relationship between power and authority. Both theories rely on 'consent' but Marxists see this as false consciousness. Discuss hegemony, ideology and ISAs.

- How are political leaders changed and does it make any difference if the class relationships remain intact?

- Both see an expanding role for the state, although some contemporary Marxists see the superficial withdrawal from areas of possible failure (health, welfare and education as well as privatisation) as an attempt to avoid a 'legitimation crisis'.

Question 4

> Refer to recent elections. Consideration of earlier results must be linked to the question.

'Successes' could be regarded as problematic. Electoral victories have been accompanied by declining support in terms of membership, loyalty, support for policies and votes.

Interactionists and others identify theoretical and methodological problems in assuming that correlations between voting and other characteristics indicate a *causal* relationship.

A good answer will attempt an *evaluation* of some of the following explanations:

- Class and partisan de-alignment, particularly the decline in working-class support for Labour. The regional divide.

- Changes in the class structure. Embourgeoisement. The shrinking of the working class. The fragmentation of the working class.

- The consumer choice model. (Industrial relations and unemployment in 1979, the Falklands and defence in 1983, but not confirmed by the salient issues of 1987, which indicated success for Labour.)

- Economic optimism.

- The ideological explanations (Dunleavy, Parkin and Marxists).

- The rise of third parties and the effects of the electoral system.

Question 5

This is a 'hybrid' question which requires a consideration of class issues as well as political developments. It does emphasise how essential a good understanding of changes in the class structure is to answering voting questions.

- Outline the embourgeoisement thesis in its original 1950s version.

- Outline the refutation by Goldthorpe *et al.*

- Present evidence for embourgeoisement over the last ten years.
  a) Rising real income and consumer boom.
  b) Increasing home and share ownership.
  c) Decline in Union support and influence.
  d) Decline of Labour Party support from the working class.
  e) Increased similarity in working conditions and job security for manual and office workers.
  f) Changes in the occupational structure.
  g) Conservative electoral victories.

- Present evidence against embourgeoisement.
  a) The persistence of poverty.
  b) The new 'instrumental' working class as described by Goldthorpe in the earlier study.
  c) The fragmented working class as described by Roberts, who saw only a small fraction embourgeoised.
  d) Proletarianisation of office work.
  e) The family does not conform to the middle-class ideal described in the 'symmetrical family'.
  f) Alternative explanations of Conservative victories.

Question 6

This question shows that knowledge from different topic areas on the syllabus can be applied to a particular question. The AEB syllabus stresses that a knowledge and understanding of theory and methods should be an integral part of the study of *all* topics. Although boards tend to ask familiar questions under a particular section of the syllabus, it is legitimate to examine any aspect of a subject which is identified on the syllabus.

The answer should present a Marxist account of the issues posed in the question. You should focus on the ideas of 'spreading ideas' and the 'political status quo' rather than the general issue of class inequality.

The phrase 'institutions such as the mass media' is an invitation to discuss other institutions such as educational, religious and legal institutions.

Discussion could include internal Marxist debates involving Gramsci, S. Hall, Bowles and Gintis, Bordieu, etc. Concepts such as Althusser's ISAs and RSAs could be applied.

Various pluralist accounts of the media, law and education could be offered as a critical alternative. You could challenge the whole idea of a 'dominant class'.

TUTOR ANSWER

Question 1

Compare and contrast elite and Marxist theories of the nature and distribution of political power.

There are both similarities and differences between Marxist and elite theories. Within each group of theories there is also some variation, as well as many common assumptions.

Both theories adopt a conflict perspective and have a 'constant-sum' view of power. That is, power is seen as being held by one group at the expense of others. This view is also shared by some pluralist writers such as Dahl, but he sees power as being dispersed through a variety of groups and not concentrated in the hands of a minority. Parsons, writing from a functional perspective, had a 'variable-sum' view of power. He saw power as being created from the authority which subjects give leaders to achieve consensual goals.

Classical elite theories follow Weber in concentrating on the so-called 'first face' of power. This is the ability successfully to influence decision-making. Later, as a response to criticism from pluralists, Bachrach and Baratz suggested that consideration be given to a 'second face' of power, where agenda-setting is seen as important in deciding what the political issues will be and which alternatives will be considered.

Lukes identified a 'third face', which is seen as crucial in modern Marxist theory. This emphasises the importance of ideology in legitimising the power of the ruling class. Their interests begin to be seen as the national interest. This Marxist view, namely that gaining the consent of the masses is an important aspect of power, has been developed in the work of Gramsci, who introduced the concept of hegemony, where domination is based on the consent of those who accept the ideology of the powerful. Althusser describes the institutions which impose this ideology as ISAs, e.g. the media and the education system. Of course this apparent 'consent' is false consciousness.

In elite theories the concept of legitimation through 'consent' is found in Pareto's distinction between 'lions' who use force and 'foxes' who use guile to rule with the acquiescence of the subjects.

Both Marxist and elite theories see power as being concentrated in the hands of a minority. For Marxists this is the ruling class, whose source of power is ownership of the means of production. Marxist revisionists, like Djilas and Burnham, see *control* over production as the basis of new ruling classes in Eastern Europe and the USA respectively.

Elite theories, some of which developed as criticisms of Marx, identify a variety of sources of power for the ruling elite. Pareto saw the psychological characteristics of individuals as important, whereas Mosca placed greater stress on structural factors, including control over organisation. This emphasis on organisation is also found in Michels' *Iron Law of Oligarchy.*

Mills is more accepting of the Marxist analysis than those above. His theory of the 'Power Elite' is not a reaction to Marxism, but a critique of post-war American pluralist theories of power. He argued that the USA was a permanent war economy, where a power elite occupied the command positions. This power elite comprised three groups whose relative power depended on external circumstances such as war, depression or prosperity. They were economic, political and military leaders respectively. The power elite were united by shared aims, common background and an exchange of personnel. They acted in concert, unhindered by weak political institutions.

Lindblom is also closer to Marxist views in emphasising the way in which business elites can veto government decisions because their actions shape the performance of the economy and thus strongly influence the government's chance of re-election.

Functionalists see power as being used to achieve consensual goals and view the moral order as the basis of power. However, both Marxists and elite theorists agree that power is not used to further common interests. Marxists see political decisions as reinforcing the existing relations of production and regard the moral order as emerging from ruling-class ideology.

Both Westergaard and Resler and Lukes emphasise the importance of looking at *who* benefits from the exercise of power. The distribution of wealth is seen as evidence of the power of the ruling class. Elite theorists also see power as being exercised selfishly to protect political and economic interests. In contrast to Marxists, wealth is seen as the possible result of power and not as its source. This could be illustrated by the illicit fortunes accumulated by dictators such as Marcos and Noriega, and by the recent exposing of corrupt regimes such as in East Germany.

Modern elite theory, influenced by pluralism, sees fragmented elites competing for power and forming temporary coalitions to gain rewards. The restricted access to such groups distinguishes this theory from conventional pluralist theory.

Explanations of the rotation of power and of the emergence of new leaders distinguish Marxist and elite theories. Marxists see the political system as part of the superstructure, and thus changing only when there are changes in the mode of production. Pareto saw elites falling when individuals lost 'their vigour'. Mosca is more influenced by Marx, in that he acknowledges the importance of economic change but also sees changes in other social forces leading to changes in political leadership. The effects of political and religious ideology could be mentioned in this respect.

Finally, both types of theory (and their pluralist critics) see the state becoming increasingly centralised, bureaucratic and important. Elite theories see control of the state as the usual basis for a governing elite. Bottomore thinks this is best illustrated by the political systems of Eastern Europe, although the ability of such elites to maintain power is currently in question.

There are, however, divisions within modern Marxism as to the role of the state. Miliband saw the state as the instrument of the ruling class, making decisions in their favour. Poulantzas has a more structuralist view, emphasising ideological domination. He also argues that the state has become relatively autonomous and that this best serves the general interests of the ruling class. Such a state appears more legitimate to the working class and will grant them the necessary concessions to prevent a legitimation crisis.

STUDENT'S ANSWER WITH EXAMINER COMMENTS

Question 2

Critically examine the evidence for the assertion that Britain has a ruling class.

> Whether there is a ruling class in Britain is debatable. Marx argues that power is held by a particular group in society, the owners of the means of production, at the expense of the rest. The dominant group furthers its interests, which are in conflict with the interests of the subject class. If the subject group accept ruling-class power as legitimate this indicates that they are falsely conscious. Power is used to maintain the existing relations of production.
>
> Westergaard and Resler argue that power can be measured only by its results. They show that wealth is concentrated in the hands of about 5% of the population who form the capitalist class. This group monopolises power and is a ruling class.
>
> Marxists argue that privilege and status are gained through inheritance and exclusive education. Those in 'elite' positions are likely to have origins in the upper class. Coates' study of the membership of the 1984 Conservative cabinet showed that 71% were company directors and 14% landowners. Scott's study of undersecretaries and ambassadors showed that they came from public schools and 'Oxbridge'. The British ruling class remains a self-recruiting and self-perpetuating stratum with shared political and economic interests. Marxists see these facts as proof that the upper/ruling class actively rule through the state, which is the 'executive committee of the Bourgeoisie' and an increasingly important part of the superstructure.
>
> Marx argues that the only way a ruling class will not exist is if a revolution occurs. This has not happened and the gap between the rich and the poor has widened.

Good working definition of a ruling class.

Simple supporting evidence.

Confuses ruling class with upper class. Good reference to the state.

> **Relevant, but isolated, point.**

Miliband argues that the British state is an instrument of the ruling class and this is demonstrated by restricted recruitment. The wealth of the ruling class ensures that they always win. In a supposedly pluralist society the state needs them to generate revenue, even Labour governments.

> **Theories of the state made relevant.**

Poulantzas would argue that, because the ruling class and state are separated, the state is presumed to be an independent, neutral arbiter so the working class accept its legitimacy. Thus rules are accepted in a way that overt ruling-class rule would prevent. There is a debate within Marxism about the independence of the state.

Elite theory is another conflict theory which argues that power in any society is held by an elite minority, not a class. Pareto and Mosca used this theory to attack Marxism. Elites owe their position in society to personal qualities of individuals or organisational ability. The elite is a cohesive minority united and organised in the face of the unorganised masses. The utopian view of an egalitarian communist society is seen as an illusion.

> **Theoretical criticism of ruling class.**

C.W. Mills wrote in 1956 that the USA was a permanent war economy dominated by a 'Power Elite' who occupied the command positions in economic, political and military organisations. They act together, with one group sometimes dominating the others. Mills is slightly Marxist in recognising concentration of power as based on other factors as well as economic ones.

Marxists criticise elite theories as failing to identify the source of power in the economy and ignoring the importance of the ruling class by concentrating on their instrument, the state.

> **Theoretical response to criticism.**

Pluralists see power as dispersed, not concentrated, in the hands of a ruling class. Functionalists argue that power is a variable sum, not constant. Society contains many groups, not just two conflicting classes. Power is dispersed through elections, shareholders, public ownership, pressure groups, accountability to Parliament and the press, etc.

> **Theoretical criticism.**

Dahl and Hewitt claim that no one group makes all the important decisions. The government is neutral and balances competing interests. Parsons' functionalist view sees power derived from authority, not ownership. The distribution of power is based on the functional importance of positions. Because power is not a fixed sum, you can make more. The more the rulers achieve consensual goals, the more power is given to them. Those in power are at the top not because they are a ruling class but because they meet the needs of the system best. Pluralists see this as applicable to any democracy such as Britain. Power is dispersed among a plurality of elites which compete to further their interests.

> **Brings in evidence but reverts to discussion of power which is not made relevant.**

> **Theoretical criticism of pluralism not made relevant.**

Critics of pluralism point out that the weak and inarticulate are excluded from the political process. Giddens argues that functionalists assume but do not demonstrate the existence of consensual goals.

Overall comments

Overall, a well-informed and critical account. However, the material is not always made explicitly relevant. The candidate needs to bring in rather more empirical evidence about Britain, e.g. using Giddens and Westergaard and Resler.

The answer is worth a C grade, but was potentially a better answer to another question on the nature and distribution of power. The ability to adapt prepared answers to variations on the expected question is important.

A Review Sheet for this chapter may be found on p. 254.

8

WORLD SOCIOLOGY AND DEVELOPMENT

DEVELOPMENT

THEORETICAL AND EMPIRICAL STUDIES

GLOBALISATION

GETTING STARTED

This chapter includes a discussion of the concepts of social change, urbanism and community, but is mainly concerned with development. The sociology of development has its roots in the early theories of social change. Its revival into a popular topic at A-level and beyond has been prompted by several influences.

1   Recognition of world economic and political problems has increased. This includes not only concern for the deprived, but also fears about the effects of growth on the environment which would in turn affect the rich.

2   The rejuvenation of the Marxist criticism of capitalism which has been applied on a global scale, and responded to, in the work of Rostow and others.

Examiners give credit for using a comparative approach and for applying theories to contemporary examples. This applies to any topic.

The main themes of questions set on this topic are:

1   **Critical evaluation of theories of development.**
2   **Examining the impact of colonialism.**
3   **Examining the relationship between development and urbanisation, industrialisation, demographic changes and the environment.**

Definitions

It is important to distinguish the following.

■ The sociology of *development*, which tries to explain why some countries are further up the ladder of progress than others.

■ The sociology of *underdevelopment*, which seeks to explain how the development of rich countries is the result of their actively promoting the underdevelopment of other countries, which therefore became (and are kept) poor.

■ *Contemporary societies* may be industrialised, post-industrial, modern, post-modern, developing, underdeveloped, rich, poor, etc.

Related topics include health, education, gender and race. The chapter on *Sociological theories* deals with social change.

ESSENTIAL PRINCIPLES

DEVELOPMENT

Bendix explained development as involving both *economic change* (i.e. industrialisation) and *modernisation* (i.e. cultural and political changes in values and institutions). This view is reminiscent of the Marxist distinction between substructure and superstructure.

Rich and poor countries have been categorised as the First, Second, Third and Fourth world, or as Developed Countries (DCs), Newly Industrialising Countries (NICs) and Underdeveloped Countries (UDCs). Remember that, as in our discussions of the other forms of inequality such as class, gender and race, the writer's political perspective has a major influence on all aspects of their work.

To simplify our consideration of many of the theoretical perspectives on development, we can continue with the idea of a classification based on political values. This amplifies the distinction already made between development and underdevelopment.

The sociology of development

It is assumed that non-developed countries are at a stage prior to (and inferior to) that achieved by industrialised nations. In order to develop they must (either alone or in contact with DCs) acquire the appropriate economic and social institutions and values. Thus aid, trade, investment and cultural diffusion are all potentially beneficial. This approach is exemplified by the work of Parsons and Rostow and is referred to as *modernisation* theory, although Parsons is more accurately a functionalist and Rostow is close to economic determinism.

The sociology of underdevelopment

It is assumed that the underdevelopment of some countries is the direct result of the development of others. The rich became (and stay) rich by exploiting the poor, who are made (and kept) poor by the continued relationship between DCs and UDCs. These theories are more or less Marxist and thus as critical of capitalism as modernisation theories are supportive of it. They tend to suggest revolutionary rather than evolutionary change.

> Use comparative examples.

We can identify variations within these broad schools by comparing *internalist* explanations, which focus on the development of a single society, with *global* explanations, which examine the impact of international relations. Again, we can differentiate *determinist* theories, which assume a single and invariable path to development caused by structural changes, from *voluntarist* theories, which see individual decisions as important.

THEORETICAL AND EMPIRICAL STUDIES

THE EARLY STUDIES OF SOCIAL CHANGE

Durkheim continued the functionalist tradition of Comte and Spencer, which was later developed by Parsons. His cross-cultural comparative studies led him to distinguish *simple societies*, characterised by *mechanical solidarity*, from *modern societies*, characterised by *organic solidarity* and individualism following the division of labour associated with industrialisation.

Marx provided a comprehensive theory of social change based on historical materialism. Revolutionary changes in the economic substructure produced appropriate changes in the superstructure.

Weber's *The Protestant Ethic and the Spirit of Capitalism* was a comparative study. It sought to explain the rise of capitalism in Western Europe rather than in other, apparently equally 'ready', areas. He saw Protestant societies as having the enterprising and individualistic values necessary for development. (See Chapter 15, *Religion*.)

There then seems to have been some loss of interest in social change as sociology became the study of modern societies, leaving comparative work on simple societies largely to anthropologists, who in the meantime had 'borrowed' heavily from functionalism.

THE MODERN DEBATE

Rostow produced an attack on communism which, nevertheless, had an oddly Marxist flavour. He argued that growth will follow the pattern of Western societies, particularly the USA, and that commission is a 'disease of transition' followed unnecessarily by some nations. (The events in Eastern Europe in 1989 provide belated support for this view.) He proposed five distinct stages of growth which, in turn, are accompanied by changes in the social structure and in values.

Parsons offered a modernisation theory which is consistent with his functionalist view of social systems. Modern culture 'fits' industrialisation, whereas traditional culture inhibits economic development. Critics see his ideas of a modern culture as an ethnocentric celebration of the USA. (See also the Tutor Answer to Question 1, below.)

Oscar Lewis wrote about how a 'culture of poverty' could inhibit economic progress in Latin America. Frank, however, responds differently to inequality in the Western hemisphere and sees it as the result of underdevelopment.

If we now look at the left-wing perspectives, we can see how modernisation and the approving view of the West is replaced by the notion of dependency and a critical view of capitalism.

Gunder Frank's *The Sociology of Development and the Under-development of Sociology* reopened the controversy over development by using Marxist notions of exploitation. But, like Baran, he saw the work of Marx himself as needing much amendment in order to explain contemporary global inequality. He described the mechanisms of neo-colonialism whereby the imperialistic relations described by Lenin could explain current world poverty (and wealth). Capital accumulation and investment, international trade, and labour markets all figure in his work, explaining exploitation of Latin America by the USA.

Hayter adds *aid* as a further cause of dependency in her critique of the Brandt report.

Illich anticipated 'green' criticisms of economic growth by attacking not just capitalism, but industrialism. He saw the ill effects of capitalism as including Western consumerist culture as well as dangerous products such as arms and drugs.

WORLD SYSTEMS THEORY: WALLERSTEIN

This Marxist approach has been developed by Wallerstein over the last twenty years. It stresses the importance of international economic relations in explaining development. His later work acknowledges the influence of political and cultural factors, but these are seen as subordinate to the world system of economic exploitation. Wallerstein describes an international division of labour and distinguishes three levels of nation:

1   The *core* nations like the USA, Japan and Britain.
2   The nations of the *semi-periphery*, such as Malaysia and Indonesia.
3   The nations of the *periphery*, which include most Third World countries.

The countries at the core exploit the other levels. However there is the limited possibility of countries moving from one level to another.

Criticism of world systems theory

- Wallerstein's theory is less rigid than Frank's, as it allows nations to change their relative status.

- Giddens sees international political relations as being separate from, though influenced by, the economic system.

- There may be different social systems at each level, e.g. not all capitalist countries are the same. East Asian capitalism is culturally and politically distinct. This is a general criticism of most theories of development which try to categorise societies in two or three types.

- World system theory is about international relations rather than globalisation. This means it concentrates on how one country exploits another without considering global capitalism, which is not always limited by national boundaries.

GLOBALISATION

SOCIOLOGY OF THE GLOBAL SYSTEM: Sklair (1993)

There is a global system structured by a global capitalist class. This system is based on:

1   Relationships between nation-states (Wallerstein's view).

2   Transnational practices which originate with non-state actors and cross national boundaries.

Sklair's account criticises Wallerstein for overemphasising economics to the exclusion of other factors.

Sklair's global system is based on three kinds of transnational practices:

- *Economic*: these are dominated by transnational corporations (TNCs). Global economic relations include trade, investment and the international division of labour.
- *Political*: these are dominated by the transnational capitalist class (TCC), which includes TNC executives, politicians, and media producers. Transnational organisations include the UN, World Bank, IMF, and from the sporting world FIFA and the IOC.
- *Cultural*: dominated by the culture–ideology of *consumerism*. Other aspects of culture are seen as far less important.

The advantages of Sklair's views are:

1 They do not overemphasise the importance of the nation-state. Class inequalities are at least as important. As he points out, poor workers in the USA do not exploit the rich of Latin America.
2 The importance of TNCs is recognised – they often have sales larger than the GNP of small and medium-sized nations.
3 The influence of political and cultural practices is recognised.
4 The influence of culture is not overemphasised.

THE GLOBALISATION OF CULTURE

Sklair has recognised the emphasis on culture as a competing model of globalisation. Several sociologists (and politicians) have expressed concern about the threat to individual, community and national identities from a global culture.

Studies have focused on consumerism (like Sklair) but also tourism, the mass media and the development of post-modern societies. A global culture is seen as a present or future possibility spread by the mass media.

Conclusions

1 The evidence for globalisation seems very strong; it has certainly convinced most sociologists.
2 The relative importance of economics, politics and culture remains a subject for debate.
3 Whether globalisation is a consequence of modernity (Giddens) or has helped to produce a post-modern era is disputed. Post-modernism is more interested in a global culture based on media representations of reality than in a global economy. However, there is no absolute distinction between economics and culture. Post-modernism recognises the increased importance of cultural images, both in selling products and as products to be sold, often by TNCs.

DEVELOPMENT AND HEALTH

The study of the relationship between development and health inevitably tends to focus on:

1 The economic causes of ill health.
2 Inequalities in the social distribution of ill health.

The interactionist perspectives tend to be neglected. These focus on:

1 The social definition of health.
2 The process of becoming ill.
3 The process of labelling the sick.

(See Chapter 18 on *Health* for fuller discussion.)

THE IMPACT OF DEVELOPMENT AND UNDERDEVELOPMENT ON HEALTH

1 Development in the First World led to a decline in mortality – particularly during the twentieth century because of:

- Improved living standards, especially nutrition owing to the agricultural revolution and the cheap imported food from the Empire.
- Environmental improvements, including pure water and sewage works.

- Medical advances. These were not really important in reducing mortality and morbidity until after World War II, antibiotics and immunisation being significant advances.

2   Imperialism and colonisation helped to spread disease. Gomm (1985) mentions the transfer of disease between colonised countries, and from Europe to the Third World – for example, sexually transmitted diseases to Africa.

3   The cash-crop economies imposed by capitalist nations worsened nutrition in Third World societies by:

- Dispossessing tenant farmers, lowering production of subsistence crops.
- Often degrading the environment and disturbing the ecological balance. Drought and swamps could be created by destroying trees and by dams and irrigation respectively.
- Encouraging production for export to pay off debts.

4   The loss of trained doctors and nurses to the First World. Gomm cites the case of Jamaica, which lost 80% of its trained nurses to the UK or Canada in 1978. The large number of Indian-trained doctors working in the NHS led to a change in training to meet British rather than Indian needs. Tropical diseases were a neglected field.

5   Capitalism has been blamed for encouraging dangerous working conditions and endangering local populations. The Bhopal chemical disaster in India is an example. Global capitalism seeks to produce where costs are low; this may be where health and safety legislation is lax.

6   Dangerous products may be sold in the Third World. Examples include products banned in the First World, such as some pesticides or dangerous products like cigarettes, where demand is falling in the First World. The selling of baby-formula milk to countries where the necessary pure water is not readily available and to mothers who could breastfeed has been widely condemned but continues nevertheless.

7   Drug companies may sell inappropriate products to Third World countries. The Third World as a whole spends a much higher proportion of its health budgets on drugs than the West. There may be more cost-effective preventive health-care schemes. Expensive complex medical care tends to be available only in the cities of the Third World, and then only to the rich.

EXAMINATION QUESTIONS

1   Why do some countries remain underdeveloped?

(UCLES)

2   Critically examine the view that education is 'the major means of achieving modernisation'.

(AEB AS-level)

3   'The problems of the Third World are a direct result of past and present exploitation by the developed nations.' Explain and discuss.

(AEB)

4   Evaluate the view that there has been a process of globalisation, in which societies operate within an integrated world-wide system.

(AEB)

ANSWERS TO EXAMINATION QUESTIONS

OUTLINE ANSWERS

Question 2

A good answer will discuss the merits of competing theories of development as well as the possible impact of education on economic growth. All material must, of course, be made explicitly relevant to the question.

i)   Evidence supporting the view can be cited, showing how education can be a key factor in promoting modern values, is an investment in human capital, and can integrate a society threatened by rapid industrialisation and urbanisation. Specific educational programmes for health and birth control could be mentioned. (See Chapter 11.)

ii) Arguments can be put forward which accept the functionalist and modernisation perspectives, but see other factors as being of equal or greater importance, e.g. aid, birth control and investment.

iii) Criticism can be made of the functionalist view of the relationship between education and the economy. Balogh, Foster and Dawes all point out the failure of vocational education in Third World countries to meet their real needs, and suggest the relative autonomy of the education system.

Marxists suggest an alternative relationship between education and the economy. Freire proposes more radical and relevant educational strategies.

iv) The rejection of modernisation theory itself, from the viewpoints of dependency theory or more voluntarist perspectives, can be considered.

TUTOR ANSWER

Question 1

Why do some countries remain underdeveloped?

Definitions of development and underdevelopment are problematic and value laden. The general, questionable, assumptions are that industrialisation on Western lines is the most advanced, and therefore the most desirable, system. Even if this were accepted, there has been no common pattern of development for industrialised nations and they have not necessarily arrived at the same destination.

Bendix defines development as industrialisation and modernisation, thus considering both economic change (like the Marxist notion of substructure) and social and political change (the superstructure).

In order to simplify many sociological explanations of *why* nations fail to develop we can make a basic division, one based less on a sociological approach than on the author's political stance.

Modernisation theories deal with the sociology of development, whereas dependency theories explain *under*development. Modernisation theories assume that non-developed countries are at a stage prior to (and therefore inferior to) development. This desirable goal may or may not be achieved. These views approve of capitalist societies in themselves and see them as potentially helpful to non-developed societies, through aid, trade or even by providing a model of success.

Dependency theories assume that the underdevelopment of some countries is the direct result of the development of others, which developed at the expense of the poor and continue to keep them poor. These views are critical of capitalism, which is seen as an international system of exploitation.

We can now critically examine these two approaches, but we also need to note that within these broad political categories there are differences based on ways of diagnosing and solving problems of development. There is the Marx–Weber debate between economic/ technological determinism and the more idealistic or voluntaristic models of change. Within the Marxist framework there is the further dispute between internal and global views of exploitation.

Parsons shows how functionalism can explain social change. The various parts of the social system adapt so that modern culture 'fits' industrialisation, whereas traditional culture inhibits it. The pattern variables associated with modern industrial society include nuclear families, mass education, individualism, rational thinking and an emphasis on achievement. Modernisation prompts economic development in an evolutionary way. Therefore UDCs need to modernise in order to develop economically.

Rostow's version of Modernisation theory is both cruder and less sociological. It claims to offer a neutral, but deterministic, view that all societies develop in an identical way, following through five distinct stages. It echoes a vulgar Marxism by claiming that social structure and values change as economic conditions change. Critics dismiss this view as little more than an ideological justification of US capitalism.

Sociological criticism of these explanations of why UDCs remain poor include the following three challenges. First, there has been no single pattern of development. Past UDCs have developed with a variety of social institutions and different values. Second, both Parsons and particularly Rostow are accused of overemphasising structural influences and being deterministic. Weberian schools of social change are more individualistic and voluntarist. Third, the major source of criticism comes from the left. They claim that modernisation ignores both international influences (such as aid, trade and imperialism) and the inevitably exploitative nature of these global relationships.

Frank and Baran have been among the most influential writers who have rejuvenated the sociology of underdevelopment within a Marxist framework. They borrow from Lenin's ideas on imperialism, which introduced the view of global exploitation by metropolitan countries and areas of satellites. Exploitation is imposed by state force (not market forces). Capitalist countries make, and keep, UDCs poor in order to benefit from cheap labour, cheap raw materials and captive markets. Slavery, unfair trade and colonisation are all part of this process.

Frank is more specific when applying this to relations between the USA and Latin America and deals with the flight of both capital and skilled labour to the USA. Other writers note the retardation and destruction of indigenous industry in UDCs and the enforced switch from subsistence to cash crops.

This last point leads us to Hayter's work on the destructive effects of aid, which may inhibit development by destroying local agriculture with free food. Aid is also seen as resulting in debt, which further underdevelops poor countries.

Illich shares the view that some countries are kept poor as a result of relationships with the DCs. He criticises not just capitalism but industrialism itself. His particular targets are the ecological damage caused by industrialisation and the effects of cultural imperialism ('CocaColonisation').

These views that some countries remain underdeveloped because of the malign influence of global capitalism can, however, be challenged. It has been shown that patterns of development vary. In some cases UDCs become NICs with the 'help' of DCs. Exploitation, if it exists, may be domestic rather than international. The importance of UDCs to the developed world may be exaggerated. The major markets for trade, labour, investment and even, arguably, aid remain within the rich world. Isolated national development has not been entirely successful (Cuba, China and Tanzania).

The search for a single explanation is perhaps doomed, whether it is a variant of Modernisation or Dependency theory. The more voluntaristic views which allow for a variety of alternatives may prove more enlightening.

STUDENT'S ANSWER WITH EXAMINER COMMENTS

Question 3

'The problems of the Third World are a direct result of past and present exploitation by the developed nations.' Explain and discuss.

> Frank, a Marxist writer, argues that exploitation of Third World countries is due to the relations they have with developed countries. He argues that the metropolis exploits the satellite to make profits. The cities in the satellites exploit the rural areas, so the labourer in agriculture is doubly exploited. He argues that colonialism and imperialism have made these countries poor. The rich are rich at the expense of the poor. The rich make satellites produce cash crops so they cannot become self-sufficient and the dependency on the metropolis will remain. Once these satellites gain independence they cannot become self-sufficient because then they need help and aid from the metropolis because they have no natural resources left.
>
> Hayter argues that the aid and loans the metropolis provides for the satellite are more beneficial to them than to the underdeveloped country. Robbin argued that giving countries loans they cannot repay creates a situation where 'aid is necessary for the system that makes aid necessary'.
>
> Frank argues that the metropolis takes all the natural resources from the satellites and in return gives them a very low price or sells them badly manufactured goods.
>
> The metropolis exploits human resources, for example, through the slave trade. Underdeveloped countries were left without young and strong men to work in agriculture. Therefore they now require aid. Also colonialism in India destroyed the textile industry.

❝ Identifies appropriate theory but too many points in one paragraph. ❞

❝ Relevant points which need developing. ❞

❝ Relevant point, but isolated from the argument. ❞

❝ Too many oversimplified and unrelated points. ❞

> Generally accurate.

Frank argues that if countries want to become independent they must have a revolution within the country - they must break contact with the metropolis. Frank's arguments are based on the relationships between the USA and Latin America.

> Worth developing Illich.

Illich argues imperialism has given underdeveloped countries false needs (a concept borrowed from Marcuse). He describes this as CocaColonisation. Underdeveloped countries are provided with inappropriate drugs and conventional medicine.

> Needs linking to previous points and the question.

Marx argued that rich countries exploit their own poor. His argument is internalist. He claims that there are fixed stages that all countries go through. These are primitive communism, feudalism, capitalism and communism. Revolution changes the economic structure and thus the whole society. So independence requires a revolution.

> Reasonable summary of modernisation. Should link explicitly to question.

Parsons proposes a modernisation theory as an alternative to dependency theory. He argues that modern rational societies fit industrialisation but traditional societies do not. So traditional societies must modernise, otherwise they will remain undeveloped. Institutions and values related to industrialisation are the nuclear family, individualism, mass education and emphasis on achievement. He disagrees with dependency theory and argues that undeveloped countries can become developed.

> Relevant alternatives, but not all suggested by McClelland.

McClelland's argument is similar to Parsons'. He says the values of the population must be changed. He argues that change is evolutionary, not revolutionary. If underdeveloped countries come into more contact with developed ones then there will be a diffusion of modern ideas. Also it can be argued that non-colonised countries can be undeveloped which is a criticism of the dependency theory.

> Not linked to question.

Rostow argues that all underdeveloped countries can become developed by passing through five distinct stages. The take-off is the most important and it is when rational scientific society replaces traditional agricultural society.

Weber argues that society is what people make it. This was illustrated by the effect of the Protestant ethic on the rise of capitalism. He argues that to become developed these countries need more contact with developed countries. Their ideology must be changed - e.g. Iran does not accept Western ideology. Weber argues these countries need a charismatic leader to make them developed.

> This is not an accurate summary of Weber.

> Critical, but should be linked to question.

Criticism of the dependency theory is that there has been no communist revolution in capitalist societies, as Marx predicted. Revolution is not due to class consciousness but vice versa.

Criticism of the modernisation theory is that even with colonialism ideas of the metropolis have not been transferred to the satellites. Not all countries want to become like the West - e.g. the Communists and Arabs. Industrialisation does not always mean capitalism, e.g. Communist China is industrialised.

Overall comments

Overall, a Grade D answer. It does demonstrate a critical understanding of different explanations but does not present a clear, logical and coherent argument. The answer lacks a clear structure and material is not always explicitly linked to the question. The terms underdeveloped and undeveloped are not used in a consistent way.

Question 4

Evaluate the view that there has been a process of globalisation, in which societies operate within an integrated world-wide system.

Since 1945 the sociology of development has been dominated by two ideologically opposed theories - modernisation and dependency theories. One is the dominant world ideology, the other opposes it. To evaluate the process of globalisation we need to break away from these theories. We must examine improvements in technology and the communication network, and assess the reasons why particular systems have become global ones.

Reassuring — has not just reproduced a general prepared answer based on modernisation and dependency theories.

Marxists identified nineteenth-century imperialism as a global system. The theory of imperialism, later developed by Lenin, influenced the development of today's dependency theories. These explanations have been used to examine the relationships between rich countries and poor countries in Latin America and Africa.

The swing away from colonialism really began after World War II, with many colonies struggling for independence from the colonial rule of weakened imperialist nations. At the same time new international organisations were formed, including the UN, World Bank and IMF. Critics have argued that these replaced the old forms of exploitation and control, which were based on colonial settlement and military force, with new forms based on loans.

The old Marxist theories were challenged by Rostow's 'non-communist manifesto', which identified distinct stages of growth through which all societies would pass as they developed from traditional societies to mass consumption. This universal theory of development suggested that there might very well be an integrated world system.

Paragraphs 2–5 build up a historically informed coherent argument. Knowledge is applied to the question and developed.

Dependency theorists such as Gunder Frank argued that the new world system was just as exploitative as imperialism. The rich countries took from the poor and made them dependent. The rich were also dependent on the poor, but despite this interdependence the relationship was not equal.

Introduces a critical view of relevant terms and concepts.

Critics of both modernisation theory and dependency theory have pointed out the problems of using terms like First and Third World or traditional and underdeveloped societies. These terms might encourage the view that nations are separate and not interrelated. Rostow falsely assumes that all societies start in the same place and that there is a single type of traditional society.

Wallerstein's world systems theory is a global theory. It tries to offer an alternative to those who see societies developing in isolation. Wallerstein identifies a core of rich countries with relationships with semi-peripheral, peripheral and finally external nations. These types are illustrated respectively by the USA at the core, Latin America at the periphery and Third World nations like Ethiopia as external areas. The core exploits the areas beyond. This approach emphasises the global nature of exploitation.

Paragraphs 7–9 address the various theories supporting globalisation. Some critical comment would help here.

Sklair said that transnational corporations such as Ford or Coca-Cola play the major role in globalisation. TNCs are growing in size and importance and are seen by both dependency and modernisation theorists as playing a major role in development. Sklair sees both the old theories as unnecessarily polarised and not giving a full picture of development.

TNCs are the centre of global power today. This is encouraged by advances in communications such as transport (jet aeroplanes) and media (satellite TV). Perlmutter wrote of the change from ethnocentric organisations operating in one country to polycentric organisations operating in several countries to geocentric organisations with a worldwide network. Giddens describes these corporations as oligopolies which dominate world markets because of their size. Many TNCs are bigger than the economies of countries they operate in. TNCs dominate the sales of cars, drugs and Cola.

> **Good evaluative conclusion related to the set question and introducing new knowledge.**

In conclusion, the evidence for a world system seems overwhelming. Nations are interdependent. World systems have taken different forms, such as colonialism and trade. The process of globalisation has been encouraged by technological advances in communication and the ideological success of Western democracies in their struggle with communism. Western culture is also spread through consumerism which, according to Sklair, is becoming the new world ideology in a global society. The interdependence of nations has integrated the worldwide system.

Overall comments

This candidate has both breadth and depth to her knowledge. She has demonstrated an in-depth understanding of the sociological issues and applied both sociological and other evidence (such as the fall of communism) to the question.

She makes specific critical points and uses an overall evaluative framework which criticises modernisation and dependency theories, and offers a variety of alternatives which support the view that there has been a process of globalisation.

Good answers will be able to demonstrate an understanding of the theory of globalisation and apply empirical studies to the set question. The reference to a 'worldwide system' should be helpful in guiding candidates to the work of writers who discuss development within a global rather than national framework.

A Review Sheet for this chapter may be found on p. 254.

CHAPTER 9

LOCALITY, COMMUNITY AND URBANISATION

PLACE, SPACE AND LOCALITY

THE CONCEPT OF COMMUNITY

CAUSES OF URBANISATION

DE-URBANISATION

STAGES OF URBANISATION

URBAN AND RURAL WAYS OF LIFE

POWER IN THE CITY

ENVIRONMENTAL SOCIOLOGY AND ENVIRONMENTALISM

GETTING STARTED

This chapter has been renamed to reflect a new set of interests, although the traditional concerns with community, urbanisation and urbanism remain. However, there is now an increased interest in environmentalism and ecology.

The approach to these issues has become more interdisciplinary. For example, geography has helped to explain the influence of place, space and locality on social life. This chapter has also been separated from the study of *World sociology and development* (Chapter 8) although both chapters still share an interest in social change, comparative sociology and critical discussions of modernity. Whereas this chapter is more concerned with Western industrialised societies, the *World sociology and development* chapter focuses more on poorer Third World countries. Note, however, that this crude dichotomy is emphatically criticised in the *World sociology and development* chapter.

Urban and rural life

Sociologists became particularly interested in the causes and effects of the urbanisation of Western Europe during the last century. They were generally concerned with the negative effects of the city as compared with the more peaceful routine of rural life. However, modern sociology has challenged this simple division between an allegedly disorderly town and a peaceful countryside, although concern about the negative aspects of city life remains, particularly where these involve conflict. We shall discuss urban riots in this chapter, although any explanation must involve an understanding of other parts of the syllabus such as inequality, poverty and deviance.

The main themes of questions set on this topic area are:

1 **The reasons for urbanisation and de-urbanisation.**
2 **The relationship between urban society and social problems, social conflict and social policy.**
3 **The similarities and differences between urban and rural life.**
4 **Different concepts of community and the loss of community thesis.**

Definitions

■ *Urbanisation* is the increase in the proportion of the population who live in large towns or cities.

■ *De-urbanisation* is the movement of the population from old towns and cities, usually to the suburbs.

■ *Community* refers to a group of people who share a common identity or set of values and often live in a particular geographical area.

PLACE, SPACE AND LOCALITY

ESSENTIAL PRINCIPLES

There is a new sociological interest in the influence of locality on social behaviour. Some theories of development concentrate on how global forces influence local social life. However, this sociological approach is concerned with a *two-way* interaction between local circumstances and histories which shape (as well as being shaped by) national and global forces. Thus even a global phenomenon like capitalism is influenced by local social structures.

Figure 9.1 The relationship between local, national and global circumstances.

The debate over the extent to which place and location influence patterns of social life can be illustrated by the term 'the inner city'. The three alternative perspectives considered below are based on evidence from three countries.

1   **Chicago: Place as the cause and location of problems**
    The inner city in the USA is clearly seen as the location of a range of social problems. This view can be found in the work of the Chicago School of the 1930s. Park and Burgess developed a theory of human ecology influenced by Darwin and Durkheim, which argues that location does influence social behaviour. Burgess produced a model of the city which divided it into *concentric zones*. The social problems of the inner city were concentrated in the *zone of transition*, just outside the central business district. In a similar way Shaw and McKay explained deviance in ecological terms, emphasising the influence of place on the nature and extent of crime.

2   **Hackney: The inner city is not a place**
    Harrison, writing about Hackney, claimed that 'The inner city is less a precise geographic location than a mode of existence....' For him the inner city was defined primarily in terms of a concentration of poverty and disadvantage.

3   **Paris: The inner city is in the suburbs**
    In France the word *banlieue* (literally suburb) has the same connotations as the term 'inner city' has in the USA and UK. The *banlieux* of some major cities like Paris and Lyon are separated from the city proper and consist of new housing estates built specifically for the disadvantaged. In France these are often ethnic minority groups

from North Africa. On these estates jobs and facilities are rare, whereas unemployment and poverty are common.

In all three cases the quality of housing is dismal.

HOUSING AND BEHAVIOUR

Does building influence behaviour? In the 1960s American writers suggested that social behaviour was influenced by architecture and planning. Tower blocks and housing with shared access and public spaces were seen as encouraging crime, fear of crime and vandalism. The solutions to such problems were identified as returning to more traditional forms of low-rise housing with no shared entrances, lifts or walkways. This was described as 'defensible space' (O. Newman). Encouraging people to walk was also seen as a way of restoring 'eyes on the street' (J. Jacobs).

> **Housing can affect behaviour.**

In the 1980s similar ideas were proposed by Alice Coleman, an English professor of geography who, supported by Margaret Thatcher, encouraged local authorities to replace or modify tower block housing to reduce crime.

There is some evidence that local authorities in Britain concentrate 'problem families' in their worst housing (O. Gill). These areas become stigmatised by the public, press and police, perhaps encouraging further deviance and certainly dissuading those who have a choice from living there.

THE CONCEPT OF COMMUNITY

Sociologists have used the word *community* in rather different ways:

> **The idea of community.**

1 *Close relationships based on a locality.* Usually they present a rather romantic view of village life.
2 A pattern of *close-knit relationships based on kinship* or perhaps on a *shared occupation* such as fishing or coal mining. (Stacey, in her study of Banbury, identified different social 'connotations' based on class, politics and interests.)
3 A *shared identity* which might define, for example, an ethnic community.

HAS THERE BEEN A LOSS OF COMMUNITY?

This has been suggested by those who see the feeling of shared identity and traditional sense of community undermined by social processes such as industrialisation, modernisation, urbanisation and bureaucratisation.

This has been opposed by:

1 Studies which have been able to identify thriving communities, whether in cities, suburbs or among the poor (see Willmott and Young).
2 Marxists, who see the real basis of community as *class*. They would see ethnic and other communities as dividing the working class and being based on false consciousness.
3 Durkheim saw the mechanical solidarity (or integration) of rural pre-industrial society as being based on shared beliefs and values, as the people were more or less the same and worked together on the land. Organic solidarity existed in industrial societies and was based on people who did *different* jobs (i.e. the division of labour) being dependent on each other. The social unrest in Paris in the Revolution of 1789 and again in the nineteenth century aroused fears of social disorganisation and conflict in cities (Durkheim called this *anomie*).
4 Tonnies made a similar distinction between community and society. In traditional rural society he identified intimate and strong *Gemeinschaft* relationships. In urban societies he identified *Gesellschaft* relationships, which were impersonal, superficial and rational. Even more than Durkheim, he was pessimistic about the future of industrial and urban society.

CAUSES OF URBANISATION

Urbanisation describes a situation where an increasing proportion of the population live in towns and cities rather than in the countryside. It is not the same thing as the growth of cities. Cities can grow without an increasing proportion of the population living in them if the rural population is growing at the same rate.

The major cause of urbanisation is people leaving the countryside to live in towns. Logically it could also be caused by:

"Factors in urbanisation."

1 Rural settlements growing so that they become towns. This has only a minor effect.
2 The population of the city growing more quickly than that of the country.
3 People migrating from the countryside to cities because of 'push' as well as 'pull' factors.

Reasons for leaving rural areas (push):

- The mechanisation of agriculture and the lowering of income for labourers may drive them away from the land.
- War may make rural areas unsafe or prevent the production of food.

Reasons for going to towns (pull):

- To find work and improve living standards.
- To change the pattern of life.

DE-URBANISATION

This refers to the movement back out of cities and large towns to suburban and rural locations which has occurred since the 1950s. The reasons for these movements include:

"Why move back to rural locations?"

1 Families having the money to fulfil the desire to be owner-occupiers.
2 The spread of housing developments outside major towns.
3 The state encouraged rehousing in 'new towns' or in suburban housing estates following slum clearance or war damage. This led to sociologists writing about 'the loss of community'.
4 Public transport, increased car ownership and a willingness to spend time commuting have allowed people to live a considerable distance from their work.
5 The decline in the physical and social environment of the inner city has encouraged those who can afford it to leave. This has left the more disadvantaged in the inner city, discouraging the setting up of new businesses and the provision of services. The decline of the inner city is then both a cause and an effect of people leaving.
6 The decline of employment in old industries which were based in the inner city and were often the reason why the city itself developed. New employment tends to be in service industries rather than in manufacturing, and these service-sector jobs are often located on greenfield sites with good rail links.
7 A combination of many of the factors mentioned above has developed because of the policy of large retailers to relocate outside cities to larger and cheaper greenfield sites which provide ample parking space. Retailing provided the major growth in economic activity during the 1980s.

Do not see de-urbanisation as the end of any process of change. Some new towns and cities are growing in population and some old cities, such as London, have begun to increase their populations, though not to the size and density of the past.

Traditional industries, such as textiles, particularly fashion clothes, remain in the inner city. Often they are similar to a hundred years ago, in other words small workshops paying very low wages to largely female and ethnic minority workers (Phizacklea, 1990).

STAGES OF URBANISATION

N. Jewson (1991) has suggested that city life is best explained by looking at the development of capitalism. He identified a series of stages in the urbanisation of Britain.

1 BEFORE THE INDUSTRIAL REVOLUTION (BEFORE 1800)

The majority of the population lived in small settlements and earned their living from the land. Fewer than 20% of the population lived in cities, which tended to be small by today's standards.

2 THE INDUSTRIAL CITY (1800–80)

"Stages in the urbanisation process."

This first stage was the result of the industrial revolution. Rapid urbanisation was the result of masses of workers being required for the new factories. Unplanned slum housing sprang up near these factories. There was little or no state provision of services. Life expectancy was lower than it was in surrounding rural areas. The urban working class did not have the right to vote, trades unions were weak, and occasionally riots occurred. Critical views of such cities are found in studies of poverty and class, and in the fiction of Dickens.

3 THE METROPOLITAN CITY (1800–1960s)

The move to the city has slowed or halted. The city has become very large in terms of both area and population. A few major cities dominate surrounding areas. Government now provides a wide variety of public services, such as houses, roads, gas, electricity, water, sanitation, schools, leisure activities and health care. The city was frequently divided into different zones for homes, work, entertainment, etc. Slum clearance led to the break-up of traditional working-class communities. The population gained political rights (see *Power and politics*, Chapter 7) and political conflict tended to be restricted to industrial action and voting rather than violence.

4 'MEGALOPOLIS', THE CITY OF THE PRESENT AND THE FUTURE (1960S–?)

The latest development of the city is associated with de-urbanisation rather than urbanisation. The city has spread over a huge area and has no clear limits. Many of the factories have gone as the old industries have disappeared and other workplaces have relocated on greenfield sites. Shops have also joined the flight from the inner city, and large shopping centres have grown up on the edge of towns. The population has become more suburban than urban, and the inner city is seen as the home of the disadvantaged. The role of local government as a provider of services has diminished, e.g. council house building has virtually stopped. Riots have again become a form of disorder, and perhaps protest.

URBAN AND RURAL WAYS OF LIFE

Urbanisation, as we have seen, refers to an increased proportion of a population living in towns and cities. This can be caused by migration from the country, or when cities have higher birth rates and/or lower death rates. In modern industrial societies, such as Britain, urbanisation has been associated with industrialisation and economic growth, whereas in Third World countries urbanisation has been associated with independence from colonialism and population growth, but not with industrialisation.

The problems associated with urbanisation in the Third World include:

1   The problems experienced by migrants arriving from the countryside, who find it difficult to adapt to urban life.
2   Population explosion. Although birth rates tend to fall in cities compared with rural areas, the problems of an increasing population are more obvious.

" Urbanisation problems in the Third World. "

3   The decline of the physical environment because of pressure on housing, sanitation, water supply and social provision, such as education and health care. This is exemplified in studies of 'shanty towns' which grow up on the outskirts of major cities.
4   Social unrest and crime. This has often been the result of family disorganisation, as single males arrived in the city first, and relative deprivation as their hopes for a better life were not fulfilled.

In *modern societies* a distinctive urban culture has been identified. The main features of 'urbanism as a way of life' were, according to Wirth:

- The *large size* of the population.
- The *increased density* of population per square mile.
- The *increased heterogeneity* of the population. This means greater variations in class, ethnicity, occupation, religion, etc.

These features created a segregation of groups and individuals, and led to the establishment of different kinds of relationships.

Relationships in *rural* areas were based on knowing the person as a member of a family and church as well as a worker, whereas in urban areas we often know people only in specialised roles, such as teacher, bus driver, neighbour, etc. – these relationships tend to be more superficial and temporary.

This unfavourable description of city life has led sociologists to see the city as a lonely place where traditional informal social controls no longer operate, leading to problems of social order which need to be solved in a formal way.

ARE CITY AND COUNTRYSIDE SO DIFFERENT?

Some sociologists have rejected the view that there is a clear distinction between urban and rural life. They have argued that:

1   There is a *rural–urban continuum*, i.e. communities are more or less urban or rural, not simply one or the other. Large rural settlements may become urban.
2   The *urban–rural distinction* is not very important, as there are inequalities and social problems in rural areas as well as in towns. Cities are not all the same. Townsend's study of poverty showed that in the 1970s, poor Salford had nearly twice the death rates at various ages as rich Oxford.
3   Industrialisation or capitalism influences social relationships more than urbanism. This would suggest that life in modern Britain is essentially similar, whether in town or country, and is markedly different from life in the Third World, whether in town or country.
4   Communities have been identified within urban areas. Willmott and Young found a thriving community in the midst of a major city. They described the 'Mum-centred' family in Bethnall Green in East London as the key feature of a close-knit neighbourhood. Later, Wilmott's study in Dagenham saw an East End type of community being reborn after being broken down by rehousing policies which had brought East Enders to a new town away from London. Other urban communities have been identified with the unifying links being ethnic or occupational.
5   Pahl argued that the *commuter* is evidence of the disappearance of the distinction between rural and urban ways of life. Commuters from rural dormitory towns and villages may have threatened the sense of community in those places. Think of the effects on housing prices which exclude the children of local people from competing for housing, as well as the lack of family and neighbourhood ties of many commuters.
6   Life in the suburbs has ingredients of both town and country. Communities are less varied and settlement is less dense than in the city.

POWER IN THE CITY

Government is often seen as representing the interests of all the community. Planners claim to encourage building to meet the needs of the whole community. Critics have suggested, however, that it is power which influences decisions about planning and the allocation of resources in the city.

Power may be held by:

1   *Businesspeople*, who decide whether to invest in factories, offices and shops, and thus provide employment. Many inner-city problems are the result of unemployment caused by the loss of jobs from the city or their relocation elsewhere. Of course, social problems themselves discourage investment. Governments may encourage investment in parts of cities damaged by riots, but businesspeople may need a lot of inducements.
2   *Central government*, which has restricted the funds available to local government to build and provide services. However, it has encouraged business by removing some restrictions on their activities in some areas of the country, such as the London Docklands.

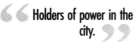 Holders of power in the city.

3   *Local government*, which was a major influence on the development of housing and services in cities, but their power has been curtailed by central government since 1979. Some local authorities, such as the Greater London Council, were abolished. Local government managers are part of the group Pahl called 'gatekeepers'. This group also includes those who lend money for housing or to business, such as bank and building society managers, and those who control access to homes, such as councils and Housing Associations.
4   The public may form organisations to protect their interests over a long period, such as tenants' associations, or to meet an immediate threat, like an unwelcome new road.

SLUMS AND THE HOMELESS

The homeless are clearly at the bottom of the housing market. Unlike other countries, there is a clear preference in Britain for owner-occupation; renting from local authorities or Housing Associations is a second choice, and renting from private landlords has tended to become less and less popular.

The 1991 census showed (1981 in brackets):

- Owner-occupied (owned outright or buying)   66%   (56%)
- Rented from local authority or New Town Association   21%   (31%)
- Privately rented (includes Housing Associations)   13%   (12%)

Although all major political parties now support the policy of increasing house ownership, it has been argued that the increase helped the Conservatives in the elections of 1983 and 1987. Certainly the Tories encouraged the sale of council houses with large subsidies. The recession of the early 1990s left many new home owners unable to afford mortgage repayments because of unemployment and unable even to sell their houses to pay off their debts.

Housing as a social problem was seen, until recently, as the problem of the 'slum' – that is, housing which was unsuitable because of its age, condition and facilities. Slum clearance by local authorities began in the last century and was advanced before the Second World War. The demolition of large areas, rather than individual houses, reached its height in the 1960s, and there were many complaints from inner-city dwellers about the destruction of traditional working-class communities, the separation of families and their being rehoused in unsuitable places without jobs, shops or recreational facilities. Frequently good housing was destroyed with the bad, and fewer homes were made available than were demolished. The demolition of the unpopular modern tower blocks which had been built to rehouse working-class communities has been identified by Jencks as the beginning of the post-modern era.

The 1990s saw an increase in those who were obviously homeless, in the sense that they were sleeping in the streets of large cities. There is also the less visible problem of those housed by local authorities in totally unsuitable bed-and-breakfast accommodation. This accommodation is paid for by the state and is associated with overcrowding, poor health, family disorganisation and insecurity.

GENTRIFICATION

Gentrification describes the process where previously run-down areas become occupied by well-off professionals and managers who choose to live in the inner city. They may occupy whole houses which were previously shared by more than one household, and are owner-occupiers rather than tenants. The attraction of 'gentrified' areas may be a combination of access to facilities and to employment, and to living in houses and districts with 'character'. The avoidance of the need to commute is balanced by the expense of buying in central areas. Many middle-class inner-city residents also choose to have their children privately educated to avoid their going to inner-city schools with low levels of achievement.

 Gentrification.

The benefits of gentrification are generally shared by the new middle-class residents and by property developers. Working-class residents may find themselves priced out of the area. The development of London Docklands has been one example of such gentrification.

URBAN RIOTS

Studies of urban life have become more popular since the riots of the early 1980s. There are debates as to whether they should be explained in terms of race, poverty, power or delinquency. Northern Ireland in the late 1960s gave an indication of the potential violence in cities directed against the police and army. The army has not been deployed in similar circumstances in Britain, but tear gas has been used and other forms of control, such as water cannon, have been deployed. The Scarman Report, written by a Lord Chief Justice for the Government after the Brixton disorders in 1981, saw the explanation for the start of the riots as lying in the relationship between the police and young black people.

Scarman was criticised from many sides. The police felt that they were being criticised for rising street crime and at the same time for their response to it, which was 'saturation policing' – that is, lots of police on the street stopping and searching young men.

Conflict theorists did not accept Scarman's view that racism was an isolated problem found only in the ranks of the police rather than being embedded in the wider society. Scarman wrote: 'Institutional racism does not exist in Britain; but racial disadvantage and its nasty associate, racial discrimination, have not yet been eliminated.' He recommended recruiting more police from ethnic minorities, but the proportion remains tiny.

It should be noted, however, that not all street disorder occurs in cities, and even when it does, it is not invariably associated with race issues. The 1980s saw violent disorder over the poll tax and the reporting of 'lager lout' disturbances in country towns rather than inner cities. The largely white housing estates were the location of many disputes.

Marx

The development of cities was seen as an inevitable part of the rise of capitalism. Although Marx wrote of the degradation of working-class life in city slums, he did see the city as the breeding-ground of class consciousness, and therefore of revolution. The peasant was seen as essentially conservative. These views have not been borne out by communist revolutions in the twentieth century in China, Cuba and Nicaragua.

Castells

Castells represents the re-emergence of the Marxist tradition in urban sociology. He sees the roots of many urban problems in capitalism rather than in urban life itself. The nature of the city is explained in terms of the role of institutions in reproducing labour. For example, he looks at public housing, hospitals and transport systems as being used to maintain the health of workers and to provide help for business.

**ENVIRONMENTAL
SOCIOLOGY AND
NVIRONMENTALISM**

Environmental sociology has developed since the 1970s, at the same time as the overall public concern with the environment has grown. There are a variety of concerns which may or may not touch on current A-level syllabuses.

In general, environmental sociology would like to examine the relationship between humans and nature, not only from a human-centred approach but also from an ecocentric or environmental-centred approach. S. Budiansky criticises many modern ecologists for romanticising the past. He suggests that they take a particular moment in history and claim that man lived in harmony with unspoiled nature. Budiansky points out that what were seen by European colonists as natural landscapes in North America, Africa and other settings were often the result of deliberate burning, reburning and other man-made practices.

EXAMINATION QUESTIONS

1 Discuss the view that urbanisation inevitably results in a 'loss of community'.

(AEB)

2 Evaluate the usefulness of housing classes in explaining why ethnic minorities are generally overrepresented in inner-city areas.

(AEB)

3 To what extent have sociological studies supported the popular stereotype of the countryside as an idyllic alternative to the stresses and strains of living in cities?

(AEB)

ANSWERS TO EXAMINATION QUESTIONS

OUTLINE ANSWERS

Question 1

This question asks you to address the old 'loss of community' debate and to look specifically at urbanisation as the cause of this loss.

1 The problematic nature of the concept of community.
2 The loss of community thesis. Tonnies, Durkheim.
3 Urbanism as a way of life. The distinctive features of urban life and the alleged absence of community ties. Wirth, Burgess, etc.
4 Empirical studies of communities in towns and cities. Gans, Willmott and Young, etc.
5 Conflict views on communities in cities:

- Rex and Moore on housing classes.
- Pahl on the influence of managers.
- Castells' Marxist view of the insignificance of urbanisation as compared with capitalism.

STUDENT'S ANSWERS WITH EXAMINER COMMENTS

Question 2

Evaluate the usefulness of housing classes in explaining why ethnic minorities are generally overrepresented in inner-city areas.

> 66 Useful introduction with early critical comments. 99

> 66 Homelessness is a good application. 99

> 66 Ethnicity and the inner city are relevant points. 99

> 66 Good use of information and analysis based on 1991 census. 99

> 66 Useful evaluation here, but could be developed further. 99

> 66 Conclusion OK — but again could be developed further. 99

The concept of housing classes was first written about by Rex and Moore in the 1960s. They wrote about Sparkbrook in Birmingham, which was a run-down inner-city area. They wanted to study why many black and Asian immigrants and their families lived in this area. They said that it was not just a question of being poor, although this was an important factor.

They suggested that there were seven housing classes. At the top were the owners of the large houses in 'good' areas. At the bottom were people in bedsits, although nowadays the homeless are arguably below this group. Ethnic minorities in Sparkbrook were mostly in class 6; this was multioccupied private housing. The reasons for ethnic groups being at the bottom of the housing classes were various: first, because they could not get council houses as they were relatively new immigrants; second, because the banks and buildings societies would not lend them money to enable them to buy their own houses. Instead, several families saved up together or borrowed from expensive moneylenders and then rented rooms to friends and relatives.

Overcrowding and lack of money made these areas even more deprived and the white population often tried to move out. Rex and Moore were concerned that a concentration of ethnic minorities in the inner city, with few jobs and little chance of getting out, would lead to riots, as in America.

The 1991 census showed that about 6% of the population of the UK classified themselves as members of ethnic minorities. These ethnic minorities are not evenly distributed throughout the country but are concentrated in certain areas of certain cities. Greater London has an ethnic minority population of over 20%, but it is not concentrated in a single inner-city area. One should not generalise about ethnic minorities or stereotype them as all living in slums. There are different minority groups who lead distinct lives, and any one minority group is divided into classes. Higher classes tend to live in the more expensive areas and the poor in the less expensive areas.

It is true, however, to say that ethnic minorities are overrepresented in inner-city areas. The inner city, according to Harrison, is a place of deprivation. There is high unemployment, low pay, poor-quality housing and many social problems, such as crime. Again this may be a stereotyped view of the inner city.

Critics of Rex and Moore say that it is primarily social class or racial discrimination which leads to the concentration of ethnic minorities, not special housing classes. Living in slum housing is the result of being low-class. Ethnic minorities may also live together by choice. This means people feel more secure and can have community-specific shops and restaurants. Rex himself later changed his mind and talked about an underclass rather than housing class.

Overall comments

A sound answer to this question must demonstrate a clear understanding of the concept of housing classes as developed by Rex and Moore and others. A good answer will evaluate the usefulness of the concept, probably by offering critical alternatives such as social class and/ or the underclass. Other empirical studies of ethnic minorities and housing could also be included.

General discussions of racial inequality are unlikely to be well rewarded.

Clear introduction to the concept of housing classes and its application to ethnic minorities.

Useful critical comment distinguishing poverty from housing classes.

The second and third paragraphs explain housing classes and add a critical comment on homelessness (good application). The issues of ethnicity and the inner city are explicitly addressed.

Paragraph four shows good interpretation and application skills using the 1991 census to answer the question in critical fashion. This helps to update the debate and gain marks for evaluation. Paragraph five continues the evaluative approach and introduces further relevant knowledge.

The conclusion helps to develop the argument by listing a series of critical points. It would be an improvement to see these developed further.

Overall this answer indicates that a concise answer can achieve a good mark. It is relevant, balanced and clearly structured. It is perhaps overreliant on Rex and Moore, and there are other critical alternatives. The use of Marxist and Weberian theory to provide a theoretical framework would improve this competent answer and move it into the top bands. Just worth a grade A.

Question 3

To what extent have sociological studies supported the popular stereotype of the countryside as an idyllic alternative to the stresses and strains of living in cities?

> **A good introduction.**

> **These ideas could have been developed further.**

> **Good points raised.**

> **Useful contrast presented.**

> **Good – but develop a little more.**

> **Sound conclusion – tails off in last sentence.**

The stereotypical view of the countryside is that it is harmonious, with a close-knit integrated community. It is different from the stereotypical view of the city, which is that it is isolated and impersonal and full of stress. These are the distinct popular views.

Tonnies distinguished *Gemeinschaft*-like communities, which are close-knit and friendly, from *Gesellschaft*-like communities, which are impersonal and isolated. Tonnies argued that there has been a move to *Gesellschaft* communities.

Durkheim argued that the separation between communities was based on the division of labour. Modern societies have moved from mechanical to organic solidarity. The division of labour means people have different jobs and are divided into different classes. He thinks that it is the differences in jobs which divide people, not differences between *Gemeinschaft* and *Gesellschaft* communities.

The stereotypical view of the countryside is not always correct. Payne and Macleod did a study of a Scottish village and found a difference between 'locals and incomers'. This village was less integrated than the stereotype suggests. The locals were close-knit, but not so for all the villagers; the incomers were seen as outsiders. Even though they lived in the same village together they had not shared the same experiences, such as the storm which had disrupted their lives. Small villages also have problems like crime, teenage pregnancy and drugs; this suggests that they are not always idyllic.

In contrast to the view of *Gesellschaft*-like communities in cities, there is evidence against isolation. Willmott and Young found a close-knit harmonious community in East London. Life was not isolated and impersonal but based on close friends and kinship ties.

Gans found that communities were not just the result of locality but were also influenced by class and patterns of marriage. Bell also argued that class influenced association more than locality. Middle-class people mixed easily with each other.

Thus despite the stereotypes there are isolated communities in the countryside and urban villages with close-knit communities in cities. Post-modernists see communities based on identities. There could be religious, ethnic and even gay communities. The closeness and integration of the community is not always based on locality. There are many different definitions of community and this can prove the stereotype wrong.

Overall comments

Good answers should go beyond 'regurgitating' a prepared 'loss of community' answer. The stereotypical views of both countryside and city are well known and are supported by sociological theory and studies. These should be explained and challenged. More contemporary material is welcomed; this might include conflict and post-modern approaches.

The answer opens well, identifying the terms of the debate. Paragraphs two and three outline the classical material, but with little development. There is a lack of evaluation so far, despite the last sentence in paragraph three. The Durkheim approach could have been developed so that the theme of integration was applied to the set question and explicitly linked to stresses, strains and idyllic rural alternatives.

Paragraph four introduces new knowledge which is applied to the set question in a critical manner. Paragraph five is a more well-known study and is quite nicely contrasted with the preceding paragraph. The sixth paragraph introduces, but fails to develop and apply, some potentially useful knowledge.

A good conclusion provides both an evaluative summary and some new knowledge. The last sentence is potentially useful but is not really applied to the question.

Overall, this is a concise but well-structured answer. It demonstrates understanding as well as knowledge and remains relevant throughout. There is a clear evaluative framework as well as individual critical points made in several places in the latter part of the answer. Perhaps some of the points could have been developed further. This answer is worth a grade B.

A Review Sheet for this chapter may be found on p. 254.

CHAPTER 10

THE FAMILY

GETTING STARTED

Most sociological debates and A-level questions can be seen as arguments between functionalist accounts of the family and a variety of critics. Interest in the sociology of the family has been rejuvenated by the popularisation of feminist and Marxist criticism.

The main themes of questions set on this topic are:

1   **Changes in the structure of the family.**
2   **Changes in roles within the family.**
3   **The causes and effects of family disorganisation.**

The most obviously related topic areas are age, gender and sociological theory. Useful references to the family can also be made in answers on health and education. Many students criticise functionalists for basing their arguments on white middle-class Americans. If you share this view, remember to point out the diversity of family life in your answers.

Definitions

Definitions of the family, and particularly the various types of family, are rather problematic and frequently ideological. Consider the dispute over whether single-parent families are 'real' families or not.

Take care to distinguish 'household' from 'family', and be aware of the diversity which exists in both. Questions may ask you to consider reasons for the existence of 'typical' families.

FUNCTIONALIST APPROACHES

MARXIST APPROACHES

FEMINIST APPROACHES

THE NEW RIGHT APPROACH

OTHER CRITICS

THEORETICAL AND EMPIRICAL STUDIES

ESSENTIAL PRINCIPLES

The major assumptions made by functionalist writers on the family include the following:

1   The family can be studied and explained only if we examine its relationships with the wider society. This includes its relationships with parts of the social system, like the economy, and indeed with the whole social system. This assumption applies to our examination of the *structure, functions* and *roles* of the family and its members.
2   The family is a 'good' thing. It is functional both for its individual members and for the wider society.
3   The isolated *nuclear* family is the dominant form of family in modern industrial society (because it is this type which is functional), whereas the *extended* family is typical of pre-industrial society.
4   There is a tendency towards increased equality within the family. This is described as the 'symmetrical family' and functionalists talk of joint conjugal roles.

CRITICS

To simplify matters we can list critics under some broad headings:

1   Marxists.
2   Feminists.
3   Historians.
4   Psychiatric critics.
5   Critics from within the functionalist camp.
6   New Right.

The Marxist approach to the family, like the functionalist approach, adopts a structuralist perspective. The family is examined by looking at its relationship with the wider social structure.

The two main themes are:

■   The influence of the economic *substructure* on family life.
■   The role of the family, as part of the *superstructure*, in reproducing the class system.

The family as a product of economic forces

The development of the family through the successive stages of history was traced by Engels and later by Marxists. This Marxist history makes a useful contrast with the 'march of progress' functionalist views.

The family as part of the superstructure

Like other institutions and ideas which form the superstructure, the family serves the interests of the ruling class by maintaining and reproducing the existing relations of production. This is why Marxists condemn the bourgeois family.

a)   The family reproduces labour power. This involves the physical and ideological reproduction of the working class by rearing falsely conscious children at no cost to the employer.
b)   Married women are a reserve army of labour, available for work when required but not seen as having a right to work.
c)   The family is a refuge from the brutality and alienation of working life. It becomes itself a source of alienation as members are obsessed with love, sex, marriage and home comforts.
d)   The family provides the consumer base for modern capitalism, as families demand family cars, consumer durables, etc.
     (See also the Marxist explanations of gender inequality in Chapter 5, particularly the answer to Question 4.)

There are a variety of feminist views on the family. Most of these owe something to Marxist theory, particularly to Engels' pioneering work. The main themes found in the feminist analysis of the family are:

1   The family is not a voluntary unit based on love and choice, but an economic unit which creates and maintains female dependence.
2   The family is not efficient at performing its functions. Many women, children and old people eventually depend on support and care from state institutions.
3   Childcare is explained, not in terms of family relations, but by its functions in industrial society.
4   Housework is real productive work, and women are exploited by men.
5   Economic dependency makes, and keeps, women falsely conscious.
    (See also Chapter 5, particularly the answer to Question 1.)

THE NEW RIGHT APPROACH

The conventional nuclear family is perceived as an ideal, and variations are seen as pathological. Single mothers are described as irresponsible and should not be encouraged by generous welfare or housing provision. New British legislation intends to pursue fathers who abandon families to ensure that they help pay for children. Many of society's problems are thought to originate or be amplified by the decline of traditional family life.

If this is interpreted as men working while women care for children, then it conflicts with New Right economics, which advocates a free market for labour irrespective of gender or marital status.

OTHER CRITICS

There are various other critics of both the functionalist approach to the family and the nuclear family itself. Among the most useful for examination purposes are the 'historians' who challenge the inevitability of the nuclear family in industrial society. There is also a collection of writers who have identified the 'dark side of the family' and examined violence, abuse, mental illness and other symptoms of family disorganisation. (See also the Tutor Answer to Question 3 below.)

THEORETICAL AND EMPIRICAL STUDIES

FUNCTIONALIST STUDIES

Functionalism dominated the sociology of the family for so long, without serious opposition, that the task of selecting only a few studies is rather difficult.

Parsons

Parsons argued that the nuclear family 'fits' the needs of an industrial society and is thus the typical form of family. The family is isolated, socially and geographically mobile, and characterised by different, but complementary, roles for husband, wife and children. It has two basic functions: the socialisation of children and the stabilisation of adult personalities.

Willmott and Young

In a series of studies of family life in and around London these authors identified progressive change, through the following four stages:

a)   The family as a unit of production in pre-industrial society.
b)   The 'Mum-centred' extended family, which provided support for insecure working-class families.
c)   The 'symmetrical family', which is home-centred and tends towards an equal relationship between spouses.
d)   They predict a fourth stage involving a more work-centred nuclear family, where conjugal roles become separate again.

Bott

Bott distinguished *segregated* conjugal roles from *joint* conjugal roles. The former she associated with close-knit social networks; the latter with loose-knit networks. The view that roles were becoming increasingly joint and equal is more or less supported by Willmott and Young and Rosser and Harris. Bott's work is a good starting point for a feminist criticism of family life.

UNHAPPY FAMILIES

Vogel and Bell

These authors are unusual in offering a critical view of the family from a functionalist perspective. They see the scapegoating of an emotionally disturbed child as functional for the stability of the rest of the family.

Other studies which highlight the *darker* side of family life (usually based on case studies, as was Vogel and Bell's work) include:

Laing and Cooper

In separate and joint studies Laing and Cooper criticised family life from a psychiatric perspective, suggesting that children are oppressed and family members made 'insane' in both abnormal and normal families.

Dobash and Dobash

Dobash and Dobash describe violence within the family and claim that it is not abnormal, but rather the predictable consequence of the position of women in marriage and in the wider social structure. (Strauss sees children in the same vulnerable position.)

Leach

Starting from an anthropological viewpoint, Leach identified the nuclear family as having detrimental effects on its members and on the wider society.

THE HISTORIANS

The relationship between family structure and industrialisation remains a popular question, linking the topic of the family with social change. The functionalist analysis of Parsons and others can be challenged by using this historical perspective.

Laslett denied the existence of a typical extended family in pre-industrial times. Anderson argued that the extended family became more common in the early days of industrialisation. Both these studies (along with Marxist views on family structure and a variety of other functionalist studies of working-class communities) accept that typical families can be explained in structuralist terms.

THE MARXISTS

Engels laid down the foundations of the Marxist approach to the family, identifying and explaining the subjugation of women. For this reason feminist writers in the 1970s took up his ideas, blaming capitalism for marital inequality. The work of Benston, Ansley, Mitchell and Oakley is more or less influenced by the Marxist analysis.

THE FEMINISTS

The family is extremely important to feminists, whether it is seen as the cause of, or only the location of, women's subjugation.

McIntosh sees 'the family' as a set of beliefs about the ideal household. However, this ideal does not exist in reality, though society is organised as if it did. The consequences include the failure of families to satisfy the needs of women (and, indeed, children, the old and even men).

Oakley pioneered the study of housework and the housewife-mother role. Her work is discussed in Chapter 5 on *Gender*, along with that of other feminist writers.

Criticism of feminist approaches

1   Martin (1984) challenged the view of women's lack of power in the home. Power was maintained by controlling relations with wider kin and through control of the home and childcare.
2   Some feminists acknowledge that women's experience in the family is mediated by class and ethnicity as well as more individual differences. Family members with disabilities will also influence the experience of family life for all members.
3   Some women remain pro-marriage and family. Housework may be perceived as creative, particularly home improvements and childcare. Housework is not supervised and the worker is relatively autonomous.

4   H. Graham (1991): An interesting effect of the employment of black women in white households on the family life of the black women was that instead of their own families being seen as places of exploitation, which would fit in with the usual British feminist analysis, they were places of resistance to exploitation and oppression. Time spent with their own children was an opportunity to be free from the work obligations imposed on them in the households of their employers or, if they were slaves, their owners.

ETHNIC DIVERSITY

Britain is a multicultural society. Many sociologists have written descriptions of the family life of various minorities. Surprisingly, many of these studies seem to confirm popular stereotypes, such as father-dominated extended families. Of course the family life of minorities is likely to be as varied as that of the majority, being influenced by class, religion and generation as well as by individual factors.

Why do ethnic minorities have distinctive patterns of family life?

> Why ethnic differences occur in the patterns of family life.

1   Economic influences
     A past history of slavery is claimed to have encouraged the development of female-led Afro-Caribbean families. Modern difficulties of immigrants finding employment and housing may have encouraged the persistence of extended family ties.

2   Cultural influences
     Traditions are more likely to be kept up when the minority maintains a distinct language and religion.

3   Discrimination and disadvantage
     It may be that racism encourages minorities to maintain their distinctive culture, whereas tolerance encourages assimilation. The family has been described by Westwood and Bhachu (1988) as a source of strength and resistance against racism.

South Asian families

People originating from the Indian sub-continent form one of the largest collections of ethnic minorities in Britain, with over 1.4 million persons. This 'Asian' population may have some common characteristics but may also be divided in various ways such as religion, country or region of origin, caste, class and language.

Common features of South Asian families

J.E. Goldthorpe (1987) reviewed several studies of Asians from different religious and national origins living in various parts of Britain and identified the following common features:

> The typical South Asian family.

1   Men exercise authority over women.
2   Parents exercise authority over children.
3   The old exercise authority over the young.
4   Marriages are arranged between kin groups.
5   The sexes are segregated, girls are chaperoned and the ideal of family honour is strong.
6   Families are extended, often living in large multigenerational households and supporting each other in getting jobs and housing.

Some of these studies were done in the 1970s and may be out of date now.

Westwood and Bhachu (1988) described Asian families as having larger *households*.

Muslim, Bangladeshi and Pakistani families are more likely to be larger than white families but are not more likely to be extended. Sikh and East African Asian households are more likely to contain three generations. Overall only 21% of Asian households are extended families but of course family ties can be maintained by living close by or through visits and the telephone.

Afro-Caribbean families

The framework for discussing Afro-Caribbean life in Britain has been strongly influenced by the study of black family life in the USA. There is a general assumption that black British families are more likely to be female-headed single-parent families than white families and that this is a 'bad' thing. In particular such families have been blamed for causing poverty and crime.

Critical thoughts

Single-parent families are seen by many as disorganised or inadequate families; however, they may be seen as *different* rather than as problem families. Marriage in the Caribbean and among black families here is later than for the population as a whole. The single mother and one child is a common outcome of relationships which may remain stable or change into a marital relationship. Indeed, the proportion of single-parent families is rising faster for white families than black families. In the Caribbean there is often support for single mothers from other females, such as grandmothers (J. Barrow 1982). Traditional types of behaviour might be expected to persist only if they are of value to individuals and the group.

The majority of black families have two parents in the household. Conventional families are most common among the middle class and church goers.

'WESTERN WAYS ARE BAD'
The following extract shows that it is not only the lives of minorities which are subject to stereotypes.

South Asians perceived English family life as cold and insecure, lacking in affection and in respect for the older generation. Families were small, young adults left home to make their own way, old people lived alone or were put into homes without good reason; marital breakdowns and sexual licence were rife. By Asian standards it all seemed outrageously immoral and inhumane.

(J.E. Goldthorpe, *Family life in Western Societies* (CUP 1987))

Stereotypes may be positive: Asians, Chinese, Greeks, Italians and Jews are seen as having warm families with strong ties.

THE FAMILY AND THE STATE

The family is threatened by the state

- F. Mount, in *The Subversive Family*, saw the family as the centre of resistance against the expansion of a collectivist (i.e. socialist) state.
- D. Marsland and others of the New Right have attacked the Welfare State for creating and maintaining poverty. He talked of single mothers being 'wedded to the state', 'the Nanny State'.
- Pessimistic functionalists have expressed the fear that the state is replacing the family by taking over its functions.

The state supports the family

- The state supports the family in the performance of its functions rather than replacing it – for example, by the provision of housing. Although many politicians seek to encourage traditional families, Housing Associations with state subsidies house those not in conventional families such as the old, young single people, and ex-psychiatric patients.
- State attitudes to fertility can be seen as generally neutral, but the state provides contraception, legal abortion and child benefits. Elsewhere the law and benefits are used actively to encourage or discourage childbearing (France and China respectively).
- Shifting attitudes and legal judgements on marital property, domestic violence and marital rape suggest that the challenge to the patriarchal nature of the family is being recognised by the state.

EXAMINATION QUESTIONS

1 'Far from being democratic the family is based on an unequal division of labour and power.' Discuss.

(AEB)

2 'Families in developing and pre-literate societies are extended; families in industrial societies are nuclear.' Discuss.

(ULEAC)

3 'Functionalist accounts of the family underestimate the extent of strain and exploitation in family life.' Discuss.

(AEB)

4 Why is divorce becoming more common in modern society? Does this phenomenon provide support for those who have argued that the nuclear family is 'dysfunctional'?

(UCLES)

5 Has the family in modern times been stripped of its functions?

(ULEAC)

6
ITEM A

Rapoport identifies five types of contemporary diversity in the family: organisational, cultural, class, life-course and cohort.

Families today organise their respective individual domestic duties and their links with the wider social environment in a variety of ways. The contrasts between 'orthodox' families – the woman as 'housewife', the husband as 'breadwinner' – and dual-career or one-parent families illustrate this diversity. Culturally, there is greater diversity of family beliefs and values than used to be the case. The presence of ethnic minorities (such as West Indian, Asian, Greek or Italian communities), and the influence of movements such as feminism, have produced considerable cultural variety in family forms. Persistent class divisions, between the poor, skilled working class, and the various groupings within the middle and upper classes, sustain major variations in family structure. Variations in family experience during the life course are fairly obvious.

(Adapted from *Sociology*,
ANTHONY GIDDENS (Polity))

ITEM B

The idea of 'the family' or 'the nuclear family' is an idea with remarkable strength and power – it is something which just about any member of our society can define and which many powerful lobbies (political, moral, religious) claim to support and revere. The image of 'the family' is quite clear.

Our traditional family model remains central to all family ideology. This is a model of a married heterosexual couple with children, and a sexual division of labour where the husband as a breadwinner provides economic support for his dependent wife and children, while the wife cares for both husband and children.

I propose that there is no such thing as 'the family' and in reality, no such things as 'normal families'. The simplest approach is at the statistical level of counting how many families do correspond to the clear image of 'the family'. Work on the 1981 Census suggested that few households corresponded to the image.

(Adapted from *The Family in Question*,
JON BERNADES (Social Studies Review 1990))

ITEM C

Preliminary results of the 1989 General Household Survey by the Office of Population Censuses and Surveys show continued growth in the number of single-parent families. The proportion of such families rose from 8% in 1971 to 17% in 1989, of which lone mothers were 15% and lone fathers were 2%.

At the same time, the proportion of households containing only one person rose from 17% in 1971 to 25% in 1989, with only 26% of households in 1989 comprising a married or cohabiting couple and children.

(Adapted from *The Guardian*,
DAVID BRINDLE (October 1990))

(a) State the increase in the percentage of lone-parent families between 1971 and 1989 (ITEM C). *(1 mark)*

(b) Identify one way in which the presence of ethnic minorities has contributed to the 'contemporary diversity' in the family (ITEM A). *(1 mark)*

(c) How far do you agree with the idea expressed in ITEM B that the 'traditional family model remains central to all family ideology'?
Support your argument with appropriate examples. *(6 marks)*

(d) Using information from the ITEMS and elsewhere, to what extent does sociological evidence support the idea that there is a 'contemporary diversity' in the *structure* of the family? (*8 marks*)

(e) With reference to any of the issues raised in the ITEMS, assess the contribution of feminist perspectives to an understanding of contemporary family life. (*9 marks*)

ANSWERS TO EXAMINATION QUESTIONS

OUTLINE ANSWERS

Question 2

" Examiners reward comparative evidence, if relevant. "

This question, which is taken from ULSEB paper 3, requires a comparative approach.

You should explain the links between economic development and family structure, provide evidence of exceptions and question the whole notion of a 'typical' family.

An outline could be as follows:

1 A brief explanation of the functionalist approach.
2 Functionalist accounts of extended families in pre-industrial societies such as Durkheim or Radcliffe Brown.
3 Parsons' explanation of the fit between industrialisation and the nuclear family. Weber also linked traditional societies with extended families.
4 Marxist views on the development of family structures as part of the superstructure.
5 Exceptions to the generalisations often made from functionalist viewpoints, e.g. Willmott and Young, Dennis *et al*, Rosser and Harris, Litvak.
6 The historical research of Laslett and Anderson.
7 Evidence of ethnic diversity and other exceptional cases, such as one-parent families.

Question 4

There are clearly two parts to this question. First, you must consider competing explanations of rising divorce rates; and second, you must explore the consequences of this increase for individual families, the family as an institution, and the wider society.

The list of causes needs to be kept sociological rather than historical.

1 Functionalists point out the decline of the extended family and its supportive functions. This can be linked to the rise of the Welfare State (see also the answer to Question 2 on marital failure, Chapter 20).
2 Changing attitudes and values resulting from secularisation.
3 Marxist and Marxist–feminist views on the tensions resulting from capitalism (McIntosh, Ansley, etc.).
4 Feminists who see rising divorce rates as evidence of women becoming conscious of their exploitation and of possible alternatives to marriage (Bernard).
5 The link between legal and social change can be mentioned.

The debate over the effects of rising divorce rates can be organised by evaluating the views of 'optimistic' functionalists (like Davis and Goode) who explain away divorce as the result of higher expectations of family happiness. They distinguish the disorganisation of individual families from threats to the family as an institution. The popularity of marriage and remarriage is cited as evidence of the continued strength of the family.

Goode sees the family adapting to these changes (rather than threats) by finding better ways of resolving disorganisation. He points out that divorce is seen as even more of a problem than the death of a spouse in the USA, but in Japan, where women can return to the extended family, divorce is not seen as a threat to the family.

These functionalist views can be contrasted with the various studies that do see the rising divorce rate as evidence of the failure of the nuclear family to meet the needs of individuals (Leach, Laing, Cooper, Dobash and Dobash, Bernard, etc.).

Vogel and Bell deal with the apparent contradiction between the family being functional for society, but threatening to its individual members.

Question 5

This question covers similar ground to questions 3 and 4. Morgan wrote that the sociology of the family could be divided into the approving and the disapproving, and the optimistic and pessimistic.

1 Pessimistic functionalists, who approve of the family, compare the security provided by the multifunctional extended family with the less important nuclear family. Leach could be included here, along with conventional functionalists like McIver. The New Right offer a similar pessimistic view.
2 Optimistic functionalists see the family as becoming more specialised and performing fewer functions more effectively. Parsons' writing about 'fit' and structural differentiation is important in this section, as is Fletcher.
3 Those who disapprove of the family have rather different views as to its continued importance. Marxists see changes in the role of the family as dependent on changes in the economic substructure, but still see it as continuing to reproduce inequality. Feminists see the family as reproducing and maintaining patriarchy and keeping its 'functions' in that sense. The psychiatric critics see the family as failing to be functional, either for individuals or for society.
4 Vogel and Bell offer the useful contradiction of the family continuing to perform its social functions, whilst failing some individuals.

Question 6

a) 9%.
b) Any relevant reference to structure (extended family), marriage roles, etc., will get the mark.
c) It is worth explaining ideology here. Reference to Marxist or feminist conceptions of ideology can fairly easily be applied to the family. You can mention religious and political attitudes to different family types. You could mention the New Right views on single parents.

   You can challenge the predominance of this idealised family by reference to welfare policies, employment practices and commercial enterprises which cater for variations on the traditional family.
d) Remember you should focus on structure (not roles or functions). The Items contain many relevant references, e.g. orthodox families, one-parent families, ethnic variations, class differences, heterosexual partners, cohabiting couples with and without children, etc.

   To argue against diversity you could distinguish families from households and identify a common basis for family structure, perhaps based on mother (and even father) and children. You could argue that families go through a fairly predictable life cycle, so although there is diversity at one moment in time, childless couples may marry, have children and these children eventually leave home, etc.
e) Good answers will be aware of more than one feminist approach, looking at theoretical differences, e.g. Marxism–feminism and radical feminism and/or feminist concern with different issues raised in the Items. These include dual careers, housework, family values/ideology, single parents, etc.

   As always, evaluation is essential. You must assess the contribution of feminism.

TUTOR ANSWER

Question 3

'Functionalist accounts of the family underestimate the extent of strain and exploitation in family life.' Discuss.

(This question requires an outline of functionalist theory and of those studies which are relevant to a consideration of 'strain' and 'exploitation'. There are many possible sources of criticism, but whichever are chosen, relevance and evaluation will gain credit.)

   Functionalist accounts of the family, though varied, share certain common assumptions. The family must be examined in terms of its relationships with other parts of the social system and indeed with the whole society. The origin, persistence, structure, roles and development of the family can be explained by looking at its functions, i.e. the ways in which it satisfies the system's functional needs of adaptation, integration, pattern maintenance, and goal attainment. In addition to being functional for the social system, it is assumed by most functionalist writers that the family as an institution is beneficial for its individual members.

Many functionalists have produced a list of the functions of the family. These vary but usually include sexual, reproductive, economic, socialisation and affective functions. The diminishing significance of some of these has been welcomed by some, such as McIver and Fletcher, who see the more specialised nuclear family performing the most important functions better than ever.

It is Parsons who dominates the functionalist sociology of the family, both as an authority and as a target for criticism. He saw the isolated nuclear family as fitting the needs of modern industrial society. This family maintained two basic irreducible functions: the stabilisation of the adult personality and the socialisation of children. The role of the family in performing just these two functions is seen as part of the more general social process of structural differentiation, where institutions become increasingly specialised and efficient.

Although they are generally optimistic about the future of the family, some functionalists have expressed reservations about the uncritical idealisation of family life. Just as the loss of some functions has been explained away, so too has the threat of rising divorce rates. Davis said they were a reflection of rising expectations of marital happiness and not of increased strain, and Gibson talked of serial monogamy as a new form of family life and not as the undermining of marriage. Goode saw family disorganisation, which he defined as functional or role failure, as a threat to individual families but not to the family as an institution. In any case, problems like divorce and illegitimacy could be accommodated by improving the ways of dealing with family members who were adversely affected, e.g. changes in property laws.

Vogel and Bell describe how certain families use children as scapegoats for their tensions and hostilities, creating emotionally disturbed children. This integrates the family and diminishes its unstable effects on society; it is thus functional for all but the victim.

Leach criticises nuclear families in industrial society by offering what sounds like a functionalist defence of the extended family. This echoes the work of Willmott and Young and Anderson, who suggest that extended families could thrive in industrial society, providing support for the insecure and disadvantaged.

Leach's description of the nuclear family as a breeding-ground for suspicion, fear and violence, both within and outside the family unit, is a theme developed by the radical psychiatrists Laing and Cooper. In joint and separate work based, as their critics point out, on case studies of abnormal families, they identify not only the damage done by families to individual members, but also the adverse impact the family has on the wider society. The dark side of the family is a view developed by Dobash and Dobash, who add violence to the mental illness described by Laing and Cooper. This violence is seen as institutionalised into society, and not as an individual abnormality. Recent concern about child abuse reinforces this view.

Cooper's work develops various Marxist themes, seeing the family as an ideological conditioning device. Other Marxist writers follow Engels and explain the brutality and exploitative nature of family life by locating the family in the superstructure of capitalist society. Here we are criticising the functionalist view of the family as an institution, rather than the image of individual happy families. The family reproduces the existing relations of production, maintaining the exploitation and oppression of capitalism. It does this in various ways: labour power is physically and ideologically reproduced at no cost to employers; women are part of a reserve army of labour; the family acts as a refuge from the brutalities of working life. This all sounds like functionalism, only in this case the beneficiary is the employer and not the individual or the wider society. The family is not just an escape from alienation, but an actual cause of it! In modern capitalist society the family is a market for goods.

Feminists revived Engels' work to argue that the main victims of exploitation were women. Some feminists see the exploiters as men rather than the bourgeoisie and condemn patriarchal, rather than capitalist, society. There is no clear distinction between Marxist and feminist approaches; rather, it is a continuum, with more or less importance attributed to class or gender.

Exploitation of women is seen in the domestic labour process. Housework is seen as real work, done by women without pay or recognition, for the benefit of men. Whereas Parsons and other functionalists saw conjugal roles as complementary and tending towards symmetry and equality, feminists see power concentrated in the hands of men. The measures of inequality of power include decision-making, control over money and violence.

Bernard argued that marriage, whilst beneficial for men in terms of career and health, had the opposite effects on women. McIntosh, in *The Anti-social Family*, argued that the idealisation of family life has harmful effects on society as well as on individual family members. It is assumed, but is not true, that the old, sick and dependent children will be well cared for within the family so that no other adequate provision need be made.

Finally, a rejoinder to feminist attacks on the family comes from Martin, who sees women as exercising control over relationships with kin and points out that many women enjoy the autonomy of housework compared with routine paid employment.

STUDENT'S ANSWER WITH EXAMINER COMMENTS

Question 1

'Far from being democratic the family is based on an unequal division of labour and power.' Discuss.

> **States a clear argument and explains division of labour.**

In both pre-industrial and nuclear families there is evidence that the family is based on an unequal division of labour and power. Boulton's study in 1983 shows that although men claim that the division of labour should be more equal and is more equal, research showed that only 9 out of 50 subjects helped 'extensively' in the house.

> **Clear argument but does not explain power.**

Structured inequalities within society have a large impact on family life. Bernard points out that social institutions such as the church, the divorce courts and the social security system have traditionally conferred authority on men in marriage, therefore many wives do consider it legitimate even if they argue about the consequences. Men have not only the power but also the authority to get their own way.

> **Good Marxist–feminist analysis. Links exploitation and decisions to the concept of power.**

Delphy concludes that men exploit women's labour. Like Marx she sees them as a working class, and as men's wages provide the means of production in the home they are like a ruling class. Because most women feel they are responsible for running the home and caring for the children they become or are made economically and socially dependent on their husbands. Final decisions which are seen as important, e.g. moving house and financial matters, are taken by husbands. Husbands wield far more power than their wives and this power is built into the marital relationship because of the wage-earning capacity of the husband, particularly when the wife is rearing young children. Edgell explains that men's greater participation in the paid labour market allows them to avoid many household tasks and dominate family life.

> **Links violence to division of labour and power.**

The continuing importance of male authority in marriage is underlined by the 1980 study *Violence Against Wives*. Dobash and Dobash argue that assault on wives is connected to cultural expectations about male authority in marriage. Violent husbands swiftly resort to force when their wives do not provide for their needs, e.g. a hot meal on the table as quickly or in quite the way he wants; or when wives question a husband's actions or opinions.

> **Relevant, but not tied into previous arguments.**

Women retain the bulk of domestic responsibility even when they are in full-time employment. Rapoport and Rapoport's study of dual-career families focused upon couples where both husbands and wives had professional or business careers. They found that although participants endorsed the dual-career pattern, the wife's career was seen as being followed for satisfaction. Both spouses placed upon the wife's shoulders the responsibility for dealing with any demands or problems the family placed on their work.

Overall comments

Overall, a C grade answer. The major deficiency is the absence of any awareness of arguments for increased democracy in the family, e.g. the symmetrical family. Rather short for an A-level answer but relevant and conceptually sound. Shows good analytical skills.

Good framework used to examine power, i.e.:

1   Influence of money.
2   Decision-making.
3   Violence.

I would like to see children and perhaps older people included in the discussion.

A Review Sheet for this chapter may be found on p. 255.

11

EDUCATION

**DIFFERENTIAL
EDUCATIONAL
ACHIEVEMENT**

**EDUCATION AND THE
WIDER SOCIETY**

**THEORETICAL AND
EMPIRICAL STUDIES**

GETTING STARTED

The sociology of education is an area in which all sociology students and teachers share some common experiences. It provides students with the opportunity to analyse their own experiences using sociological concepts, and to evaluate theories using their own experiences.

This topic illustrates the relationships between sociology and social policy. Sociological research seems to influence education policy, such as encouraging the expansion of opportunity. On the other hand, social policy has been a topic of research itself and has also influenced the social reality we wish to study. For example, recognition of gender and ethnic inequality has changed the experience of many pupils and their actual levels of achievement. Therefore, note the dates of research studies as apparently contradictory evidence could be the result of studying similar subjects at different times.

The main themes of questions set on this topic are:

1 **Examining the relationships between education and the economy.**
2 **Examining the relationship between education and inequality, including consideration of social mobility and meritocracy.**
3 **Evaluating competing explanations of differential educational achievement.**
4 **Examining research on classroom interaction between teachers and pupils and within groups of pupils.**
5 **Examination of the formal curriculum and the 'hidden curriculum'.**
6 **Explaining educational policy and evaluating its effectiveness.**

Definitions

- *The curriculum.* This is the sum of learning experiences offered by schools.

- *The hidden curriculum.* This is the unofficial consequence of school experience. Not just knowledge, but what is experienced as a result of the organisation of the school.

- *Meritocracy.* This is a system where rewards depend on merit, that is, on ability and effort, and not on ascribed characteristics.

- *Vocational Education.* This is learning which is seen as directly related to work. It takes the form of either specific training or preparation for employment in general.

Related topics include types of social inequality (class, race and gender), the family, work and development. Sub-cultural theories of differential achievement reflect similar theories of deviance.

ESSENTIAL PRINCIPLES

A major sociological problem is explaining the mass of evidence which indicates a correlation between educational achievement and class, ethnicity and gender. The changing sociological explanations reflect developments in sociology in general, such as the rise of interactionist and modern Marxist theories. Explanations can be grouped under four broad headings:

1 Innate ability

This is a psychological rather than a sociological explanation. Functionalist sociologists frequently assume, but do not attempt to demonstrate, natural inequality in order to support the meritocratic ideology. The Liberal sociologists deny the significance of innate differences in explaining the differential achievement of groups, as opposed to individuals.

2 Out-of-school factors

These are generally structuralist explanations, identifying a variety of causal factors under the sub-headings of material deprivation and cultural deprivation. A number of material factors have been mentioned in research, including poverty and bad housing. Cultural influences include parental expectations, values, and childrearing styles, which are seen as class specific, and also language development and usage.

 Most of the research in Britain has been on class, whereas in the USA race has always been a major concern. These studies tend to play down the significance of individual differences and the experience of school, and to locate the problem in the family and neighbourhood.

3 In-school factors

Education provision can influence success. Schools vary in the quality of staff and buildings. However, most explanations which identify the school as the most significant factor in explaining educational achievement tend to be interpretive accounts.

 Interactionists focus on the teacher–pupil relationship and often draw on labelling theory or refer to the self-fulfilling prophecy. There is also a body of work on the formation of pupil sub-cultures.

 Ethnomethodology has criticised the interactionist approach for underestimating the active part played by pupils in making sense of the experience of school.

4 Marxist accounts

Modern Marxists recognise the importance of both out-of-school deprivation and differential treatment in school. Deprivation is seen as a symptom of socially structured inequality. Thus Bordieu talks of the working class lacking 'cultural capital', which makes them less educable in the majority of schools which conform to the dominant ruling-class values.

 Differential treatment by teachers is seen as reinforcing existing social categories (occupation, race and gender) rather than as being based on the interaction of individuals. This conforms with the feminist view that the school reflects and reinforces the prevailing inequalities of the society.

This section deals with the contributions of functionalist and Marxist sociology to the understanding of the role of education. In particular, it is concerned with the relationship between education and the economy, education and inequality, and education and social control. This involves a consideration of both educational institutions and ideas.

THE FUNCTIONALIST APPROACH

Functionalists explain the development of the education system by examining its relationships with other social institutions and the contribution it makes to satisfying the functional needs of the whole system.

 The main functions identified are the *economic function*, which meets adaptation needs, and the more general *socialisation function*, which is concerned with integration and social control.

The economic function

Educational systems are perceived as responding to demands for skilled labour and contributing to economic growth. Economic growth, in turn, can provide additional funding for the expansion of educational provision (see also the Outline Answer to Question 2, Chapter 8).

The extent to which education does, or should, provide specific vocational preparation is debatable. The selection and role allocation function is probably more significant. The development of the 'New Vocationalism' in English education could be seen more as the result of political direction than of economic forces. A further criticism is that the supply of skilled labour seems to respond to pay, rather than to the provision of places for training. Such places, as in the cases of nursing and teaching, often go unfilled.

The socialisation function

Consensual values are transmitted through the education system either manifestly (for example through religious instruction) or latently (for example the effects on pupils of studying in a hierarchical institution). The distinction between *manifest* (overt and deliberate) functions and *latent* functions (not intentional or even diagnosed consequences) is similar to the Marxist distinction between the official and hidden curricula. The transmission of culture involves the content of the course, the organisation of the school, and the teacher–pupil relationships.

THE MARXIST APPROACH

Marxists see the education system, both the institutions involved and the ideology they transmit, as part of the superstructure of capitalist society. Systems are shaped by the economic substructure and in turn reproduce the existing relationships of production. The role of education is thus to perpetuate capitalism. This involves the preparation of the workforce for its intended role and the reinforcing of ruling-class hegemony.

Comparison with the consensus-structuralism of functionalism can be made as follows:

1   Both study education by looking at its relationship with the wider society.
2   Both link education with the economy. Marxism sees education as reproducing capitalism, whereas functionalists see it as fitting the needs of industrial society. Functionalists emphasise training and role allocation, whereas Marxists emphasise the production of deskilled obedient workers.
3   Both identify a cultural reproduction role. The functionalists stress the integrative effects of transmitting consensual values, whereas the Marxists talk of ruling-class ideology and of maintaining false consciousness.
    (See also the Tutor Answer to Question 1 below.)

THE NEW RIGHT APPROACH

The virtues of traditional education are extolled and many post-war reforms condemned. Anti-sexism, anti-racism and multiculturalism in the curriculum are condemned. The teaching of both Literature and History should emphasise English national glory, and religious teaching should be primarily Christian. The teaching of Sociology has been singled out for particular condemnation! (See Chapter 23 on *The nature of sociology*.)

THEORETICAL AND EMPIRICAL STUDIES

EDUCATIONAL ACHIEVEMENT

These will be summarised under the headings of class, gender and ethnicity. But first some warnings to consider when evaluating evidence.

1   Findings of studies carried out *at the same time* are sometimes contradictory. But this should be distinguished from situations where findings of studies at *different times* disagree. The latter is by no means necessarily contradictory!
2   The nature and extent of differential achievement change over time. Some groups seen as disadvantaged have subsequently improved their performance. Therefore *dates* of studies are highly relevant.
3   Definitions of class, gender and ethnicity are problematic. They are socially defined and their meaning is socially constructed.
4   Classes are divided by race and gender.
5   Ethnic groups are divided by class and gender.

6   Gender groups are divided by class and ethnicity.

7   Different ethnic groups perform differently.

8   The definition and assessment of educational achievement are problematic.

9   Ethnic minorities and females may succeed in terms of examination results, but still be disadvantaged if schools reinforce stereotypes and allow discrimination.

10 If the issue is the existence of a meritocratic society, it must be noted that educational success alone does not eliminate other forms of inequality in the job market.

GENDER

Out of school

The family, peer group and media can socialise girls into early leaving, marriage and 'women's jobs'. The division in the labour market often encourages underachievement, with nursing and secretarial work having low entry qualifications as compared with men's professions and skilled jobs.

Sharpe (1976) described how girls learned the priorities of love, marriage, husbands, children, jobs and careers (in that order). McRobbie (1978) looked at the content of romantic magazines and their influence on girls' expectations. Griffin (1985) suggested that early leaving was seen by working-class girls as an escape from their responsibility for housework, as employment raised their status in the family. Fuller argued that West Indian girls were determined to get jobs which would ensure their independence from men.

It should be noted that despite different treatment at home, girls are raised in the *same families* as boys. Therefore the influence of the family on such things as language will be less significant for gender than for class and ethnic groups.

In school

The influence of curriculum choice and content has been indicated by the following. Deem (1980) showed how girls were encouraged into 'feminine', and thus low-status, subjects by the school. Blackstone (1980) showed how girls were allowed to avoid science in mixed schools, but to a lesser extent in single-sex schools. Oakley (1982) suggested that the hidden curriculum was a reflection, rather than a cause, of women's position in society.

Teacher–pupil interaction is a significant factor according to Wolpe (1977), who wrote that girls were 'taught' to smile at male teachers, to be passive and to develop self-discipline earlier than boys. Delamont (1980) showed how different expectations began in nursery school, and in a subsequent study showed how the YTS pushed girls into feminine jobs. Stanworth (1983) reported that teachers were more likely to know the boys' names and to interact with them in class, whereas they underestimated the abilities and ambitions of girls. Despite all this evidence, Spender found that teachers denied any such favouritism.

Pupil–pupil interaction remains significant in the social control of girls. Both boys and girls share the sexist attitudes of the society in which they live. Whyte showed how boys denied girls equal access to bricks in nursery school and to science equipment in secondary school. Lees (1988) showed how sexist language such as 'slags and sluts' is used to intimidate and inhibit girls. She also reports physical intimidation of girls in school. Spender found that teachers tolerated such behaviour and persisted in the use of 'man-made language'.

ETHNICITY AND RACE

American studies of the 1960s tended to replace the notion of innate intelligence as a cause of black underachievement with descriptions of a deficient culture and a pathological family life. However, Labov (1975) challenged the application of Bernstein-like ideas to black dialects.

Rex and Moore (1967) explained underachievement in class, rather than cultural, terms. Most recent studies have concentrated on the teacher and school as the source of inequality. Coard (1971) saw racism as the explanation of the overrepresentation of black children in ESN schools, while Pakistani children were underrepresented. Performance in relevant tests failed to explain these differences. Tomlinson (1972) found evidence of low teacher expectations for ethnic minority pupils. Driver (1981) found evidence that, despite considerable improvements in the numbers getting five or more higher-grade CSEs or O-levels and in A-level grades, children of West Indian origin still underachieved. However, girls did better than boys. Green showed that white boys got more attention from teachers than girls or ethnic minority pupils.

Separate small-scale studies in London and Bradford in the late 1980s have actually shown pupils from most ethnic minorities achieving more than their white classmates. These studies need a careful consideration of the class background of the children, as indeed do all studies on this issue.

CLASS

Out-of-school studies have not concentrated on the home in isolation from the school. But they have tended to take the school for granted, seeing it as reacting in a neutral way to children who arrive at school in a more or less educable condition. Halsey suggested that neither 'material circumstances' (housing, father's class, etc.) nor 'family climate' (parental encouragement, linguistic competence, etc.) have a strong influence, provided children were in the same school.

Coates and Silburn argued that poverty disadvantaged children in a variety of material and cultural ways. Bernstein, who claims he has often been misrepresented, made language a major area of concern in the sociology of education. He sees differences in the ability of working-class and middle-class children to use the elaborate code of language favoured by teachers.

In-school studies have looked at the formation of pupil sub-cultures which conform more or less to the values of the school (Hargreaves 1967, Lacey 1970 and Ball 1981). Sub-cultures seem related to streaming within schools as well as to class. Ball sees the school as offering a 'cooling-out' process where ambition is lowered. Willis (1979) describes a similar process, but sees the pupils as playing a more active part.

Teacher–pupil interaction has been described by Becker, who relates it to labelling theory. Nash emphasises that teachers' expectations are based not on the 'real' class characteristics of children, but on the teacher's perception of class. Keddie identified the way in which teachers offered a different curriculum to low-stream pupils and interpreted their questions and behaviour differently.

FUNCTIONALIST STUDIES

Durkheim

Durkheim saw education as the methodological socialisation of the young. It provided them with the general qualities necessary to be members of a society and with the specific skills to fill particular occupational roles. Thus education systems contribute towards satisfying the functional needs of integration, social control and role allocation.

Parsons

Parsons identified the basic values underlying education in the USA as equality of opportunity, competition and individualism. Children cease to be judged by the particularistic standards of the home, which are replaced by the universalistic standards of the whole society. Subsequent inequality is thus legitimised. Education thus reflects the consensual values which integrate the society.

Davis and Moore

Davis and Moore emphasise the role allocation function, seeing education as the mechanism by which the most qualified people are channelled into the most important jobs.

MARXIST STUDIES

Althusser

Althusser described education as an 'Ideological State Apparatus' which reproduces inequality. Both the ideology underlying the curriculum, and the institutions which transmit it, contribute to this reproductive process.

Inequality is legitimised and reinforced. Schools claim to treat pupils in a neutral fashion and teachers and pupils believe this. Althusser sees the process of ideological reproduction as 'unconscious'. This is a common theme in his Marxist–structuralist approach, which owes a debt to Durkheim as well as to Marx. The school is mistakenly seen as independent of the economy.

Willis

In contrast to Althusser's structuralism, Willis offers a more action-based Marxist analysis. He describes how working-class boys are not integrated into the culture of the school, which is middle class. The school is seen as offering them nothing which is relevant or useful, and they demand nothing. Thus the school does not 'brainwash' them and has no specific effect, beyond reinforcing the view that education is not for them. They fail, not in their own terms, but in the view of the school.

Bowles and Gintis

In a series of empirical and theoretical studies of schooling in the USA, Bowles and Gintis developed their correspondence theory of education. They argue that there are interdependent relationships between the family, education and work. The work roles of parents influence the socialisation of children, thus the family influences educational achievement. The school corresponds to the workplace, thus work roles are influenced both by socialisation in the family and by achievement in school.

Examples of the correspondence between school and work include:

1 The fragmentation and stratification of school knowledge is similar to deskilled and fragmented work.
2 Pupils rely on teachers for knowledge, as workers rely on managers.
3 Both school and workplace motivate and control through extrinsic rewards.
4 Pupils learn to be submissive to authority.
5 Both school and workplace are hierarchically organised.
6 Rewards appear to be based on merit, which thereby legitimises inequality.

EXAMINATION QUESTIONS

1   'The expansion of educational provision in Western industrial societies is a direct consequence of the demand for an increasingly skilled workforce.' Explain and discuss.

(AEB)

2   Assess the extent to which educational reforms in Britain over the last fifty years have created a meritocratic society.

(AEB)

3   What is meant by the 'hidden curriculum' in schools? How have sociologists contributed to our understanding of this aspect of education?

(WJEC)

4   Assess the strengths and weaknesses of interactionist explanations of differential educational achievement.

(AEB)

5   **ITEM A**

Cultural reproduction refers to the ways in which schools, along with other social institutions, help carry on social and economic inequalities across the generations. This concept directs our attention to the means whereby, via the hidden curriculum, schools influence the learning of values, attitudes and habits. Schools reinforce variations in cultural values and outlooks acquired early in life. When children leave school, this has the effect of limiting the opportunities of some, whilst enhancing those of others.

Source: adapted from A. GIDDENS, *Sociology*
(Polity) 1989

ITEM B

The strengths of the structural-functionalist approach to education lie primarily in the emphasis that it gives to interrelationships between the education system and aspects of the wider social structure. In particular, as a result of highlighting the links between education and the economy, the processes of selecting and differentiation within schools and the resulting distribution of 'life chances' become issues of central concern in the sociology of education.

Source: adapted from STEPHEN BALL, *Education*
(Longman) 1986

ITEM C

The policy-makers of the 1960s saw a direct relationship between educational reform and economic well-being: a skilled and educated workforce would facilitate economic growth which would, in turn, constitute a firm basis for sustained educational expansion. But this simple philosophy was shattered by the economic recession of the early 1970s which served to undermine all the liberal and expansionist beliefs of the previous decade. The Callaghan government of 1976–79 was anxious to distance itself from 'progressive' educational opinion and tried to build a new educational consensus around more central control of the school curriculum, greater teacher accountability and the more direct subordination of secondary education to the perceived needs of the economy. But this was by no means 'radical' enough for the Far Right of the Conservative Party, which began to question the nature and purpose of a 'national system of education, locally administered'.

5

10

Source: CLYDE CHITTY, 'The Education System Transformed'
(*Sociology Review* Volume 2 No. 3 February 1993)

a) Name the sociological perspective which is usually associated with the idea of cultural reproduction expressed in ITEM A. (*1 mark*)

b) Suggest *three* ways in which the local administration of the education system has been weakened since 1970 (ITEM C). (*3 marks*)

c) Evaluate the importance of the hidden curriculum in schools to the 'learning of values, attitudes and habits' of schoolchildren (ITEM A line 4). (*9 marks*)

d) For which social groups have schools had 'the effect of limiting the opportunities' (ITEM A line 6)? (*3 marks*)

e) Using information from the ITEMS and other sources, assess functionalist and Marxist approaches to the relationship between education and the economy. (*9 marks*)
(*Total 25 marks*)
(AEB)

ANSWERS TO EXAMINATION QUESTIONS

OUTLINE ANSWERS

Question 2

You must start with a clear idea of meritocracy in order to judge the impact of educational reforms. Accurate, if not detailed, knowledge of educational reforms is necessary.

i) Explain meritocracy. The necessary tests of educational reforms should be:
   a) Is education the dominant means of access to highly rewarded positions?
   b) Does educational achievement depend on merit?

ii) Consider the effectiveness of some of the following by referring to relevant sociological studies.
   a) Free secondary education for all.
   b) Comprehensive schools.
   c) Raising of the school leaving age (ROSLA) from 15 to 16.
   d) Expansion of higher education.
   e) 'Vocationalism'.
   f) The Education Reform Act: the national curriculum and City Technology Colleges.

   The first question is discussed in mobility studies (males only!), particularly by Halsey *et al.* Race is covered by the Swann report and gender by Equal Opportunities Commission publications.

   The second question is covered by a wealth of studies including Ford, Ball and Rutter. More recent studies dealing with the YTS, etc., make a refreshing change for examiners, e.g. K. Roberts and Parris *et al.*

iii) Marxist criticism, which sees meritocracy as an ideological myth and the educational reforms aimed at reproducing and legitimising inequality. Bowles and Gintis, Willis and Jencks, offer different interpretations of this theme.

Question 3

This question requires an examination of the concept of the 'hidden curriculum' and an evaluation of relevant studies.

i) Provide a definition of the 'hidden curriculum' and distinguish it from the knowledge and practices which comprise the formal curriculum.

ii) Indicate the application of the concept to class, and to race and gender inequality. Mention the organisation of the school, its rules and rituals, the relationships between pupil and pupil, and between teacher and pupil, and the 'hidden' content of school books, e.g. reinforcing nationalism, racism and sexism.

iii) Marxist explanations, which see the 'hidden curriculum' as ruling-class ideology and emphasise the significance of economic relations outside the school. (Bowles and Gintis, Althusser and Willis, can be used.)

iv) Interactionist explanations, which see pupils playing a more active and conscious role in pleasing teachers in order to gain rewards. (Jackson and Hargreaves.)

v) Illich provides a similar analysis to the Marxists but uses the concept to criticise the school and teachers rather than capitalist society.

vi) You could include a critical view of the concept, comparing it with functionalist views of the latent functions of education. Also point out that what is latent or 'hidden' in one situation may be overt and formalised in other circumstances: e.g. religious or political education, the promoting of co-operative or competitive games, and the current emphasis on vocational education.

Question 5

a) Marxism.

b) Any three changes, e.g. CTCs, grant-maintained schools/opting out, national curriculum, FE colleges leaving LEA control, etc.

c) The answer needs to present a balanced critical account. The role of the hidden curriculum can be assessed in Marxist, feminist, interactionist or even functionalist terms. One critical approach might be to develop the view that the transmission of values, etc., may be planned and deliberate.

    Alternatively, other non-school (religion, media, family) sources may have more influence on values. You can look at the organisation of the school, rules, content of the formal curriculum, etc.

d) Any three from girls, boys, ethnic minorities, working class or similar alternatives.

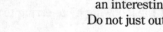

e) You should draw on all three Items and use evidence to point out the strengths and weaknesses of the two approaches. You will be rewarded for pointing out similarities and differences between the two approaches. You could mention preparation for employment, vocational training, selection, ideological reproduction of the workforce, the links between economic development and education (modernisation theory), etc. Bowles and Gintis are particularly useful to argue the Marxist case, and Willis offers an interesting view from the pupil.

Do not just outline the two approaches in sequence; you must evaluate each explicitly.

TUTOR ANSWER

Question 1

'The expansion of educational provision in Western industrial societies is a direct consequence of the demand for an increasingly skilled workforce.' Explain and discuss.

The growth of educational provision in Western Europe and the USA has occurred throughout the twentieth century and particularly since the Second World War. However, the pattern of growth and the nature and extent of increased provision vary between nations. Britain, for example, has a smaller proportion of the population in higher education than most of its competitors.

    Both functionalist and Marxist writers tend to explain this expansion by linking it to economic development, although neither give as narrow an explanation as that offered in the question.

    Functionalism explains the origin, persistence and development of social phenomena by identifying their functions. Functions are the contributions the phenomena make towards satisfying the functional needs of the system, thus ensuring the survival and stability of the society. Growth in educational provision would be seen as 'fitting' the needs of an industrial society. Certainly the demand for a skilled workforce is seen as one of those needs. Mass education arrived with industrialisation and, as well as providing suitable workers, could be seen to depend on the economic surplus created by the new methods of production. Advanced industrial societies are characterised by a growth in office, managerial, professional and skilled technological work at the expense of less skilled manual work. These new jobs require educated workers.

This kind of functionalist argument has been used to explain both the expansion of higher education and the development of 'vocational' education. However, functionalists do not see the provision of trained or skilled workers as the sole economic function of education. The selection or allocation function is seen as equally important. The education system provides for the assessment of pupils' abilities and aptitudes, so as to allow the best qualified to fill the most functionally important positions. This is a major theme in Davis and Moore's theory of stratification. Parsons, following Durkheim, also attaches importance to the role of education in integrating society by transmitting consensual values and morality.

Berg has offered critical research which suggests that better-educated workers are not necessarily more productive workers. (Although managers may assume that their better workers are more educationally qualified.) Educational qualifications help people to get jobs, but not to perform them well. Debates about education and stratification also raise doubts as to whether the bases for success in education are ability and effort, and thus whether the education system *does* allocate people to suitable positions.

Marxist theories also emphasise the importance of economic influences on the educational system. The organisation of schools and the curriculum are seen as part of the superstructure of capitalist societies. The explanation of the expansion of education lies then, not in the demands of industrial society, but in the effects of capitalism.

Bowles and Gintis, like the functionalist writers, see employment as a major influence on the nature of the education system. Their 'correspondence' theory argues that there are interdependent relationships between work, education and the family. The way in which school corresponds to work is the most important element of their study for this answer. If capitalism is to function efficiently, then a disciplined and hard-working labour force is required. Possible worker resistance is minimised by the training received in school. Workers are prepared for working for cash in jobs by working for extrinsic rewards at school. They also learn to rely on experts for knowledge and to respect authority. The hierarchy of the workplace corresponds to the hierarchy of the school. Competing for rewards at school prepares the more successful to compete for promotion at work. In both cases, conformity is rewarded.

Other Marxist writers, such as Althusser, also explain the functioning of education by showing how it supports the interests of capitalism. The reproduction of labour power is seen as involving the reproduction of ideology more than suitable skills. Much employment in advanced industrial societies has become deskilled and it is a docile, rather than qualified, labour force which is required. Schools are seen as places which 'cool' ambition rather than encourage competition. Willis explains how pupils play a more active role than many Marxists acknowledge in settling for the same working-class jobs as their parents. Clarke and Willis argue that the training schemes of the early 1980s were set up not to bridge the alleged skills gap, but to divert attention from structural causes of unemployment and to locate the problem with the young and the schools.

Marsden has questioned the links between educational expansion and the demand for labour (which is central to both functionalist and Marxist sociology) as well as the stated aims of both Conservative and Labour governments. He sees the education system as responding to other demands, such as equality of opportunity (which is in keeping with functionalist theory). However, he also argues that there is a degree of autonomy, as illustrated by the continued control over the curriculum exercised by the universities and examination boards. Recent government initiatives have challenged this alleged autonomy, and have tried to bring them into line with perceived economic needs.

Collins, in the USA, also argues that the contribution of educational expansion to economic growth has been exaggerated and that the US labour force might be over-educated beyond what is necessary to acquire job skills. In support of this view we could cite the economic growth of the 1950s, which was not driven by educational expansion, and the failure of the expanded Higher Education sector to produce the extra scientists and technologists which the Robbins Report advocated. The early 1980s saw a contraction in university places at the same time as the demand for such places was highest. The demand for more higher education for women has been fuelled not by the predicted labour shortage of the 1990s, but by the demand for equal opportunities since the 1970s.

STUDENT'S ANSWER WITH EXAMINER COMMENTS

Question 4

Assess the strengths and weaknesses of interactionist explanations of differential educational achievement.

> Interactionist views do not assume that there is any objective social reality. Instead of looking for cause-and-effect laws they look for the reasons why individuals are defined as successes or failures. They do not use official statistics in their explanations of differential educational achievement, seeing them as social constructions. Interactionist sociologists criticise positivist sociologists for their 'out-of-school' explanations of differential achievement because they fail to consider processes in school and are no better than a layman's explanations of sociological phenomena.
>
> Becker saw teachers' views of the pupils as affecting their performance in school. He found by interviewing teachers that they had notions of what made an 'ideal pupil'. Cicourel and Kitsuse found that teachers' judgements of pupils, supposedly based on objective factors such as IQ and performance in class, were actually judgements based on the perceived class of pupils. Keddie related this theory to streaming, where pupils were judged and grouped according to their perceived ability.
>
> Rosenthal and Jacobson studied the self-fulfilling prophecy in an experiment in a school. They gave the pupils an IQ test to rate their ability and then told teachers that certain pupils were more likely to improve in class. These pupils were in fact chosen at random. They retested the pupils after a period of time and found that not only did the teachers perceive the chosen children as being more attentive and better behaved but also the children's actual performance had improved more than that of other children. Rosenthal and Jacobson found that the teachers had forgotten the original list of 'spurters' but their attitudes and attention to the children had improved their performance.
>
> Ethnomethodological approaches stress the role that pupils play in the classroom situation. They see the pupil's attitude to the teacher as playing an equally important part as the teacher's attitude to the pupil. Whilst following an interpretive approach, ethnomethodologists have criticised other in-school explanations of differential achievement as regarding the pupil as a non-active participant in classroom interaction.
>
> Interactionist approaches have been criticised using positivist out-of-school explanations which show that external influences still affect pupils' performance in school. This may be seen more recently where schools have become more equal with more racial and gender equality. It may be seen that when this happens external influences such as class and class-based differences play a greater role in differential achievement.
>
> The Marxist approach is similar to the interactionist approach, in that teachers are seen as treating children unequally, but it also takes into account out-of-school factors.

" Good start. Not a prepared run-through on differential achievement. Attempts comparison with other explanations. "

" Relevant studies, but not developed. "

" Relevant, but not related to ethnicity, class or gender. Not criticised. "

" Shows diversity of interactionist approaches. Needs studies. "

" Good logical criticism. "

Overall comments

Overall, a short but successful attempt to outline and assess interactionist studies. Sound on concepts but thin on evidence. The candidate was short of either time or knowledge. This is a typical last question. The application of a general understanding of relevant concepts to this question deserves credit. Should discuss class, race and gender. Worth a C grade.

A Review Sheet for this chapter may be found on p. 255.

GETTING STARTED

There is considerable overlap between sociology of work and some closely related topics, especially *Social class* (Chapter 3) and *Organisations* (Chapter 13).

The best guide to what should be covered in this section is perhaps offered by examination questions. However, good answers frequently benefit from, or even require, reference to other topics. In this chapter we refer to the Marxist criticism of 'Taylorism' which is a central part of recent debates on the nature of both office and factory work, but see Chapter 13 for a more detailed account of Taylor's original work.

Other chapters which offer related material include *Professions* (Chapter 14), *Gender* (Chapter 5) and *Education* (Chapter 11).

The main themes of questions set on this topic are:

1 **Alienation and job satisfaction.**
2 **Industrial conflict.**
3 **The relationship between work and non-work.**
4 **Unemployment.**

Students should show an awareness of the increasing significance of studies of women at work (including housework), white-collar work and unemployment. The nature of a post-industrial society based on knowledge and information workers, and service-type occupations, has implications for stratification and development as well as for this topic.

Definitions

- *Alienation* is the separation or estrangement of the individual from his true self, from others and from the world he inhabits. The workplace is seen as the main location and cause of alienation, but the concept is also used in the sociology of religion, the family, race and deviance.

- *Industrial conflict* occurs in a variety of forms, not just strikes.

- *Job satisfaction* is often considered as involving *intrinsic* sources of satisfaction found in the work task itself, and *extrinsic* sources of satisfaction found in working conditions, and especially pay.

- *Work* is generally seen as paid employment.

- *Unemployment* is the undesired absence of paid employment.

- *Fordism* describes the old use of technology for mass production of standardised products using a deskilled workforce.

- *Neo-Fordism* is the use of technology to save labour and improve quality whilst still maintaining both the vertical and horizontal division of labour.

- *Post-Fordism* is the breakdown of the division of labour as employers emphasise the need to innovate (new products and processes).

- *Flexible specialisation* describes the producers' responsiveness to new markets, leading to changing work roles, ability to respond to technological change, and the loosening of management control.

ALIENATION AND JOB SATISFACTION

INDUSTRIAL CONFLICT

WORK AND NON-WORK

THEORETICAL AND EMPIRICAL STUDIES

**ALIENATION
AND JOB
SATISFACTION**

ESSENTIAL PRINCIPLES

A framework for answering questions on both work satisfaction and industrial conflict can be provided by grouping theories under three headings:

- Conditions in the workplace.
- Marxist approaches.
- Interactionist approaches.

CONDITIONS IN THE WORKPLACE

Conventionally such studies have concentrated on production technology, debating the degree to which technology determines satisfaction (Blauner and critics). We can also consider here the influence of managerial control (Weber and Taylor) and informal work groups (Mayo). There is an overlap with organisation theories discussed in the next chapter.

MARXIST THEORIES

Alienation results inevitably from the relations of production found in pre-communist societies. It is at its worst under capitalism which '... perfects the worker and degrades the man'. The inseparable causes are:

- The wage contract which exploits the employee.
- The nature of factory work (and later office work).

Marxists see the organisation of work as having the dual purpose of maximising profits and controlling the workforce. This results in such alienating conditions as the extreme division of labour, deskilling, mechanisation and bureaucratisation. The worker is motivated solely by pay.

Modern Marxist studies deal not only with factory work, but also with white-collar and female workers. These themes are pursued in the discussions about 'proletarianisation' (p. 118) and the position of women and ethnic minorities in the labour market (pp. 119 and 120).

INTERACTIONIST STUDIES

These reject structuralist explanations which identify external causes of the workers' attitudes and behaviour at work. Instead the reasons for workers' experiences are to be found by understanding their motives and the *meanings* they attribute to work. These meanings are influenced by the workers' prior experiences, both inside and outside work. Thus, neither capitalism nor working conditions have inevitable and uniform effects on workers.

**INDUSTRIAL
CONFLICT**

The three groups of explanations above can be used to explain both the *extent* and *type* of industrial conflict found in particular firms, industries and countries.

The interactionist approaches concentrate on the meaning which conflict has for the participants, and can be used as the basis for a critical account of strike statistics.

Marxists debate the real meaning behind conflict with the interactionists. The essence of the argument is whether the pursuit of any goal, except that of a change in the relations of production, is to be seen as false consciousness.

A final way to categorise theories of industrial conflict is to distinguish *consensus* from *conflict* theories. The former see peaceful industrial relations as normal and strikes as pathological, whereas the latter see conflict as normal and apparent peace as evidence of bourgeois hegemony.

Since 1979 the industrial relations climate has changed dramatically in the UK, generally in the favour of employers. Trade-union membership has declined, unemployment has risen to unprecedented post-war levels, the occupational structure has continued to change, legislation has curbed trade-union power, and previously strong unions such as the miners, printers and dockers have suffered probably irreversible damage.

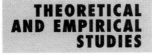

WORK AND NON-WORK

Definitions of work, non-work and leisure must be regarded as problematic. S. Parker provided widely accepted definitions which were little changed by Elias and Dunning.

- *Work* is paid employment.
- *Work obligations* are voluntary, done outside normal working hours but associated with a job.
- *Existence time* is the satisfaction of needs such as eating and sleeping. *Non-work obligations* are domestic duties, such as childcare and cleaning.
- *Leisure* is free time when people choose activities or inactivity.

McIntosh rejects the work of both Parker and Elias and Dunning as restricted to men. The degree of choice and separation is not, she claims, available to women.

You might organise your answers by distinguishing the following approaches:

1   Marxists, who see both work and leisure activity as produced by capitalism.
2   Those like Parker, who see work as related to leisure.
3   Feminist critics, who see women's leisure opportunities to be as restricted as their work chances.
4   Interactionists, who see the previous arguments as overdeterminist and are concerned with the meanings attached to work and non-work activities.

Unemployment

The main issues are:

1   Problems of definition, which form the basis of a criticism of the official statistics.
2   Explaining the distribution of unemployment by class, race, age, gender and region.
3   Explaining the causes of unemployment.
4   Examining the effects of unemployment.

ALIENATION AND JOB SATISFACTION

THEORETICAL AND EMPIRICAL STUDIES

In-work studies

Blauner sees alienation as the consequence of the type of technology used in industrial production. He distinguishes four types of technology and sees alienation as increasing as technologies become more complex. This trend is (optimistically) reversed when the most modern form of technology is employed. Alienation is measured along four dimensions: powerlessness, meaninglessness, isolation and self-estrangement.

Wedderburn, Gallie and Mallet, in separate studies, all query Blauner's overemphasis on technology. They suggest alternative influences on satisfaction, including managerial practices and the national culture.

Weber rejects Marx's view that bureaucracy is a form of control exclusively linked to capitalism and inevitably bad for workers. Some aspects of bureaucracy are alienating, as they reduce the autonomy of the worker, but others provide him with security and a career. (See Chapter 13 on *Organisations*.)

F. Taylor's theory of 'scientific management' claimed to meet the employers' need for efficiency, and the profit this generated then allowed the workers' need for cash to be satisfied.

Mayo's 'human relations' approach seemed to have discredited Taylorism as early as the 1930s. Social rewards gained from informal work groups were seen as more important than economic rewards gained by individuals. Control was seen as friendlier and more democratic.

Trist and Bamforth pioneered the socio-technical systems approach. This argued that managerial practice can influence satisfaction within the limits set by technology. The reorganisation of conventional car assembly lines by Volvo and Saab-scania followed their recommendations.

Marxists

Marx's work on alienation developed from his study of philosophy and religion. He predicted an optimistic future for man, who would express his true self through creative work. This, however, can happen only after the fall of capitalism. The alienated worker does not own his product, works only for cash, has no control over production and is isolated from himself, his fellow workers and his employers.

Carchedi follows C.W. Mills in extending the concept of alienation to white-collar workers. He writes of the proletarianisation of office work. The causes of this process include: bureaucratisation, fragmentation and the subsequent deskilling of office workers. Feminisation of this workforce is a contributory factor. Mills extends the argument from routine office workers to managers and professionals. Salaman develops Braverman's criticisms of the work of Weber, Taylor and Blauner. The design of work is aimed not just at efficiency, but at controlling the workforce. This is the purpose of the fragmentation of work and the deskilling of workers. Mayo's proposals are dismissed as simply more subtle forms of control, suitable for higher-grade workers, managers or for those likely to resist.

Weberian studies

Goldthorpe and Lockwood used their Weberian-influenced 'action approach' to point out the significance of the instrumental attitude to work. Their 'affluent workers' saw work as a means to an end, namely cash, rather than the seeking of intrinsic satisfaction or social rewards in the workplace.

The source of this instrumental attitude was not the boring work, but the privatised family life they experienced *outside* work.

Blackburn and Beynon echo this view. The workers' expectations, and the meaning they give to work, influence the degree of satisfaction they experience. Thus skilled day-shift men, with high expectations, were more alienated than part-time and night-shift women who did less skilled work but had a more instrumental attitude to their jobs.

THE EFFECTS OF NEW TECHNOLOGY ON THE WORKERS' EXPERIENCE OF WORK

The debate about the relationship between technology and job satisfaction has until recently been focused on the work of Blauner and critics. This means it is not only discussing the technology of the 1950s and early 1960s but also tends to be restricted to manufacturing rather than service industries and office work (or even home-working and housework). This is a problem with much of the traditional sociology of work.

What is new technology?

A convenient description would be to consider the use of information technology for:

Computer-Aided Manufacture (CAM) such as robots.
Computer-Aided Design (CAD), which can test buildings and cars before they are built.
Information processing in offices such as word-processors.

The effect on manufacturing industry

A. Phizacklea (1990) challenged Blauner's technological determinism. She suggested that the introduction of new technology in the fashion industry depended on factors other than its development and availability. These factors were:

1   The stage of the production process: the design and cutting stage is more likely than the manufacturing stage to use computers.
2   Markets: fashion requires short runs and quick responses to seasonal and other demands. Therefore it is less suitable for mass production.
3   Labour markets: the labour market is divided by class, race and gender. The supply of labour in different European countries influences the employment of new technology. In Britain successive waves of immigrants have been able to set up small businesses with very little capital (a sewing machine) and have employed other immigrants, particularly women, cheaply.

Has new technology in the office led to the alienation and proletarianisation of clerical workers?

Lockwood (1989) has updated his *The Blackcoated Worker* (1966), which tested the Marxist theory that white-collar workers had become proletarianised. (See Chapter 3 on *Social class*.) In 1966 he argued that the class situation, work situation and status of clerks were still superior to those of factory workers.

Lockwood has reconsidered Braverman's modern Marxist view that capitalists have extended their drive to control work and workers from the factory to the office. Braverman talks of the 'degradation' of office work as it becomes *fragmented* and *deskilled.* Again Lockwood refutes the Marxist hypothesis as either inaccurate or not proven. He points out that:

1   There are few, if any, machine-minding jobs in offices.
2   'Technology itself does not dictate the use that is made of it.' In general computers are underused.
3   The effects on the skills and autonomy of the worker depend on managerial strategy.
4   Lockwood predicts that the computerisation of large organisations which employ mostly white-collar workers – such as banks, insurance companies and the civil service – is more likely to lead to the *abolition* of jobs than to their degradation.

The pessimistic view
Gill (1985) predicts the polarisation of jobs, reduced promotion, isolation of workers, and increased monitoring and control of work and workers.

The optimistic view
Daniel (1987) looks forward to job enrichment, increased skills and responsibility, an increased range of tasks and higher pay as jobs are upgraded.

And women?
Phizacklea reminds us that women's skills are devalued because it is women who perform them. Therefore, what appears to be deskilling may be feminisation of the task, which remains as skilled as before.

Huws (1984) noted the alienation of female home-workers using computers. They complained of isolation and the pressure of being constantly reminded of housework. Phizacklea and Wolkowitz (1995) remind us that class and ethnicity influence women's experience of home-working and their pay.

Pringle (1983) argues that secretaries have retained skills and power despite feminisation and mechanisation. Status has declined as secretarial work became a woman's job. She sees the possibility of technology removing boring routine jobs like copytyping, but others note that it may remove jobs altogether.

INDUSTRIAL CONFLICT

In addition to the writers above, the following offer explanations of the extent and type of conflict based on working conditions.

Kerr and Seigel see integrated communities as more likely to sustain collective conflict, such as strikes, than fragmented groups. In 1985 the miners of Nottingham and Derbyshire did not, on the whole, support the strike. Unlike other miners they lived in mixed housing in terms of class and occupation.

Gouldner suggested that organisational change and managerial practice encouraged a strike in a gypsum mine among underground workers whose work was less suitable for bureaucratic control than that of surface workers.

Hyman emphasises the need for an 'action approach', while supporting the view that conflict is to be regarded as normal. This point is also made by Lane and Roberts in their study of the previously peaceful Pilkington glassworks, where specific demands were formulated by the workers *after* the strike began.

Dahrendorf agrees that strikes can be seen as normal and argues that the Marxist notion of inevitable revolution has been undermined by the institutionalisation of class conflict in the arena of industrial relations.

Taylor and Walton, in a study of industrial sabotage, borrow from interactionist studies of deviance to examine the reasons behind allegedly motiveless vandalism.

WORK, NON-WORK AND LEISURE

Parker reviewed existing studies which linked occupation with non-work activities. He then produced a theory, which suggested three kinds of patterns of work–leisure relationships. These were the opposition, complementary and extension patterns. His work represents a good starting point in answers involving subsequent criticism.

1 **The extension pattern**
Leisure activities were often similar to work. The function of leisure was to 'develop the personality'. This pattern was found where work was a central life interest and associated with workers who enjoyed their work, e.g. professionals, artists, musicians and athletes.

2 **The neutrality pattern**
Leisure activities were somewhat different to work. The family or leisure was the central life interest. Typically work was not satisfying. The function of leisure was relaxation. This pattern was associated with clerical workers and factory workers.

3 **The opposition pattern**
Leisure activities were definitely unlike work and the central life interest was outside work. Work was likely to be alienating. The function of leisure was escape and recovery from work. This pattern was associated with unskilled manual workers, particularly in 'extreme occupations' such as mining.

In addition to work, Parker saw education and the amount of time available as influencing leisure. He argued (1982) that the rigid separation of work from leisure caused by total rather than gradual retirement deprived the retired not only of money and social contacts but also of a sense of usefulness.

Criticism of Parker

Parker himself recognised that in some circumstances his definition of leisure as time free from working was more appropriate for men in full-time work than it was for those who do not do paid work. Parker saw the *unemployed* and *housewives* as special cases.

Age and family life cycle. Rapoport and Rapoport (1975)

In contrast to Parker, Rapoport and Rapoport identify family lifestyle as a more significant influence on leisure than work itself. They are interested in age, marital status and parenthood, and they also recognise the influence of other correlates such as class, gender and health. They identify a fixed sequence of four phases which shape leisure, beginning with adolescence and ending with retirement.

Roberts used the phrase 'domestic age' to describe a concept that combines chronological age with family relationships and responsibilities. He saw adolescence as an exceptional period in that the family is not the focus of leisure activities.

Deem (1986) replicated the Rapoport and Rapoport study. She distinguished four major periods affecting the lives of women in Milton Keynes. She saw sexual orientation and ethnicity influencing the extent to which boys were a major leisure interest for teenage girls.

Feminist criticism

1 Feminist sociologists see housework as real work usually performed by women (for men).

2 Women do not always have free time. They may enjoy leisure whilst performing an obligation, e.g. chatting at work or watching TV while ironing clothes.

3 Leisure activities are influenced by age, marriage and children. Because of childcare obligations mothers' leisure is frequently taken at home with the family. Single and childless women have more free time and are more likely to be in paid employment.

4 Women are limited in their freedom to go out. Husbands, fathers, and girls and women themselves have views on suitable and safe places to go. Bingo and church are seen as more suitable than pubs. Travelling unaccompanied may be seen as a problem. Daughters as well as mothers may spend more time at home. McRobbie wrote of a 'bedroom culture' of teenage girls based on friends and music.

5 Deem suggested that leisure might be a state of mind rather than specific activities, e.g. having a relaxed meal. Activities such as cooking and eating could be work, non-work obligation or leisure, depending on why they are done.

Marxists

Marxists argue with the view that leisure is *free* time because:

- It is usually paid for.
- It involves control.

Clarke and Critcher (1985) examined leisure both as a commodity and in cultural terms.

They claimed that 'Leisure is now central to capitalist economic and cultural domination.' Leisure, they argued, must be examined within the framework of contemporary capitalism; thus the influence of both the market and the state must be examined. They see leisure as a distinct set of activities demarcated from work by time and space, and as the product of the capitalist mode of production.

1   Leisure has become *products* which consumers are persuaded to buy – e.g. sport has moved from the park to the leisure centre and requires expensive kit. Consumers buy recorded music rather than playing instruments.
2   Leisure is a means of *social control.* The young unemployed are seen as a problem which can be solved by providing organised leisure activities to keep them off the streets and out of mischief. Many leisure activities are controlled by the state – e.g. where and when you can drink, dance or even walk.
3   Clarke and Critcher make the very important observation that the consumer has become the ideological justification of capitalism. Consumption is portrayed as freedom, and this can occur only within a capitalist society. Leisure 'demonstrates why capitalism works'.

Conclusion

Further problems of defining work and leisure arise in considering home-working, housework, household production such as growing vegetables and making clothes, professional sport and artistic careers.

K. Roberts claimed that leisure was growing; it was no longer just a residual part of life, and the use of leisure time depended on choice rather than class, status, work, or any other single element.

UNEMPLOYMENT

The problem of unemployment

Sociology syllabuses and textbooks rarely mentioned unemployment until the 1980s, probably because it was seen as a problem of the 1930s which had been cured by post-war government policy.

Because of dramatic increases in the level of unemployment since the late 1970s, it is once again seen as:

A social problem.
A sociological problem.

Social problems

1   Problems experienced by the unemployed and their families. These include poverty and a sense of worthlessness.
2   Problems the unemployed are seen as causing for others. These include:
    a) The cost of paying benefits to the unemployed, some of whom are seen as 'scroungers'.
    b) The threat of disorder, particularly from the young unemployed.

Sociological problems

Sociologists are interested in:

1   The lives of the unemployed.
2   Defining and measuring unemployment. Criticising unemployment statistics.
3   Examining the causes of unemployment.
4   Examining the social distribution of unemployment by class, ethnicity, gender, age and region.
5   The effects of unemployment on society.

The definition and measurement of unemployment

The Department of Employment defined the total unemployed as those 'unemployed and able and willing to do any suitable work' (1987).

The Government's decision in 1982 to use *claims for benefit* to measure the level of unemployment rather than registration as *seeking work* has reduced the overall level of apparent unemployment, and underestimates the numbers of certain sections of the population, particularly married women.

Unemployment is usually distinguished from *non-employment.* It suggests being available for work (i.e. both willing and able) and being unable to find employment.

Sociologists and politicians have debated the accuracy of the unemployment figures.

Underestimating unemployment

1 *Married women* are unlikely to be eligible for benefit. D. Sanders and J. Reed (1976) found that less than one-third of self-defined unemployed women were registered.
2 Those *under eighteen* are not normally eligible for benefit. They may be compelled into training schemes or be reluctant students.
3 Those *over sixty,* or *disabled* or *sick*, are encouraged to claim other forms of benefit even if they are still seeking work.
4 Those not 'actively seeking work' may be refused benefit. The Government decides what this actually means.
5 When jobs are scarce some of those without jobs may see themselves as *unemployable* rather than unemployed.

In a depressed labour market marginal workers such as the sick, people with disabilities, the old, the young, and those of low intelligence may decide not to seek work.

Overestimating unemployment

The Government, some newspapers and New Right sociologists have argued that even the new unemployment figures are an overestimate of the real number seeking work. They have mentioned:

1 Fraudulent claimants who work in the black economy.
2 The 'workshy'.
3 The high level of welfare benefit, which acts as a disincentive to find work. Claimants become 'welfare-dependent'.

Critics of this New Right view:

1 See a poverty trap caused by low wages and deductions from benefits rather than high benefits.
2 Pahl estimates that the black economy is more likely to recruit from the ranks of the employed than those who claim benefits, and in any case increased surveillance and threat of prosecution contain the number of 'scroungers'.

Causes of unemployment

1 **New technology** has reduced the number of manual workers in heavy industry or factory work. In the 1990s this has begun to happen in office work. For example, cashpoint machines have replaced many bank workers. (New technology can also reduce unemployment, as it makes goods cheaper so more people can buy them, and creates new products.)
2 **International competition** has reduced the market share of UK firms both domestically and in international markets. (The cure is to be more competitive at home and abroad.)
3 **Changes in the occupational structure** have led to a decline in employment in manufacturing and an increase in employment in service industries. The impact of this varies between different groups in the workforce and different parts of the country. (The cure would include training, retraining and education, so people could learn new skills.)
4 **Cyclical changes in demand** for goods and services both nationally and internationally lead to fluctuations in the total level of unemployment. (The cure was to use Government spending to influence demand. This was how Conservative and Labour governments controlled unemployment until the 1970s.)
5 **The money supply** influences inflation, and thus the competitiveness of industry, and thus unemployment. (The cure includes cuts in taxation and public spending and keeping wages low. This is seen as encouraging people to set up new businesses.)

The social distribution of unemployment

Those most likely to be unemployed are people in low-paying and insecure jobs, the very young and oldest in the labour force, people from ethnic minorities, people from among the disabled and the handicapped, and generally those with the least skills and living in the most depressed areas.

Sinfield wrote this in 1981, and it remains true. Note that his list does not consider gender, although in the same book Sinfield does point out that women are less likely to register as unemployed.

Be prepared to discuss the relationship between unemployment and *class, race, gender, age* and *disability*.

Unemployment can be seen as both a cause and an effect of socially structured inequality.

NB: Pahl argued that it is not appropriate to stereotype the unemployed and see them as a distinct population. People go in and out of unemployment.

The social effects of unemployment

In addition to considering the impact of unemployment on those without jobs we can examine some of the alleged effects on the wider society.

1 **Effects on workers**
   Workers feel less secure; this permits employers to exercise more control and is likely to reduce wage demands.
      Mobility between jobs is reduced as workers feel safer where they are.
      Weakens trades unions and disciplines workforce.
2 **Regional unemployment**
   Specific communities may be affected, e.g. coal-mining areas. The consequences of job losses tend to be cumulative as local businesses suffer from the reduced demand for goods and services.
      Unemployment is unevenly spread between regions. England has lower rates than the rest of the UK. The South-east had lower rates, but not in the 1990s.
      Within regions it is concentrated in the so-called 'inner-city' areas.
3 **Unemployment and social control**
   Unemployment is disproportionately experienced by particular age and ethnic groups, and concentrated in specific neighbourhoods. Attempts have been made to link unemployment with crime, riots and political protest.

Conclusion

The disadvantaged are the most likely to experience unemployment, and the most probable consequences of unemployment are the problems of poverty. 'What unemployment does before anything else is to make those who experience it poor' (Clarke and Critcher).

EXAMINATION QUESTIONS

1 Examine the view that distinctions between work and leisure have become increasingly blurred.

(AEB)

2 Evaluate the explanations sociologists have offered for different levels of strike activity and other forms of industrial conflict.

(AEB)

3 Assess the different ways in which sociologists have explained alienation in industrial societies.

(AEB)

4 Examine the view that industrial conflict is an inevitable feature of industrial society.

(AEB)

5

ITEM A   ESTIMATES AND PROJECTIONS OF THE CIVILIAN LABOUR FORCE: GB

16–19-year olds   A-level recruits

Fewer than 20 large employers currently account for the employment of over half of the estimated 27,000 leavers with A-level and Scottish Higher School Certificates looking for work. Employers' demands, if anything, are likely to increase over the next few years. However, the numbers at this level available for employment will fall to 22,000 by 1995.

ITEM B   GREAT BRITAIN – UNEMPLOYMENT (seasonally adjusted)

quarters

ITEM C   CHANGE IN EMPLOYMENT 1984–1987

	thousands
Agriculture, forestry and fishing	−35.7
Extraction of minerals/manufacture of metals and metal goods	−63.5
Engineering	−64.9
Distribution, hotels and repairs	+235.8
Transport, communications	+65.0
Banking, finance	+428.4

Source: Department of Employment Labour Force Surveys
Reproduced in Labour Market, Quarterly Report, July 1988.

a) Referring to ITEM A, suggest *two* reasons why the number of A-level leavers available for employment will fall by 1995.   (2)

b) How far do the official statistics of unemployment accurately reflect the number of people looking for work?   (6)
c) Using the statistics in ITEM C, describe the changing patterns in the occupational structure between 1984 and 1987.   (4)
d) Examine the implications of the statistics in ITEMS A and C for the employment prospects of 18–20-year-olds in the labour market.   (6)
e) Assess sociological contributions to our understanding of the effects of unemployment.
                                                                              (7)
                                                                   (*Total 25 marks*)
                                                                              (AEB)

ANSWERS TO EXAMINATION QUESTIONS

OUTLINE ANSWERS

Question 1

Although definitions such as those used by Parker attempt to distinguish work and leisure they do, in addition, introduce other categories of activity, such as non-work obligations.

You can explore these terms and examine in detail problem areas like sport and housework. The existence of enforced leisure through unemployment and the growth of the black economy can also be discussed.

Question 2

This question requires a different emphasis to Question 5, where a more general overview of conflict is permissible. Here, both the level and type of industrial conflict must be considered.

The answer can be constructed using the Marxist, technology and interactionist frameworks outlined above. You should refer to studies of strikes and other forms of conflict which attempt to explain variations in levels, such as community integration, technology, culture, etc.

Types of conflict could be discussed by distinguishing:

a)   Individual from collective forms.
b)   Overt from institutionalised conflict between employers and unions.

(If you have not prepared the appropriate studies of strikes, etc., it is still relevant to refer to the problems of measuring conflict and to examine the official statistics debate.)

Question 5

Marxists might argue that there is an inevitable conflict of interest between employer (capital) and employee (labour) in *capitalist* society.

Dahrendorf sees industrial relations as the institutionalisation of class conflict.

Writers such as Blauner see the problem lying in the technology employed in *industrial* rather than capitalist society.

Interactionist approaches deny the 'inevitability' of social phenomena. They study the meaning behind manifestations of conflict from the viewpoint of the parties involved.

The human relations approach, and other consensus perspectives, suggest that conflict is pathological and can be controlled.

TUTOR ANSWER

Question 5

a)   Referring to ITEM A, suggest *two* reasons why the number of A-level leavers available for employment will fall by 1995.

1   There will be a relatively small age cohort owing to a falling birth rate eighteen or so years before.
2   A larger proportion of the age group is likely to go into higher education.

b)   How far do the official statistics of unemployment accurately reflect the number of people looking for work?

The official unemployment figures are based on those who claim unemployment benefit. Thus those looking for work, but not eligible or willing or able to claim, are excluded from the figures. However, the figures will also include those who claim benefit, whether legitimately or fraudulently, who may not actually be looking for work.

The statistics can be criticised on the basis of their *reliability*, which is threatened by frequent changes in the basis for collection, and their *validity*, as they reflect current social definitions of 'unemployment' rather than any objective rate. In addition, the Government has been criticised by political opponents and professional statisticians for manipulating the criteria of unemployment to make the figures look lower.

Those who may be looking for work, but not eligible for benefit, include those under eighteen. Muncie estimated that 300,000 unemployed youth were hidden in the YOPS training programme. The largest group is married women, who soon cease to be eligible for benefit and may 'disappear' into the home.

This group raises the problem of defining unemployment. Less employable workers, such as married women, the old, the sick and disabled, the unskilled, ill-educated and illiterate, may regard themselves, and be seen, as unemployable rather than unemployed. The Marxist concept of a reserve army of labour reminds us that some groups are seen as available for work when required, but are not seen as entitled to work.

If the definitions and methods of collecting data were kept constant, even if the numbers were inaccurate, there would be a useful indicator of trends of unemployment.

c)   Using the statistics in ITEM C, describe the changing patterns in the occupational structure between 1984 and 1987.

The first two figures indicate a decline in primary (extractive) industry.
    The third figure indicates a decline in secondary (manufacturing) industry.
    The other three figures indicate increases in the tertiary (service) sector.
    The largest change is the increase in office jobs in banking and finance. This, as with the expansion of other service industries, is likely to provide more employment in traditionally feminine jobs.

d)   Examine the implications of the statistics in ITEMS A and C for the employment prospects of 18–20-year-olds in the labour market.

Item A indicates a fall in the supply of 18–20-year-old labour. It is also likely that the decline will be proportionately higher among the better educated, who are likely to proceed into higher education. Other things being equal, this will enhance the employment prospects of those who are available, particularly the more educated and better trained.

Item C illustrates probable changes in the demand for labour. Those living in rural or mining areas will have to travel, or hope that alternative employment in service industries, e.g. tourism and leisure or 'sunrise' industries, will expand.

Banking and finance remain concentrated in the South-east, particularly in London itself. Workers will have to commute and it is possible that demand will be for the more educated.

The other service industries recruit more semi-skilled labour, and this suggests that prospects will be good for levels of employment, if not for those seeking interesting careers with high pay.

The expansion of employment is biased towards the more traditionally feminine occupations. The way in which we view such jobs may change, as employers compete more for workers. Nursing has already anticipated a major shortfall in traditional recruits.

e)   Assess sociological contributions to our understanding of the effects of unemployment.

Unemployment is claimed to have detrimental effects on individuals and their families. Fagin and Little see the effects in terms of 'loss'. The losses include self-esteem, sense of purpose, routine, relationships and, of course, income. Unemployment correlates with several measures of ill health. It may be that ill health contributes to unemployment or that both sickness and unemployment are more common in the lower classes. Caution is necessary when interpreting figures. Lower income can adversely affect diet and housing conditions, affecting the unemployed and their families. Smoking, alcoholism and suicide are all more prevalent among the unemployed (see also Chapter 18, especially the answers to Question 3 and Question 4).

The effects on the wider society are also open to discussion. The Marxist concept of a reserve army of labour would suggest that certain sections of the workforce are more likely to be unemployed. However, despite high unemployment in the 1980s, more and not fewer married women joined the labour market. Unlike Germany, Britain could not 'export' unemployment by limiting the numbers of migrant workers.

The regional nature of unemployment in the UK has led to social and political divisions. The Labour Party has lost virtually all its seats in the South, except in inner London. The Conservative Party has lost virtually all its seats in Wales and Scotland.

Union membership and power have declined, although this may be due to legislation and to changes in the occupational structure, as well as to unemployment.

Racial tension in the early 1980s was associated with unemployment, but in the USA the worst violence occurred during periods of prosperity. Crime has also been seen as a result of unemployment, but the crime rates of the 1930s do not confirm this view. J. Young sees relative deprivation as a more important factor.

Finally, Pahl has argued that the unemployed have been stereotyped and are not, in fact, different from other sections of the working class. Working-class life has often been characterised by insecurity, unemployment and poverty. The unemployed are not a distinct group, as workers continually move in and out of employment. However, over a quarter of Britain's unemployed have been without work for over two years.

STUDENT'S ANSWER WITH EXAMINER COMMENTS

Question 3

Assess the different ways in which sociologists have explained alienation in industrial societies.

> **Successful description of alienation.**

Marx said that what singles out humans from other species is the capacity to control nature by creative activity. Work can be an expression of human intellect and creative capacity, and through work man can express his true essence. Alienation is the separation of man from his true essence and occurs when work is debased and made a burden. The alienated worker is seen as brutalised and greedy as he works for money.

> **Capitalism identified as cause; design and control point good.**

Marx felt that capitalism produced the most alienation. Workers are tied to machines performing meaningless tasks. Labour power becomes a commodity and human activity is bought at the cheapest price. The product of labour is owned and sold by the capitalist and the worker is exploited. Owners design and control the whole work process, so creativity and intellect are stifled and controlled by others. The worker has no control over what is made or how, when or at what price.

> **Modern Marxists do discuss deskilling and proletarianisation of office work.**

For Marx the only way to overcome these aspects of alienation is to abolish the economic relations which create it. However, it is not clear whether a communist society could sustain abundance through high productivity and still abolish alienation and allow men to realise their true selves.

Marxist theory concentrates on factory work rather than office work and so do other theories.

Weber, Taylor, Mayo and Blauner all feel that alienation is caused by conditions within the workplace. Unlike Marx, Weber feels that bureaucratic control is not exclusively a feature of capitalism, nor is it necessarily harmful, but it will persist because it is efficient.

> **Not directly linked to alienation or question.**

Taylor pioneered Scientific Management, which involved minute division of labour, the separation of the worker from the decision-maker and payment by results. Mayo indicated that informal social relations were more important to workers than economic rewards.

Weber, Taylor and Mayo all suggest ways in which work can be organised efficiently, i.e. profitably, and their ideas have been applied to the workplace. Alienation is seen as the unfortunate product of efficiency.

Blauner also disagrees with Marx's assumption that alienation is a product of capitalism. He feels that it is caused by production technology. Blauner measures alienation along four dimensions: powerlessness, meaninglessness, isolation and self-estrangement. He divides technology into four types. Craft, machine-minding and assembly-line work produce increasing amounts of alienation. However, the fourth, most modern type, process production, is less alienating and caused Blauner to be optimistic about the future.

> **Good brief summary.**

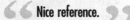

> Nice reference.

> Salaman should be linked to Marxist ideas. A quote about design and control has been used in a past question.

Blauner's description of alienation has been used by women to describe housework. Oakley interviewed 40 housewives who described their work in similar terms as assembly-line workers.

Salaman disagrees with the idea that alienation is caused by working conditions. He claims that the most important cause is the design and control of the work, which can be explained by the capitalist system. Work is organised by owners or managers to meet two interrelated needs. These are profit and control. Sometimes one is seen as more important than the other.

Braverman also stresses the control of the proletariat. It is easier to control the workers when they are under one roof. This, he claims, was the main reason the factory system replaced domestic production. Deskilling and fragmentation ensure that only the boss knows the whole process. This reduces the worker's bargaining power and cheapens labour. This may have either the effect of fragmenting solidarity or the opposite effect of increasing class consciousness.

In contrast to those sociologists who see alienation caused by capitalism or conditions in the workplace, interactionists feel that alienation is an individual response which depends on the attitude of the workers. Workers' experience of work depends on the meaning they attribute to work which is influenced by the workers' present and past experience both inside and out of work. Individuals respond differently to the same objective conditions.

Goldthorpe and Lockwood's Luton Studies found that workers had an instrumental attitude to work. They worked for money not job satisfaction. Therefore if financial rewards were high they were not dissatisfied. The source of the instrumental attitude was thought to be outside in the privatised family.

Blackburn and Beynon agree, finding that part-time women workers and night-shift men had low expectations of job satisfaction but worked for the pay. They were generally satisfied despite their boring jobs. However, day-shift skilled men, despite having more interesting jobs, were dissatisfied because of higher expectations.

> Good use of studies.

McKinnon conducted a similar study in Canada but concluded that instrumental attitudes were a response to boring work, not a reason for choosing high-paid but alienating work.

Overall comments

Overall, a sophisticated and critical account with a variety of relevant studies. An A grade answer.

Odd parts could be directly related to the question explicitly.

The candidate would be rewarded for considering alienation in other contexts apart from the context of work, e.g. religion or family.

A Review Sheet for this chapter may be found on p. 255.

ORGANISATIONS

CHAPTER 13

GETTING STARTED

Some students, or even teachers, find this a rather dry topic, perhaps because most of the literature on the subject is about work organisations. You might find this chapter more relevant if you try to relate what is often dated and remote material to your own experiences. You may not have direct experience of even part-time work, but you will have been a customer, client, patient, and certainly a student, of bureaucratic and other types of organisation.

The main themes of questions set on this topic are:

1 **A critical view of bureaucratic organisations.**
2 **The need to study informal as well as formal organisations.**
3 **A critical evaluation of management theories, particularly 'Scientific Management' and 'Human Relations' theories.**
4 **Can organisations be democratic?**

The most obvious related topics are work and the study of professions, professional associations and trades unions.

Definitions

- *Organisations* are groups with a structure and values, set up to achieve specific goals.

- *Informal organisation* describes the social order which emerges from a work group, rather than being imposed from above.

- *Formal organisation* describes the planned allocation of authority and tasks.

- *Bureaucracy* is a form of organisation based on rational principles. It is hierarchical, impersonal and governed by rules.

- *Effectiveness* refers to success in achieving goals.

- *Efficiency* refers to minimising costs.

BUREAUCRACY

FORMAL AND INFORMAL ORGANISATION

MANAGEMENT THEORIES

CAN ORGANISATIONS BE DEMOCRATIC?

THEORETICAL AND EMPIRICAL STUDIES

ESSENTIAL PRINCIPLES

Weber saw *rational-legal* or *bureaucratic authority* as increasingly typical for government and business organisations in modern industrial societies. His ideal type of bureaucratic organisation is easier to remember and analyse if we use Littler's scheme, which divides the characteristics into two categories.

1   Bureaucratisation of the structure of control. This includes the division of labour and the hierarchical control over jobs rather than individuals. This is sought by leaders in order to maintain control.
2   Bureaucratisation of the employment relationship. This describes the career of individuals, where appointment, salary and promotion are based on rational and not personal criteria. This is often sought by workers to provide security.

The case for bureaucracy

“ Is bureaucracy bad? ”

It is suited to the efficient management of large-scale organisations in predictable conditions. Its technical superiority can be likened to mechanisation in factories. Action is 'rational' (i.e. individuals can calculate the best means to achieve ends) rather than effective or traditional.

The case against bureaucracy

Weber himself recognised certain limitations: inefficiency in times of crisis; 'specialists without spirit' and efficient organisations with evil purposes. Either now, or at the end of the chapter, try and illustrate these points, both from the studies and from your own knowledge and experience.

Later critics develop these and other points. The main themes are:

1   Ineffectiveness and inefficiency in achieving goals.
2   Adverse effects on staff in terms of job satisfaction.
3   Adverse effects on inmates, patients and clients.

FORMAL AND INFORMAL ORGANISATION

You need to:

1   Define organisation.
2   Distinguish formal from informal organisation.
3   Explain why informal organisation develops, despite being unplanned.
4   Offer both Marxist and interactionist perspectives on informal organisation.

Remember that formal organisation can usually be equated with bureaucracy as it involves the planned and rational allocation of tasks and authority. Informal organisation describes actual, rather than ideal (i.e. desired by management), behaviour. Authority and control exist in informal organisations but are often 'traditional' rather than rational. Mayo suggests that norms emerge because of the structure of the work group, whereas interactionists see order as negotiated.

MANAGEMENT THEORIES

These can be arranged into the various schools which have criticised the work of F. Taylor.
Taylor's basic assumptions were:

1   Workers want high wages.
2   Bosses want low production costs (i.e. efficiency).
3   Scientific Management could satisfy both bosses and workers.

Taylor's critics include:

■   Mayo and the Human Relations school, who deny Taylor's view of cash-motivated individuals. They accept his aim of efficiency for profit but suggest a variety of more participative and democratic management methods.
■   Marxist critics who challenge the possibility of consensual aims between employer and worker. More specifically, they are concerned with the alienating effects of the fragmentation of tasks and the deskilling of workers.
■   Action theorists who deny the view shared by these essentially structuralist writers: namely, that the organisation can be seen as a social system which exists independ-

ently of the members and which can determine their attitudes and behaviour. Instead, organisational order is seen here as being negotiated by individuals.

CAN ORGANISATIONS BE DEMOCRATIC?

Consideration of the issues raised by this question should go beyond a discussion of Michels' work. The meaning of 'democracy' in this context could be outlined. Generally it implies the sharing of power and the participation in decision-making.

We can look at democracy inside the organisation and examine the extent of participation rather than imperative control. We can also look at the effects which the organisation has on outsiders, such as clients, patients and the wider society.

Whereas Michels and, in a different way, Marxists see organisational democracy as impossible, other writers suggest the possibility of democracy, either for some kinds of organisations rather than others or for some individuals in the organisation rather than others.

THEORETICAL AND EMPIRICAL STUDIES

BUREAUCRACY

Burns and Stalker, Gouldner and Crozier all suggest that bureaucracy is inefficient in unstable and unpredictable circumstances, such as scientific research, mining and factory maintenance.

Blau showed how rule-breaking in a bureaucratic organisation enhanced efficiency in the work of employment agencies. Roy made a similar case for rule-breaking in a factory, where workers saved unnecessary journeys by taking more tools from a storeroom than were allowed.

Selznick argued that bureaucratic organisations develop their own internal needs, such as survival and expansion, which can conflict with their stated goals. The effects of this are described in Michels' work.

Merton's criticism takes the form of identifying the *dysfunctions* of bureaucracy. As above, he sees it as inappropriate for conditions of change or flexibility. In addition, he sees the possibility of 'ritualism' developing, where workers become obsessed with means (rules and red tape) rather than ends. All the above critics have taken the organisation's goals for granted and concerned themselves with the issue of 'efficiency'.

Marxists see bureaucracy as an organisational form which is part of the superstructure of capitalism and has inevitably adverse and alienating effects on both individuals and the wider society. Neo-Marxists, such as Burnham and Djilas, see the top managers and administrators who control, rather than own, the means of production as forming new ruling classes in the USA and communist Eastern Europe, respectively.

Silverman and other interactionist critics reject the bureaucratic approach, not on the grounds of its inefficiency nor on those of its alienating effects, but because it fails to explain the workings of organisations. It is individual actors, not organisations, who have needs and goals. Social order is imposed not by impersonal organisation rules nor through ruling-class hegemony but *negotiated*, as individuals attribute meaning to the behaviour of themselves and others. Goffman shows the very 'real' effects of this interaction process on inmates of Total Institutions, such as psychiatric hospitals.

FORMAL AND INFORMAL ORGANISATION

Weber's model of bureaucracy can be used as the dominant example of a type of formal organisation.

Blau explains how informal organisation develops in order to achieve organisational aims.

Ditton's 'Fiddling bread salesmen' and the illegal price-fixers described by Geis show how organisations tolerate and even reward law-breakers who serve their own and organisational interests. (You might consider the 'insider trading' scandals of 1988 in this light.)

Etzioni summarises interactionist criticism of the approaches above which overemphasise the possibility of harmony and fail to consider non-business organisations. These interactionist approaches (see Silverman above) are more concerned with the processes by which order is negotiated rather than imposed by either exploitative or enlightened managers.

MANAGEMENT THEORIES

Taylor's work was completed before the First World War but remains influential, despite its early apparent discrediting by the Human Relations school. Marxists argue that its principles remain the basis for the organisation and control of work in capitalist society, and subsequent management theorists see his work as a benchmark to be rejected or amended.

The main principles are:

1   Scientific work-study can find the best ways for engaging in the work activity.
2   'Suitable' workers should be selected and trained to work scientifically, motivated by cash incentives.
3   Management should be separated from workers and should also be governed by scientific principles.
4   Piece-rates can be scientifically calculated and should not be reduced if workers earn a lot; they should share in the firm's prosperity.

Mayo: the studies at the Hawthorne Works led him into laying the foundations of the 'Human Relations' school of management, which perhaps even now dominates academic writing and the ideology of management in the workplace. The studies emphasise the importance of informal work groups in setting norms of production and the significance of social as well as economic rewards. Managers are advised to seek consensual solutions to problems and to develop structures and skills which enhance the communication between workers and managers.

Burns and Stalker argued that there is *no* ideal management system and instead suggest a 'contingency approach', where technology, markets, human skills and motivation are all considered. They distinguish *mechanistic organisation* (similar to Weber's bureaucracy) from *organismic organisation*, which is more flexible, less hierarchical and more suited to conditions of change. Their main example is in the field of electronics, where firms require continual research and development.

EXAMINATION QUESTIONS

1   Assess the proposition that all organisations are inevitably oligarchic.

(ULEAC)

2   'Scientific Management and Human Relations are different approaches to the study of organisations but they share the same aim of controlling the workforce.' Discuss.

(AEB)

3   'Informal social processes reduce the efficiency of organisations.' Examine this view.

(AEB)

4   Examine the view that Bureaucracy is always an efficient form of organisation.

(AEB)

5   'Organic systems of organisation may be effective in innovative high-technology firms; they are unlikely to be effective in large-scale manufacturing industry.' Discuss.

(UODLE)

6   Explain and evaluate the different approaches of functionalists and interactionists to the study of organisations.

(AEB)

ANSWERS TO EXAMINATION QUESTIONS

OUTLINE ANSWERS

Question 1

This question occurs in the politics section of the paper. It requires reference to wider political issues and not just a narrow critique of bureaucracy, although this is relevant.

The essence of the answer should be an evaluation of the theoretical and empirical arguments for and against Michels' 'iron law of oligarchy'.

i) Explain and illustrate Michels' proposition. He can be seen as an elite theorist critical of Marxist views on the liberating effects of a revolution.
ii) Subsequent studies which support Michels can be cited, e.g. Selznick on the TVA. Include criticism of the governments of socialist countries, but perhaps mention the democratisation of Eastern Europe in 1989.
iii) Subsequent studies which criticise him can be cited. Include Gouldner's theoretical criticism, where he points out the need for leaders to get the consent of workers or subjects and sees oligarchy not as inevitable, but as in competition with democracy. Collective bargaining in British industrial relations is an example. Other studies can be used, such as Lipset *et al*, who see the possibility of democracy in unions but are generally pessimistic. Marxists see the cause of oligarchy in class relationships, not in the organisation itself. Etzioni sees some organisations as democratic.

Question 3

There is the opportunity here to use material on bureaucracy in answering questions on information organisation.

i)   Define and distinguish formal and informal organisation.
ii) Define effectiveness and efficiency.
iii) Ask 'efficient for whom?' and discuss at this point, or later, the Marxist analysis of organisations and their emphasis on control (Braverman, etc.)
iv) Consider Weber's view that rationally planned organisation (usually bureaucratic) is the most efficient.
v)   A variety of studies from different perspectives can be cited which support the proposition in the question. Taylor and Walton's interactionist study on industrial sabotage, Beynon on resisting management control of the pace of work, and studies of working to rule (easily linked to criticism of bureaucracy). Ditton, Mars and others who have studied theft in the workplace note how theft from customers may be permitted, encouraged or even institutionalised into work roles. However, this threatens the employer when the techniques are applied to theft from the organisation.
vi) The other side of the argument can be examined, i.e. that informal social processes could enhance organisational efficiency. This is found in studies by Blau, Mayo, Etzioni and Roy. Separate studies of receptionists and nurses in a dressings clinic show how people develop unofficial, but sometimes approved of, discretionary powers in order to make their jobs more interesting and more efficient.

Question 5

This is a more *specific* variant of those questions on organisations which are concerned with the effectiveness and efficiency of bureaucracy, formal organisation and particular methods of management.

i)   Outline Burns and Stalker's work. Their mechanistic type of organisation can be equated with Weber's bureaucracy to provide greater opportunity for criticism.
ii) The effectiveness of mechanistic forms in mass production is supported by Weber and Taylor and also by those critics of bureaucracy who see it as unsuitable in unpredictable circumstances but efficient in large-scale manufacturing.
iii) The need for less bureaucratic types of organisation has been argued by Handy, who sees more organic forms as suitable for the development of new technologies. Drug manufacturers mass-produce but are also dependent on continual research and development. The place of scientists in such organisations varies, from a leadership role to being outsiders working on research contracts.
iv) The development of the atomic bomb pioneered the bureaucratisation of scientific research, which Burns and Stalker later argued was inappropriate.

Question 6

Look before you leap! Candidates often try to reinterpret questions on organisations as critical discussions of Weber on bureaucracy. That is *not* likely to be a successful strategy here.

Functionalist theories examine organisations as systems of interrelated parts. They see the most important issues as the effectiveness, efficiency and even survival of the organisation. Thus Weber's ideal type, which he sees as the most efficient form of organisation, can be criticised by other functionalist writers such as Merton, Blau and Selznick.

Interactionist theories are concerned with the negotiation of order and how individuals attach meanings to behaviour. Weber's interest in different forms of social action is thus a relevant influence on later writers such as Silverman. Well-known studies such as Goffman's *Asylums* can be explained here.

Marxist analysis offers a critical view of both approaches, although arguably it shares the structuralist approach of the functionalists. Nevertheless, the aims of the organisation are seen from a critical viewpoint.

TUTOR ANSWER

Question 4

Examine the view that Bureaucracy is always an efficient form of organisation.

For the purposes of this essay, a bureaucratic organisation will be defined as one which conforms more or less to Weber's ideal type. Efficiency will be looked at from the managerial viewpoint of achieving goals at minimum cost. This can be distinguished from effectiveness, which is measured by the extent to which goals are achieved.

Weber saw bureaucracy as proliferating in modern industrial societies because of its 'technical superiority' in maintaining social order and in achieving goals. Bureaucracy is based on rational rather than effective or traditional social action. The rational actor calculates the best means to achieve deliberately chosen goals. Bureaucracy then avoids arbitrariness, both in the treatment of staff and clients (or patients, inmates or subjects, depending on whom the organisation serves). This ensures that the most suitable staff are appointed and promoted. Control is ensured by making behaviour conform to rules, and thus be predictable. The results of actions can be calculated in advance. This permits continuity for the organisation, since individuals become dispensable as the rules apply to their *positions* and not to them personally. Such information is kept in files, and not by individuals. Weber saw bureaucracy as ensuring efficiency by reducing both personal and material costs, because of the strict subordination of staff to rational rules.

Gouldner is better known for his criticisms of bureaucracy, but he does identify four positive functions which enhance organisational efficiency. First, the 'explication function' where desired behaviour is made explicit by managers to subordinates. Second, the 'screening function' where the manager is protected from resentment by the impersonality of the rules. This reliance on bureaucratic authority also helps solve the problem of replacing the sometimes charismatic founder of business and other organisations. Third, the 'remote-control function' where individual managers need not be present to supervise work as the rules substitute for close observation and control. Gouldner cites the example of the forest ranger who follows state rules and procedures whilst working in isolation. Finally, there is the 'legitimate punishment function' where rules allow punishment for rule-breaking without provoking unmanageable personal tensions.

So far it has been argued that bureaucracy can be efficient, at least in some circumstances. However, Weber himself recognised certain problems. He saw it as 'inefficient in times of crisis' as well as having adverse effects on staff, or being used to achieve evil aims, albeit efficiently. This last point acknowledges the Marxist view that the bureaucratic state is used as an instrument of class domination. (See *Power and politics*, Chapter 7.)

The theme of inefficiency in the face of crisis, or even of unpredictability, is common to a number of critics. Crozier, in a study of a tobacco factory, noted that the mass production of a standardised product was ideally suited to bureaucratisation. However, the unpredictable nature of *machine failure* meant that the work of *maintenance staff* could not operate under a bureaucratic system. Some organisations have adopted planned maintenance schemes, where routines are followed whether or not such work is actually necessary. Critics see this as a ritualistic attempt to ensure that workers at least look as though they are working.

Gouldner, in the study of attempts to bureaucratise a gypsum mine, documented the conflicts which arose when a new manager was appointed. The new manager had to contend not only with the unpredictable nature of mining, but also with resistance from a workforce which had integrated into the local community to such an extent that supervisors were not prepared to enforce rules against theft against their neighbours, friends and relatives.

Burns and Stalker use different terminology but again emphasise the unsuitability of bureaucracy (or mechanistic organisation) for work where initiative, creativity and flexibility are required. They argue that organismic organisation is more appropriate for successful research and development in the electronics industry. The difficulties faced by scientists and other professionals working under bureaucratic control have been described by Cotgrove, Merton and (in a more Marxist context) Mills, who sees alienation resulting. Professionals working in bureaucratic organisations may fail to serve the needs of clients.

Blau showed how the actual breaking of bureaucratic rules could enhance organisational efficiency and increase the job knowledge of federal employment inspectors. This suggests either that the particular rules were unsuitable, or that bureaucratic rules cannot be produced for some situations.

If we regard the term 'efficiency' as problematic, we can ask: efficient for whom? Goffman's study of a psychiatric hospital does not take the existence of bureaucracy for granted, but does see social order emerging from the negotiation of reality by the 'actors' involved in the situation. However, he also sees those with most power, namely the staff, imposing rules on the patients. The effects of imposing these rules is the opposite of the purpose of the organisation, which is therapeutic.

Marxist and other conflict critiques of bureaucracy see efficiency as always being judged from the point of view of the employers or the state. The organisations will then have alienating effects on staff, clients and subjects.

Efficiency does not always imply effectiveness. The NHS uses short waiting lists and short stays in hospital as indicators of efficiency. This disregards the fact that patients drop off lists if they cannot attend the hospital on the nominated day, even if they are never treated. Early discharge from hospital may inhibit recovery or even encourage return for further treatment. Similar observations can be made about prisons, where harsh (and cheap) regimes may encourage reoffending.

Michels saw the tendency towards oligarchy, even in organisations with democratic aims, as inhibiting effectiveness and efficiency. Similarly, Selznick saw organisations developing their own survival and expansion needs to the detriment of efficiency.

STUDENT'S ANSWER WITH EXAMINER COMMENTS

Question 2

'Scientific Management and Human Relations are different approaches to the study of organisations but they share the same aim of controlling the workforce.' Discuss.

> Clever links with Marx and Weber.

Scientific Management was an idea developed by F. Taylor in 1912. Its principles reflect Weber's contemporary writing on bureaucracy. Weber's theory is based less on technology and more on methods of organisation and control. Weber rejects the Marxist view that bureaucracy is a form of capitalist control which has ill effects on workers.

Taylor, like Weber, suggested that the optimum efficiency of the workers would be achieved only by treating them as an extension of machines or organisations and as isolated individuals. This was opposed to treating them as a united workforce with thoughts and minds of their own. Taylor advised standardisation and specialisation of tasks and removal of all intellectual work from workers. Decision-making and control should be placed in the hands of managers. He thus pioneered the ideas which were later taken up by Ford such as deskilling, fragmentation of work and mass production on an assembly line.

> Brief but thorough account of Taylor.

Taylor also advocated payment by results. He decided that the workers were motivated solely by money and would produce more goods more efficiently if paid piece-rates.

In direct conflict with Taylor's theory Mayo produced the Human Relations theory. He carried out a series of studies at the Hawthorne works of Western Electric in Chicago. He wanted to test Taylor's theory that there was an optimum illumination level to maximise productivity. He discredited Taylor's theory by discovering that illumination itself had no effect but the fact that the workers knew they were being studied did. When they were aware of being observed productivity increased. Mayo then argued that social factors affected workers' performance.

Mayo carried out follow-up studies in the 'bank wiring room'. He studied fourteen workers for six months. They were paid by a productivity bonus scheme. He discovered that despite being paid by results there was a unity among the workers not to individually maximise their production for extra bonuses but instead the group established its norms of production. There was group disapproval against those who produced either more or less than the norm. The Human Relations theory also argues that people need security, companionship and identity. They need to feel that they can communicate with the management. These people have to work with one another, on a collective basis, otherwise the worker will experience alienation and this will lead to a fall in productivity.

66 **Brief but adequate account of Mayo.** 99

Braverman and Bowles and Gintis suggested that although the Human Relations theory was preferable to Scientific Management they both shared the common aim of controlling the proletariat. They said management serves two main purposes, these are efficiency and profitability and secondly to control the workers, thus inhibiting the development of workers' autonomy. Braverman says that the decline of domestic production was not due to new machinery but because the bourgeoisie had a vested interest in keeping the proletariat controlled in one area, that is, the factory. He also suggests that the fragmentation of tasks and the deskilling of workers makes them easy to replace and reduces their bargaining power as the manager knows the whole process and the workers do not.

66 **Good critical use of writers; should identify as Marxist.** 99

Salaman agrees with Braverman that Taylorism is a form of organisational control but he also believes that Human Relations is a way of concealing exploitation. The sympathetic treatment of workers keeps them falsely conscious. Salaman explains the design of work in Marxist terms, arguing that bureaucracy is not, as Weber claimed, inevitable but a product of capitalism, not industrial society. Both management theories control workers but in different ways using different forms of rewards.

66 **Accurate and relevant. It is he, not Braverman, who criticises human relations.** 99

Modern Marxists claim that Taylorism is still used today despite the view that Mayo discredited it in the 1930s. The evidence is found at the lower end of the job market where workers are deskilled and are extensions of the production line. Mayo's theory is used more with higher-level and managerial workers where the need for social rewards is greater.

66 **Apt comment.** 99

We can conclude that both theories are indeed just ways of controlling the workforce and means of exploitation, but Human Relations is less insensitive and thus preferable.

66 **Forceful, if arguable, conclusion.** 99

Overall comments

Overall, this is a succinct and well-argued account. It shows the differences between Scientific Management and Human Relations and successfully identifies the Marxist criticism of these in the question.

Worth a Grade B. Could be improved by clarifying the Human Relations section and by linking the Braverman study more explicitly to Taylor.

A Review Sheet for this chapter may be found on p. 255.

PROFESSIONS

GETTING STARTED

Questions on the professions are set regularly. They frequently require you to challenge the view that they are distinctive occupations with a particular commitment to public service.

Criticism has tended to come from conflict theorists, but it is interesting to note the more recent attacks from the 1987 Conservative Government. The Government's commitment to market forces, competition and efficiency has encouraged challenges to the restrictive practices of lawyers, to the professional autonomy of doctors and to the job security of university lecturers.

The main themes of questions set on this topic are:

1 **A critical evaluation of the role of professions in society.**
2 **A comparison of professional associations and trades unions.**
3 **The problems experienced by professionals working in bureaucratic organisations.**

Related topics include:

■ *Stratification.* Some critics examine professions in class terms.

■ *Work.* We could examine attitudes to work and the relationship between work and non-work.

■ *Organisations.* Professionals are increasingly salaried employees rather than fee earners.

■ *Health, education, welfare, science* and even sociology itself all provide employment for professionals.

Definition of the key term 'profession' is problematic and is indeed part of the answer to the most popular questions (see pp. 141–4 below). The professions can either be seen favourably as special occupations, or more critically as a class or classes.

THE ROLE OF PROFESSIONS IN SOCIETY

PROFESSIONAL ASSOCIATIONS AND TRADES UNIONS

PROFESSIONALS IN ORGANISATIONS

THEORETICAL AND EMPIRICAL STUDIES

THE ROLE OF PROFESSIONS IN SOCIETY

ESSENTIAL PRINCIPLES

We can summarise the various approaches as follows:

- **Consensus perspectives:**
  - Trait approach.
  - Functionalist accounts.
- **Conflict perspectives:**
  - Marxist accounts.
  - Weberian accounts.
  - Illich.
  - Feminist accounts.

This provides a useful framework for some answers.

CONSENSUS PERSPECTIVES

These offer an approving view of the professions, demonstrating the special contribution they make towards satisfying the needs of individuals and the functional needs of the social system.

The trait approach

This defines professions in terms of their possession of distinctive traits or characteristics which make up an ideal type. This allows us to distinguish real professions, such as medicine or law, from semi-professions, such as teaching and nursing.

A typical list of traits is:

a) Altruism. A commitment to serving the client and society.
b) A specialist body of knowledge acquired during a long period of education and training.
c) Control over training, qualification, recruitment and expulsion.
d) A code of ethics.
e) Fee earning.

These five characteristics all enhance both individual and occupational autonomy.

   (**NB:** You might use this list of traits to structure an essay. You could examine each one from both consensus and conflict viewpoints.)

Functionalist accounts

These see the professions as playing a unique role in meeting the needs of the social system. The professional's work deals with important values, where the client lacks expertise and thus has to rely on the professional's integrity and skill. Professional norms, such as those found in codes of ethics, protect the client from exploitation and ensure that the public interest is served. The high status and rewards enjoyed by the professions are explained by their functional importance (see the functional theory of stratification: Davis and Moore, Chapter 3 on *Social class*).

CONFLICT PERSPECTIVES

Marxist accounts

These see professionals as serving the interests of the ruling class. They tend to consider not just the traditional professions but also managers and bureaucrats. Professional knowledge is seen as part of the superstructure of capitalist society, e.g. the law or definitions of health.

Weberian accounts

These emphasise the ways in which the traits of professions can be used as strategies to maintain or improve their market situation. The key Weberian concept employed is *social closure*; this means restricting access to both the rewards and the opportunities for achieving them in order to maximise those rewards.

   Although the state may help to secure a monopoly for a profession, the relationship is not a simple one. Some professions (or even levels of a particular profession) are more supported by, and in turn support, the state than others.

Illich

The distinctive contribution of Ivan Illich has been to examine in detail the *harm* done by professions to individual clients and to the wider society (see Illich on *Health*, Chapter 18).

Although he shares some common ground with other conflict approaches, he does not attack capitalist or patriarchal society in general, but rather the professions themselves.

Feminist accounts

Feminist critiques of the professions are concerned with two main issues. First, the exclusion of women from high-status and highly rewarded professions, or at least the higher ranks within the occupations. Second, the harm inflicted on women as clients, for example the medicalisation of pregnancy. (See also Chapters 5 and 18.)

PROFESSIONAL ASSOCIATIONS AND TRADES UNIONS

Generally, consensus theorists see the two types of organisation as quite distinct, and are uncritical of the role of professional associations. On the other hand, conflict theorists see them as essentially similar, but explain the 'apparent' differences as attempts to legitimise the privileged position of the professions.

Questions which require comparisons are best constructed by choosing a *particular* characteristic and then considering it from the viewpoint of the two institutions (or in other cases, the theories, approaches or methods) to be compared. This works much better than just describing the two institutions in separate parts of an answer.

You could compare their:

- objectives
- methods
- memberships
- values and ideologies

(See also the Tutor Answer to Question 1, below.)

PROFESSIONALS IN ORGANISATIONS

The major issue is the effects which follow from professionals losing their traditional autonomy by becoming salaried employees of organisations rather than fee earners.

There are a variety of possible relationships between the professional and the organisation (see Hall below).

These may produce a number of problems:

1   The more bureaucratic, and thus less professional, the employing organisation, the more likely is the possibility of *role conflict*. Involvement in work becomes less moral (i.e. based on shared values) and more calculative (i.e. instrumental) or even alienated.
2   The organisation's *efficiency* and *effectiveness* can be adversely affected if decision-makers are less knowledgeable than the professionals they control. Judgements of competence are now made by managers, and not by peers. Weber failed to anticipate the split between bureaucratic authority and the professional authority which is based on expert knowledge, not rank, and is not confined to the needs of the organisations.
3   The professional–client relationship may be undermined. Potential *solutions* to these and other problems lie in:

   i)   Separating professional tasks and personnel from bureaucratic tasks and officials.
   ii) Professionals themselves adapting to bureaucratic needs.
   iii) Changing the organisational structure, so that professionals are granted more autonomy.

THEORETICAL AND EMPIRICAL STUDIES

THE ROLE OF PROFESSIONS IN SOCIETY

Durkheim sees professions as a stabilising force, integrating industrial society where social solidarity is threatened by the division of labour. He emphasises their commitment to community, and not to class or selfish values.

Barber, writing in the post-war USA, repeats this point about the altruism of professionals, describing them as dedicated to community interests.

Parsons illustrates the above, describing how scientists employ their knowledge rationally to solve community problems. He also identifies the functional role of the doctor, who authenticates the sickness, thereby allowing the patient temporarily to abandon work and other responsibilities (see Chapter 18).

Davis and Moore explain the high rewards enjoyed by professionals in terms of their functional importance and the need to attract and motivate the most able recruits.

The following *conflict theorists* tend to see the professions in class terms, rather than just as an occupational category.

T. Johnson points out that different professions and, just as important, the different ranks within a profession enjoy various levels of occupational control and reward. This inequality is a result of the changing class structure of capitalist society.

Althusser shares the Marxist view, and emphasises the importance of professions in transmitting ruling-class ideology and their role in both ISAs and RSAs (see also Chapter 11).

Navarro explains state intervention in medicine by pointing out the need for a healthy (i.e. fit for work) workforce to serve employers.

Mills anticipates the proletarianisation of professionals, together with other white-collar workers (see also Chapter 3).

Friedson sees the importance of state intervention in professional activity from a Weberian rather than a Marxist perspective. Professional autonomy is dependent on restricting knowledge, and the state can protect or undermine professional monopoly.

Parry and Parry show how professionals try to maximise rewards by restricting competition. Professionalism is an occupational strategy which can be understood only in relation to the class structure.

Illich specifically identifies the harm inflicted by doctors and other health professionals on individual patients and society. He describes *iatrogenic* illness, which is caused by medical intervention.

PROFESSIONAL ASSOCIATIONS AND TRADES UNIONS

Parker offers a clear comparison between the two types of organisation.

T. Johnson shows how different sociological perspectives could be applied to the comparison, particularly how conflict perspectives blur the distinction.

J. Jackson describes the process and the effects of the professionalisation of both occupations and society.

PROFESSIONALS AND ORGANISATIONS

Hall proposes four types of relationship between professionals and organisations:

1   Private practice (e.g. traditional partnerships).
2   Professional-led organisations (decisions made by experts, e.g. US hospitals).
3   Heteronomous organisations (organisations of professionals under external control, e.g. English hospitals and schools).
4   Professional departments within bureaucratic organisations (the professional is in a subordinate position serving the needs of the organisation; e.g. lawyers employed by commercial companies).

Merton identifies role conflict for scientists employed in large organisations.

Cotgrove sees scientists in industry as abandoning professional values and serving organisational goals by becoming instrumental rather than private professionals.

Mills sees lawyers as serving the interests of corporations, not the public, and the increased bureaucratisation of professions.

Burns and Stalker suggest that *organismic* rather than *mechanical* organisation is better suited to solving scientific problems (see also Chapter 13).

EXAMINATION QUESTIONS

1   Examine the similarities and differences between Trades Unions and Professional Associations. Illustrate your answer with examples.

(AEB)

2   Compare and contrast consensus and conflict approaches to the study of 'professions'.

(AEB)

3   Assess sociological explanations of the high income and status associated with professional occupations.

(AEB)

4   Describe and explain the differences between 'professions' and 'semi-professions'.

(AEB UODLE)

5   Examine the relationship of professions to bureaucratic organisations.

(Author's question but the wording comes from the new AEB syllabus)

ANSWERS TO EXAMINATION QUESTIONS

OUTLINE ANSWERS

Question 3

Critical analysis, not just description, of the competing explanations is required for a good answer. Do not just outline different approaches to the professions, but focus on 'high income and status'.

Reference to more general explanations of inequality by the various approaches will add theoretical depth to the specific studies of professions.

- Trait approaches see professions as distinctive and superior occupations. You should critically evaluate the distinctive features, asking whose interests are served in each case. Also regard the term 'professional' as problematic.

- Functionalist approaches share the approving view of professions but explain their high status and rewards as a necessary mechanism for ensuring effective role allocation and performance to functionally important positions. Select relevant criticism of Parsons and Davis and Moore to challenge this view.

- Conflict theories tend to derive from Marxist or Weberian explanations of inequality. The former emphasise the ideological role of professions and the latter the occupational strategies that restrict competition.

Remember that positive, as well as the more obvious negative, criticism scores marks.

Question 4

Some detailed description of the characteristics of professions as perceived by the various approaches is obviously required. However, as in all answers, credit is given not just for remembering descriptive material but more importantly for the ability to analyse and evaluate arguments.

We can, as above, use consensus and conflict approaches as the framework for the answer.

Trait theories distinguish degrees of professionalism, on the basis of the possession of a list of distinctive traits. Traditional professions have most of these traits, whereas semi-professions have fewer. Give illustrations and perhaps explain development in terms of the historical role of the state. Functionalism explains the professionalisation of society and occupations and sees full professions as performing the most valued tasks, and employing the rarest skills.

Marxist theory sees the relative status and rewards of different occupations (and ranks within an occupation) as reflecting the needs of a developing capitalist class structure.

Weberian theories see the distinction between real and semi-professions as no more than their respective ability to control competition through closure strategies.

In conclusion, it is worth pointing out that any distinction between professions and semi-professions should not be seen as fixed. All the above theories see the possibility of threats to traditional professions, e.g. bureaucratisation and the increased professionalisation of other occupations.

Question 5

The instruction to 'examine' requires a detailed and critical analysis of the various relationships which can exist between the professions and bureaucratic organisations.

You could use Hall's four types of relationship to organise an answer, and in each one consider the problems that are likely to occur. Alternatively you could write separate sections on problems for the professional, the organisation and the client. Hall's types could then be offered as potential solutions to conflict.

A good answer is likely to put the process of bureaucratisation in a theoretical context, referring to Marx, Weber and Durkheim.

TUTOR ANSWER

Question 1

Examine the similarities and differences between Trades Unions and Professional Associations. Illustrate your answer with examples.

There are three main views as to the similarities and differences between Trades Unions (TUs) and Professional Associations (PAs).

First, despite acknowledging that both are organisations of workers, they are seen as distinct in terms of their role in society, objectives, methods, ideology and membership.

Second, they are seen as essentially similar, but the public acceptance of professional ideology conceals this so that PAs seem superior.

Third, both similarities and differences are recognised and a tendency for a degree of convergence between the two is identified.

Definitions of the PAs and TUs must be regarded as problematic, because their characteristics are changing rather than fixed and their role is perceived differently from the various sociological perspectives.

Those writers who see the two types of organisation as largely different tend to accept at face value their 'ideal types' and to be uncritical of the distinctive traits of the professions.

I shall now contrast the two by distinguishing their objectives, methods, membership and values. The main stated goal of PAs is to serve the client and community through the rational application of their particular expert knowledge and the maintenance of high standards of practice. They are thus committed to social service rather than to the selfish interests of the members. In contrast, the TUs are seen as defensive and not altruistic organisations. They try to redress the bargaining disadvantage of individual workers in their relationship with employers.

The methods used by each to achieve their objectives can also be contrasted. PAs strive for, and in many cases achieve, autonomous job regulation. They gain this independence by exerting control over recruitment, training and qualification. They also may devise and enforce their own code of ethics. The main methods used by TUs are collective bargaining (backed up by sanctions such as strikes) and joint consultation (or even participation) with employers at plant, company, industry and national level. This co-operation at national level with employers, and also with government, has been diminished in recent years by the current Government's distaste for 'corporatism'.

Perhaps the most superficial distinction can be made by looking at membership. PAs are organised on an occupational basis and comprise highly educated recruits to, and usually from, the middle classes. TU membership largely consists of manual workers, organised perhaps on an occupational or craft basis but also possibly as an industrial or general TU. The total membership of TUs has declined dramatically since 1979, but the non-manual membership has risen, in both proportional and real terms. This distinction is thus diminishing, particularly as some white-collar unions seek professional status and some PAs adopt TU methods.

In terms of values and ideology, considerable differences are perceived. PAs are individualistic in outlook, despite a sense of community based on their positive attitude to work; whereas TUs are collectivistic in outlook, their solidarity being based on tradition or instrumentalism. (These concepts are developed in the work of Lockwood and Goldthorpe.) TU members see society in class terms ('them and us') whereas professionals see social inequality as based on individual achievement. The PAs are seen as conservative, supporting the status quo but generally above partisan politics, whereas the TUs in most industrial societies are associated with left-wing parties.

If, in the second part of the answer, we argue that the two types of organisation are essentially similar, then the professions must be looked at more critically.

From a pluralist view, both can be seen as secondary work organisations which bargain in the industrial relations system and represent members' interests in the wider political system. However, a better case for similarity is found if we adopt the conflict perspectives argued by Marxist and also Weberian writers.

The objectives of PAs are seen here as either serving ruling-class interests or as being intrinsically selfish, but legitimised by ideology. Their methods are similar to, but often more effective than, those used by TUs. The closed-shop, restrictive practices, pressurising of government and using industrial muscle are all employed by PAs. The autonomous job regulation which was effectively destroyed by Rupert Murdoch of Fleet Street is virtually unchallenged on Harley Street. However, both dockers and university lecturers lost job security in the 1980s.

The special traits which define the professions can be negatively evaluated to argue that they are merely strategies of 'closure' used by PAs to maintain or improve the market situation of professional workers.

If we now, for the third part of the answer, argue that the similarities and differences cannot be regarded as fixed but develop in response to wider social changes, then some tendency to convergence can be argued.

Professionalisation of individual occupations and society as a whole has been remarked upon by functionalists and Weberians. This process is explained by the increased rationalisation of society and the successful application of scientific and other expertise to society's problems. Functionalists see the effects as stabilising the social system, Weberians as increasing efficiency and improving the rewards of professionals.

Marxists have predicted the 'proletarianisation' of professionals along with other white-collar workers. Unionisation of lower professionals, such as teachers and nurses, and the bureaucratisation of the employers of higher professionals, such as doctors, are threats to the autonomy described above. Those professions, or ranks of professions, which have been most 'feminised' in membership are perhaps the most vulnerable.

Braverman saw TUs emerging and maturing as a response to Taylorism, which led to the loss of occupational self-control of craft workers through deskilling. Similar threats to the control of knowledge and technique enjoyed by professionals may lead PAs to develop TU tactics.

In conclusion, it might be wisest to abandon attempts to argue that TUs and PAs are either identical or distinct categories, but instead to see a continuum between the two which is changing and not fixed.

STUDENT'S ANSWER WITH EXAMINER COMMENTS

Question 2

Compare and contrast consensus and conflict approaches to the study of the 'professions'.

66 Should identify functionalism as a consensus theory. 99

66 Not clear if the income of the professional or the ruling class is referred to. 99

66 Sounds more like Weberian than Marxist analysis. 99

The role of people in the professions is seen by functionalists as satisfying the functional needs of the social system. Davis and Moore state that certain positions in society are more important than others and require special skills which only a few people have the talent to perform. Therefore the high rewards for the professions are one way of making sure that important positions are filled by the best people.

However, Marx argues that they are servants of the ruling class, keeping the working class falsely conscious and using their positions to legitimise power and rewards of higher income and prestige.

Many of the long-established and influential professions have bodies which have a legal right to test the competence of prospective members. Such bodies as the BMA and the Law Society control the right of individuals to practise and can therefore control the number and type of practitioners in a particular field.

Whereas functionalists would say that this system maintains standards and protects clients by preventing exploitation, conflict theories suggest that it is their way of restricting entry. By controlling members it creates a closed shop.

Marshall and Barber respectively see professionals as unselfish and dedicated to the interests of the client and the community, but in fact the client is rarely given the opportunity to express satisfaction or dissatisfaction with the service received. Professionals usually insist that only fellow professionals are qualified to assess their performance. Their own ethical codes may prohibit one professional from criticising another.

One important characteristic of professionals as seen by functionalists is that they have a distinctive body of knowledge acquired through formal training which is expertly applied. Marx says the language used in training denies access to the working class by making it difficult to understand. Today in some professions, e.g. the law, it seems easy for them to demand large sums of money from the working class to translate complicated vocabulary in documents drawn up by themselves.

Weber thinks the professions are part of the redistribution of power to bureaucratic organisations which increasingly employ professionals: the upper and middle classes providing a service for themselves.

Durkheim, however, says the professions integrate modern societies by serving the community, not themselves. They bridge the gap between capitalism and the extension of the bureaucratic state by being dedicated to community interests.

Professionals are seen by some Marxist revisionists as part of a new ruling class rather than just servants of it. This new ruling class controls, rather than owns, the means of production. Parsons, however, argues that scientists serve the community rather than class or selfish interests.

Women's health seems to be controlled in most cases by doctors. Statistics show that far more women are patients than men. Feminists feel that in most cases, such as pregnancy, women are able to take care of themselves.

Illich attacks the professions as selfish occupations, not part of a particular class. For example, in *De-schooling Society* teachers are seen as obstacles to education. They control pupils through the monopolisation of knowledge. We can all be made into potential patients by doctors.

Good comparative point.

Functionalism and critics, but not identified as such.

Not clear if it is the client or the prospective professional who is exlcuded by language.

Yes.

Yes.

Djilas and Burnham and criticism.

Feminist critique of professions could be developed.

More to be said on Illich and critique of medicine.

Overall comments

Overall, a competent and critical account, worth a C grade; it could be improved by:

1 Developing the Weberian views of Parry and Parry to discuss the self-interested behaviour of professions, using concepts like market situations, status and power. The potential for exclusion should be pointed out.
2 Explaining more clearly the distinction between consensus and conflict theories.
3 Distinguishing Marx from Marxists.

A Review Sheet for this chapter may be found on pp. 255–6.

15

RELIGION

GETTING STARTED

The sociology of religion is concerned with the role of religion in the wider society and the way in which religion helps people to make sense of the world. The intention of sociology is neither to affirm nor to challenge religious belief but to examine religion from the point of view of social actors or to identify the impact of religion on social behaviour.

The main themes of questions set on this topic are:

1 **Critical evaluation of the major theories of religion of Marx, Durkheim and Weber.**
2 **Comparison of the major theories and their application to issues such as social order, social change and social inequality.**
3 **The secularisation debate.**
4 **The significance of the growth of sects.**

Credit will be given for comparative material and for the ability to apply theories to contemporary events.

Definitions

- *Religion.* There is no agreed definition, but sociologists are concerned with these three aspects of religion:
- *Religious belief.*
- *Religious practice.*
- *Religious institutions.*

- *Secularisation.* Involves the decline in the influence of religion on the wider society and the reduction in the spiritual content of religious belief. Any definition must be regarded as problematic.

- *Sects.* According to Wilson, these are 'Exclusive bodies which impose some test of merit … faith, knowledge or obedience …'.

- *Cults.* Are arguably religious groups whose beliefs and practices are more concerned with this world than with more spiritual matters.

Related topics include *sociological theory, development, stratification* and other areas which are concerned with *belief, knowledge* and *ideology.*

MARXIST PERSPECTIVES

FUNCTIONALIST PERSPECTIVES

WEBER

FEMINIST PERSPECTIVES

THE SECULARISATION DEBATE

SECTS

THEORETICAL AND EMPIRICAL STUDIES

ESSENTIAL PRINCIPLES

Certain shared assumptions about the role of religion in society are to be found in the work of Marx and in subsequent Marxist accounts.

1   Religious beliefs and institutions are part of the superstructure of exploitative (pre-communist) societies.
2   Changes in the economic substructure produce changes in religion.
3   Religion helps to reproduce the existing relations of production.
4   Religion is a form of alienation. It was made by men to ease their suffering, but also perpetuates it.
5   Religion is the 'Opiate of the masses'. First, it eases the pain produced by capitalism and second, it distorts reality so that the source of pain is concealed. The working class is kept falsely conscious. Suffering, deprivation and poverty are seen as divinely ordered. Justice will come to the righteous and meek in the next world. Some religions await imminent divine intervention which cools revolutionary fervour.

Critics

Weber attacked the alleged economic determinism of Marx. He saw religious belief as influencing the economic organisation of society, rather than vice versa.

Functionalists recognise similar effects of religion on the wider society, e.g. Durkheim saw it as diminishing the significance of social stratification and Malinowski saw it as easing emotional stress. However, they emphasise the positive, integrative effects of religion, rather than seeing it as reproducing inequality.

Modern Marxist writers have questioned the continued importance of religion as ideology. Abercrombie sees ideological control as generally less important as the employment relationship provides sufficient control of the working class. This criticism would apply to the media and other sources of ideology. Clarke and Critcher are among those who see 'consumerism' as the contemporary legitimation of capitalism.

Functionalists, following Durkheim, include social anthropologists like Malinowski and Americans like Parsons and Davis and Moore. They share certain common assumptions about the nature of society and the role of religion in society. The origin, persistence and form of religion can be explained by identifying the contribution it makes towards meeting the needs of the social system.

The functional needs satisfied by religion are:

1   *Integration*: shared beliefs, rituals and sacred objects provide a basis for social order based on consensual values. Durkheim saw religion as the worship of the moral order which makes up society.
2   *Social control (pattern maintenance)*: religion provides divine backing for important rules and the certainty of justice in the next world.

Critics

Critics question both the desirability and existence of social solidarity based on consensus. Even if these were demonstrated, religion could be the cause of disharmony and disunity.

Weber's study *The Protestant Ethic and the Spirit of Capitalism* is seen as having a wider significance than its explanation of the substantive issue of the rise of capitalism in Western Europe.

1   It provides a critical view of the Durkheimian approach to sociology, whereby the scientific study of social facts is advocated. Weber shows how the social meanings given to behaviour offer an alternative topic of study.
2   It is more obviously a critique of Marxist economic determinism. Whereas Marxists see ideas emerging from the substructure, Weber argues that ideas and beliefs (i.e. the Protestant ethic) can influence the economic organisation of society. Whereas Marxists see religious belief as inhibiting social change, Weber saw religious belief as a potential cause of change.

Weber's study argued that Protestant beliefs contributed towards the rise of capitalism in certain specific cases. It was a necessary, but not a sufficient, cause and was not an example of a universal social law.

The basis of the argument is that the Protestant beliefs associated with Calvinism, such as concern with deeds in this world and predestination, encouraged thrift and individualism, which in turn encouraged the development of capitalism. The individual is seen as working hard, in a rational manner, and investing the proceeds in order to improve productivity and profitability.

Critics

Marxists maintain that the apparent link between Protestantism and capitalism is not, as Weber suggests, an 'elective affinity' but the result of Protestantism being a suitable ideology to legitimise inequality.

Other critics, whilst accepting the possible relationship between religious belief and economic development, argue that a variety of other factors may have been more influential in explaining the rise of capitalism and are therefore more appropriate explanations of economic development in general. The alternative causal factors include religious freedom, liberal democracy, and the influence of 'marginal groups' such as immigrants.

FEMINIST PERSPECTIVES

Religious beliefs can be seen as patriarchal ideology. Both religious institutions and beliefs help to legitimise gender inequality. Women may be denied some religious roles, perhaps because of perceived 'impurity'.

RELIGION AND FAMILY LIFE

Religion frequently supports the ideology of family life. The family is the location for the social control of women and children. This control is often expressed in terms of the need to protect women and children from the sexual desires of outsiders and sometimes from their own sexuality. In addition, religious beliefs may legitimise male ownership and inheritance of property, and a division of labour based on gender.

Obedience to husbands may be legitimised by religion.

There may be conflict between feminism and religious ideas over the abortion issue.

RELIGION AND SCHOOLS

There are as yet no state Muslim schools. Private Muslim schools are single-sex and nearly always for girls. Single-sex schools are supported by some feminists as giving girls more opportunities, but this assumes a curriculum similar to that available at mixed schools or boys' schools, not one which emphasises traditional gender roles.

THE SECULARISATION DEBATE

Marx, Durkheim and Weber are all concerned with the relationship between religion and the wider society. They emphasise the effects of religion on various aspects of social life, such as social change. All three, in fact, predict the emergence of more secular societies and see the rise of modern industrial or capitalist society as an influence on this process.

The main sociological issues involve the problems of:

- defining secularisation.

- assessing the extent of secularisation.

- attributing meaning to behaviour, particularly attendance at religious ceremonies.

SECULARISATION: SOME ADDITIONAL CONCEPTS

- **Desacralisation** is the loss of the ability to experience a sense of the sacred or mystery in life, and ceasing to believe that supernatural forces control the world.

  Weber refers to this as **disenchantment** following the rise of scientific and rational thinking. This refers to what is going on in the mind of the individual and group, whereas secularisation refers to the declining impact of religion on society.

- **Disengagement** is the separation of church from everyday society.

- **Structural differentiation** is the specialisation of social organisations such as the church or family and is, according to Parsons, a feature of modern society; e.g. churches have abandoned some of their education and welfare functions to focus on specifically religious matters.

■ **Individuation**: according to Bellah, members of modern society are not materialistic, rational and secular. They are religious as individuals, not as church members. Critics of Bellah say his definition of religion as a search for meaning in life is itself a widening of the definition of religion to such an extent that it is evidence of secularisation.

SECTS

The early studies of sects were concerned with the categorisation of religious organisations, in particular with distinguishing sects from churches. The major emphasis of most studies was on Christian sects. Subsequently, interest has shifted to explaining the links between religious movements and other aspects of social life. The origin, growth and future development of sects and cults have been explained in a variety of ways, relating changes to other aspects of social change. Non-Christian sects and non-religious cults have been studied and their roles in society examined (see p. 000).

THEORETICAL AND EMPIRICAL STUDIES

MARXIST STUDIES

Modern Marxists are far less interested in religion than Marx himself was. This is because there now appear to be more effective ways of reproducing ruling-class ideology, e.g. education and the mass media (see Marxist sections of Chapters 11, 16 and 22). Althusser and Gramsci are certainly interested in notions of hegemony and ideological control, but primarily acknowledge the effects of secularisation rather than religion in Western capitalist societies.

FUNCTIONALIST STUDIES

Durkheim provided the basic ideas which are found in modern functionalist approaches and which were outlined above. He did offer the distinctive view that religion was, in fact, the worship of society, or more specifically the moral order. In describing religion in aboriginal society he said 'the God of the clan is the clan itself'.

Durkheim offers the rather Marxist-sounding view that religion can integrate societies by making inequalities seem less significant and making people feel less aggrieved by them.

Malinowski, like Durkheim, applied the functionalist approach to the study of religion in simple societies. He does not accept Durkheim's view that religion is the worship of society. He offers, instead, the view that the functions of religion apply to more restricted areas of social life than the establishment of the collective conscience. Religious beliefs and rituals integrate societies when solidarity is threatened by emotional stress, e.g. following death, or by uncertainty resulting from the inability to predict nature, e.g. the impact of bad weather on fishing.

Herberg offers a functionalist account of the role of religion in contemporary American society which, incidentally, indicates the way in which religion itself can become secularised. Religion helps to integrate an immigrant society by:

a) providing churches which cut across ethnic divisions.
b) providing organisations to which individuals in a competitive individualistic society feel they can belong.
c) 'Americanising' the major denominations of Christianity and Judaism.

Berger and Luckman – an interactionist view of religion

Every society has a body of knowledge by which it makes sense of the world, and this 'universe of meaning' must be constantly justified and reinforced. Religion puts mankind in a central position in the whole universe. Berger and Luckman see the 'universe of meaning' as a *social construction*, not just an individual making sense of the world.

The universe of meaning can be destroyed from outside if gods and kings are shown to be impotent – e.g. the Spanish invaders of South America undermined the Inca religion.

RELIGION AND SOCIAL CHANGE

Both Marxists and functionalists see religion as essentially a conservative influence on society. There are, however, various studies which challenge this view.

Thompson identifies the roots of English socialism in the Methodist Church, not in Marxism, and thus sees the potential for religious beliefs to support social change.

Worsley, in a study of 'cargo cults' in the South Pacific, suggests that religious movements can be transformed into radical political groups challenging imperialism.

Friere, in discussing the rise of 'liberation theology' within the Roman Catholic Church in Latin America, argues that authentic Christianity involves the 'critical analysis of social structures'.

The role of religious movements in the struggle for civil rights in the USA and against apartheid reinforces the reformist, or arguably revolutionary, potential of religion. Islam is identified as a conservative influence in some societies, and as a force for change in others.

FEMINIST STUDIES

G. Sahgal and N. Yuval-Davis (1990), *Women and Fundamentalism*

These authors have criticised the negative effect on women of the rise of fundamentalism in Britain. Although Islam has, since the Rushdie affair, been the most publicised example, they are equally concerned with what they perceive as the development of fundamentalism among Christians, Jews, Hindus and Sikhs.

They describe:

- Conservative fundamentalism, which asserts traditional social and religious values.
- Radical fundamentalism, which rejects corrupt and impure forms of religion and wishes to return to original roots.

Both kinds reject pluralism and liberalism, and both are seen as threats to women's freedom. The role of women is seen in a family context, where women play a vital part in biologically and culturally reproducing the religious community. For feminists this involves the reproduction of patriarchal ideology.

The writers acknowledge that racism may contribute to the rise of fundamentalism (along with the anomie and alienation associated with modern industrial society).

Critical thoughts

Fundamentalism may challenge the beliefs of an imperialist society, whether these beliefs are seen as Christian or secular. In particular, separate single-sex education may protect minority girls from both sexism and racism, and the wearing of the *hijab* can be seen as a symbol of resistance to both racism and being seen as a sex object. This is an argument heard from educated women in Iran as well as the UK.

C. Butler (1995), *Religion and Gender: Young Muslim Women in Britain*

Butler notes the adverse media image of Islam in Europe. She argues that Asian women are perceived and portrayed as victims. They are seen as being controlled by men – kept at home and forced into arranged marriages. Butler challenges this view, pointing out the diversity which exists within the Muslim community. Although most British Muslims are of Asian origin, many come from other places.

Butler has studied Muslim women from the Asian communities, and points out that within these communities there are also considerable differences based on generation.

Findings of interviews with second-generation Muslim women:

1 Continued commitment to religion based on the family.
2 Racism has strengthened, not weakened, religious identity. Britain is perceived as home, but their identity is not British.
3 Rejection of Asian or Indian sub-continent identity and customs. Arranged marriage, dowries, and caste are seen as 'un-Islamic' and borrowed from Hindu culture. Identity is more Muslim than Pakistani or Bangladeshi, but they still feel pushed into an Asian identity by, for example, racism.
4 Women may also reject patriarchy as part of a man-made culture, not part of Islam. Islam is seen as a defender of equality, not a source of oppression.
5 The women want a life outside the home, education and jobs.
6 Some see parents as living in the past. Attitudes in Pakistan have moved on, but parents remember it thirty years ago.

Conclusion: the media view is an inaccurate stereotype.

Critical thoughts

1 Many of the sources date from the 1970s and 1980s.
2 1990s' generational conflict may involve religious children challenging parents'

accommodation to secular Western values. Religion may not always support traditional values – it can challenge them.

STUDIES OF SECTS

Wilson explained the growth of sects as a response to secularisation, unlike Martin's view that they were evidence against secularisation as they represent a movement towards pure and fervent religion. Wilson sees sects as attracting seekers of mystery, ecstasy, a stable social order, a sense of identity and a feeling of belonging. In addition they attract those who reject the impersonal, rational, bureaucratic and wicked world. He does not accept that all such groups would be regarded as religious in the everyday sense of the word.

Wilson distinguished eight types of sect and cult based on their attitude to the wider society which influences their beliefs, practices and organisation. He sees significant differences between 'conversionist' and 'withdrawn' groups and also between 'world affirming' and 'world rejecting' groups.

Wallis explained the development of various kinds of new religions and new cults in terms of their members' rejection of modern industrial society. He identified the alienating effects of work, curbs on individual freedom, secularisation and materialism. The new converts were frequently adolescents who sought success or peace of mind in this world, or an escape from it. The reference to secularisation is similar to Wilson's earlier views. Wallis also offers a view, influenced by Merton's anomie theory of deviance, suggesting that blocking opportunities to achieve consensual goals by legitimate means encourages membership of world affirming groups such as Scientology or Christian Science.

Wallis distinguishes cults, which offer success in this world, from the new religions which may also be world rejecting or world accommodating. The new religions include:

a) Fundamentalist sects of Jewish-Christian origin, which tend to be evangelical and puritanical.
b) Imported sects of Eastern religions, which are puritanical and reject materialism.
c) Hybrids, like the 'Moonies' (the subject of a participant observation study by Barker), whose church is an amalgam of Eastern and Western religions and is pro-capitalist.

STUDIES OF SECULARISATION

Wilson has argued for the secularisation thesis (see also Tutor Answer to Question 4). He cites as evidence:

a) The decline in religious practice, such as church attendance, observing rules and participation in rites of passage.
b) The decline in religious knowledge and belief.
c) The decline in the influence of religious institutions, particularly on secular matters such as politics and education.
d) The declining numbers, influence and prestige of an ageing clergy.
e) The growth of sectarianism.

Martin has presented an opposing view, questioning the validity of the behavioural measures listed by Wilson. He claims that religious beliefs and meanings continue to have considerable influence on people's lives. He sees people and religious organisations as becoming more, not less, religious.

Bellah has argued that the declining influence of religious institutions is not evidence of secularisation, but simply of a change to a more individual form of religious belief and practice. Martin saw this as the natural development of the Protestant tradition of individualism.

Parsons sees the persistence of religious belief and values in the secular morality of Western societies. He is concerned with the integrative and social control functions of religion. Fellow functionalists Davis and Moore see a minimal amount of religiosity as 'indispensable' because of the functions associated with religion.

EXAMINATION QUESTIONS

1   Examine the view that religious ideas and institutions are necessarily conservative forces.

(AEB)

2   'The growth of religious sects and cults can be understood mainly as a response to social and economic deprivation.' Examine this view.

(AEB)

3   Does the growth of new religious movements throw doubt on the idea of secularisation?

(UODLE)

4   What problems do sociologists face in attempting to define and measure secularisation?

(AEB)

5   Compare and contrast Marxist and Weberian explanations of the relationship between religious belief and social change.

(AEB)

ANSWERS TO EXAMINATION QUESTIONS

OUTLINE ANSWERS

Question 1

This question requires a critical discussion of the role of both religious belief and organisations in the wider society. The simplest organising framework is to use the three classic theories and some modern examples. Note the different interpretations of the term 'conservative' and their implications for the answer.

1   Marx and the Marxists:
   Religion is conservative in the sense that as part of the superstructure of exploitative societies it helps to maintain the existing substructure. The opiate of the masses keeps the working class falsely conscious.
2   Durkheim and the functionalists:
   Religion is implicitly conservative in that it helps to maintain the equilibrium of the social system. It stops people feeling aggrieved and makes inequality less noticeable. Note the similarity with Marx. Change, if it occurs, is evolutionary rather than revolutionary. Religion integrates society and helps maintain social order. Herberg suggests that religion integrated US society.
3   Weber:
   Religion is not necessarily conservative. Calvinism helped to promote the rise of capitalism. The Islamic revolution in Iran, the Liberation Theology of the RC Church in Latin America, and Worsley's 'Cargo Cults' all illustrate similar changes encouraged by religion.
4   You could also discuss whether churches are conservative whereas sects are not (this is a generalisation to be challenged).

Question 2

You must explain, criticise and offer alternative views to the claim that deprivation is the main explanation for the growth of sects.

1   Social and economic deprivation does explain the growth of sects:
   a)   Marx sees all religious beliefs and institutions as part of the superstructure.
   b)   Weber writes of a Theodicy of suffering.
   c)   Glock and Stark see the development of religious groups as a response to deprivation of various kinds, including social and economic deprivation.
   d)   The success of Black Muslims in the ghettoes of the USA is an example of responding to deprivation.
2   Alternative explanations of the growth of religious groups:
   a)   Wilson suggests that sects arise as a response to secularisation.

b) Martin sees sects as evidence of a religious revival.
c) Niebhur sees sectarianism, and the subsequent consolidation of some sects into denominations, as a recurring process.
d) Wallis offers a variety of possible factors encouraging new groups, including alienation, anomie and the rejection of materialism.
e) Glock and Stark suggest other forms of deprivation, such as ill health, which sects compensate for.

Question 3

This is not an uncommon question and it requires consideration of material both on sects and on secularisation.

Yes:

1 Churches have lost members and influence but new movements have thrived, indicating that religion is developing, not in decline (Martin).
2 This is a continuation of historic tendencies towards sectarianism to regain purity and/ or follow a charismatic leader (e.g. Christians and Sikhs).

No:

1 Sects are a response to secularisation, not evidence against it (Wilson).
2 Growth is explained by social disorganisation and change (Wallis).
3 Growth is explained by social and economic deprivation (Glock and Stark).

TUTOR ANSWER

Question 4

What problems do sociologists face in attempting to define and measure secularisation?

Sociological debates about the extent of secularisation in modern industrial societies focus more on the problems of definition and assessment than on the 'facts' about religious events. Definitions of both religion and secularisation are disputed, and in the absence of a consensual view of what secularisation would involve there can be no agreement on the extent of the phenomenon.

Durkheim saw religion as a unified system of beliefs and practices about sacred things. The emphasis on unity suggests that the influence and functions of religion decline when there is religious diversity or scepticism. Wilson suggests that we should see religion as the behaviour and organisations which are 'in the everyday sense of the word religious'. He is trying to avoid the problem of perceiving any novel magical, mystical or supernatural belief and practice as evidence of some kind of religious revival.

The major arguments against secularisation in Britain have come from Martin. He sees secularisation as referring first to changes in thought, attitude and belief, and second to changes in institutions, custom and practice. Secularisation would involve the declining importance of religion at both the institutional level and the personal level. His concern with belief, as well as practice, is central to the problem of assessment.

A less partisan position is taken by Shiner who, in an attempt to unravel the complications caused by the term secularisation being used in so many different ways, offers a simplified view. Based on a review of the literature, he suggests that there are two dominant themes. First, the secularisation of society, which involves a decline in the influence of religion over the wider society. Second, the secularisation of religion itself, which involves religious ideas and institutions becoming less spiritual and more worldly.

A final view, from an interpretive perspective, comes from Berger and Luckman. They saw religion as providing a 'universe of meaning' whereby individuals made sense of the world. Religion legitimises beliefs and institutions. They are doubtful whether more rational beliefs could explain ultimate mysteries, such as death.

Assessment of the extent of secularisation usually involves consideration of three dimensions of measurement of religion. These are: religious belief, religious behaviour and religious institutions. The reliability and validity of such measures will be considered below.

The main problems of assessing the extent of secularisation can be summarised as follows:

First, the problem of agreeing on definitions so that sociologists can decide what should be observed and measured. This has been discussed already but one outstanding issue is the extent to which change in religious belief, practice or institutions should in itself be regarded as evidence of secularisation.

Second, the problems of identifying the meaning behind behaviour. Even if the reliability of, say, church attendance statistics could be taken for granted, the significance of church-going as a measure of religiosity could be disputed. There are of course technical problems involved in the gathering of church attendance figures, such as which institutions should be included, as well as problems of interpretation.

Third, there is the problem of assessing the degree of *past* religiosity, which is of course necessary in order to compare the current position with the past. Such a comparison is to demonstrate the decline or otherwise of religion. Many of those who simultaneously describe and deplore the trend towards a more secular society may have a romanticised view of some non-existent 'golden age' when religion flourished.

These problems can be illustrated by considering some of the major disputes over interpreting events which, it has been argued, are evidence of secularisation. The most important of these is the problem of the motives and meanings attributed to religious behaviour. There has been a decline in church attendance and in participation in rites of passage. This could be taken at face value, or the meaning of this could be questioned by pointing out that religious belief does not require church attendance and that individual practice, for example in the home, still flourishes. Conversely, religious practice may have alternative meanings; for example, people may follow dietary rules for secular reasons and church attendance may be motivated by the desire to participate in social activities.

The declining influence of religious institutions has been cited as evidence of secularisation. However, Parsons has argued that the withdrawal of churches from political and educational roles is evidence of structural differentiation, and that the churches are now more religious. Martin sees the declining influence of the church as a natural progression of the individualism of the Protestant tradition, which he supports.

The development of rational, secular ideas in politics, the sciences and professions seems to represent a threat to the traditional religious ideas. Marx, Freud and Darwin have all been used to challenge religious beliefs. Durkheim, Weber and Marx all predicted the decline of religion in more rational industrial societies. Critics have suggested that the secular alternatives are no more rational than religious belief. Berger talks about 'scientism' as an ideology involving unquestioning faith in the ability of science to explain the universe. However, as stated above, Wilson pointed out that not all irrational beliefs could be regarded as authentic religion.

The view that religion itself has become secularised by accommodating itself to the various changes in society has been used to sustain the secularisation thesis in the USA, where religious identification and practice remain at high levels. Examples can be found of the bureaucratisation of religion, the development of business aims by religious organisations and the modernisation of religious beliefs and practices to conform to the secular values of a secular society. However, it is also the case in the USA, and throughout much of the Islamic world, that there has been a revival of religious fundamentalism which challenges the secularisation thesis.

Thus, it can be seen that the debate over secularisation is as much a debate over the appropriate definition of concepts and methods of assessment as it is a dispute over evidence.

STUDENT'S ANSWER WITH EXAMINER COMMENTS

Question 5

Compare and contrast Marxist and Weberian explanations of the relationship between religious belief and social change.

> Two completely different concepts in sociology are Marxist and Weberian explanations of religion. Marx believed that the relationship between religion and social change was that religion inhibited and suppressed social change. Weber, on the other hand, believed that religious belief could and did cause social change.
>
> However, before we compare and contrast these two views, it must be said that both Marx and Weber adopted different approaches to the study of religion. Weber attempted the interpretive understanding of social action and employed the comparative method. Marx believed that action is constrained by the economy. Many Marxists believe history is a mechanical process directed by economic forces.

" Suitable introduction. "

" Should link history to social change. "

> Change 'Religion creates' to 'Religion helps to create'.

> Good on ruling class. How is inequality legitimised?

> Insert 'or possibility' after need.

> Insert *may* before cause.

> The need for religious belief declines as profit becomes an aim in itself.

> These three paragraphs contain good comparative material.

> Why does Protestantism particularly suit capitalism?

> Appropriate critical use of Durkheim.

> Should deal with belief.

> Not 'determined' may be 'encouraged'.

Marx sees the role of religion as supporting ruling-class interests. Religion creates a falsely conscious society, unaware of its exploitation and fitting the needs of capitalist employers.

The falsely conscious society is created by easing the pain of exploitation. The working class are led to believe that their suffering is a virtue and that they will be rewarded in the next world. Their exploitation and inequality are justified by God. It is not only the working class who are influenced by religion but also the ruling class. However, for them religion is a force which can justify their wealth at the expense of the workers.

Therefore Marx believed that religion acted as an opiate to dull the pain produced by oppression. It creates a distortion of reality and provides many of the deceptions which form the basis of ruling-class ideology. Religion does not solve the problem of exploitation but is instead a misguided attempt to make life bearable. As the workers are under the influence of religion and falsely conscious they see no need for social change. Therefore, religion acts as a restraint over any type of reform and smothers thoughts of revolution.

Weber sees religion as a dynamic force which causes social change rather than discourages it. In *The Protestant Ethic and the Spirit of Capitalism* Weber concentrates on the effects of Calvinism on the promotion of capitalism. He describes how Calvinistic beliefs encourage individualism. Instead of trying to attain success in the next world they attempt to find success in this world. Rather than putting their energies into religious activities, as some religions do, the Calvinist puts a lot of effort into economic production. The profits gained from production are saved and invested in new ventures rather than lavishly spent.

Weber concludes that Calvinism underlies the practice of capitalism and that making money becomes both a business and a religious ethic. As evidence of his theory Weber points out that where Calvinism did not prevail economic development was slower than in Protestant Western Europe.

Therefore, unlike Marx, Weber believes that religious belief encourages social change. Although, in itself, religion is not able to do so, it does provide individuals with the right attitudes and values to adopt social change.

The major contrast between Marx and Weber is that Marx believed that religion was shaped by economic factors but Weber rejected this view and believed that religion was able to influence economic behaviour.

However, both Marx and Weber did agree that ultimately religion would be wiped out. In Marx's case a communist society would banish exploitation, therefore the need for religion and superstition would vanish as there would be no pain to ease. Weber sees the growth of science and rational thinking as leading to the decline of religion.

Marx believed that Protestantism particularly suited capitalism. As part of the superstructure it met the requirements of the ruling class. Weber saw Protestant beliefs as a necessary ingredient in the rise of capitalism.

Both Marx and Weber can be criticised by the functionalist view of religion. Durkheim saw religion as reinforcing social norms and promoting solidarity, not false consciousness. He believed that religion forms a collective consciousness, not individualism. This creates order, control and social stability.

Marx can be criticised by the fact that religion continues to flourish in Eastern Europe. Also church leaders have been involved in protest, e.g. Martin Luther King and Desmond Tutu.

Weber's work is harder to criticise as he claims that Calvinism is not the only cause of social change and the rise of capitalism but that many factors were involved. However, England was never like the Western European countries Weber describes as its religious beliefs were not Calvinistic. Also many believe that early capitalism actually preceded and largely determined Protestantism.

> Therefore, we can see that Marxist and Weberian explanations of the relationship between religious belief and social change are contradictory. However, Weber's theory did come about as a direct attempt to criticise Marx.

Overall comments

Overall, a good C grade answer. It needs to deal more specifically with belief rather than religion in general. The link between Calvinist beliefs and the rise of capitalism could be explained more clearly.

Comparative points must be made explicit throughout the essay.

There are better modern examples of the relationship between religious belief and social change, e.g. the influence of Islam on the Iranian revolution.

A Review Sheet for this chapter may be found on p. 256.

16

THE MASS MEDIA

THE MARKET MODEL

THE MASS MANIPULATIVE MODEL

THE INTERACTIONIST MODEL

THE NEW RIGHT APPROACH

THEORETICAL AND EMPIRICAL STUDIES

GETTING STARTED

Sociological interest in the mass media has developed through a series of focal concerns which often reflect more general developments in sociology. However, public interest remains concentrated on the issue of the adverse effects of the media on antisocial behaviour. The need for censorship and control because of the perceived effects of sex and violence in the media is still on the political agenda. It is an issue which has produced an unlikely alliance of feminists and traditional moralists. The Government announced another research project in December 1989 which will begin by reviewing existing research.

The main sociological interests have shifted to the ideological role of the media in relation to class, gender and ethnic issues. Both sociologists and politicians remain interested in the partiality of TV news, for example the rows over the reporting of Northern Ireland and the American bombing of Libya.

The mass media provide a fruitful source of subjects for student research and hopefully this chapter will suggest some suitable hypotheses for further investigation.

The main themes of questions set on this topic are:

1 **Explanations of the relationship between ownership, control and output of the media.**
2 **Critical examination of bias in the presentation/selection of the news.**
3 **Examination and explanation of media representation of gender, ethnicity, age and class.**
4 **The role of the media in the amplification of deviance.**
5 **Evaluation of studies of the effects of the media on attitudes and behaviour.**

Definitions

■ *The mass media* is the system of communication which transmits messages to large audiences. It includes TV, radio, newspapers and magazines. Some writers would also consider including discs and tapes as well as popular design in the definition.

Related topics include *deviance, race, gender, politics* and *stratification*.

ESSENTIAL PRINCIPLES

Early research on the mass media emphasised the effects of media output on attitudes and behaviour. The methods and explanations were frequently influenced by psychology.

The shift from studying short-term effects to more general cultural effects has been accompanied by attempts to place the media in a broader social context. The main concern has become the relationship between ownership, control and output. There often seems to be more interest in analysing the content of the media and in making various assertions than in demonstrating possible effects on the audience. The various relationships between ownership and production have been evaluated by Cohen and Young, who favour the interactionist model explained below.

THE MARKET MODEL

This is the model which conforms to the principles of a liberal-democratic society with a market economy. The audience is seen as made up of consumers who thus influence the output of the media by providing profit for the owners. Owners, and thus controllers and producers, seek audiences. They compete to provide what is demanded. There is no conspiracy between owners or government. A wide range of opinions are offered, and only the illegal and the unsellable are excluded. Events in the news are seen as having an objective reality and are selected for broadcasting or publication by journalists and editors on a professional basis. In the USA the free press is seen as an important watchdog, helping prevent state abuse of power.

Pluralism, like the market model, is associated with democratic societies. The pluralist approach emphasises not only the diversity of ownership but also importance of access to the media for competing interests.

Criticism

This comes from Marxists who raise the issue of oligarchic control of the media, and from liberals who claim state interference and control.

THE MASS MANIPULATIVE MODEL

This is seen by Cohen and Young as being the opposite of the market model in that the audience, instead of being the major influence on the media, are the passive and uncritical receivers of media messages. The Christian 'right', epitomised by Mary Whitehouse and the American 'moral majority', still support the pre-war 'hypodermic syringe' view and see a conspiracy to corrupt conventional morality through the portrayal of sex, violence and other challenges to traditional morality. The Marxist version of this model is much more common among sociologists. There is an internal Marxist debate (found also in the sociology of the state) between instrumentalists, such as Miliband, and structuralists, such as Althusser and Marcuse (see also Chapter 7). The former view sees fairly direct control over media production by the ruling class, whereas the latter view sees journalists and editors as being influenced by ruling-class ideology, and willingly conforming to the interests of capitalists.

Criticism

Coming from *both* liberals and interactionists it suggests that the evidence of concentration of ownership, or even bias in output, is insufficient to demonstrate particular effects on the audience.

THE INTERACTIONIST MODEL

This combines some elements of the previous theories. The media are seen as reflecting the existing attitudes of the audience, as well as helping to create and reinforce a consensual view of the world.

The prevailing consensus is identified by writers within this perspective as pro-capitalist, sexist and racist. Thus this model has become associated with the left, at least in Britain.

The selection and presentation of news is seen as being influenced by both technical and ideological factors. In this sense 'the news' is seen as socially constructed, rather than a neutral description of real events. The process is described by Cohen and Young as the 'manufacture of news' and the outcome as 'agenda-setting'.

Criticism

This has come from ideological opponents who accuse these writers of political bias in their selection and interpretation of broadcasts.

Ethnomethodologists see the interpretation of news by academics as a similar process to the manufacture of news by journalists. Sociologists, like other viewers and readers, interpret media output according to their own 'commonsense assumptions'. Meanings are read into stories and images according to the audience's expectations.

THE NEW RIGHT APPROACH

There are two conflicting strands to the New Right view of the media.

■ The free-market view (like the market model above) which argues that Government should not broadcast or publish themselves and should minimise regulation of those who do. The state can prevent monopolies, and competition will provide the audience with choice.

■ The conservative moralistic argument from the political and often religious right, which advocates censorship of media output which challenges the conventional moral order or is seen to encourage bad behaviour.

EFFECTS OF THE MASS MEDIA

THEORETICAL AND EMPIRICAL STUDIES

Katz and Lazarsfeld rejected the 'hypodermic syringe' model which had developed in both academic and popular circles to criticise the effects of Hollywood films on the young. They replaced it with their two-step flow model which saw the audience as made up of *groups* influenced by opinion leaders, rather than as an undifferentiated and uncritical mass.

McQuail, Blumler and Brown emphasised the different uses people made of the media, which therefore satisfied different needs.

Belson conducted in-depth interviews with adolescent boys to assess the effects of TV violence on their behaviour. He claimed that a high exposure to TV violence increased the degree to which they engaged in serious violence.

Among a variety of methodological criticisms of his study is the problem identified by Murdock and McCron of using the boys' memories as sources of data, on both the exposure to violent programmes and the committing of violent acts.

Eysenck and Nias supported the view that the media can cause violence. Their approach and methods are psychological, but they are worthy of note as authorities for those who seek evidence for extending control over the media.

Thus a series of studies, using methods such as case histories, interviews, surveys and laboratory experiments, have produced inconsistent and contradictory results. Imitation, desensitisation to violence and cathartic effects have all been noted.

D. Morley rejected the view of the passive homogeneous audience. He demonstrated that the social characteristics of the TV audience, e.g. occupation and ethnicity, influenced the effects of the programmes on that audience. However, he did argue that the fact that families all over Britain watched the national news helped to 'construct the nation'.

POLITICS AND THE MASS MEDIA

Blumler and McQuail (1959 election) and Butler and Stokes (1964 election) minimise the short-term effects that the media have on political attitudes and electoral behaviour. The earlier study even suggested that the partisan press might repel support. The latter study saw a friendly press as preserving loyalty during a difficult period for the government.

Goldsmith's media research group conducted a study of press reporting of London councils. They claim that a negative campaign damaged Labour's vote in the 1987 election. They investigated a series of invented stories which discredited councils and reinforced the perception of them as 'loony left'. They claim that stories which portray councils as obsessed with minority interests had the following effects: they distracted electors from real social problems like employment and housing, they divided the Labour Party, they marshalled support for control of council spending, and they fuelled a dislike of minorities and of those involved in equal opportunities policies.

The Glasgow University Media Group (GUMG) criticised TV news coverage of the Falklands Campaign. The main charge was weakness and laziness in the face of a Ministry of Defence policy of managing the news to maintain public support.

INDUSTRIAL RELATIONS

The GUMG, in a series of studies based on a detailed analysis of the presentation and selection of industrial relations reporting, saw evidence of a systematic bias against employees and trades unions.

M. Harrison, in *TV News: Whose Bias?*, accused the GUMG of the very selectivity and bias they themselves saw in news broadcasts. The GUMG claim the mantle of 'social scientists', but are no less subjective than journalists.

Palmer and Littler described management as 'invisible heroes' in media reporting of industrial relations. They point out the frequency of reports of trades union and TUC statements which give the workers' views and the apparent absence of employer statements. This is because the employer viewpoint is often presented as an objective one, not requiring attribution. They also noted the emphasis on *symptoms* of disorder and conflict, rather than *causes*.

RACE

Hartman and Husband described how the media helped to create a 'framework for thinking' about race relations. The media did not define the situation in isolation, but within the existing culture, with its imperialist legacy.

They provide some useful data on media effects on schoolchildren, as well as explaining the media output in terms of 'news value'. Race is newsworthy when familiar negative stories can be written about violence and immigration.

Troyna, in a study of press reporting of race in 1974, found different *attitudes* in the *Guardian*, *Times*, *Mirror* and *Express*, but agreement on the *issues*. The agenda comprised immigration control, hostility and discrimination, legislation and Enoch Powell.

GENDER

McRobbie, in a study of the girls' magazine *Jackie*, suggested that the presentation of femininity as attractiveness was tied in to the need to fall in love. The magazine reinforced traditional gender stereotypes with romantic love as the motive force.

Tuchman, in an article based on content analysis, argued that women were 'symbolically annihilated' by the media through their absence, condemnation and trivialisation. Perhaps the most hostile reporting of women came with the Greenham Common story, where the peace issue became an attack on feminism.

Ferguson, in a study of women's magazines, showed the persistence of themes like 'getting your man' and 'self-improvement', but also the change in emphasis over a 25-year period.

DEVIANCE

Ditton and Duffy demonstrated the overreporting of violent and sex crimes. Though only a small proportion of the total extent of crime, they dominate the crime stories in newspapers. This, and the sensationalisation of crime, helped to promote fear of crime.

Hall looked at the role of the media in reinforcing ideological views on law and order. The media helped to promote hegemony when the perceived 'right' of the ruling class to lead was being undermined by economic crisis. The need to be more coercive was legitimised by the combined threats of race, youth and crime.

Cohen explained the role of the media in the amplification of deviance. The alleged seaside 'riots' of the 1960s were, in fact, initially only minor disturbances and they were described as such in local papers. The hostile social reaction, fuelled by the media and their predictions of trouble, helped to increase the levels of perceived and real deviance. (See also Chapters on *Race and ethnicity*, *Deviance*, *Gender*, *Work* and *Power and politics*.)

EXAMINATION QUESTIONS

1   What factors influence the content of 'the news' in the mass media?

(UODLE)

2   Assess the sociological evidence for and against the view that the effects of the mass media vary according to the social characteristics of the audience.

(AEB)

3   How have sociological approaches to the study of the mass media changed over the last forty years?

(AEB)

4   Assess the extent to which the ownership of the mass media can influence the content of the mass media.

(AEB)

5   'The mass media may not tell us what to think, but they do tell us what to think about.' Explain and discuss.

(AEB)

6   a)   What part is played by the mass media in the formation of public opinion in the United Kingdom?   *(13)*

    b)   To what extent does television provide balanced information for citizens?   *(12)*

(*Total 25 marks*)

(SCE)

ANSWERS TO EXAMINATION QUESTIONS

OUTLINE ANSWERS

Question 1

This is a similar question to 4 except for its more narrow focus on 'the news' rather than media output in general. The issue of ownership will, of course, be considered but need not dominate the answer. The concept of 'the news' should be treated as problematic. The framework of the three basic approaches, identified above, can be used, and this offers different interpretations of what is newsworthy.

i)   The 'market' model offers a liberal-democratic view of news reporting. The selection and presentation of real-life objective events is influenced by a combination of consumer wants and professional judgements. Critics provide evidence of interference by owners, and particularly government, and cite examples of bias. Supporters point to the diversity of views and resistance to censorship.

ii)   The 'mass manipulative' view can propose both Marxist views on hegemony and evidence of censorship or even direct control by governments. Marxist approaches tend to assume rather than demonstrate effects, but there is plenty of evidence of interference by governments.

iii)   The interactionist view provides much empirical evidence of bias. The content of the news is seen as the product of both ideological and technical influences. Critics suggest that the bias is frequently in the eye of the beholder. Harrison's critique of the GUMG analysis of the Falklands news reporting is a good illustration.

Question 2

This question requires an emphasis on the diverse nature of audiences in terms of class, gender, ethnicity, age, political viewpoint, educational experience, etc.

    The chronological development of sociological explanations (and their divergence from psychological studies) could be an appropriate framework if each theory or study is evaluated in terms of whether it addresses the issue of a differentiated rather than a mass audience.

    The best answers will evaluate the evidence from theoretical and methodological standpoints as well as the findings.

1   The **hypodermic syringe** and **mass society** models fail to acknowledge the

existence of a diversified audience but do assert that the mass media can affect attitudes and behaviour.

2 The **two-step flow** model argues that the effects on the audience depend on the mediation of opinion leaders in smaller social groups.

3 The **uses and gratification** approach is similar to the market model described above and sees the audience as both discerning and differentiated. Morley's 'Nationwide' study supports this view.

4 The absence of convincing evidence of specific or short-term effects has led sociologists to study the role of the media in the creation and reinforcement of cultural images, norms and values. The critical approaches from Marxists, feminists and interactionists emphasise the ideological role of the media, set it in a broader context of inequality and emphasise the effects on the less powerful.

Question 3

This is a very broad question, where the candidate must provide the focus if a coherent answer is to be developed in 45 minutes. The best answers will trace changes in approaches to the study of the media and try to link them with the development of sociology in general.

i) Early studies influenced by psychology concentrated on assessing the effects of the media on audiences. The attempts to utilise scientific kinds of methods could be linked to the predominance of the positivist paradigm in sociology and behaviourism in psychology. Apart from violence, the effects of TV on political attitudes was a popular issue as TV was becoming the dominant medium.

ii) Cohen and Young edited a selection of studies on the 'Manufacture of News' which were more or less influenced by the rise of the interactionist approach. These studies concentrate on the output of the media, rather than on the effects on the audience. The interest in deviance and social problems is apparent in work on moral panics (seaside riots and mugging), race relations and strikes.

iii) The 'rejuvenation of Marxism' analysis is reflected in media research which concentrates on the issue of the relationship between ownership and output. Often a reference to the media is only a part of more general and critical views of the role of the state in capitalist societies, as found in the work of Althusser, Marcuse, Miliband and Westergaard and Resler.

iv) The influence of *semiology* (the science of signs), popularised by Barthes, can be found in media studies which concentrate on the representation of youth, ethnic groups and women in the media. Stereotyping is often seen as ideological by Marxists and feminists. The choice of women or ethnic minorities in such studies reflects the rising interest in sociology (and in society in general) in such issues.

Question 6

a) A good answer will emphasise the absence of academic consensus on this issue. The advertising and public relations industries are evidence that government, political parties and business all see the media as influential.

i) Hypodermic syringe model: explain and illustrate with a current example.

ii) Two-step flow model: criticise the view of an uncritical mass society and point out the importance of opinion leaders.

iii) Consider Hartman and Husband's view that the media provide a framework for thinking about issues, but do not form attitudes and opinions.

iv) Consider the Goldsmith's media group claim that adverse press reports damaged the support for the Labour Party in 1987.

b) It is worth briefly considering the difference between 'balanced' and 'objective'. Balanced implies allowing more than one view on an issue, whereas objective suggests that reporting could be value free.

This part of the question specifies television and it is likely, but not essential, that news broadcasting will be the major issue. In addition, documentaries, current affairs programmes and drama could also be considered.

i) Studies of the impartiality of the news by Cohen and Young and the GUMG on industrial relations and the Falklands.

ii) Consideration of government interference with news and current affairs, e.g. the arguments over bombing Libya and interviews with the IRA.

iii) Consideration of the way that television drama represents groups or ideas, e.g. race and gender.

TUTOR ANSWER

Question 4

Assess the extent to which the ownership of the mass media can influence the content of the mass media.

There is no single pattern of ownership of the mass media, either internationally or even within the UK. There are, however, recognisable tendencies for concentration into fewer hands. This means corporations do not simply accumulate more newspaper titles but also extend ownership over different kinds of media. Golding and others have documented this process of accumulation, citing the Murdoch and Maxwell multinationals as examples. Obviously any Marxist interpretation of such accumulation is open to criticism, but the pattern of ownership itself is more varied than such an analysis suggests.

The BBC is a public corporation financed by a government-set licence fee and the extent and manner of interference is disputed. Independent TV is currently owned by shareholders who have temporary franchises awarded by publicly responsible bodies and are subject to scrutiny from them. It may be that the conglomerates expand their empires into press, TV and news media, like satellite and cable TV, but new technology and the changing industrial relations situation in the newspaper industry have led to the publishing of new independent titles, such as *The Independent*.

Examination of the content of the media can take various forms. Marxists focus on very general effects on the audience, which is seen as relatively passively soaking up messages which maintain false consciousness. Content of media production is read in this light. Other, equally critical, studies focus on more specific issues, such as industrial relations, race and gender stereotyping or political bias. Cohen and Young, in *The Manufacture of News*, suggested that most analyses of the relationship between ownership, control and production of the media can be seen to fall into three broad categories.

First, the market model, which assumes the working of economic forces in a free market. Owners will seek to maximise profits. The sources of profit include the cover price of the paper, the cost of hiring cable or satellite facilities, and advertising revenue. The content of the media is thus indirectly determined by readers and viewers, as owners and editors seek to maximise audiences (in the case of tabloids and popular TV) or to reach a selective audience (as in the case of quality papers and specialist TV or magazines). Within this model, there is the possibility of editors and journalists satisfying both owners and the public by operating as independent professionals with a commitment to quality and truth. This might be exemplified by Woodward and Bernstein taking on President Nixon. The audience can use market forces to gain their preferences, which are sufficiently varied to ensure that there is a broad spectrum of opinion.

Second, the mass manipulative model, which is predominantly, but not necessarily, Marxist, reverses this causation. Instead of audiences influencing content through owners, the owners influence the audience (which is seen as passive and spongelike) through the content of the media.

Marxist theory would not isolate the particular issue of ownership of the media as being especially important. The owners of the means of production will control the media, whether they are in private or state ownership. Althusser sees the mass media as increasingly important as an ISA, reinforcing ruling-class hegemony. Miliband sees the process of control as more subtle than a simple conspiracy. He identifies four control mechanisms:

1   Direct ownership and control.
2   The use of advertising revenue to determine content.
3   The use of the state to control output openly or covertly.
4   The ideology of the personnel who produce the content. This high-conspiracy view sees control over journalists and editors as implicit. They willingly accept bourgeois ideology or benefit from co-operating, e.g. tame lobby correspondents. Those who dissent can be excluded (journalists had to be approved to accompany the Falklands task force or to be admitted to briefings).

Golding and Murdock saw the Fleet Street papers as opinion-making flagships, which made losses for their conglomerate owners. Now, of course, most are very profitable.

The third model follows an interactionist approach and emphasises the existence of a 'consensual paradigm' which shapes media content. This consensual paradigm is a limited framework for thinking about issues, which is therefore both a cause and an effect of media output. Thus, neither audience nor owners determine the content of the media in isolation, as claimed by the previous explanations. Content reflects the prevailing culture of society. This is seen not as genuinely consensual but as influenced by the powerful. The output also helps create and reinforce this consensual paradigm. Thus selection and presentation are identified as the key processes influencing output, and ownership is only one influence to be considered.

The GUMG emphasise the role of ideology, whereas Cohen and Young see technical influences as also significant. These include decisions about the placing of cameras and the influence of deadlines. The news, then, is 'manufactured' in the sense that it is pre-planned. Hoggart reinforces this theme by talking of four filters through which TV news must pass. These are the effects of time and resources, the news value, the visual value, and the prevailing culture. Again, there is mention of both ideology and practical considerations in the setting of agendas.

A final alternative to these three views is suggested by Tunstall, who sees the influence of media professionals as being of more significance than the other models suggest. He accepts many of the points made in the interactionist view, such as Cohen and Young's view of the importance of periodicity (time scales) and consonance (fitting in with existing views of what is newsworthy). Organisational and professional needs can be divorced from the issue of ownership. However, editors and journalists do get sacked.

STUDENT'S ANSWER WITH EXAMINER COMMENTS

Question 5

'The mass media may not tell us what to think, but they do tell us what to think about.' Explain and discuss.

> Good exam technique; straight into answer.

> Cohen and Young use the term 'consensual' in a critical way.

> Perhaps too much detail for exam. Good conclusion.

> Selection and presentation are key processes.

The interactionist approach argues that the media reflect existing attitudes and values. The content of the media is explained by the wider society, i.e. the prevailing consensus. Hartman and Husband judged the effects of the media on attitudes and the way the audience 'defined the situation' in a study about race relations. They conducted a comparative survey of schoolchildren in areas of both high and low immigration and in schools within these areas with high and low numbers of immigrants. They found that the rate of immigration was perceived as high, rising and threatening. There was little awareness of either the real rate of immigration or immigration controls. In areas with many immigrants competition for jobs and housing was seen as a problem, but in areas with few immigrants riots were seen as a problem. Where the media and not experience was the main source of information then conflict was more likely to be perceived. They conclude that attitudes are neither formed nor changed by the media but the media interact with cultural values to produce a 'framework for thinking' about race relations. The framework may be hostile due to society being hostile because of the imperial legacy and the news value of conflict.

Interactionists argue that the media help to create and reinforce consensual values. Items are selected and presented to conform to these beliefs. Media output is in line with the prevailing consensus and can thus be examined for bias. *Bad News* by the GUMG is a left-wing critique of industrial relations reporting alleged bias against workers. Selection is illustrated by the editing of a speech by Harold Wilson on the economy. The initial news item was restricted to the BL strike and a later item omitted criticism of management. Presentation bias is identified in language, e.g. bosses make 'offers' and workers make 'demands' and usually bosses are in offices whilst workers are on picket lines. The framework here is industrial action as threatening and disruptive, similar to the selection as news of high immigrant birth rates and omission of falling immigration. Reports used words like 'invade' when forty illegal immigrants were found.

" Agenda-setting is a key concept. Sophisticated theory. "

Cohen and Young in *The Manufacture of News* show how much of the news is planned agenda-setting. News does not therefore consist of real-world objective events but is a social construction which tells us what issues to think about.

" Only critics talk of race relations 'industry'. "

The CRE showed that conflict and bad news dominate reporting of race. The race relations industry is seen as composed of villains who discriminate against the white community. Content analysis showed how black unemployment and blacks as victims of crime are not considered newsworthy.

" Not linked directly to question. "

Goldsmith's Media Research Group linked race to anti-left stories in media coverage of the GLC, e.g. *The Sun* reported the banning by Camden council of the word 'sunshine' and *The Star* reported the banning of 'Baa Baa Black Sheep' by Hackney. The reports were fabricated by journalists.

" Good introduction. "

All this research shows how the media form a type of framework of particular issues. But Marxists argue that the media are part of the superstructure reinforcing the existing relations of production (not consensus). Althusser argues that institutions such as the media promote false consciousness through ISAs rather than coerce the working class.

Cohen and Young argue that 'the Manufacture of News is largely an elitist endeavour', i.e. for the purposes of the bourgeoisie to control and tell the masses what to think about. The output promotes false consciousness which therefore demonstrates who controls it and therefore sets limits on thought by (a) lies and distortions in the news (b) the opium of the masses (c) creation of false needs as argued by Marcuse. The bourgeoisie replace the chains of iron with chains of gold.

" Not entirely clear, but good points. "

Miliband argues that because of the function the mass media play in this economic and political context they can only affirm and not challenge existing patterns of power and privilege. Therefore they are an instrument in the hands of the ruling class.

" Good conclusion. "

The Marxist account argues, unlike the interactionists, that it is the ruling class, not consensual values of society, that tell us what to think about.

Overall comments

Overall, a thorough and conceptually sophisticated answer. Occasionally material is not made explicitly relevant. Not enough on the difference between 'what to think' and 'what to think about'. Hartman and Husband do illustrate just this point, as do some modern Marxists.

There are of course studies on attitude formation and change which are neither Marxist nor interactionist. This is worth a B grade.

A Review Sheet for this chapter may be found on p. 256.

GETTING STARTED

Many sociologists regard the study of poverty and the poor as part of the more general issue of social inequality. However, there is a long tradition, going back to the last century, of regarding poverty as a distinct area for research. The study of poverty frequently includes the relationship between social policy and deprivation; indeed, a discussion of the effects of the Welfare State remains central to both sociological and political debates. It is important to remember that the study of poverty is invariably an ideological activity, with the values of researchers being influential in determining the ways in which poverty is defined, measured and explained.

The main themes of questions set on this topic are:

1 **The problems of defining poverty.**
2 **Evaluating sociological explanations of poverty.**
3 **Examining solutions to poverty.**
4 **Discussing the roles and effectiveness of the state, community, voluntary organisations, the family and private sector in the provision of welfare.**
5 **Explaining the distribution of income and wealth and examining the impact of taxes and benefits on the rich and the poor.**

Definitions

Poverty does not have a generally accepted sociological definition. Rather, a variety of alternative definitions exist.

- *Absolute poverty* means lacking the basic necessities of life. Health and even life itself are threatened.

- *Relative poverty* exists when people earn so much less than average pay that they are unable to participate in what have come to be regarded as ordinary living patterns.

- *Subjective poverty* is the feeling of being left out of everyday life because of lack of money.

- *The culture of poverty* is a set of values, norms and behaviour patterns which distinguishes the poor from the rest of society.

- *The Welfare State* describes government intervention in society to deal with social problems and provide social services for all. The main services are health, education, social security and housing. Left-wing sociologists would include a wider range of governmental activities which are seen as benefiting the richer more than the poorer.

- *Social problems* are issues of public concern. Sociologists have conflicting views on who defines social problems. They may be objectively defined or socially constructed.

- *Sociological problems* are questions which sociologists wish to explain.

- *Social policy* is the ideology which underlies the management of social institutions in order to achieve particular societal goals. The most discussed aspects of social policy include state/health education and welfare provision.

Related topics include *stratification*, *age* and *health*.

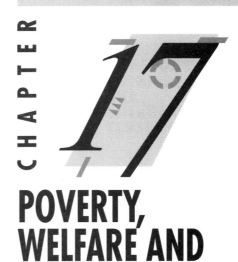

CHAPTER 17

POVERTY, WELFARE AND SOCIAL POLICY

THE PROBLEMS OF DEFINING AND MEASURING POVERTY

EXPLANATIONS OF POVERTY

THE CULTURE OF POVERTY

THE WELFARE STATE

SOCIOLOGICAL APPROACHES TO SOCIAL POLICY AND THE WELFARE STATE

WELFARE STATE AND INEQUALITY

ESSENTIAL PRINCIPLES

Defining poverty is a political as well as a sociological problem. Both definitions and explanations of poverty often reflect the ideological views of writers.

ABSOLUTE POVERTY

Rowntree tried to define poverty in a scientific way by calculating a poverty line based on the minimum income necessary to maintain a healthy life. This method involves selecting a 'shopping basket' of necessities such as food, clothing and housing, and calculating the family income required to buy it. He distinguished *primary poverty*, caused by low income, from *secondary poverty*, caused by spending unwisely.

Rowntree also discovered the *cycle of poverty*, which demonstrated how people could move in and out of poverty during their lifetime as their income and commitments changed.

Criticisms of absolute definitions include:

1   Deciding what is a necessity is problematic. There is no universally accepted list. The distinction between necessities and luxuries is historically and culturally specific. For example, in rural areas and other areas not served by public transport you might need a car to work and shop. Even the 'necessary' intake of food, in terms of calorific and nutrient values, depends on occupation or age.
2   It may be that the poor, even if they do have the minimum income required, will lack the opportunity and understanding to spend as the experts recommend. This has led some sociologists to argue that there is a 'culture' of poverty.
3   Basic needs change. Longer life expectancy and smaller families increasingly mean that people have to provide for their own old age. In fact the reduction in the real value of most state provision has led to the need for 'defensive spending' to protect families against ill health, unemployment and even crime. The cost of maintaining children in higher education has also shifted substantially from the state to the family.

RELATIVE POVERTY

Here the poverty line is estimated by listing not just what is required for subsistence but in addition what is needed to take part in everyday life. Townsend produced his own list of items which he said were necessities. In 1954 this included newspapers but not contraceptives. By 1979 his list had twelve items covering diet, social activities and housing.

Mack and Lansley (1985) did a sample survey asking the public which of a list of 35 items they regarded as necessary for a minimum acceptable standard of living, not just survival or subsistence. They calculated the numbers of the poor and the depth of their poverty by identifying those who lacked a number of the 26 items that most of the subjects in the survey regarded as 'necessities'. They found, using this measure, that 22% of the population were on the margins of poverty and 5% in intense poverty.

The problems with this approach include:

1   Ensuring that those who lack items do so through lack of means rather than by choice. For example, people may not eat meat for cultural or ethical reasons.
2   Being aware that what is seen as a need may change, so lists must be updated regularly.

OTHER MEASURES OF POVERTY

Another way of calculating relative poverty is to look at changes in the distributions of income and wealth in the country. This can produce a variety of indicators of the nature and extent of poverty:

1   *The real income of the poor.* Townsend (1991), using the Government's own figures, claimed that from 1979 to 1989 the income of the poorest 20% *fell* by 4.6% while the income of the richest 20% *rose* by 40%.
2   *Comparisons with average earnings*:
    ■ Piachaud (1991) calculated that the income of a married claimant of unemployment benefit had fallen from 35% of average earnings in 1979 to 27% in 1990.
    ■ J. Williams (1992) showed how the proportion of individuals with below half

average income had increased from 10% of the population in 1979 to 20% in 1990. An income below half of average income has increasingly become the way in which the Government has defined the poor, although it does not state an official poverty line.

In a practical sense the level of income at which *income support* begins dictates the Government's view of a poverty line. The outcome of the political debate as to whether there should be a minimum wage and at what level it should be will also contribute to an understanding of the Government's view on what constitutes the poverty line.

EXPLANATIONS OF POVERTY

The first three explanations suggest that poverty is not just lack of money but may be a situation caused or perpetuated by the poor themselves. These cultural explanations are often associated with the political right.

The later explanations concentrate on structural causes and tend to emphasise inequality as a major cause of poverty. They tend to be favoured by the political left.

BLAME IT ON THE POOR

Poverty has been seen as the deserved result of weakness or wickedness. In Victorian Britain the poor were criticised for having large families and for spending their money unwisely, particularly on alcohol.

The tabloid press still tell us about 'scroungers' who neither need nor deserve benefits. Those in rich countries often perceive Third World poverty in these terms.

The *solution* was seen as encouraging the poor to behave better through schools and churches. Missionaries did not only travel all over the world, they also ventured into the 'uncivilised' inner cities.

Critics of Spencer's view of the dissolute poor emerged during the nineteenth century. Rowntree, for example, identified poverty among families in York, where the head of the house was in full-time work.

THE UNFORTUNATE POOR

After the Second World War it was widely thought that the problem of poverty was disappearing, for the following reasons:

- The expansion of the Welfare State.
- Economic growth bringing higher wages.
- Full employment.

The few who were still recognised as poor were seen as special individual cases, such as the old, sick or disabled.

The *solution* was seen as improved benefits for all, or at least the needy.

Critics point out that by the 1960s poverty had been rediscovered among the low-paid. Indeed, since the 1980s full employment has not been seen as a realistic political aim, suggesting that the unemployed poor will become, and remain, a substantial number and a long-term feature within society.

THE CULTURE OF POVERTY

Some explanations suggest that poverty is not just lack of money and imply that the poor are *different* from the rest of society.

Oscar Lewis pioneered this view in studies of the way of life of the poor in Latin America. He saw the poor as sharing a distinctive set of attitudes and behaviours. They were said to feel helpless, dependent, inferior and living for today rather than planning for the future. Families were often headed by single mothers, and the poor did not participate in organisations like political parties and trades unions.

This distinctive culture has been associated with the idea that there is a poor underclass (see below). In the USA it has been used to explain the disproportionate number of the poor who are members of minority groups.

There are different views on the relationship between this culture and living in poverty. The alternatives include:

1 Culture (seen as inferior) causes poverty.
2 Poverty causes (an inferior) culture which maintains poverty (O. Lewis).

3   Poverty causes (a positive adaptive) culture which helps the poor survive (C. and B. Valentine).

This third viewpoint does not blame poverty on the poor. Neither does Gans' view, which suggests that it is the culture of the non-poor which encourages the inequality that helps to maintain poverty.

The *solution* would be to change the culture rather than give the poor higher benefits. In the USA there were educational initiatives in the 1960s 'war on poverty' which tried to help children escape from the cycle of poverty; here low income was seen as limiting the opportunities for educational success.

Critical views

1   May question the very existence of a distinct culture.
2   May suggest that values and behaviour are the result, not the cause, of poverty.
3   May point to other, usually structural, causes.
4   May see the whole concept of a culture of poverty as an ideological device to blame poverty on the poor.

SITUATIONAL CONSTRAINTS

Critics of the cultural explanations claim that it is primarily economic conditions which limit the opportunities of the poor. Low pay, high unemployment and racial disadvantage all prevent the poor from improving their position.

The *solution* would require increasing opportunities for people to acquire adequately paid jobs. Minimum wages might be considered. Racial discrimination in the workplace and in appointment outcomes could be tackled, and improved childcare made available for single parents.

THE FAILURE OF THE WELFARE STATE

Critics of the Welfare State with left-wing views such as Westergaard and Resler, and Kincaid, assert that if the aim of the Welfare State is to redistribute incomes from the rich to the poor, it has had very limited success. The level of benefits is seen here as inadequate, with some of the poor not even entitled to benefits. *Critics* include some New Right sociologists who claim that poverty is perpetuated by making the poor dependent on benefits.

The *solution* would be to ensure that benefit levels are adequate either by raising them for all or by targeting them on the very poor. Alternatively, policies could be directed towards attacking the inequality which is seen as the real cause of poverty.

Another solution would be to ensure that benefits do not exceed possible earnings and to make people work for benefits. This is called 'Workfare'.

WEBERIAN-INFLUENCED ACCOUNTS: THE POWERLESSNESS OF THE POOR

The poor may be weak not just because of their lack of money but also because they lack the power which comes through membership of organisations such as political parties, pressure groups or trades unions. Vulnerable groups may include the old, the young, women, the sick and people with disabilities.

Rex applied this Weberian analysis to ethnic minorities and immigrants, emphasising their weak position in the markets for work, education and housing (see Chapter 4 on *Race and ethnicity*). The *solution* would be for the poor, perhaps with the help of others, to acquire more power. Recruitment drives to encourage the poor to join organisations and even to register for the vote (join the electoral register) might be considered here.

MARXIST-INFLUENCED ACCOUNTS

Poverty is seen as the inevitable result of the inequality arising from the exploitation of the working class in capitalist societies. The poor and the unemployed have a 'warning effect' on those in the working class who are in work and relatively well paid. They are a reserve army of labour.

The *solution* here would be seen as the end of exploitation and the redistribution of income following the revolutionary overthrow of capitalism (Miliband, Kincaid, Westergaard and Resler).

Critics argue that the poor are a distinct group in society, not just those at the bottom of a homogeneous working class. Weberians see them as distinctive in terms of being disadvantaged in the distribution of power; cultural explanations emphasise the distinctive behaviour of the poor.

WOMEN AND POVERTY

Feminists have argued that women are particularly vulnerable to poverty. Women are seen as a distinctive group in the labour market(s). They often work part-time and tend to do 'women's jobs', which are frequently low-paid. Marriage and motherhood may make women dependent on men or, in many cases, on the state.

The *solution* is for women to have equal opportunities in finding well-paid work. More equality within marriage, better childcare facilities and more flexible working hours would help to achieve this.

A *critical alternative* to feminist accounts of women's poverty comes from New Right sociologists who have spoken of single mothers being 'married to the state'. Those in the New Right might thereby seek to discourage single parenthood.

THE NEW RIGHT

The American author C. Murray (1984 and 1990) suggested that the poor, found largely in the inner-city areas, are to blame for their poverty and are mainly poor by choice. The culture of poverty is passed on to children who are influenced by their immediate neighbourhood, especially by inappropriate role models such as relatively successful criminals, and by widespread welfare provision which creates dependence. This underclass is characterised by the unwillingness of the young to work, criminality and broken families. Members of the underclass are seen as a threat to the rest of society and are often identified with the ethnic minorities.

British politicians, the media or sociologists of this persuasion tend to emphasise ethnicity less but share the views on welfare dependence. This is a revival of those versions of the 'culture of poverty' argument which blame poverty on the poor and seek to limit, rather than improve, welfare benefits.

Critics are convinced that the existence of an underclass which shuns work has been asserted rather than just demonstrated. Poverty exists among those whom the New Right do not wish to stigmatise, such as the old and those with disabilities who are unable rather than unwilling to work.

Rising unemployment is not an individual matter but the result of national and international economic changes which have little to do with the particular individuals or groups who lose their jobs.

THE WELFARE STATE

WHAT IS THE WELFARE STATE?

In the Welfare State the Government uses its power to modify market forces, adopting one or more of the following strategies:

1   Ensuring a minimum family income, whether people work or not.
2   Tackling the effects of problems such as sickness, retirement and unemployment.
3   Offering good services to all, irrespective of class, race or gender.

Early attempts to provide for the disadvantaged have included workhouses for the poor (described in *Oliver Twist* by Charles Dickens) and old age pensions, introduced in 1908. However, the Welfare State in the UK is generally seen as dating from the Beveridge Report of 1942, which laid down a number of key principles. The various post-war Acts which came into force in 1948 put some of these principles into practice.

Beveridge wrote that the state should battle with the 'five giant evils' which included physical want itself and the four other evils which contributed to physical want. The five evils he named were:

■ Poverty.

■ Disease.

■ Squalor.

■ Ignorance.

■ Idleness.

Most current social policy and administration can be seen as aimed at dealing with one or more of these evils. Conventionally the Welfare State includes social security, the NHS, housing aid, education and personal social services provided by social workers. Left-wing sociologists would also wish to include tax allowances, occupational pensions, sick pay and all government economic policy affecting employment and wages, as part of welfare policy. At present many of these seem to benefit the well-off in addition to the poor.

SOCIOLOGICAL APPROACHES TO SOCIAL POLICY AND THE WELFARE STATE

SOCIAL DEMOCRATIC REFORMIST SOCIAL POLICY

This has been proposed by many social democratically inclined British sociologists. They include T. H. Marshall and R. Titmus, writing in the early days of the post-war Welfare State, and P. Townsend, who has been influential in discussions on poverty, welfare and health issues for the last 30 years. Such writers have suggested that the Welfare State is, at least potentially, the solution to poverty by providing a safety net for those who are temporarily or permanently unable to support themselves. They believe that all citizens have a right to basic levels of welfare provision including education, health services and pensions, and that these should be universally provided.

Critics

1   The market liberals from the New Right are critical of the increasing cost of providing universal welfare benefits, the alleged unfairness of supporting 'scroungers' and the debilitating effect which state support is thought to have on its recipients, i.e. the creation of a culture of dependency.
2   Marxists see the gains as an illusion (see below).
3   Feminists see the existing structure of the Welfare State as perpetuating the subjugation of women (see below).

Even those sympathetic to the aims of universal provision are concerned about the increasing costs resulting from the perceived failure of government economic management to maintain full employment. Such concerns are reinforced by the increasing costs of providing medical care for an ageing population, and of fewer people in work supporting more people in retirement through universal pension entitlements.

THE FUNCTIONALIST APPROACH

Functionalism has generally presented a sympathetic view towards the development of the Welfare State. This may surprise those who associate functionalism (particularly American functionalism) with the political right. Functionalists since Durkheim have expressed concern about the threats to social solidarity resulting from the division of labour, industrialisation and urbanisation. Parsons and Smelser see the possibility of state-provided welfare systems as *integrating* such societies. This is also a theme in some of the work of the British Social Democratic writers mentioned above.

Critics

1   Conflict theorists question the extent to which modern societies are integrated.
2   New Right critics point to the adverse fiscal effects of government spending and also the detrimental effects of welfare dependency.

MARXISTS

Marxists see the Welfare State either as an illusion which fails to redistribute income or as a successful safety valve to dampen down protest and maintain 'false consciousness'. The Marxist view of the state (p. 64) emphasises its role in *legitimising capitalism*. However, if other sources of legitimacy can be found to gain the support of the working class, then the Welfare State can be reduced. This is the explanation some contemporary Marxists have given for the apparent public acceptance of the aim of reducing welfare spending proposed by Conservative governments since 1979.

The *new legitimacy* comes from:

■ Increasing home ownership following council house sales.
■ Wider share ownership following privatisation of publicly owned businesses.
■ The increased commitment to consumerism.

■ The working class having been more or less successful in their struggle for concessions from employers. These gains include the setting up of the Welfare State itself.

THE MARKET LIBERALS OR THE NEW RIGHT

These thinkers see the Welfare State as perpetuating poverty by keeping the poor dependent and removing the incentive to improve their situation. They often point to unemployment and poverty 'traps', whereby the benefit/tax system penalises those trying to improve their circumstances. The withdrawal of benefit from and imposition of tax on the low-paid as their incomes increase are seen as a major disincentive to effort. The solutions advocated by the market liberals often involve curtailment of benefit provision. They do not see the redistribution of income and wealth as a legitimate goal for the state. Where the continued existence of welfare services is accepted, it is argued that the discipline of the market will help to provide better-quality services at lower cost.

Market forces have been brought into public services in a variety of ways:

■ Open enrolment and some managerial independence for schools and colleges. The introduction of vouchers for nursery and post-16 training.

■ The internal market in the NHS where, for example, hospitals compete with each other to provide surgery and care. The encouragement of private health provision and GP fundholding.

■ Local authorities putting out some services to competitive tender by private suppliers and using private old people's homes, etc.

Critics

The Social Democrats argue that the free market itself generates problems for the disadvantaged and invariably fails to deal with them.

FEMINISTS

Feminists tend to be critical not so much of the principle of the Welfare State as of its administration. The system of taxation benefits is seen as supporting a family household which maintains patriarchy (see *Gender*, Chapter 5). This family structure is seen by Marxist-feminists as reproducing labour power and providing capitalism with a reserve army of labour (RAL). However, there have been some attempts to support women's interests, such as the introduction of child benefit paid directly to mothers and tax allowances on childcare costs for working mothers.

Critics include other feminists who have challenged the view of women as an RAL. They argue that men and women often do not compete for the same jobs, as the labour market is largely segmented by gender. Also, it is women who are increasingly working, as unemployment rates are growing faster for men.

WELFARE STATE AND INEQUALITY

To what extent does the Welfare State reduce inequality and, in particular, redistribute resources between rich and poor? This is not entirely a factual question. As we have seen, there are different ideological viewpoints on this:

WHAT IS INEQUALITY?

When we considered stratification in Chapter 3, *Social class*, it was suggested that inequality could be measured using three dimensions:

1   The distribution of rewards, e.g. income, wealth and power.
2   Opportunity, i.e. access to rewarded positions (life chances).
3   Subjective measures, e.g. the experience of deprivation.

We can now examine how the system of taxation and benefits influences inequality.

TAXATION

■ *Progressive taxes* redistribute income, e.g. different rates of income tax, with the richer paying a higher proportion of their incomes in tax.

■ *Neutral taxes* affect people equally by taking the same proportion of the incomes of rich and poor.

- *Regressive taxes* favour the better-off by taking a smaller proportion of their incomes, e.g. a ceiling on National Insurance contributions for all earnings over a particular level.
- *Direct taxes* are charged on income and are usually progressive, e.g. income tax.
- *Indirect taxes* are charged on spending and are usually regressive, e.g. VAT on buying certain goods and services means that both rich and poor pay the same absolute amount of tax.

Since 1979 the overall burden of tax has increased slightly but shifted from direct to indirect taxes. The rich have benefited, particularly from a lowering of direct rates of tax. All governments tend to increase taxation, but the Conservatives are particularly committed to low marginal direct tax rates, which they see as encouraging enterprise. Preferential tax treatment for performance-related pay serves the same purpose. Wealth is not effectively taxed, and the distribution of wealth is much more unequal than the distribution of income.

BENEFITS

1   Many benefits have increased in value, but not relative to earnings. The UK spends less on social security as a proportion of GNP than other EU countries, but slightly more than the USA. It is nevertheless now the biggest item of public expenditure, whereas in the past it was exceeded by defence and education. Social security spending has increased at a fairly constant rate since the 1950s, irrespective of which party has been in power. In fact the highest rate of increase was between 1979 and 1984 because of dramatic increases in the numbers of unemployed. The Conservatives do, however, spend much less on subsidising housing than governments prior to 1979.
2   Tax allowances on private health, education and housing spending all favour the better-off. Other sources of private welfare, such as occupational pensions and sick pay, are also tax-allowable for employers.
3   The poor may not take up benefits because of ignorance or pride. There may be administration problems in claiming benefits for some of the most needy, for example the homeless.
4   Some groups have ceased to be eligible for particular benefits. For example, entitlement to unemployment benefit has been removed from the under-18s, and full-time students can no longer claim housing benefits or maintenance benefits during holiday periods.
5   Some benefits are *targeted* on those who can demonstrate need, usually through a means test of income and assets, e.g. family credit. Other benefits are *universal*, e.g. child benefit, old age pensions and access to the NHS. Expenditure on roads and subsidies on items such as rail fares and the opera benefit those who are better off.

CONCLUSIONS

1   Even before 1979, Townsend claimed that, 'The richest 20% of the population gained nearly four times as much from the social services as the poorest 20% ... particularly via education and housing benefit.'
2   Westergaard and Resler argue that any redistributive effect is *within* rather than *between* the classes. The healthy, working, better-paid lower classes pay for the sick, unemployed and dependent lower classes. The family life cycle influences whether you pay or receive. For example, families with dependent children or the retired are more likely to receive benefits than families without dependent children.
3   Residual models of poverty suggest that the poor are special cases, and support selective help through means-tested benefits. Politicians refer to this as targeting benefits. Marsland has supported this view that universal benefits are wasteful and encourage a dependency culture. Conversely, Jordan argues that universal benefits allow the poor to seek work without the disincentive of losing all benefits and thus being worse off. Structural models of poverty see it as the result of inequality. They suggest a major redistribution of rewards or foresee revolution by the disadvantaged as a real possibility.
4   Gans suggested that welfare professionals are some of the major beneficiaries of the Welfare State through their salaries. This view is also shared by New Right writers such as Marsland.
5   The problems of quantifying the number of the poor and their condition remains,

partly because of disagreement over definitions. The real income of the poor has risen since the Second World War (not every year), but they are now relatively worse off compared to average earnings.

EXAMINATION QUESTIONS

1 Assess the argument that different definitions and explanations of poverty reflect different ideologies.

(AEB)

2 'The provision of universal welfare benefits is responsible for the continued existence of poverty.' Evaluate the arguments for and against this statement.

(AEB)

3 'Despite many sociological studies on poverty, it is still not possible to define a "poverty line" which will be supported by all.' Critically examine the arguments for and against this view.

(AEB)

4 Assess the view that official statistics misrepresent both the nature and extent of poverty in the United Kingdom.

(AEB)

5 The claim that 'the poor are themselves to blame for their poverty' is a feature of some explanations of poverty. Critically examine the sociological arguments for and against this statement.

(AEB)

ANSWERS TO EXAMINATION QUESTIONS

OUTLINE ANSWERS
Question 3

This question requires the candidate to demonstrate an understanding of different definitions of poverty and of ways of measuring it. You should mention:

- Absolute definitions of poverty, e.g. Rowntree.
- Relative definitions of poverty, e.g. Townsend.

Perhaps also consider subjective definitions of poverty.

Even where there is some agreement on the definition of poverty used, there is still some debate about setting the poverty line. For example, Mack and Lansley were dissatisfied with the measurements used by Townsend, though they share his view that poverty must be defined in relative terms.

Governments may change the poverty line for economic or electoral reasons, or they may refuse to define a poverty line at all. The definition of poverty by both politicians and sociologists is influenced by ideological considerations.

Question 4

This question may begin to be a little out of date, as John Major's Government seems reluctant to publish poverty statistics at all! Townsend criticised the discontinuation of the publication of health statistics by social class. Candidates need to deal with the following:

1 The *meaning* of poverty, i.e. different definitions of poverty and also the changing nature of poverty.
2 The *extent* of poverty. This depends largely on how it is defined and where the poverty line is drawn. (If indeed a poverty line is recognised.)

The ideological influences on the statistics can be considered (see Question 1). The implications of the acknowledged extent of poverty for social welfare policy could be explored.

A discussion of the validity and reliability of official statistics can be found in *Suicide and official statistics*, Chapter 20.

Question 5

This question can be answered by assessing the various theories after clarifying whether they support or reject the proposition in the question. Most sociological explanations of poverty can be fairly easily divided into those that blame the poor and those that examine socially structured inequality.

Generally, cultural theories are more likely to blame the poor. However, this was not the intention of Lewis, although he is often seen in this light. Similarly, New Right theorists may see themselves as critical of the Welfare State rather than the poor.

STUDENT'S ANSWERS WITH EXAMINER COMMENTS

Question 1

Assess the argument that different definitions and explanations of poverty reflect different ideologies.

> **Appropriate introduction.**

> **The start of a systematic review of ideologies.**

There are different definitions and explanations of poverty. Absolute poverty means living below a subsistence level of income. Deciding the definition of the minimum income may depend on the political beliefs or ideology of the person who fixes it. Relative poverty involves defining poverty in relation to average income.

Marxists see poverty as the result of the class inequality which is inevitable in capitalist societies. Marxists define class in terms of ownership. The owners' need for profit leads to the exploitation of the workers, who do not receive the value of what they produce. The contradictions of capitalism produce a constant pressure to reduce wages to maintain profits; this increases inequality and poverty. The poor act as a reserve army of labour. Miliband wrote about poverty in modern Britain and argued that the only solution was a restructuring of society based on social, not private, ownership and the production of goods for their social value, not for profit. The Marxist approach supports the view in the question that explanations of poverty reflect the ideology of the authors.

> **Good critical comments.**

> **Useful contrast for Marxists.**

However, the New Right see poverty in terms of culture rather than inequality. Their ideological view discounts structural explanations of inequality and thus of poverty. Murray, without offering much evidence, blamed the poor for their poverty. He accused the poor of being idle hedonists who live for the moment. His view was criticised by F. Field, who said that most people want to work. Some critics have argued that the dependency culture is the effect, not the cause, of poverty. People without jobs or on low pay feel deprived and apathetic. The ideology of the New Right is evident in their arguments, which blame the victims. Critics point out that the poor are not a separate group with a distinctive culture: many people move in and out of poverty during their life cycle, often ending up poor when they are old.

> **Again relevant critical comments.**

> **Useful evaluation.**

Functionalists also have a conservative ideology. Their explanations of poverty tend to justify inequality, which ensures that all necessary jobs get done. The poor and those just above the poverty line strive to do better. These ideas are developed from the functionalist theory of stratification. Tumin sees stratification as dysfunctional because it limits opportunity. Functionalism is ideologically conservative because it justifies the status quo.

The Social Democrats' explanation of poverty reflects their reformist ideology. They explain poverty in structural rather than cultural terms. Poverty is maintained by situational constraints, not by the laziness of the poor. Their ideas are supported by the view of a cycle of deprivation and poverty. Poverty leads to bad housing, which leads to ill health and absence from school. Educational failure leads to low-paid work or no work, and the probability of continued poverty. Whereas the New Right want to cut benefits, the Social Democrats want to improve the Welfare State.

> **Could have gone further here.**

In conclusion, it seems that definitions and explanations of poverty do reflect different ideologies and political goals. Like all sociology, they reflect the values of the sociologist. Sociology cannot be value free.

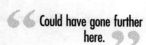

Overall comments

This answer includes material on both definitions and explanations of poverty. The student shows knowledge and understanding of a variety of sociological theories and is able to apply these to the question. The structure of the answer is rather list-like, but sections are often linked by critical comments. The issue of ideology is explicitly, though briefly, addressed. Evaluation was present both as specific points and in a critical framework which favoured Social Democrat and Marxist views. Overall this answer achieves a good A-level standard, perhaps on the A/B borderline.

Question 2

'The provision of universal welfare benefits is responsible for the continued existence of poverty.' Evaluate the arguments for and against this statement.

> **Good reference to question.**

It was not until the Beveridge Report and the introduction of the modern Welfare State in the 1940s that benefits were made available by the state. However, there are studies which show that poverty was a part of our society long before this. Thus it is a very important point against the claim in the question, as poverty continued to exist in our society in the past, even when benefits were not available.

In the light of this, then, we can say that poverty has existed in our society for many years and that 'the continued existence of poverty' should be studied with this in mind.

> **Relevant critical approach.**

Another criticism of the view expressed in the question comes from the Weberian view which maintains that the Welfare State is important for those in poverty as a form of 'protection' for the 'weak'. This is, to an extent, quite true because it provides a safeguard against the low status/power of the poor. Certainly, the poor are among the weakest groups who lack access to power and are non-union/low-paid workers. Here benefits may enable them to live 'normally' by providing income.

> **Good use of knowledge and understanding.**

Even from the functionalist perspective the Welfare State is seen as a 'safety net' to catch those unable to look after themselves. This is further supported by studies which define poverty in an absolute way. From these we can see improved living standards and diets for most people, suggesting that the Welfare State has actually helped those in poverty. Thus it can be argued that the Welfare State, rather than causing the continued existence of poverty, has allowed those who are most susceptible to poverty to live above the levels of destitution.

Moreover, those who are actually in poverty may not feel subjectively so because welfare benefits provide opportunities (even though they are limited) for those on benefits to live according to the social norm.

> **Again good critical approach.**

Also, from the Marxist perspective, poverty is an inevitable feature of capitalist societies and so welfare benefits are not the reason why poverty persists but, rather, the fact that the whole society operates in meeting ruling-class requirements. Similarly, feminists would argue that because of the patriarchal structure of our society poverty persists.

On the other hand there is also a considerable level of support for the view offered by the question.

First those from the New Right suggest that welfare benefits promote dependency among those in poverty and in turn the culture of poverty is maintained.

> **Good reference back to question.**

Major New Right theorists such as Murray and Marsland have talked about the laziness and unwillingness to work among people in low economic classes. They say that benefits make those in poverty dependent. Therefore we can see some agreement with the claim in the question from the New Right perspective.

> **Good use of studies.**

Furthermore, studies such as those by Coates and Silburn say that poverty is the result of a range of factors including poor housing, poor opportunities, poor education, and so on. Thus money, or rather lack of it, is not the only factor in causing poverty. Instead poverty is seen as a deep-rooted and complex problem. At this stage it seems that the provision of welfare benefits, according to this view, doesn't necessarily reduce the level of poverty.

However, we can apply this by bringing in the issue that those on benefits are often stigmatised by the rest of society. This may in turn lead to a feeling of inadequacy, etc., among the poor, perpetuating a culture of poverty which in effect becomes a self-fulfilling prophecy whereby those in poverty become trapped in a vicious circle of poverty in both cultural and material terms. In this sense, then, it can be said that the claim put forward in the question does indeed have some truth attached to it.

From another light we can look at research which points to the social facts that the rich benefit more from the Welfare State than society as a whole. Townsend, in 1991, claimed that from 1979 to 1989 the income of the poorest 20% fell while the income of the richest 20% rose. ('The Services'.) Westergaard and Resler also argue that any redistributive effect is within rather than between classes.

Here, then, we may say that because some welfare benefits such as child benefit are universal, even those who are not 'needy' receive money from the Welfare State, and so there is not a 'fair' system of redistribution. In turn it can be argued that those who really need the additional income are deprived of their entitlement by money going to those who do not really need it. Thus we can say that this is a major cause of poverty.

Overall, then, it is an extremely difficult task to come to a single decision about the view expressed in the question. Varying and conflicting evidence and theories are relevant, each supporting a different perspective. However, I feel that generally welfare benefits, although not always adequate, are helpful in reducing poverty by providing the poor with means to live above the level of destitution.

Overall comments

This is clearly a Grade A answer. It is particularly strong on interpretation and application. This is not just a general answer on poverty and/or the Welfare State which the candidate prepared before the examination. The candidate really does attempt to address the set question. The answer could have been improved by more emphasis on 'universal benefits' rather than the Welfare State in general. The candidate's knowledge and understanding of theories is stronger than his/her knowledge of studies but it would be difficult to include much more under examination conditions.

A Review Sheet for this chapter may be found on p. 256.

HEALTH

GETTING STARTED

This relatively new topic is a useful vehicle to discuss broader issues in sociology, such as theories, approaches and methods. It makes a refreshing change from suicide and crime in the critical discussion of positivism and the use of official statistics. It is also a good topic to use to illustrate interactionist theory and provides material to discuss social policy issues.

The main themes of questions set on this topic are:

1   **The social definition and construction of health.**
2   **The social distribution of health chances and health care by class, age, gender, ethnicity and region.**
3   **Relationships between doctors and patients.**
4   **The development and effectiveness of health care by the NHS, private sector, community and family.**

Most questions focus on the social distribution of health, but it is wise in any question to treat health and related concepts as problematic. The best answers do not rely on journalistic accounts of inequality or even on the amassing of sociological research studies, but instead apply and evaluate sociological approaches.

Related areas include:

1   The *professions*; particularly doctors but also nurses.
2   *Poverty* and the *Welfare State.*
3   *Deviance* and *suicide* are studied in similar ways, and *mental illness* in particular links them to the study of health.
4   *Class, age, gender* and *development* are all related to the *social distribution* question.
5   *Sociological theory* and *methods.*

Definitions

Definitions are problematic and are often a critical issue in questions.

■   *Disease* is a pathological abnormality with an objective biological cause (you have a disease).

■   *Illness* is a patient's subjective response to real or imagined disease. It involves the experience of pain, discomfort or abnormality (you feel ill). Disease and illness need not coincide.

■   *Health* can be defined as the absence of sickness (either disease or illness), or in a more positive way as a sense of well-being. Good health is falsely assumed to be normal, in fact a 1978 survey indicated the reverse: that health problems were normal.

THE TRADITIONAL MEDICAL MODEL

POSITIVIST APPROACHES

INTERACTIONIST APPROACHES

CONFLICT APPROACHES

FUNCTIONALIST APPROACHES

THEORETICAL AND EMPIRICAL STUDIES

INEQUALITIES IN HEALTH CARE

GENDER AND HEALTH

MENTAL ILLNESS

ESSENTIAL PRINCIPLES

The sociology of health can be simplified by regarding it as a series of familiar sociological approaches applied to a range of sociological issues.

The issues include:

1   The definition of health.
2   The social distribution of health chances and health care.
3   The role of health professionals and others who care for the sick.
4   The effectiveness of the NHS.

The approaches to be considered are:

1   The traditional medical model.
2   Positivist.
3   Interactionist.
4   Conflict.
5   Functionalist.

THE TRADITIONAL MEDICAL MODEL

This non-sociological approach has been the basis of the public's commonsense view of health and health care for some time, although it is increasingly challenged as lay experts and the general public become better informed or more critical of experts.

Disease is seen as the cause of ill health and disease is often equated with external attacks on the body by micro-organisms, i.e. bacteria and viruses. Good health is perceived as normal and ill health as an objective state producing predictable illness behaviour in individuals who are seen as either unfortunate or perhaps inadequate. This moral dimension of 'getting sick' is treated somewhat differently by the functionalists below, but in this approach getting sick can be seen as the result of choosing a bad diet, smoking, poor personal hygiene or sexual misdemeanours.

Medicine is seen as treating individual symptoms in a professional and rational way and advances in health as depending on finding cures.

POSITIVIST APPROACHES

The major difference between this and the non-sociological approach above is the view that ill health can have social, rather than purely individual, causes. Thus the emphasis is on the comparative method to identify social and economic patterns of ill health. These approaches are strongly influenced by Durkheim's *Suicide*. Definitions of health and sickness are seen as objective and tend to be taken for granted. Studies seek to establish the biological or social causes of disease. Health statistics are seen as a useful source of data. Explanations of the inequalities in health revealed by positivist research involve either examining the different lifestyles of the rich and poor or examining differences in the availability of health care. Conflict theorists use positivist studies to attribute blame for sickness to socially structured inequality rather than to individual misfortune.

INTERACTIONIST APPROACHES

These present similar criticisms of positivism to those found in the sociology of suicide and deviance. Health statistics, which record differences between the mortality and morbidity of different social groups, are seen as a social construction. In the same way that police and judicial processes produce crime statistics, and coroners' verdicts are the source of suicide statistics, it has been argued that health statistics are produced by doctors' diagnoses.

Studies of disease, and particularly mental illness, may adopt the labelling approach popularised by Becker. Health, disease, illness and even death are seen as social constructions. There are no 'real' rates of ill health to be discovered. Such rates are seen as a result of the interaction between doctors, patients and others. The negotiation of reality by doctors, patients, relatives and the media can be used as part of functionalist, Marxist, feminist and other conflict approaches. The conflict approaches tend to stress the importance of power in these interactions.

CONFLICT APPROACHES

MARXISTS

Marxists argue that disease is caused by capitalism and not just by industrial society. Direct causes include pollution, dangerous products and the stress and poverty caused by exploitation.

Definitions of ill health and the institutions which are involved in the treatment of the sick are seen as part of the superstructure and thus help to reproduce the existing relations of production, e.g. health has been equated with being fit to work. The views that ill health is the result of individual misfortune or that the solution to health problems lies in medical treatment and scientific breakthroughs which will produce miracle cures are seen as false consciousness.

Doctors and the NHS are seen as serving the interests of the ruling classes by keeping the working class 'fit' and docile. Medical care is seen as a form of social control, e.g. the definition of mental illness and the control of patients with drugs or in locked wards. The health industries divert attention away from the real causes of ill health by focusing on cures rather than prevention. The Welfare State, through the tax system, transfers the cash of the working class to private industry, such as drug companies and hospital builders and suppliers.

FEMINISTS

Feminists argue that disease results from the inequalities of patriarchal societies. Women are seen as being at greater risk of disease than men because of inequalities in the home and at work. An additional cause of stress is the role many women play as unpaid and unrecognised providers of primary health care within the family, whether nursing the temporarily sick or the permanently infirm or disabled. Feminists see doctors as exercising control over female bodies and feminine behaviour.

ILLICH

Illich specifically criticised doctors and drug companies for the 'medicalisation of life' which produces *iatrogenic* illness. This means illness caused by health care. The source of the problem is seen as lying in industrial, rather than specifically capitalist, society. He distinguishes three forms of iatrogenesis:

1 *Clinical iatrogenesis* is the result of harmful medical intervention in the form of unnecessary or incompetent surgery, side effects or addiction to drugs and accidents in hospital.
2 *Social iatrogenesis* describes the medicalisation of life, e.g. fertility, pregnancy or unhappiness. Social problems, such as abortion or 'mercy killing', become technical problems and are left to doctors rather than to politicians or priests to resolve.
3 *Cultural iatrogenesis* involves individuals giving up independence and allowing experts to control their lives. A similar process is described in his critique of education where teachers are seen to be preventing the education of children in the same way that doctors 'expropriate health' (see also Chapter 14).

FUNCTIONALIST APPROACHES

Parsons' work on the functional effects of the 'sick role' is not based on the coincidence of consensus perspective and positivist approach we have come to expect after Durkheim. The patient's adopting of the sick role is legitimised by doctors. It results from a negotiation between the two parties. It is functional as it allows the patient temporarily to drop out from responsibility without challenging consensual norms.

Doctors are seen as competent professionals, committed to the public good and to the interests of their patients. Their high rewards are justified by their functional importance (see also Davis and Moore on *inequality*, Chapter 3, and *Professions*, Chapter 14).

THEORETICAL AND EMPIRICAL STUDIES

INEQUALITIES IN HEALTH

This was the title given to the Black Report, a study of the social distribution of health commissioned by the Labour Government in 1974 and published in 1980 amid some controversy. It reviewed the research of others and summarised the explanations for the continued correlation between health and class under four headings. Criticism of the explanations can be found in the Black Report itself and in later research such as 'The Health Divide', 1987.

The artefact explanation

This suggested that there was no real evidence that low income caused ill health. The apparent relationship was based on the fact that definitions of class based on occupation concentrated on the old (and thus less healthy) in the lower classes, because there were fewer new recruits to the shrinking ranks of unskilled manual workers. Criticism in a later study called 'The Health Divide' indicates that poorer civil servants are less healthy than richer ones.

The selection explanation

This argument reverses the causation in the relationship between class and health. Instead of poverty being seen as the cause of ill health, ill health is seen as a cause of downward social mobility and good health as contributing to upward mobility. A similar argument has been offered to suggest that the unhealthy are more likely to be unemployed.

Criticism of this view has been based on longitudinal studies which demonstrate that only 3% of the seriously ill are downwardly mobile and that only 10% of the differences in infant mortality between the classes can be explained in this way.

The cultural deprivation explanation

This is reminiscent of the culture of poverty argument put forward by Lewis and others, which is alleged to blame poverty on the poor. In this case disease is blamed on the inadequacies of the poor who choose an unhealthy lifestyle involving smoking, drinking and too many chips (former Health Minister Edwina Currie's famous speech). In addition, the lower classes are seen as failing to use the available health care effectively.

Critics see poverty and ill health as the result of socially structured inequality, rather than of cultural deficiency. Also the evaluation of culture depends on time, place and power. What are regarded as unhealthy eating habits may depend on *who* displays them. For example, when potatoes were the food of the poor whilst the rich ate meat, the latter was held in higher health regard; since then the relative values of these foods have been re-examined.

The material deprivation argument

This was the explanation preferred by Townsend, who was on the Black committee. It was also the implications of this that probably led the Government to dismiss Black's recommendations as unrealistically expensive. Numerous studies have suggested that the following can have detrimental effects on health and that the lower classes are more at risk.

Bad housing has been linked to stress and contagious diseases. Unemployment has been linked to stress-related diseases, suicide, increased drinking and smoking, and of course the effects of reduced income to eating a less nutritious diet. Working conditions can also provide risks, such as accident, exposure to toxic substances and stress.

'The Health Divide' was able to offer only minimal criticism of this view, by largely supporting the cultural argument. Poor civil servants, for example, do indeed have worse smoking and dietary habits.

INEQUALITIES IN HEALTH CARE

The social distribution of health may depend on access to health care as well as on inequalities in health chances. Internationally, it is evident that there are enormous differences in the availability of medical treatment. In general, developed countries have healthier populations and certainly spend more on health care.

In the UK, there is an ideological commitment to equality of treatment and to free care, at least for acute problems. The extent to which the NHS fulfils this commitment, and who is to blame for any inequalities in health care provision, is of course a party political issue.

The two main concerns are:

1   The provision of health care, which depends on the allocation of resources.
2   The effective use of health care, which may be inhibited by practical or cultural barriers.

There are methodological problems in assessing the effective use of services.

1   The needs of groups to be compared must be held constant. That is, the age structure

and other risks must be controlled in order to see whether provision is fair.

2   Measures of use are problematic. Quality of care is as important as the frequency of visits to GPs, or the duration of stay in hospital.

3   Health statistics may be seen as a social construct, with the 'need' of groups assessed only by using the previous diagnoses of doctors.

4   More expensive care may not be better care. The cost of patient care will be increased if the prices of drugs or hospital buildings rise, without improving quality.

PROVISION OF HEALTH CARE

Private health care is available for individuals who can, and wish, to pay. Employers provide private health insurance for key workers and perhaps for their families.

Allocation of resources within the NHS is also an influence on the care available to different groups. The allocation of resources can be based on social policy, political decisions and market forces. We can explain the allocation of money in different ways.

Marxists would consider the benefits to the ruling class of, for example, spending on health in order to keep the workforce fit. Illich would see the emphasis on high-technology hospitals orientated towards cures, rather than prevention, as evidence of the medicalisation of life. Doctors may prefer to spend time and resources on those who can be cured rather than on, say, the care of the terminally ill.

Successive governments have planned to reallocate spending to even out spending patterns between regions. In the past, the South and urban areas were better provided for than the North and rural areas; this does not reflect a simple class bias. The majority of spending is still on hospitals rather than on community care, and within the hospital sector geriatric, psychiatric and disability attract less funding than acute medicine.

Research in 1990 claimed that the quality of care is a major influence on the survival of cancer patients, and that the provisions of such care varies considerably between regions.

THE USE OF SERVICES

Even where services are open to all, the middle classes have been shown to use them more effectively. The working class in general uses the NHS more, but by most measures they are less healthy and thus have a greater need. The middle classes use preventive care more, including screening for cancer, dentistry, immunisation, antenatal care, and family planning.

The middle classes seek earlier treatment, get longer consultations, and are able to communicate more effectively with GPs. Howlett and Ashley overcame some of the methodological problems mentioned above by studying prostate operations (prostate disease occurs more or less equally in all classes of men) and finding that the middle classes were more likely to seek early treatment and gain admission to teaching hospitals. The working-class male was more likely to wait until the condition was chronic and go to less well-equipped general hospitals.

GENDER AND HEALTH

The main concerns are:

1   Women as providers of health care.
2   The influence of gender on health. This involves consideration of the differential health chances of men and women and also the differences in the extent and type of health care used by men and women.

As with most gender issues, the emphasis in recent research has been on women rather than men.

WOMEN AS PROVIDERS OF HEALTH CARE

This can be related to the study of housework and inequalities within the family (see pp. 41–2).

Most paid NHS workers are women, but they are underrepresented in the higher-status and higher-paid jobs.

Women as mothers, wives and daughters provide unpaid health care within the home. This is rarely recognised by the social security system which does, however, provide support for men to employ care where wives are not available. This responsibility contributes to the perception of mothers as less suitable employees.

WOMEN AS USERS OF HEALTH CARE

Nathanson wrote: 'Women get sick but men die'. Despite their longer life expectancy, women use the health care services more than men. This is not the cause of their living longer, nor is the extra health care the reason they live longer. The most intensive use is whilst women are fertile, between the ages of about 15 and 44.

Mental illness rates are twice those for men, as calculated by GP diagnoses, and 50% higher if admission to hospital as an in-patient is used as a measure. The type of mental illness diagnosed is different for women, with more depression and less psychosis.

Explanations

1   Women are biologically more at risk, particularly whilst of childbearing age.
2   Women are socially more at risk, because of their role within the family. Graham found that marriage in effect depressed the class of women by reducing their access to resources. As compared with single women, she found that married women ate less well than single mothers living on lower household incomes. Bernard found that marriage itself had an adverse effect on health.
3   Interactionists argue that the illness behaviour of women is different. Women are more likely to go to the doctor, perhaps because they are less likely to be in paid employment. They are also encouraged to seek medical explanations for, and solutions to, problems associated with housing, poverty, marriage and sex.
4   Women are diagnosed differently from men. They are more likely to be perceived as mentally ill and are more willing to accept a diagnosis which allows temporary respite from household stress through hospitalisation or drugs. Men can often avoid stress through absence from work, and mental illness may be concealed as it is deemed harmful to one's career. Illich has described how the concept of the medicalisation of life can be applied to the fertility and pregnancy of women.

MENTAL ILLNESS

Positivist studies of mental illness have largely accepted the medical model of mental illness and followed Durkheim's positivist methodology. Interactionist critics have questioned the possibility of an objective definition of mental illness (or indeed any other kind). Conflict theorists are concerned with *who* defines people as mentally ill and for *what purpose.*

Lemert distinguishes primary and secondary mental illness, the latter resulting from social reaction; this also applied to deviance. He argues against the medical view that paranoia is the result of delusions and claims that the social misfit is in fact excluded from normal interaction and that this produces increasingly deviant behaviour.

Goffman's *Asylums* is a useful study of organisations as well as of the 'career' of the mental patient. He describes how 'total institutions' produce rational responses to the rules, which are often perceived as madness, e.g. hoarding or wishing to leave. This last point is demonstrated by the difficulty encountered by Rosenhan and others who faked the symptoms of schizophrenia to study a psychiatric hospital from the inside and needed legal help to get out. Getting out requires the patient to accept the sick label and then, after treatment, to conform to a model of 'well behaviour'.

Szasz dismissed mental illness as a myth and psychiatry as a form of social control. He comments on the role of the law in defining madness and the custodial role of psychiatric hospitals. Deviance is redefined as illness and is alleged to be susceptible to scientific diagnosis and treatment; e.g. until the 1960s the American Psychiatric Association defined homosexuality as an illness. His work is a largely conservative attack on 'the therapeutic state'.

EXAMINATION QUESTIONS

1   To what extent would you agree that what constitutes health and illness is a matter of social definition?

(ULEAC)

2   How might sociologists contribute to our understanding of the relationship between doctors and patients?

(AEB AS)

3   'Whether people are sick or healthy is not a chance occurrence but something produced by the society in which they live.' Explain and discuss.

(AEB)

4   Examine sociological explanations of class, gender and regional variations in the distribution of health and illness.

(AEB)

5   'The Welfare State has not significantly redistributed health resources in favour of the most needy.' Critically examine the sociological arguments for and against this view.

(AEB)

ANSWERS TO EXAMINATION QUESTIONS

OUTLINE ANSWERS

Question 1

This is similar to those questions which ask you to consider the extent to which deviance, suicide, madness, genius, old age, youth or gender can be regarded as objective categories or as socially defined and constructed.

i)   Traditional medical model: where health and illness are objectively defined in physiological terms.
ii) Positivist approach: following Durkheim, illness is seen as abnormal and differential patterns of ill health are explained by identifying social causes.
iii) Interactionist approaches: see health, disease and illness as socially defined and constructed. The negotiation of reality between doctors and patients is emphasised. Parsons' functionalist explanation of the adopting of the 'sick' role can be included here.
iv) Marxist approaches: often use positivist explanations of disease but also point out the ideological nature of definitions of health and sickness.
v)   Feminists: echo the views of Illich on the 'medicalisation' of life. Doctors have medicalised fertility, pregnancy and childbirth.
vi) Other non-Marxist conflict theorists: have argued that the definition of mental illness is a form of social control.

Question 2

This is a general question where a variety of good responses are possible. The general rule to remember is that credit is given for evaluating, as well as for examining, the sociological contributions.

The different approaches provide an appropriate framework for an answer, which could deal with a variety of material depending on your knowledge of this and related parts of the syllabus.

One outline could be:

i)   Interactionist theories influence all the following approaches. Each suggests different reasons why doctor–patient interaction has particular outcomes. Explain the theoretical approach and illustrate. Examples include Gibson, Goffman, Lemert and Duff and Hollingshead.
ii) Parsons on the functions of the sick role. Perhaps other functionalist views on professions.
iii) Marxist approaches emphasising the role of medicine as a form of social control. This is found in non-Marxist conflict theory, e.g. Szasz and Zola.
iv) Feminist approaches where (male) doctors control women, e.g. through the medicalisation of pregnancy.
v)   The work of Illich on iatrogenic illness.

Question 5

This question requires an application of knowledge of welfare policies and the Welfare State as well as more specific knowledge about the social distribution of health chances and health care.

The aims and effectiveness of the Welfare State and NHS can be discussed using a variety of theoretical frameworks such as Marxist, interactionist, feminist and New Right.

i) 'Need' can be regarded as problematic.
ii) The needy can be identified in terms of class, gender and ethnicity, age, region, poverty and unemployment.
iii) The distribution of health resources can be looked at in terms of region (the North–South divide and the overprovision in London) and different types of health problems (for example, the underfunding of psychiatric and geriatric care compared with acute services). The influence of market forces and social policy can be considered. The reduced public spending and tax cuts of the Thatcher years may be made relevant.
iv) The benefit to the most needy depends on effective use of resources as well as their provision. You can introduce debates about doctor–patient relationships and the use of preventive care.

TUTOR ANSWER

Question 4

Examine sociological explanations of class, gender and regional variations in the distribution of health and illness.

Explanations of the social distribution of health and illness must consider the problematic nature of health statistics which can be seen as socially constructed. Morbidity and mortality statistics record doctors' diagnoses and coroners' decisions and thus variations (as in suicide and crime rates) may not represent the real rate of sickness, if indeed there is a real rate. The three variables mentioned in the question can be separated logically, if not in practice. Regional differences may be influenced by class, and within classes there are gender differences. Separate explanation of each variable requires that the other two be held constant. In each case, the distribution of health and illness will be influenced by both the health chances of each group and the availability and use of health care.

There is as much variation within regions as between them. Localities within regions may have characteristic patterns of ill health. Separate studies by Harrison in Hackney and Skrimshire in Newham, both in east London, indicate low standards of health. Harrison identified access to care as a major cause, whereas Skrimshire blamed industrialisation in Newham compared with rural Oxfordshire for high rates of bronchial and respiratory disease.

Unemployment is related to ill health. This may be the effect of unemployment itself or the effects of loss of income. Certain categories of people are more at risk of unemployment, such as ethnic minorities, women, the lower classes and the unfit. Unemployment is concentrated in particular regions of the UK, such as Northern Ireland and Scotland, which also have the worst health records.

Cultural differences may be regionally based. Ethnicity may influence diet, smoking and drinking habits, family size and the experience of violence. Doyal's Marxist study *The Politics of Cancer* suggests that industrial processes are a causal factor, and industry is of course concentrated in particular regions. For example, high levels of radioactivity, whether man-made or natural, have been linked with cancer.

Gender also correlates with ill health. 'Women get sick but men die' (Nathanson). Women live longer, but use health care more. Most of the extra use is not in old age, but during the fertile years. Women have higher rates of mental illness and have different kinds of mental illness.

There are a variety of related explanations for these variations. Feminists identify social causes: Bernard blames marriage itself and Graham suggests that women get less than their fair share of family resources. The comparatively confined lives led by women mean that their chances of death through accident or violent crime are less than those for men.

Sex, as well as gender, may be influential, with women's reproductive capacity exposing them to health risk. This last point can be seen from an interactionist view. Illich's claim that fertility and pregnancy have been 'medicalised' explains the more frequent contact with doctors. Similarly, women may be more likely to be diagnosed as mentally ill and more likely to accept the diagnosis. Women are encouraged by the family, school and media to seek medical resolutions for emotional and social problems, such as poverty, housing, sexuality, marriage and unhappiness.

There is a massive amount of available data on class and ill health. Both internationally and within the UK health correlates with class. This can be explained by looking at both health chances and health care. Within the UK, the NHS is supposed to offer equal care, but Titmus and Anderson argue that the middle class have more access to, and make better use of, the available services. Resources are allocated on the basis of the market and social policy. Marxists see the decisions as serving the interests of the ruling class, concentrating on getting workers fit for work. Howlett and Ashley have shown how the middle class seek earlier treatment and are more likely to use preventive care.

The Black Report on inequalities of health suggested four possible links between class and health. Two of these explained away class differences as either 'artefact' because lower classes had a higher average age or the result of ill health causing downward mobility and unemployment. Evidence published in 'The Health Divide' in 1987 refutes these explanations, as few of the ill are downwardly mobile and poor civil servants are less healthy than rich ones.

The other explanations focused on the material and cultural deprivation of the working classes. This includes housing, diet, smoking and drinking habits, etc.

Doyal and Pennel offer a thorough Marxist analysis of the social distribution of health, identifying capitalism as the cause of ill health. Thinking of ill health as a random event is regarded as false consciousness. The actual causal mechanisms are identified as poverty, industrial accidents and diseases, pollution and unsafe and unhealthy products. Health care is seen as diverting attention from the real causes of disease, transferring public funds to big business, and as a form of social control.

STUDENT'S ANSWER WITH EXAMINER COMMENTS

Question 3

'Whether people are sick or healthy is not a chance occurrence but something produced by the society in which they live.' Explain and discuss.

> **Straight into the answer. Not elegant style, but practical exam technique.**

> **Relevant arguments demonstrating social causes.**

> **This is where the other side of the argument should be presented. She misses the opportunity. Ill health is seen as objective and as a chance occurrence, e.g. random infection by bacteria or virus.**

> **Good explanation of the social construction of health with examples.**

> **Class influencing care is adequately explained.**

> **Should be Marxists not Marx.**

Marxist theories suggest that ill health is caused by capitalism and for working-class people to think it is a chance occurrence is false consciousness produced by capitalist ideology. Poverty, accidents at work and diseases developed from occupational hazards mean ill health is a result of capitalism.

Statistics indicate that mortality and morbidity rates show better health for higher than lower classes. Within the UK health is unequally distributed in terms of getting sick and getting care. The Black Report 1980 found that 'material deprivation', i.e. low income, which has an effect on diet and housing, and 'cultural deprivation' among working-class people contribute to ill health.

The public's commonsense view is that ill health is an objective state and needs to be cured. Medicine is seen as treating symptoms in a professional scientific way.

Interactionists challenge the medical system by saying good or bad health is diagnosed by labelling and is a social construction resulting from the negotiation of reality between doctors, patients and their relatives and the media, etc. Lemert found in his studies that the socially inadequate were made paranoid by real, not imagined, exclusion. Homosexuality, not screaming, and the absence of skin disease have all been socially defined as forms of illness.

The middle class have had better access to and made better use of available health care services, conclude Titmus and Anderson. They use preventive care, e.g. screening, dentistry, antenatal care, immunisation and family planning. They seek earlier treatment, get longer consultations and are better known to doctors. Private health care is more available to people who are better-off because they can afford it and employers usually offer it to valued employees.

Marx sees medical care used as social control, e.g. mental illness and control of women's fertility. Treatment is promoted to keep workers healthy. Illich uses the term iatrogenic illness to describe sickness induced by medical care. He believes that health care causes disease through side effects of drugs prescribed, immunisation, unnecessary operations, and has

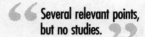

> Better to start new paragraph for Illich. Good description though.

> Completes Illich; should be in same paragraph.

> Relevant argument.

> Good material; extends discussion from class to gender. Could have developed the social construction issues.

> Several relevant points, but no studies.

led to the 'medicalisation of life', producing changed definitions of health and illness behaviour. Screening and preventive health education are seen as ineffective and increasing the number of patients. Being pregnant, wishing to control fertility, being old, ugly, unhappy or mad have been medicalised, seen as ill health and requiring medical treatment.

He states that improvements in morbidity and mortality rates are due to public hygiene or higher living standards. Unemployment, class and ill health seem to be related. Unemployment is more common in lower classes and ill health is too. Sickness causes downward mobility, e.g. the ex-mentally ill patient cannot get the same position in the job market. 'Fit for work' is a social not a medical category and depends on the labour market.

Women use health care more often than men; according to Nathanson women get sick but men often die. Mental illness rates are twice male rates for diagnosis by GP and 50% higher than males for in-patient admissions. Explanations could be that they are biologically more at risk (fertility) and socially because of stress in the family. Women are encouraged by the media and their families to seek medical resolutions to social problems like housing, marriage, poverty and sexual problems.

For ethnic minorities racism, racial discrimination and racial harassment may cause stress-related diseases and access to medical care may be hindered by language and cultural differences.

Overall comments

Overall, a well-developed but one-sided account. The theoretical issues could be developed further and the discussion needs to be more critical. A well-informed answer showing knowledge and understanding of this topic. Worth a B grade.

A Review Sheet for this chapter may be found on pp. 256–7.

GETTING STARTED

It seems that, somewhat in common with Sunday newspapers, sociology examinations are more concerned with deviance than with social order. As deviance helps us to identify rules which might otherwise be taken for granted, this topic is a useful source of examples for many sociological issues. The value of a comparative approach to sociology, which is emphasised by some examination boards, is highlighted by the culturally specific nature of deviance.

The main themes of questions set on this topic are:

1   **The relationships between power, social control and deviance.**
2   **Evaluation of sociological explanations of deviance.** Questions may cite particular theories by name for you to consider, or may present you with a problem to explain, such as differential conviction rates.
3   **Discussion of specific forms of deviance.** These may include football hooliganism, drug abuse, white-collar crime, etc. **Suicide** and **ill health** are discussed in other chapters.

Related topics include:

■   *Suicide.* This develops in detail the debate over positivism.
■   *Media* and their role in deviance amplification.
■   *Methods questions.* Deviance studies offer a rich source of examples to evaluate methods and to illustrate theoretical problems in doing research.
■   *Health.* The debate as to whether health can be objectively defined or whether it is a social construction is the same as that over the definition of deviance.
■   *Sub-cultural* theories of deviance contribute to discussions of *education* and *youth cultures.*
■   As expected, *class, race* and *gender inequalities* manifest themselves in the sociology of deviance.

Definitions

The definition of *deviance* is problematic, and is itself a central issue in some questions, as we shall see later in this chapter.

DURKHEIMIAN THEORIES

INTERACTIONIST THEORIES

MARXIST THEORIES

FEMINIST APPROACHES

THEORETICAL AND EMPIRICAL STUDIES

ESSENTIAL PRINCIPLES

The best way to organise answers on this topic is to use a simplified grouping of theories, approaches and studies. This provides the framework for comparative and critical answers.

The three main headings used here are:

1   Durkheimian.
2   Interactionist.
3   Marxist.

There are differences *within* these broad groupings, but some common assumptions which apply to most studies can be identified.

DURKHEIMIAN THEORIES

The general perspective is consensus structuralism. The major theories are functionalism and sub-cultural theories. The dominant approach to research is positivist.

Deviance is defined as breaking consensual rules and deviants are defined as rule-breakers. The main question is 'why do some people break the rules?'

A common method of enquiry is to compare the biographies of known deviants with those of normal people, and to see the differences as causes of deviance. Crime statistics are seen as a useful resource which can be used in comparative studies.

The police and courts are seen not as problematic, but as neutral. The role of the media is to reinforce consensual values.

The main types of deviance studied are crime and other serious offences.

Critics

Interactionists challenge the definition of deviance, the positivist approach and related methods.

Marxists deny the existence of genuinely consensual values.

INTERACTIONIST THEORIES

The shared perspective is individualist rather than structuralist. Some writers acknowledge the influence of power in the creation of social order. The major theoretical influences are symbolic interactionism and ethnomethodology. The dominant approach is anti-positivist. It is this that unifies these various studies.

A deviant is seen not as a rule-breaker but as someone who has been processed as a deviant, i.e. successfully labelled deviant. The main question is 'why are some people more likely to be so labelled?'

The methods associated with this approach try to describe the interaction or negotiation between 'offenders' and various forms of social institutions and agencies such as the police, the courts and the media. Crime statistics are seen not as a useful resource, but as a subject to study. It is suggested that they describe police and judicial procedures, rather than the criminals. The role of the media in amplifying deviance and causing moral panics can be a question in its own right. Minor non-criminal deviance, or even non-offenders, are studied as well as criminal deviance. Studies include mental illness, stuttering and the innocent.

Critics

Positivists claim that interactionists avoid the most important issue, which is explaining crime.

Marxists share the view of differential law enforcement and the problematic nature of crime, but criticise interactionists for not considering the influence of structural inequality on justice.

MARXIST THEORIES

The shared perspective is conflict structuralism. The major theories are varieties of Marxism. The sociological approach may be positivist. Deviants are seen as real or alleged breakers of ruling-class law. The main questions are 'who makes the rules and how does their enforcement serve ruling-class interests?' The results of research, whatever the method, are interpreted in a Marxist light. Crime statistics are seen as a device to blame social problems on the working class and as evidence of unequal enforcement. The police, courts and the law itself are seen as part of the superstructure. The media reinforce ruling-class ideology. Studies often describe crimes of the powerful and the policing of the working class.

Critics

The possibility of genuinely consensual norms and values is avoided. As with interactionist approaches, there is the tendency to excuse or even glorify offenders and to ignore victims.

Interactionists see Marxist studies as overdeterministic: the effect of structural influences is exaggerated.

FEMINIST APPROACHES

The New Criminology, like most of the old, neglected women and crime.

(Abbott and Wallace 1990)

Much of the sociological interest in women and crime has focused on women as victims rather than offenders – particularly of crimes related to their position in a patriarchal society: that is, as victims of domestic violence and sexual crimes.

One of the reasons that women and crime has been a neglected area in sociology is that women appear to be remarkably non-criminal.

(Abbott and Wallace)

Women are very underrepresented in crime statistics, and criminal behaviour is seen as unfeminine. Prostitution and shoplifting are possible exceptions to this rule.

Abbott and Wallace have examined:

1 The amount of crime committed by women.
2 The kinds of crime committed by women.
3 Recent changes in the amount and types of crime committed by women.

Studies of convicted women show:

1 The motive for theft is want or need.
2 Women commit all types of offences.
3 Women fear the criminal label.
4 Women are seen as double deviants. They offend against notions of femininity as well as the law.

THEORETICAL AND EMPIRICAL STUDIES

DURKHEIMIAN STUDIES

Durkheim saw some deviance as potentially functional. It tests the usefulness of current norms and reinforces the collective consciousness. The causes of deviance include too much or too little integration. *Suicide* provides the model for studying deviance.

Erikson followed Durkheim and argued that the authorities created crime waves to clarify and reinforce norms. He cites witchhunts as examples.

Merton developed Durkheim's concept of *anomie* to explain deviance in the USA. The socially disadvantaged lacked the opportunities to achieve consensual norms by legitimate means; therefore some rejected either the means or the ends themselves. This produced four kinds of deviance.

SUB-CULTURAL THEORIES

These present an 'internal critique' of Merton. They question his assumption of consensual values and his view that deviance is an individual response.

A. Cohen sees deviant sub-cultures opposing middle-class values.

Miller sees them as part of mainstream working-class culture. Their 'focal concerns' of smartness, toughness and excitement are common to English football hooligans.

Cloward and Ohlin combine sub-cultural theories with Merton to suggest that responses can be either individual or collective, depending on the perception by the deviant of the causes of his or her disadvantage.

DJ. West is an English criminologist who responded to S. Cohen's interactionist criticism of positivism by refining his research methods to study delinquents before they had been caught. West is a good critic to use when discussing labelling.

Young and Lea revived sub-cultural explanations in their New Left Realism.

INTERACTIONIST THEORIES

Becker asks why some people, and acts, are labelled deviant. He sees the consequences of the acts as important in this labelling process, rather than the acts themselves. In other words, social reaction to the acts and the characteristics of offenders and victims are important factors. He also asks 'who makes the rules?'

Cicourel provides, perhaps, the best interactionist critique of crime statistics. He also introduces the ethnomethodologist's concept of *commonsense assumptions* to explain the behaviour of law enforcers (see also Chapter 20 on *Suicide and official statistics*).

Lemert emphasises the importance of social reaction in transforming primary deviance to secondary deviance. (See Chapter 18 on *Health*.)

J. Young gives an interactionist account of the role of the police in the amplification of deviance. He provides a useful account of crime waves, which can be used to criticise crime statistics. In his more recent work, which has been described as 'left realist', he measures crime in a more positivist way through victim studies.

MARXIST THEORIES

S. Hall provides a link between interactionist and Marxist theory by explaining the interaction between the police, media and black youth in terms of the crisis of capitalism.

Marx himself saw the state, the law, agencies of social control and definitions of morality all as part of the superstructure of capitalist society. Criminals form part of the reserve army of labour and the threat of crime legitimises oppression.

Althusser sees deviance being defined and contained by both 'Repressive' and 'Ideological State Apparatuses'.

Chambliss illustrates how specific laws and enforcement procedures can serve ruling-class interests. He cites tax law in colonial East Africa and medieval vagrancy laws as examples. In his study of Seattle, he argues that those in power were part of organised crime.

Pearce confirms this view, discussing corporate crime and other crimes of the powerful.

The new criminology of the 1970s combined interactionist and Marxist views. English interactionist writers, such as J. Young, I. Taylor and Walton, felt that labelling theories failed to relate policing and other forms of social reaction to wider issues of power and inequality. As stated above, Young further refined his ideas, seeing these views as failing to give sufficient consideration to victims who, like offenders, usually come from the working class.

NEW LEFT REALISM (YOUNG AND LEA)

Main assumptions

1 **Crime is a real problem** for society in general, and working-class inner-city communities in particular. Young's earlier work was interactionist and tended to see 'offenders' as victims of the police and courts and crime as a moral panic, not a real problem. Other writers, such as Gilroy, have defended crime as political protest or 'Robin Hood' behaviour.
2 **Emphasis on the victim.** Victim studies offer a more accurate picture of crime than official statistics give of the extent of crime (much is unreported) and what is seen as serious crime. The disadvantaged are most likely to be victims. Young notes the greater risks of victimisation for women.
3 **The police are losing the fight against crime, particularly in the inner city.** Better policing with community support is the best way to reduce crime, although **the causes of crime are structural.**

The causes of crime

1 **Marginalisation**
The unemployed, particularly if they are working class and/or black and/or living in the inner city, are excluded from society by not working. Work, trades unions and

political parties give the working class some power; these opportunities are not always open to those often referred to as an underclass (in the Weberian rather than the New Right version). Riots and fights over territory are ways of asserting power.

2 **Relative deprivation**

This is also a Weberian concept. It describes the feeling of being denied access to rewards (see Chapter 17 on *Poverty, welfare and social policy*). The young are encouraged to desire and expect material success by the media, etc. If this success is not forthcoming, they perceive injustice. This idea was used as a partial explanation of 1960s' urban riots in the USA.

3 **Criminal sub-cultures**

These are adaptations to economic conditions. This also is an old explanation. The sub-cultures emphasise individualism, aggression, competitiveness and masculinity.

NLR: a critical evaluation

1 Hughes questioned whether it was New, Left or Realistic. He saw it going back to old ideas like anomie, sub-culture, relative deprivation, etc.

Marxists see it as underemphasising capitalism as the source of the problem and blaming the working class for crime.

2 Gilroy and others see it as racist or at least providing ammunition for racists to use. It seems to encourage the view of black criminality.

3 NLR overemphasises street crime as the main form of serious crime. White-collar and corporate crime is acknowledged, but not seen as so threatening.

4 There is an overemphasis on victims as a source of data and insufficient attention paid to offenders. Interactionists, like Young in his younger days, used offenders to describe their own motives and meanings.

 Good points.

5 Alternative responses to marginality and relative deprivation such as politics or religion are mentioned but not explored.

6 Overemphasis on class and insufficient attention paid to gender, ethnicity, community.

7 Riots and collective disorder are distinguished from individual crimes. Causes of riots are not just criminal gain but response to relations with the police and housing and unemployment.

8 On the positive side it may be more useful than:

- *Right-wing views* that see punishment and repression as the solution to crime, which is caused by individual wickedness rather than inequality.
- *Left-wing views* that celebrate crime as resistance to oppression.
- *Interactionist views* that deny there is crime problem and see offenders as victims of the police and courts and fear of crime as moral panics. These theories do not explain crime; NLR does.

FEMINIST STUDIES

Social control theory (Heidensohn 1986)

Women comprise only 12% of known offenders for all crimes, and even less for the most serious crimes: robbery, wounding and murder. The reason is that women are generally more conformist because they are more constrained.

They are controlled by:

1 **Their general position in society**

Women are not seen as aggressive and they learn not to be violent. The ideology of femininity defines appropriate behaviour for women. Being unfeminine is in itself deviant, although it does not constitute a crime. Unconventional family life exposes offenders to double condemnation. (Cook 1987 on social security fraud argues that single mothers are punished for their lives as well as their crimes.)

2 **Their position in the family**

Women are constrained by subordinate family roles and domestic responsibilities. This private control limits their opportunities to commit crime.

Criticism

Carlen (1987), whilst she is sympathetic to Heidensohn's feminist perspective, argues that the social control theory fails to explain why some women do commit crimes.

She argues that women calculate the costs and benefits of deviant behaviour. They make a class deal to work and a gender deal to act in a feminine way. Women make these deals because they accept the ideology of a patriarchal and capitalist society. This ideology is transmitted through the family, school and the media.

A few women are perhaps marginalised because of their exclusion from 'normal' family life. They may feel they have nothing to lose and prefer law-breaking to poverty and isolation.

Women who break the law but keep the gender deal and remain 'proper' daughters or wives tend not to be criminalised even if they are caught.

EXAMINATION QUESTIONS

1   How far has the work of labelling theorists and interactionists helped us to understand why some people become criminals and others do not?

(UCLES)

2   Assess the explanations sociologists have offered for the relatively low rate of convictions for white-collar and corporate crime.

(AEB)

3   Examine sociological contributions to our understanding of
EITHER a) soccer hooliganism
OR b) deviancy amplification.

(AEB)

4   Outline and assess Marxist explanations of crime and deviance.

(AEB)

5   Assess the evidence and arguments which suggest that female crime and delinquency are significantly underrepresented in official statistics.

(AEB)

6   'Members of ethnic minorities are no more prone to commit criminal acts than any other sections of the population, but are overrepresented in criminal statistics.' Explain and evaluate this statement.

(AEB)

ANSWERS TO EXAMINATION QUESTIONS

OUTLINE ANSWERS

Question 1

The key point is that becoming a criminal must be distinguished from actually offending.

Interactionists distinguish crime from rule-breaking. The criminal is someone who has been successfully labelled as a deviant. Interactionist theory deals with this process of being labelled.

Becker says this depends on:

i)   The consequences of the act.
ii) Social reaction to the act.
iii) The characteristics of both offender and victim rather than the act itself.

Lemert distinguishes primary deviance from secondary deviance which follows social reaction.

Cicourel concentrates on the role of law enforcement in creating crime and criminals.

Young describes the role of the police in amplifying deviance whereas S. Cohen emphasises the media.

(Half the answer could criticise interactionist theories).

Durkheimian theories argue:

i)   It ignores the origins of actual crime.
ii) Deviants can be identified before they have been labelled (West).
iii) Becker's sympathy for the underdog lies with the offenders who commit trivial crime, not with the victims of serious crime.

Conflict theories argue:

i) It avoids the issue of the relationship between deviance and power. Who makes and enforces the rules, and in whose interests?

ii) It accepts official definitions of crime.

iii) It ignores the active part that offenders may play. You might conclude by looking at S. Hall, who attempts an interactionist approach within a Marxist framework.

Question 2

Here you must consider *convictions* as well as, or instead of, the actual extent of crime. Define both white-collar and corporate crime.

i) Durkheimian theories: these suggest reasons for a low rate of crime rather than just convictions. Merton's anomic theory would see ritualism as a middle-class response but the other responses as characteristically working class.
(Critics question the consensual basis of rules and the neutrality of law enforcement.)

ii) Interactionist theories: these see the explanation for differential conviction rates as lying in the reactions of police and the judicial procedures.
(Critics say they take the law for granted and fail to explain offenders.)

iii) Conflict theories: here the law and its enforcement must be seen within the context of the class structure of society. Who makes the law and in whose interests is it administered? (Carson, Chambliss, Pearce and Gordon all offer Marxist studies.)

An interesting conclusion might be based on Sutherland's pioneering pre-war studies. These begin by pointing out the low level of recorded white-collar crime and seeing it as the result of low rates of reporting and detection and conviction. He then discredits conventional explanations of (low-class) crime and offers the new theory of differential association.

Question 5

i) Discuss the theoretical and methodological issues associated with the reliability and validity of crime statistics applied to the question of gender. Consider whether women commit less crime and/or whether they are less likely to be caught.

ii) You could critically apply the traditional explanations of variations in crime rates to women. Abbott and Wallace assess biological, anomic, sub-cultural theories, labelling and Marxist accounts as explanations of women's behaviour.

iii) Evaluate specifically feminist explanations of the amount and type of crime committed by women. These include Heidensohn's social control theory and critics.
A good answer may raise issues about *the definition of female deviance* and its relationship with conventional gender roles.

iv) You might mention the overrepresentation of women as *victims* of certain kinds of crimes related to patriarchy such as domestic violence and sexual assaults.

Question 6

Some ethnic minorities are overrepresented in some criminal statistics. Generally this is interpreted as their appearing disproportionately as 'offenders'.

It could also mean being overrepresented as victims of racially motivated or any other kind of crime.

Recent miscarriages of justice suggest that black, Asian and Irish minorities may more frequently be victims of false arrest and imprisonment.

Logically there are two major explanations for ethnic minorities appearing to commit more crimes or more of some kinds of crime:

i) They commit more crime.

ii) They are more likely to be caught and processed as offenders.

Both these statements could be true.

In some cases the overrepresentation of minorities in lower classes and in inner-city areas may explain part or all of the ethnic differences in crime rates.

You should be able to apply the major theories of deviance to the particular case of ethnicity.

i) Merton's anomic theory.

ii) Sub-cultural theories.

iii) Labelling theories.

iv) Marxist theories.

There are also specific accounts of ethnicity and crime in Britain.

S. Hall applies a combination of Marxist and interactionist perspectives to explain both a higher rate of black offenders for some crimes and a racist response to all the black population from the public, police, media and Government. His *Policing the Crisis* focuses on the moral panic over mugging in the 1970s.

P. Gilroy is associated with the New Criminology. He explains high black crime rates in terms of class and racial inequality. He argues that crime is an act of resistance to oppression.

Black crime is an act of resistance to racist oppression. It is a form of defence and/or a way of hitting back. He claims that colonialism continues in Britain today. Marches, demonstrations and even riots are acts of resistance which occurred in colonies and continue now. These acts bring minorities into conflict with the police.

Gilroy cites the example of Rastafarianism which, in addition to being a religion, is a protest against colonialism and expresses a desire to return in freedom to Africa.

Young and Lea's New Left Realism denies that the disproportionate number of black convictions is simply the result of police racism. They point out that 92% of crime is reported to the police by the public; therefore the statistics are not mainly the result of police decisions – although they do see policing as exaggerating the black crime rate.

They write that black offenders do commit more of some kinds of crime (e.g. street crimes) but acknowledge that they are less likely than white offenders to commit other crimes (burglary). Overall, the crime rate is higher for black people but lower for Asians than for white offenders.

They explain the higher rate in the black population by reference to:

i) Relative deprivation, where achievements do not match aspirations. Interestingly, the crime rate for first-generation immigrants from the Caribbean was lower than for the white majority. Perhaps their aspirations were lower and unemployment was rare.

ii) Marginality refers to the experience of exclusion from mainstream society, particularly exclusion from work.

iii) Sub-cultural responses to racism and deprivation may vary. Religion and criminality are two alternatives.

Question 3a

This question requires evaluation of the various sociological approaches, not just a history of soccer hooliganism. The best answers will link the development of different approaches to changes in sociology in general.

A chronological account is just as appropriate as the more conventional list of approaches to deviance found elsewhere in this chapter.

i) Marsh *et al.* wrote a psychological/ethological account, arguing that football hooliganism was not, in most cases, real violence but orderly rituals perceived as disorderly by outsiders.

Williams thought that this was taken up by sociologists for political reasons, as it appeared to blame the problem on social reaction and not on the alleged hooligans. Their study does neglect to consider structural influences on behaviour. The same emphasis on social reaction is found in S. Cohen's study of moral panics.

ii) The CCCS studies introduce a Marxist perspective to studies of youth in general. The rituals and symbols of youth are explained at a sub-cultural rather than an individual level and are seen as resistance to capitalism, e.g. skinhead style and behaviour was explained by looking at the changes in traditional working-class communities. The acceptance of these theories, which tend to be assertions rather than based on empirical studies, was helped by the rising popularity of Marxist sociology in the 1970s.

iii) The Leicester work of Williams, Dunning and others attempts to trace a continuous, but changing, history of soccer hooliganism. They identify lower-working-class masculine aggressiveness as a continuing theme. Changes in the class structure, such as higher incomes permitting travel, and changes in race relations help to explain the changing extent and nature of the hooligan problem.

The prolific nature of the Leicester work can be explained by the current perception of hooliganism as a social problem and by the existing tradition of sports research.

TUTOR ANSWER

Question 3b

Examine sociological contributions to our understanding of deviancy amplification.

Deviancy amplification can be approached from a range of sociological perspectives, though the concept is particularly associated with the interactionist view. Deviance amplification can mean one or more of the following:

i)   More deviant acts are being committed.
ii) More serious acts are being committed.
iii) There is an increased perception (true or false) and/or fear (justified or not) of crime.

A combination of these can produce a crime wave.

The various interactionist studies share a basic common assumption: that it is societal reaction which explains the increase in real or imagined crime rather than the biographies of deviants or social facts external to individuals. The foundations of the interactionist approach are found in Becker's view that labelling can encourage the development of a deviant career. Wilkinson addressed more specifically the notion of a deviancy amplification spiral, where a perceived increase in deviance produces increased social reaction from the public, media and police, which in turn produces more visible deviance and thus more reaction, and so on.

S. Cohen describes how 'Folk Devils' and 'Moral Panics' can be created and amplified by the media. Minor seaside disorder was described as a riot, worse was then predicted, and this led to the polarisation of 'mods' and 'rockers' who went to the resorts where the press had promised violence. More effective policing meant more arrests and therefore crime, which here depended on social reactions; for example, obstructing the police requires a police presence. Soccer violence and lager louts are more recent examples of moral panics. The violence may be real, but public perceptions and fears change irrespective of rises and falls in *actual* events.

Young looks at 'the role of the police as amplifiers of deviancy, negotiators of reality and translators of fantasy'. He describes in detail the special role of the police and courts in amplifying deviance associated with drug abuse. Law enforcement isolates drug users, puts drug sales in the hands of professional criminals and makes real the imagined distinction between corrupted innocents and wicked pushers. Typically, victimless crime rises in response to more active policing – importuning in public lavatories and insider trading are examples. The willingness of victims to report, say, rape or child abuse has a similar effect on public perception of crime.

Moving to non-criminal deviance, Lemert argued that social reaction could be a cause (rather than an effect) of secondary deviance. He was able to apply this to stuttering and mental illness. Atkinson's early work on suicide showed how social reaction from media, academic research, and families could influence not only the reported rate of suicide by affecting coroners' verdicts but also the real rate of student suicide.

Conflict theorists have challenged the interactionist approach. S. Hall, in *Policing the Crisis*, provides a Marxist context for the moral panic about mugging in the 1970s (see Victim studies, Chapter 20). He accepts the interactionist process described above but explains why it occurs by arguing that it legitimises the need for more repressive policing, which is really required because of the coming crisis of capitalism. The panics about strikers and social security scroungers can be seen in a similar light.

Gouldner, specifically criticising Becker, argues that the interactionist view takes the nature of deviance for granted and sees the offenders as too passive.

Functionalist theory since Durkheim has also been able to offer an alternative and more structuralist approach to moral panics and deviancy amplification. Durkheim saw the function of social reaction against crime and criminals as reinforcing the collective conscience. This was taken up by Erikson, who saw the creation of crime waves by the authorities in Puritan New England as an attempt to clarify and reinforce the existing religious moral standards. More recently M. Douglas cites the persecution of Jehovah's Witnesses in pre-war USA for not saluting the flag. This was initially perceived as a threat to national unity during a period of anomie, until Pearl Harbor served to reintegrate US society by finding a new enemy within and abroad. The integrating effect of the scapegoat echoes Hall's work on the racist undertones of the mugging scare.

STUDENT'S ANSWER WITH EXAMINER COMMENTS
Question 4
Outline and assess Marxist explanations of crime and deviance.

Theories of crime and deviance can be divided into three broad categories. The first of these is the functionalist theory investigated by the positivist approach of Durkheim, Merton and others. This assumes consensual rules for the good of society. Rule-makers and enforcers have legitimate power which is approved by all sections of the population. Deviance is rule-breaking and explanations are sought from within the structure of society.

> **Definitions and explanations of deviance, but not linked to question.**
>
> **Should start here.**

The interpretive approach of a more individualistic perspective is advanced by followers of Weber, including Becker and Young. For them the deviant is the person who is caught and labelled deviant. There is an emphasis on the effects of social reaction and the role of the police as amplifiers of deviance.

The third view of crime and deviance is the conflict theory of Marx and others. Marx considered that the state agencies of social control, the law, judiciary and social definitions of deviance and morality are all part of the superstructure of society, produced by and reinforcing and supporting the economic substructure. Therefore social order is imposed by the powerful on the powerless and is not based on shared values. It serves the interests of the powerful and not the maintenance of social integration. Conformity to rather than compliance with the rules is false consciousness and, according to Marx, even laws which appear to support working-class interests like the legal entitlement to join a union are, in fact, only supporting false consciousness.

> **Good comparative points on order and integration.**
>
> **Attitudes to violence against children are culturally and historically specific.**

However, critics of this view claim that there does seem to be a genuine consensual view of some deviance. For example, there is a general abhorrence of violence against children which does not appear to be false consciousness.

The functionalists see power as granted by populations to rulers to allow them to enforce consensual rules and not to support ruling-class interests. However, if, as Marx claims, rules are not consensual but laws legitimise the power of the ruling class, then deviance (i.e. the breaking of rules) can be seen as a threat to the interests of the powerful. There is much evidence that enforcement of rules is applied differently to different groups who commit the same crime and working-class crimes are policed more conscientiously than higher-class crimes. Although other sociologists agree with these findings they do not share Marx's explanations and feel that they have not been demonstrated through research.

> **Differential enforcement also argued by interactionists.**

Marx claimed that crime supported the economic infrastructure. Criminals can be thought of as part of a reserve army of labour. Crime is a protection against poverty and theft is redistribution of income within the working class. The working class are generally both victims and criminals. During economic slumps there are more criminals and more police are needed to control the 'crime wave'.

> **This could link up with Hall in para 8.**

This explanation of crime as a normal response to inequality may appear to glorify crime and can be criticised for failing to explain why the majority of people appear to keep the rules.

Crime is seen as being a threat to ruling-class interests and because the ruling class feel their property to be under threat it legitimises their efforts to produce better means of protecting it. They acquire more locks, better security and a larger police force. This strengthens the power of the ruling class to control the working class as a whole and enables them to deal better with union activities or other threats to their domination.

> **Not clearly argued. Crime prevention provides a legitimate reason for strengthening law enforcement which can be used against the working class.**

One of the strengths of the Marxist theory compared with others is that it asks 'who makes the rules?' and looks for the answers within the economic and political structure of society. In contrast the interpretive approach restricts itself to individual encounters and might criticise

Gouldner.

Marxist theories for being deterministic and failing to consider individual interpretations of situations at all.

Another strength of Marxist theory is that whilst Becker's labelling theory criticises the police, social workers and other 'caretakers' it does not mention the 'master institutions' of the state and the ruling class who control the lower levels.

Marxists also question official definitions of deviance whilst others do not.

Marxist explanations do not conflict with the interactionist critique of 'crime waves' and Young's account of deviance amplification. These can be explained within the Marxist economic structural view. S. Hall claims that the media, representing the interests of capital, create moral panics. If it is believed there is a crime wave, especially if it can be blamed on a section of the public such as black youth, this can be used as an excuse to increase the police force and perhaps add to their powers or change laws and thus legitimise a more repressive state more able to control the workers.

If the Marxist view of crime as part of the superstructure is correct, then countries with similar levels of economic development should have similar patterns of crime. In fact they do not. This suggests that causes of crime and deviance are more complex than Marxist theories imply.

Another important issue which Marxist theories do not explain is the very marked sex difference in criminality. The Marxists are not alone here as other theories of deviance also neglect this.

This explains paras 6 and 8.

Last two paragraphs are not integrated into the answer but sensibly add relevant points to gain extra marks. It is often appropriate to consider gender or ethnicity.

Overall comments

Overall a good B/A grade answer with comparative and critical structure.

The opening could have been improved. You must address the question, not reproduce arguments in the order that your notes or textbook present them. Given time and space actual Marxist studies could have been included, e.g. Chambliss, Pearce, Gordon and the 'New Criminology'.

A Review Sheet for this chapter may be found on p. 257.

20

SUICIDE AND OFFICIAL STATISTICS

POSITIVISM

THEORETICAL AND EMPIRICAL STUDIES

STUDIES OF CRIME STATISTICS

GETTING STARTED

This chapter will deal with questions on official statistics, particularly crime statistics, as well as the various debates on suicide. It provides a link between various topics and with the more general issues of sociological approaches, methods and theories.

Suicide is a popular, but difficult, topic. Standards of answers tend to be high because it is covered so thoroughly by teachers and textbooks. The main problems appear to be in understanding some complex ideas and then applying them to the demands of specific questions. Far too often examiners see well-prepared answers to questions that candidates were hoping would be set, rather than to the ones which were actually set.

The AEB syllabus says that students should 'consider the sociological issues raised by the study of suicide'. This means that you must debate methodological and theoretical issues, as well as the studies of suicide itself.

The main themes of questions set on this topic are:

1 **Explaining variations in suicide rates between different groups.**
2 **Evaluating Durkheim's functionalist explanations of suicide.**
3 **Explaining the social construction of suicide.**
4 **Evaluating the positivist approach to the study of suicide.**

In addition to questions which mention suicide specifically, you can use the arguments in this chapter to answer questions on:

■ *Methods*: particularly the comparative method and the use of official statistics.

■ *The nature of sociology*: for example, should it be the scientific study of 'social facts'?

■ Evaluating *structuralist* and *action approaches*.

■ The problems of defining and measuring *deviance, crime, religious belief, marital failure, strikes* and *health*, all of which can be seen as social constructions.

Definitions

■ *Official statistics* are social statistics gathered and published by the government or its agencies.

■ *Positivists* are sociologists who use empirical, scientific research to test cause and effect laws.

■ Interpretive sociologists study subjective meanings not objective facts.

ESSENTIAL PRINCIPLES

Durkheim chose to study suicide in order to demonstrate that his 'rules of sociological method' could explain even this apparently most individual of acts. The debates over suicide involve a critical consideration of his positivist approach and the use of the comparative survey as the most suitable scientific method. Supporters question the specific variables which Durkheim identified as causes of suicide, but accept the existence of social facts which constrain individual behaviour.

The most difficult idea to grasp and explain is the argument that there is no real rate of suicide that can be discovered and objectively measured. Atkinson is not just accusing coroners of making mistakes (for A-level students to expose!) but is arguing that they themselves create the suicide statistics.

The contrasting views of positivists and their critics to official statistics such as suicide statistics can be summarised as follows:

Positivist sociologists	use	official statistics	to study	objective social facts
Durkheim	used	suicide statistics	to study	the social causes of suicide rates
Anti-positivists	study	official statistics	as a form of	socially constructed reality
Atkinson	studied	suicide verdicts	to discover	coroners' commonsense assumptions

This distinction can be illustrated by the different ways in which we regard other kinds of description. We can compare the positivist use of statistics with the way a geographer uses an aerial photograph to study landscape or a botanist uses paintings of flowers to study their structures.

The interpretive approach to statistics can be compared with the study of photographs or paintings as constructions in their own right which, if they tell us anything, describe the techniques by which they were produced and perhaps tell us something about the producer.

DURKHEIM

Durkheim found, following an exhaustive study of the suicide statistics of various countries, that despite variation between the suicide rates of different societies, any given society or group within that society had a stable suicide rate. This suggested that social causes rather than individual characteristics should be studied.

The social causes he discovered involved the degree of integration and moral regulation. This led him to distinguish four types of suicide. The first two were characteristic of simple societies or close-knit groups within a modern society. The second two were typical of industrialised society.

- *Altruistic suicide*, caused by too much integration.
- *Fatalistic suicide*, caused by overstrong moral regulation.
- *Egoistic suicide*, the most common type, caused by under-integration.
- *Anomic suicide*, caused by too little moral regulation.

OTHER POSITIVISTS

These tend to support Durkheim's approach and his comparative analysis of statistics but have either offered alternative explanations (Henry and Short) or tried to refine his methods (Gibbs and Martin).

Sainsbury supports the integration hypothesis and reminds the critics below that in the USA ethnic groups have distinct rates which resemble their countries of origin, rather than rates which vary with individual coroners in different states of the USA.

PSYCHOLOGICAL APPROACHES

Despite Durkheim's rejection of psychological causes, such as mental illness, modern studies continue to link suicide with individual disturbances. Pritchard estimates that 2/3 of all suicides in England are mentally ill. A study dealing with jumping in front of trains claims that schizophrenics are 1,000 times the normal rate more likely to commit this act, and that this form of suicide clearly indicates the victim's intentions.

Stengel makes a valuable distinction between suicide and attempted suicide, based on the motivation of the victim rather than the outcome in terms of life or death. Thus failed suicide is distinguished from faked suicide.

INTERPRETIVE APPROACHES

The following critics are more concerned with challenging Durkheim's approach than with his specific explanations.

Douglas rejects Durkheim's positivist approach and his view of social causes. Instead he argues for the need to search for the social meaning of suicide, which varies between cultures and individuals. These variations in meaning in turn influence coroners' decisions, which themselves produce the official suicide rate. He advocates the study of suicide notes as a useful source of data on meanings. His interactionist view of the statistics is that they are the product of the negotiation of reality by involved parties, particularly coroners.

Atkinson has described the development of his sociological work through three phases. First, as a positivist seeking to refine Durkheim's work. Second, as an interactionist supporter of Douglas when he became concerned with the labelling process. Third, as an ethnomethodologist claiming that there was no possibility of discovering the 'true' rate of suicide. The focus of these studies ceases to be either suicide or even coroners, and concentrates on nothing more than the way in which humans make sense of themselves and each other. His actual research does give us some insight into the ways in which deaths become categorised as suicide. First, he studied the social processes leading to student deaths being categorised as suicide; and second, he conducted an experiment where English and Danish coroners were given the same case notes, but found that the latter gave more suicide verdicts. Crucially, he denies the existence of a 'real' rate of suicide.

Sacks also offers an ethnomethodological account of social life in general, using suicide as an example. He examined the transcripts of telephone conversations in a suicide prevention centre to see how suicides and staff make sense of the situation. His own interpretation is, of course, no better or worse than anyone else's.

NB: Recent examination questions often require more thorough knowledge of Atkinson and Douglas at the expense of Durkheim.

STUDIES OF CRIME STATISTICS

Critical discussion revolves around two stages in the production and use of crime statistics.

1   The gathering of data. Have the figures been collected fully and accurately? Are they reliable or could the process be more accurate?
2   The interpretation of the data. Are the figures a valid measure of crime and criminals or are they a description of police and judicial processes?

Conventionally crime figures have been the official collections of crimes known to the police (CKP) and data about convicted criminals.

Following criticism from the interactionist school, both positivists and interactionists, and even governments, have become interested in alternative types of figures.

SELF-REPORT STUDIES

These have permitted a check on the reliability of CKP figures. Hood and Sparkes, in a study in Utah, found that 93% of a sample of young people had offended, yet hardly any of tens of thousands of offences had been detected and even fewer acted upon. D.J. West used *self-reporting* to overcome the criticism which labelling theorists had made of conventional studies linking delinquency to deprivation by identifying differences before the offenders had become known to the police.

VICTIM STUDIES

Victim studies, such as the British Crime Survey and Young and Lea's work in Islington and on Merseyside, have shown a greater extent of crime than the CKP figures suggested, and have also produced data on the fear of crime as well as on crime itself.

The reasons for unreported crime include:

1   Victims being afraid or ashamed, e.g. rape, domestic violence and incest. Illegal immigrants in California began to report crime when their resident status was no longer threatened.
2   Victims seeing reporting as a waste of time because the offence was trivial, or there was no realistic chance of detection or because property was uninsured, e.g. indecent exposure and petty theft. As insurance becomes more widespread, the amount of reported, though not actual, crime will rise.
3   Victims are unaware or unconcerned, e.g. theft from work.
4   'Victimless' crimes which require detection by the police, e.g. prostitution, drug abuse, bribery and importuning in public lavatories.

Cicourel demonstrated the social construction of crime statistics by explaining the variation between two similar Californian cities in terms of policing policies and practices. A similar explanation has been given for dramatic rises in arrests both for importuning and for possessing obscene publications in Greater Manchester.

Finally, S. Hall's study of the crime figures for 'mugging' in the early 1970s illustrates the way in which the debate can take technical, theoretical and ideological forms.

Waddington claims that the figures Hall quotes actually show the increase in street crime which his study denies. Hall sees the moral panic developed through media reaction as evidence of the labelling process and of the importance of social reaction in defining deviance. Hall explains the moral panic in terms of racism and the need for the ruling class to 'Police the Crisis', whereas Waddington argues that in the absence of any objective measure of what is a reasonable social reaction to crime, dismissing reaction as a moral panic is ideological.

SECONDARY SOURCES

Secondary data is information which has been collected not by the sociologists themselves but by others. It exists in either a quantitative or a qualitative form.
  Secondary sources used by sociologists include:

1   *Social statistics.*
2   *Organisational records.*
3   *Media output.*
4   *Diaries, autobiographies and other personal documents.*
5   *Published sociological research.*

Social statistics

Social statistics are produced by a variety of bodies. Those produced by the Government are called Official Statistics. They cover a wide variety of areas including births, marriages, divorces and deaths, crime, employment and unemployment, health and educational achievement. Non-government bodies produce statistics on similar activities and also on church attendance, racial disadvantage and job opportunities for women.

Organisational records

Employers, schools and colleges, churches and other organisations keep records which may be of use to the sociologist.

R. Revans compared five Manchester hospitals by looking at their records of absenteeism, wastage of student nurses during training, labour turnover, and patients' recovery rates. He argued that these were measures of the morale in the hospital.

Media output

The mass media produce newspaper reports, TV and radio broadcasts, recorded music and also books and magazines.
  Sociologists have analysed these in both quantitative and qualitative studies.

Personal documents

We can use diaries and other personal accounts to find out how people in the past felt about issues. The complex relationship between class, race and gender can be examined by reading accounts of domestic labour written by employers, owners, servants and slaves (H. Graham).

Published sociological research

G.P. Murdock is famous for his argument that the family is a universal institution. He based this argument on published research about some twenty societies. His critics also used the same published research to attack his views.

EXAMINATION QUESTIONS

1 'What is defined as suicide is more a matter of what the coroner thinks, than what the dead person intended.' Discuss with reference to recent studies of suicide.

(AEB)

2 What use are official statistics to sociologists trying to understand EITHER crime OR marital failure?

(UCLES)

3 Durkheim's study of suicide has been criticised on theoretical and methodological grounds. Outline Durkheim's study and examine these criticisms.

(AEB)

4 'Statistical analysis always gets a bad press. The notion that you can "make statistics prove anything you like" dies hard. But, ironically, a great deal of emphasis is placed on official statistics when recommendations are being made and new policies introduced. You are more likely to be allowed to build 10,000 new council houses if you can show that 20 per cent of a city's population is living in substandard housing than if you provide five or six detailed, but personal, accounts of living in damp and decaying conditions.

Official statistics drawn up by Government departments, trade unions, the census office and other organisations are obviously a useful source of information for sociologists, but they need to be used carefully.'

(Jane L. Thompson: *Examining Sociology*)

a) Give *two* sorts of official statistics 'drawn up by Government departments, trade unions, the census office and other organisations'. (*2*)
b) Explain why some sociologists use official statistics in their work. (*8*)
c) Some sociologists would argue that 'detailed but personal accounts' are more informative than official statistics. What advantages do such accounts have? (*7*)
d) Why do official statistics 'need to be used carefully'? Illustrate your answer with a variety of sociological examples. (*8*)

(*Total 25 marks*)
(AEB)

ANSWERS TO EXAMINATION QUESTIONS

OUTLINE ANSWERS

Question 1

This is an unusual question. Instead of the usual debate using Durkheim, his work is scarcely relevant. You must contrast:

i) Those theories which deal with the work of coroners (Douglas and Atkinson).
ii) Those which focus on the intentions of the deceased (Taylor, Stengel and Giddens).

The coroner's verdict is based on a complex set of commonsense assumptions which involve the media, families, police and sociologists' research. The suicide is defined *after* the event.

Theories which deal with intention are clearly more interested in what happens *before* death. Work with the Samaritans and suicide notes is helpful.

Durkheim can be made relevant if you emphasise his rejection of psychological explanations or use him as the springboard for Atkinson's and Douglas' criticism.

Question 2

NB: 'either/or' so do only ONE.

Crime

You should critically consider what sociologists can *use* official statistics for.

i) The positivist approach to crime uses official statistics as a more or less accurate and representative description of the real extent of crime. Historical and cross-cultural analysis can be carried out, as well as correlations made with the social characteristics of criminals.

ii) Technical objections to the uncritical use of official statistics by some positivists might question the methods used to gather and interpret data. The 'dark figure of crime', victim studies and white-collar crime could be mentioned.

iii) The interpretive critique could form the major part of this answer. Official statistics are seen as a social construction telling us about police and judicial processes. Labelling theory and the work of Cicourel could be discussed.

iv) A brief reminder of Marxist criticism of the above and of the suggestion that official statistics are produced by agencies which are themselves part of the superstructure, using categories defined by the ruling class.

Marital failure

i) Statistics which may be used to describe the extent and effects of marital failure include: divorce figures, number of single-parent households, poverty statistics and figures for domestic violence and health, particularly mental illness.

ii) Positivist approaches might use divorce statistics to link marital failure with other variables, such as class, occupation, number of children, age at, and duration of, marriage.

iii) Functionalists, such as Davis, question whether rising divorce rates should be seen as evidence of a threat to the family as an institution. Instead they see them as indicating the higher expectations people have of marriage. Gibson sees serial monogamy as indicating discontent with partners, not with marriage itself.

iv) Interpretive sociologists would also question the meaning of the statistics and the process of producing them. The problematic nature of 'marital failure' could be discussed.

v) Practical criticism of divorce statistics as an index of marital failure might mention the effects of legal changes on the figures and the broken marriages which are never recorded as divorces or even legal separations. Goode's discussion of family disorganisation is potentially useful.

TUTOR ANSWER

Question 4

a) Give *two* sorts of official statistics.
   Crimes known to the police and unemployment figures.

b) Explain why some sociologists use official statistics in their work.

The decision to use official statistics either as a source of data or as a topic of study can be made on theoretical or practical grounds. In addition, if sociologists wish to influence social policy they may find it more effective to quantify a social problem and to support their arguments with official statistics.

Positivist sociologists use statistics as a more or less accurate description of an objective social reality, such as the extent of crime, the number of broken marriages, or the suicide rate. Durkheim's *Suicide* remains the model for such studies. The statistics were used as data for a comparative survey which tested various hypotheses. Analysis of the statistics might also generate new hypotheses, such as those found in the Black Report once class differences in health had been established.

The virtues of using statistics relate to the desire to be detached, to avoid contaminating subjects or being influenced by them, and to be scientific. The data is seen as reliable and available for others to test.

Practical points include the fact that such statistics may be the only source of data, such as the historical studies of Laslett and Anderson. The statistics also allow sociologists to study large numbers of subjects dispersed over a large geographical area quickly and cheaply. Studies based on divorce statistics by Gibson and Ross, and on strikes by Hartman, illustrate this point.

Interpretive sociologists do not 'use' official statistics as much as regard them as a social phenomenon worthy of study in their own right, for example, Cicourel's study of crime statistics and Atkinson's study of suicide figures. Rather than describing the objective social phenomena they claim to describe, the statistics are seen as revealing more about the processes by which they were produced.

c)   Some sociologists would argue that 'detailed but personal accounts' are more informative than official statistics. What advantages do such accounts have?

The use of 'detailed but personal accounts' is advocated by interpretive sociologists who would wish to produce the accounts themselves, based on their own experiences, rather than use other people's as a form of secondary data.

The theoretical justification for participant observation, which is a major way of producing personal accounts, is illustrated by Weber's view that sociology should aim to provide 'interpretive understanding of social action'. It is seen as crucial that the sociologist identifies the meanings which individuals give to social interaction, the motives which individuals have for action, and the commonsense assumptions which individuals use to make sense of situations. Participant observation allowed Becker to understand the experiences of becoming a marijuana smoker and of working as a dance band musician. Conducting informal interviews, whilst joining in with students' everyday lives, allowed Aggleton to develop systematic as well as impressionistic data.

The theoretical arguments for participant observation and other methods which produce personal accounts are not restricted to anti-positivist sociology. Malinowski pioneered the use of participant observation by social anthropologists who shared his functionalist perspective. It enabled the researcher to see how apparently strange behaviour fitted the needs of simple social systems. He rejected the work of those who allowed missionaries and colonial officials to mediate between them and their subjects.

> **There are no inevitable links between theoretical assumptions and methods.**

There are also practical arguments that detailed personal accounts might provide more valid data. In pre-literate societies which have not been previously studied there may be no secondary data available. Social groups which are secretive or indulge in illegal or shameful activities can be studied from their point of view only if the researcher gains their trust, or joins in and observes covertly.

Barker's study of the Moonies involved her in openly participating in their meetings. Humphrey's study of casual homosexual encounters was based on covert participant observation, whereas Polsky advocates that the researcher be open when studying criminals.

It may be that the sociologist need not choose between the use of official statistics and methods producing more personal accounts, but instead can regard a variety of methods as complementary. Newby makes just this point in order to justify the use of a variety of methods in his study of farm workers.

d)   Why do official statistics 'need to be used carefully?' Illustrate your answer with a variety of sociological examples.

Positivists do not accept the use of official statistics uncritically. They are concerned with technical problems, which may arise at either the gathering or interpretation stage, and adversely affect the accuracy of the figures or the conclusions drawn from them. Positivists see the use of such secondary data as requiring caution, but feel that the difficulties could be overcome, or at least minimised.

Positivist critics of Durkheim's *Suicide* have pointed out the inconsistent nature of pathological investigations at the time; and Gibbs and Martin have suggested a more precise definition of the concept of integration.

Different techniques of collecting data produce a variety of problems. Daniel's study of racial discrimination was hampered by the absence of a complete sampling frame which listed the non-white population. This remained a problem until the 1991 census overcame previous political objections and included a question on ethnicity, although the categories used have been criticised. Where the source of data is interviews, the problem of interviewer bias identified by Hyman and others arises.

Interpretive sociologists raise theoretical rather than practical objections to the use of official statistics. They deny the possibility that the statistics can be an impartial description of an objective social reality. They may deny the existence of such a reality or see the statistics as inevitably failing to describe it.

Thus for Cicourel, crime statistics are produced by police and judicial processes; and for Atkinson suicide figures are a list of coroners' decisions. Similarly, critics of health statistics see them as socially constructed by the negotiation of reality between doctors, patients and others. Indeed, Sudnow sees death itself as a social construction.

Finally, *ideological* criticisms of the ways in which statistics have been produced, analysed and published have been raised. Moser, ex-head of the Government Statistical Service, has expressed concern that the Government has threatened the integrity of its official statistics by, for example, changing the basis for calculating unemployment and also health spending figures. Townsend complained of the suppression of the Black Report and the subsequent omission from published data of class differences in health. S. Hall criticised the decision to publish the race of offenders for some crimes but not others. Media interpretation of statistics raises a host of other issues about bias through selectivity and presentation.

STUDENT'S ANSWER WITH EXAMINER COMMENTS

Question 3

Durkheim's study of suicide has been criticised on theoretical and methodological grounds. Outline Durkheim's study and examine these criticisms.

Durkheim's positivist approach to sociology led him to believe that the subject matter of sociology is social facts and that individual behaviour is based on the culture of the society in which he exists.

> Should be between groups in the *same* society. The stability of rates should be mentioned.

> Smokers?

To prove this he decided to study suicide as this is the most individual and personal act and if his study was successful it could be used to examine other social behaviour.

Using the official statistics he studied the suicide rates on a national basis. He found that they varied between communities and also between groups in different communities.

> Not an assumption but a hypothesis.

He decided to dismiss certain social and health factors, e.g. mental illness, race and smoking and non-smoking, and assumed these variations must be based on integration.

Based on his belief that integration was the independent variable, he found that suicide could be put into four types:

i) Anomic - when social rules cease to exist, e.g. Wall Street.
ii) Fatalistic - too much integration, e.g. Eskimos.
iii) Altruistic - too much integration.
iv) Egoistic - the most common and caused by too little integration, e.g. single-person households.

> Examples are not helpful.

> No reference to Catholics. The variable was Protestant or Catholic, as well as religious and non-religious.

He then studied Jews and Protestants in Germany and found a higher suicide rate among Protestants who were less religious and concluded that religion caused more integration. For example, family life and stability had a bearing on suicide statistics.

Anti-positivists disagreed with the way Durkheim did sociology and his view of the nature of society. They thought that each individual determined the nature of his particular society and decided on his own social action and that there is no objective social reality. They disagreed with the way suicide statistics were produced and interpreted. They believed that suicide statistics should be the subject of a study. Douglas thought that it was the meaning of the act that was crucial. He studied suicide notes, some of which were real and some of which were a cry for help.

> Obscure.

> No real rate of suicide.

> They saw statistics as a social construction rather than as being inaccurate. They should be studied as a topic in their own right.

Coroners' reports were also criticised. The way they categorise suicide and the fact that they use commonsense assumptions based on information from doctors and families of suicides and also based on age, sex and mental illness.

Atkinson conducted a study on students that showed how shared definitions can influence suicide verdicts.

Although Durkheim rejected mental illness Pritchard's study of suicide showed 2/3 were mentally ill.

> Atkinson thought that coroners' reports were unreliable because they were based on records and measurable.
> Durkheim ignored the fact that because religious people were more integrated they were also more likely to hide suicides in the family because of shame.

Overall comments

Overall, a brave attempt which raises the major issues but often fails to develop them. Few candidates seem to be able to distinguish between the inaccuracy of suicide statistics because coroners make mistakes and the view that there is no real rate of suicide.

Atkinson deserves a more thorough treatment. His study of English and Danish coroners could be mentioned and his ideas on commonsense assumptions based on mode and circumstances of death used as illustration. Worth a D grade.

NB: 'Theoretical' refers to his explanations based on integration and moral regulation. 'Methodological' refers to the debate over the value of a positivist approach to sociology.

A Review Sheet for this chapter may be found on p. 257.

METHODS

GETTING STARTED

All the syllabuses cover the use of sociological methods. Some of the examination papers have separate questions on methods, either in the form of critical essays or as part of structured stimulus questions. Where coursework is required, the ability to employ methods successfully and to evaluate their use critically is rewarded.

A critical understanding of the use of methods is helpful in understanding and criticising *any* topic on the syllabus.

The main themes of questions set on this topic are:

1 **Critical evaluation of a particular method or group of methods.**
2 **Comparison of the uses of particular methods or groups of methods.**
3 **Why do sociologists choose particular methods?**
4 **What is the relationship between theoretical assumptions and methods?**
5 **The relationship between choice of method and the desire for a scientific and value-free sociology.**

Definitions

These terms are not used consistently by different writers.

- *Methodology* is the analytical study of the ways in which sociological research is conducted.
- *Methods* are systematic ways of collecting and analysing data, e.g. a survey.
- *Quantitative methods* collect and interpret data in a systematic way. Data can be expressed numerically.
- *Qualitative methods* collect both objective and subjective data which is descriptive rather than numerical.
- *Techniques of data collection* refer to the stage in research when information is gathered, e.g. an interview.

Specific methods and techniques are defined and explained below.

The use of secondary data, particularly official statistics, is discussed in the *Suicide* chapter. Other related areas are *theory* and *the nature of sociology*. *Methodological* issues arise when considering sociological research on any subject.

ESSENTIAL PRINCIPLES

(Some examples of studies using the method are given.)

Primary	Secondary
Quantitative	

Primary	Secondary
SURVEY:	SURVEY:
1 QUESTIONNAIRE (Townsend: Poverty)	1 OFFICIAL STATISTICS (Durkheim: Suicide)
2 STRUCTURED INTERVIEW (Rowntree: Poverty) (National Sex Survey)	2 RECORDS e.g. absence from work or school
	PRESS REPORTS (K. Pryce: Reports about black community in St Paul's)
3 UNSTRUCTURED INTERVIEW (Dobash and Dobash: Domestic violence)	PUBLISHED SOCIOLOGICAL STUDIES (G. Murdock: Comparative study of families)
4 OBSERVATION	
EXPERIMENTS (W. Daniel: Racial discrimination)	CONTENT ANALYSIS OF MASS MEDIA (GUMG: War and Peace news) (G. Loban: Sexism in reading schemes)

Primary	Secondary
Qualitative	

Primary	Secondary
OBSERVATION (S. Ball: Beachside School)	CONTENT ANALYSIS OF MASS MEDIA (A. McRobbie: 'Jackie')
PARTICIPANT OBSERVATION 1 COVERT (Humphreys: Homosexuals)	DIARIES, NOVELS
2 OVERT (Polsky: Criminals)	PERSONAL DOCUMENTS (Leicester University study of young people's images of attendance at football matches is both qualitative and quantitative)
UNSTRUCTURED INTERVIEW (A. Oakley: Pregnant women)	
PERSONAL DOCUMENTS	
CASE STUDY (P. Willis: A school)	
EXPERIMENT (Atkinson: Coroners' decisions)	

- Many studies use a *variety* of methods to get different sorts of data. (E. Barker: Moonies)
- Different methods allow checking of findings and improve reliability. (Humphreys: PO followed up by interviews)
- They may adopt different sociological perspectives which encourage particular methods.
- (A. Phizacklea: Fashion industry. Primary and secondary. Interviews and observation.)
- (W. Daniel: Racial discrimination. Experiments [objective data] and interviews [subjective data]).

This section will examine the reasons why sociologists choose particular methods and techniques. In particular we will discuss the assertion, made in many questions, that theoretical assumptions are the dominant influence on choice. The following discussion has been strongly influenced by Bell and Newby's *Doing Sociological Research*, which asked contributors to describe how they *actually did* their research, instead of merely asking for a prescriptive list of how research *should be done*.

The factors influencing the choice of method in this list should not be seen as alternatives, as they are often interrelated. For example point 6 involves all the others.

REASONS FOR CHOOSING METHODS

The various reasons behind the choice of particular methods include the following:

1	Theoretical assumptions.	4	Chance and inspiration.
2	Practical restraints.	5	Moral and ethical issues.
3	The topic to be studied.	6	The sociology of sociologists.

THEORETICAL ASSUMPTIONS

The sociologist's perspective on society and approach to sociological problems can be a major influence on the method chosen.

Positivist sociologists prefer methods which can be employed scientifically. Research should be reliable, valid, generalisable and above all verifiable; e.g. Durkheim chose the comparative survey method using official statistics. This is also consistent with his functionalist perspective on society, as he sees the behaviour of individuals as being constrained by external structural influences.

Interpretive sociologists choose methods which provide insights into the social construction of reality by revealing the subjective experience of those studied. They are looking for the ways in which actors attribute meaning to their own, and others', behaviour, and at the commonsense assumptions which underlie the way people define social situations; e.g. Becker chose participant observation to study deviants by sharing their experiences. Sacks chose to study conversation between potential suicides and staff at a suicide prevention centre.

Feminists often choose interpretive methods to allow women to speak for themselves.

There are exceptions to these generalisations. Both positivists and interpretivists use official statistics, albeit in different ways. Experiments are associated with positivist scientific research but have been employed by Garfinkel, Atkinson and Rosenthal and Jacobson in non-positivist research. Goldthorpe and Lockwood used the survey method in research influenced by social action theory. Participant observation was used by the functionalist Malinowski.

Many sociologists have used more than one method in a study in order to provide complementary forms of data. Daniel's study of racial discrimination used three methods. Humphreys followed up his participant observation with interviews. Newby recommended the use of a variety of methods to gather different sorts of data in his *Deferential Worker*.

PRACTICAL RESTRAINTS

The practical or technical advantages or disadvantages of particular methods are discussed below. They include the following points:

- Participant observation involves problems of access to powerful, exclusive, secretive or deviant groups.

- Sample surveys must compromise between cost and representativeness. The different sampling techniques have particular advantages and disadvantages.

- Postal questionnaires reach people cheaply if dispersed over a wide area, but have low response rates.

- Different types of interview can be compared on the basis of reliability and insight.

Use the studies below to illustrate these points.

THE TOPIC TO BE STUDIED

- Historical studies usually require the use of secondary data such as diaries, documents or official statistics; e.g. Anderson or Laslett's studies of the family.

- Large-scale studies often use secondary data (e.g. Murdock's cross-cultural study of the family in 250 societies), or sample surveys, such as studies of voting behaviour.

- The study of secretive and deviant groups often employs covert participant observation. Humphreys, Barker and Wallis all followed up participant observation with interviews or questionnaires.

- The study of pre-literate societies often involves participant observation, because of the absence of written records and the need to learn new languages. Malinowski and Mead lived among simple societies. This is, of course, a constraint on those who wish to avoid long-term research.

CHANCE AND INSPIRATION

Most people know the stories of 'chance' scientific discoveries by Archimedes, Newton and Fleming. There have been similar events in sociology. Malinowski was on his way to Australia when the Great War began. In order to avoid internment as an enemy alien he stopped in the Trobriand Islands and began a lengthy participant observation study. Ditton was working as a bread salesman and happened to come across the institutionalisation of theft into the work role; he continued as a participant observer.

ETHICS AND MORALITY

Sociologists must make ethical decisions which may conflict with theoretical or practical demands. Polsky has condemned Humphreys' advocacy of covert participant observation on ethical, as well as on practical, grounds.

Covert research involves both deception and invasion of privacy. Participant observation of deviants may involve joining in, or having knowledge of, crime. Polsky suggested that the researcher should make clear what kinds of activities he wishes to avoid.

Those who choose to conduct experiments must be prepared to interfere in their subjects' lives. This is seen as justifiable if, as in medical research, the subjects or the public benefit.

THE SOCIOLOGY OF SOCIOLOGISTS

There are sociological explanations of the behaviour of sociologists, just as there are for any other occupation. The previous five reasons could all be covered by this heading. The main issues identified by Bell and Newby are the problems of funding and 'institutional setting'.

Atkinson explained his conversion to interactionist sociology as in part a result of getting an appointment at Essex University in the company of those pioneering this approach in England.

Burgess pointed out the difficulty of writing a detailed research proposal to do participant observation and thus the difficulty of getting research funds. This problem can be overcome if the topic is seen as a social problem, e.g. Williams' *Hooligans Abroad*.

Gouldner criticised the domination of positivist research, which he saw proliferating because it gave insecure American sociologists the respectability they craved during the attacks on academic freedom in the 1950s. (See the discussion of value freedom in Chapter 23 on *The nature of sociology*).

DOING FEMINIST RESEARCH

Oakley, in her *Sociology of Housework* (1974), pioneered the view that doing sociological research involved feminist issues. In the summary below, the views of Oakley and other feminist writers, including Roberts (1981), Abbott and Wallace (1990) and Skeggs (1992), are presented. They offer a critical view of conventional research, which they call 'malestream', and offer feminist alternatives.

A COMPARISON BETWEEN:

CONVENTIONAL 'MALESTREAM' RESEARCH	& FEMINIST RESEARCH
1 Ignores women as subjects or restricts study to the family.	1 Studies women.
2 Ignores or underestimates the significance of gender in relationships. Male behaviour is seen as normal.	2 Emphasises the importance of gender (power) relationships. Masculinity is not a norm from which women deviate.
3 Male researchers: ■ are bosses; females are assistants. ■ control careers of women. ■ dominate subjects.	3 Women are researchers. They treat subjects as equals.
4 Malestream sociology seen as neutral. Feminist sociology seen as ideological.	4 Malestream sociology not neutral thinking; it is the result of ideology. Malestream knowledge controls women.
5 Scientific, objective, quantitative positivist sociology is seen as superior. Detachment from subjects is an aim.	5 Interpretive, subjective research from a woman's point of view is usually a good strategy, but there is no best method. Involvement may help discover more. Women, and perhaps men, will reveal more to women. Women can get access to 'women's spaces'.
6 Research should be value free (achieved by positivist approach).	6 Feminist sociology should improve women's lives. Value-free research preserves the (patriarchal) status quo.

Feminist methodology: a critical view (based on Hammersley [1992] and Skeggs [1992]

1 In addition to gender one must consider class, race, age and sexuality.
2 Methods must be open to criticism by others in order to check reliability.
3 It is useful to study the motives of the oppressor (men) as well as the oppressed (women); therefore research by men would be useful.
4 Interpretive research in general, not just feminist research, recognises the ethical and practical problems of imposing reality on the subjects. However, the subjects' perception of the situation is not the only form of data. Objective structural factors limit subjects' behaviour.
5 Both Comte and Marx argued, like the feminists, that social science should try to change the world, not just explain it. However, feminists may disagree on the significance of race and class for gender. Angela Davis (1981) criticised white feminists for underemphasising race.

Hammersley concludes that feminism provides valuable explanations, but does not offer a distinctive methodology.

Criticism of Hammersley

Ramazanoglu (1992) argues that Hammersley has criticised the subjectivity of feminism by repeating the unquestioned assumption of male sociology that objective rational methods are best: 'He has waved a manly sword in striking down straw women.' Gelsthorpe (1992) argues that he did not consider the diversity of opinion within the feminist camp on methods and aims.

Skeggs argues that empathy is possible between women and essential for research. However, she asks whether the researcher should risk spoiling research by challenging the racism and sexism of subjects.

She also points out that women researchers may be denied access to some spaces through threat or discrimination.

THEORETICAL AND EMPIRICAL STUDIES

Critical evaluation of the various methods used in sociology should involve a consideration of theoretical, practical and ethical issues. There is no 'best' method. Sociologists are influenced by their theoretical assumptions but still have to balance often conflicting practical constraints.

Studies of large numbers of subjects tend to be more reliable and representative, but lack depth and insight. Minimising personal involvement reduces the problem of contamination, but limits the depth of possible understanding. High levels of control make research more reliable, but run the risk of making that research artificial.

THE SURVEY

The survey method involves both the collection and analysis of data. Many cases are studied, and data is quantified and analysed in a systematic way. The survey can be used to test hypotheses, for instance, seeking correlations between variables by using multivariate analysis, as in Durkheim's comparative study of suicide.

Comparative surveys can be:

a) Longitudinal; e.g. the 1971 health longitudinal survey.
b) Cross-cultural; e.g. Durkheim's *Suicide*.
c) Historical; e.g. Laslett's study of changes in household size.

Methods of data collection used in surveys include:

a) The use of secondary data; e.g. Durkheim.
b) (Postal) self-completed questionnaires; e.g. Wallis' study of Scientologists.
c) Interviews which can be more or less structured; e.g. Willmott and Young in Bethnal Green and Oakley's study of housework.

- *The sample survey* involves selecting and studying a small proportion of the population. This saves time and money. If the sample is *representative*, the results can be *generalised* to the whole population.

- *The population* is all those who could be included in the study and all those whom the study claims to describe.

- *The sampling frame* is a list of the population from which the sample is chosen. Daniel had no suitable list of ethnic minorities (see Chapter 4).

- *The sample* is those selected for study.

SAMPLING METHODS

Sampling methods are ways of choosing representative samples. They include the following.

a) *Quota* or *Stratified* samples are chosen by dividing the population into strata with particular characteristics, and by selecting individuals from each stratum in proportion to their numbers in the population. This method is cheap and quick, but the relevant strata must be known in advance.
b) *Random* samples are chosen mathematically from the whole population so that each unit has an equal chance of selection (like playing 'Bingo').
c) *Stratified random* samples are chosen randomly from predetermined strata, and not from the whole population. This ensures that relatively rare strata are represented even in a small sample.
d) *Purposive* samples are chosen so that specific subjects are included, and may sacrifice representativeness to achieve this. This may be the only solution if no sampling frame exists. Goldthorpe and Lockwood selected subjects from Luton to test the embourgeoisement thesis on the basis that if it had not occurred in such suitable conditions, it would not have occurred anywhere.
e) 'Snowball' samples are chosen by allowing subjects to introduce the researcher to other

suitable subjects. This is unlikely to be representative, but it does permit access to secretive subjects.

INTERVIEWS

Interviews may provide structured data for surveys or take the form of unsystematic records of subject responses (see answer to Question 3 below). Surveys generally employ more structured and formal interviews, using standardised questions which can produce quantifiable and reliable data. The advantage of formal interviews over subject-completed questionnaires is that the interviewer can explain and probe, e.g. Goldthorpe and Lockwood.

Less formal interviews are favoured by sociologists who wish to avoid imposing their views on their subjects, thereby limiting the validity of their responses. The advantage over other qualitative methods, such as participant observation, is speed; e.g. Oakley on housework.

Interviewer bias is the problem caused by interviewers affecting the responses of the subjects. The issue here is reliability. Different or even individual interviewers may act inconsistently. This problem can be minimised by training and by the standardisation of questions. Research has shown that the class (Katz), gender (Hyman), race (Williams) and political values (Rice) of interviewers can affect responses. Labov argued that the interview situation itself might intimidate some subjects. Becker, however, felt that the aggressive interviewing of teachers actually got them to reveal their true feelings.

QUESTIONNAIRES

Questionnaires are lists of pre-set questions used to measure attitudes, opinions and behaviour. They can be used to gather data from large numbers of perhaps widely dispersed subjects. If questions are standardised, such data can be easily quantified and analysed.

Postal questionnaires, as employed by Wallis and Hite, risk low and unrepresentative response rates. The questions themselves can be criticised. Slight variations in wording can produce different responses. Pilot studies for the EEC referendum produced a 20% variation in results by using different wording to seek approval for continued membership. Opinion research on abortion, commissioned by interested pressure groups, has produced results actually supporting the opposing side's position.

A study by La Piere showed that answers may not indicate actual behaviour, as restaurants which had admitted a Chinese couple later answered a questionnaire saying they would not. When racial discrimination is not acceptable, the opposite response might be found (Daniel).

AN EXAMPLE OF SURVEY RESEARCH

THE NATIONAL SURVEY OF SEXUAL ATTITUDES AND LIFESTYLES (1992)

(Wellings, Field, Wadsworth and Johnson)

The aim of this study was to identify patterns of sexual behaviour and to identify patterns of sexual attitudes with particular reference to AIDS.

METHOD: SAMPLE SURVEY
TECHNIQUES FOR GATHERING DATA: STRUCTURED INTERVIEW
SELF-COMPLETED
QUESTIONNAIRE
(A related research project conducted in France used telephone interviews.)

POPULATION: ADULTS 15–59 GREAT BRITAIN
SAMPLE: 19,000 FROM 50,000 ADDRESSES
(This was the largest survey of sexual behaviour using interviews. It was hoped that a large sample would reveal unusual behaviour.)

SAMPLING METHOD: RANDOM
(Kinsey used volunteers for 17,000 interviews in USA in 1940s.)

RESPONSE RATE: Typical of survey research.
(The topic was not a problem. The researchers said people were more secretive about their incomes!)

PILOT STUDY: Was conducted to refine questions and see if subjects would answer.

(It was intended that the subjects, rather than the researchers, should be able to define and describe behaviour. Questions on masturbation turned out to be embarrassing for subjects and were dropped rather than risk refusals to participate.)

FUNDING: Originally the Government, who dropped it for political reasons.
The Wellcome Trust (a medical research charity) took over.

(They said it was 'Worth doing and going to be well done'. The cost according to the press was £½m. It was funded because AIDS is seen as a SOCIAL PROBLEM.)

PROBLEMS OF RESEARCH INTO SEX

- People do not use explicit language.
- They may not understand questions.
- They may be embarrassed or shocked.
- Behaviour is private.
- People may deny or exaggerate activities.

SOLUTIONS

The researchers:

- Used a pilot study to ensure subjects would respond.
- Used a self-completed questionnaire, rather than interviews, for the most intimate questions.
- Allowed subjects to respond using a number code instead of words.
- Subjects were guaranteed anonymity.
- Checked data against external sources, e.g. abortion records, and within the questionnaire. They noted that people are inconsistent.
- People respond to the interviewer, not the topic. Subjects were 'More willing to discuss sex than earnings'.

(Source: *BBC Horizon programme* 3 December 1992)

THE EXPERIMENT

The experiment involves the manipulation of an independent variable (cause) and the observation of a dependent variable (effect), whilst controlling extraneous variables. Observation and surveys may be similar to experiments, in that they look for naturally occurring differences rather than manipulate them; e.g. studies of the effects of unemployment on suicide. Experiments can take place in the laboratory (to maximise control) or the field (for naturalness).

In the natural sciences, the experiment is seen as the 'superior' method because of the possibility of control and reliability. We might expect that this method would be favoured by positivists but, in fact, it is rarely employed because of practical, theoretical and ethical reasons. Durkheim advocated the use of the comparative method as a substitute for experimentation. Positivist research using experiments is rare, unless we consider social psychological experiments which have sociological implications, such as Milgram's *Obedience to Authority* or Zimbardo's study of the effects of allowing students to role-play prisoners and wardens. Daniel used an experiment to test the extent of racial discrimination. Mayo began the Hawthorne studies with an experiment to test the effects of illumination on productivity and found that simply being in an experiment influenced the behaviour of subjects. This obviously has wide implications for research, as does Rosenthal and Jacobson's demonstration of the self-fulfilling prophecy.

Interpretive sociology has surprisingly shown a willingness to use the experiment. Garfinkel used experiments to show that everyday behaviour is governed by 'commonsense assumptions'. He created rule-breaking situations (e.g. responding to questions with random answers or getting students to act as lodgers in their parents' homes), and then observed how subjects made sense of these novel situations. Atkinson had a similar intention of revealing the commonsense assumptions which coroners use to define suicide when he presented English and Danish coroners with identical case notes to see if they reached equivalent suicide verdicts or not.

CONVERSATIONAL ANALYSIS

This method is also employed in ethnomethodology to describe how people arrive at the meanings they give to social situations. Sacks used his own commonsense assumptions to study tape recordings of conversations between staff and callers at a suicide prevention centre. He noted that both parties saw the suicidal person as having 'no one to turn to', though that was precisely the role of the centre.

(**NB:** Refer back to the *Suicide* chapter and note that Sacks is not interested in suicide itself, only in the ways in which people make sense of the world.)

CONTENT ANALYSIS

Content analysis involves the systematic analysis of written documents or broadcasts. It has been used in studies of the mass media to demonstrate bias in the selection and presentation of news by the GUMG and others.

Content analysis of school books has alleged that they reinforce racist stereotypes (Wright on geography textbooks) and sexist stereotypes (Loban on reading schemes).

OBSERVATION

As regards **observation**, Shipman has argued that all research in the natural and social sciences depends on observation. He sees it as an active process where the researcher uses his mind to interpret what he sees and hears.

Examination questions tend to focus on participant observation, which is joining in the everyday lives of subjects. Gold has distinguished four ideal types of observation, ranging from complete participation to complete detachment. The general aims of participant observation are to study subjects in natural situations, thereby avoiding some of the problems of involvement.

Since Malinowski, functionalist social anthropologists have favoured participant observation to discover how apparently strange behaviour can be explained by looking at the way it 'fits' with other behaviour and contributes to social stability.

Interactionist sociologists have advocated participant observation as a means of sharing the experiences of subjects to discover the meanings they give to situations. Becker and Polsky have produced accounts of 'real' participation as a musician and poolroom player respectively. Hargreaves was able to show that actual teaching was different from teachers talking about teaching. Cicourel, in a study of juvenile delinquents, was able to describe the labelling process by joining in the routine activities of probation officers and sharing their conceptions of people and events.

Involvement, which is clearly the justification of participant observation, is also the source of most of the criticism directed against it, whether from a theoretical, practical or ethical viewpoint. Whyte's admission that he both influenced, and was influenced by, gang membership is often quoted. Interference can be reduced in different ways. King found that being over six foot, remaining standing and avoiding eye-contact allowed him to move among infant schoolchildren with minimal involvement. Polsky encouraged subjects to see him as a neutral observer rather than as an official, thrill–seeker or rival. He also stressed the importance of learning the language of subjects – in this case, the slang and non-verbal signals of pool hustlers. This is obvious when conducting anthropological studies of other societies, but is less so when studying deviant sub-cultures. Ditton noted the distinction between 'fiddling' (stealing from employers) and 'knocking-off' (from guests' hotel rooms); only the latter was condemned.

EXAMINATION QUESTIONS

1 Read the following extract written by a sociologist proposing to carry out research on a religious sect and answer the questions which follow.

I have always been sceptical of those who argue that sociology should model itself on the natural sciences. For me, studying people is not the same as studying natural objects such as chemicals or rocks; studying human actions presents its own particular problems and requires its own special techniques and approaches.

5   Although I accept that to some extent sociologists should maintain some detachment from their subjects, I think that we also have to get involved if we are to understand human behaviour. For this reason I have decided to carry out research on my chosen group by using ethnographic methods. For example, I intend to go along to a prayer meeting and pretend to be a potential convert genuinely interested in their

10   beliefs. I shall not reveal my true identity or intentions, but use covert research methods. I believe that 'going underground' in this way will enable me to discover how the worshippers really behave as unaffected by my presence as possible. Although such methods do raise both practical and ethical or moral issues, I believe they can be justified because it's the best way to study people by disturbing them as little as

15   possible.

a)   What term is used to describe sociologists who model sociology on the natural sciences (line 2)?   (*2*)

b)   What are the differences between studying people and studying natural objects (lines 2–3)?   (*6*)

c)   What do you understand by the term 'ethnographic methods' (line 8)   (*3*)

d)   Using research studies from any areas of social life to illustrate your answer, outline the *practical* advantages *and* disadvantages of covert research (line 10).   (*8*)

e)   What do you think might be the 'ethical or moral issues' referred to in line 13 above? How could you criticise this sociologist's approach on ethical grounds?   (*6*)

(*Total 25 marks*)
(NEAB)

2   The most common type of survey is the *cross-sectional* or snapshot survey. The researcher gets information from a cross-section of the group under study at one point in time. Thus the findings are gathered fairly quickly and cheaply to provide useful information....

5   A less common and more expensive type of social survey is the *longitudinal* survey. In this, a selected group is studied over a period of time. This enables the researcher to gain not only current information but also insights into the way people are changing their attitudes or behaviour over a much longer time-span.

Almost always used as part of a social survey is the questionnaire. This is where

10   the sociologist designs a set of questions about a particular subject to be answered by respondents (the people being surveyed). Questionnaires are difficult to write but are worth the effort because the sociologist can get a lot of information from respondents. However, some types of questions are easier to handle than others.

(Adapted from R. Power *et al: Discover Sociology*)

a)   According to the passage, what advantage does the longitudinal survey have over the cross-sectional survey?   (*1*)

b)   Name *two* different types of question (line 13) which may be used in a questionnaire, and give an example of each.   (*4*)

c)   '... the people being surveyed' (line 11) are chosen by different types of sampling. Discuss the advantages and disadvantages of different sampling techniques.   (*8*)

d)   Examine the advantages and limitations of using questionnaires.   (*12*)

(*Total 25 marks*)
(AEB)

3   My aim is to provide an overview of the sorts of considerations that sociologists take into account when designing research and deciding which methods to use. These considerations can be thought of as falling into four groups. First, what is to be the researcher's *standpoint* in relation to the research? Is the researcher going to do the

5   research, evaluate the research done by other people, or commission someone else to do the research? Second, what is the researcher's *approach*? Is the aim to produce positivist, interpretivist, ethnomethodological or structuralist explanations of whatever aspects of the social world are under study? Third, what *strategy* is the researcher adopting: a case study, a sample survey or an experiment? And fourth, what *techniques*

10   is the researcher going to use to collect and analyse data? For example, will it be an observation or an interview study? Will the data be quantified and statistically analysed or used raw in illustrative quotations?

(from *Principles of Methods* – Peter Halfpenny)

a)   Name *two techniques* used by researchers, other than those in the passage.   (*2*)

b) What does the author mean when he talks of data being 'used raw in illustrative quotations' in sociological research (line 12)? (*5*)

c) Explain what is meant by the term 'case study', and why sociologists might accept this strategy (line 9). (*8*)

d) Examine the relationship between a researcher's *approach* and her or his *technique*. (*10*)

(*Total 25 marks*)

(AEB)

4 Compare quantitive and qualitative methods of collecting sociological data. Illustrate your answer with examples.

(AEB)

5 Theory and Methods

ITEM A

The Economic and Social Research Council's 16–19 Initiative was launched in 1986 to investigate the wider social and psychological implications of youth's new condition. A representative sample of over 5,000, drawn from four parts of Britain (Kirkcaldy, Liverpool, Sheffield and Swindon), was surveyed by mailed questionnaire in 1987, 1988 and 1989. In each area, sub-samples were studied in greater depth through home interviews, and further ethnographic fieldwork was undertaken in Sheffield and Kirkcaldy.

(Adapted from *Young Citizens in Social Science Teacher*, 20.2 Spring 1991,
KEN ROBERTS)

ITEM B

Eichler's 'Nonsexist Research Methods' can be thought of as a handbook describing how every practicality of research can be sexist and how this can be avoided. The examples which are most readily recognised concern the construction of questionnaire items. In many ways, the art of writing good questions is a matter of constructing them in down-to-earth language. One drawback of this feature is that it becomes all too easy to pull in the sexism which resides in everyday talk. The classic example of this is when question-writers use 'he' when they are inquiring about persons-in-general. As an example, consider the following question on racial attitudes:

'If someone wanted to make a speech in your community claiming that blacks are inferior, should he be allowed to speak or not?'

(Adapted from *Feminist Methodology in Developments in Sociology*,
Vol. 8, RAY PAWSON)

ITEM C

Intensive, informal interviewing is another characteristic method in qualitative research. Respondents whose social situation or behaviour is the object of study are selected, and they are questioned at length. Instead of using the structured, pre-coded type of interview schedule, such interviews use many more open-ended questions and may be more conversational in character. Dennis Marsden's study 'Mothers Alone' tried to make the interview as much like a conversation as possible; while in Frank Coffield *et al*'s case study of four deprived families, the research began with unstructured interviews and developed into something akin to friendship, though with the research purpose explicit throughout. This is unusual for intensive interviewing, but completely different from the conventional large-scale survey interview, involving one visit to ask largely pre-structured questions.

(Adapted from *Social Science and Social Policy*,
MARTIN BULMER)

a) Suggest two reasons why the researchers in ITEM A might have wanted to carry out home interviews with sub-samples of the original 5,000 respondents. (*2*)

b) Re-write the question on racial attitudes in ITEM B so that it avoids 'the sexism which resides in everyday talk'. (*1*)

c) Assess the usefulness of mailed questionnaires as a method of sociological research (ITEM A). (*8*)

d) (i) What do sociologists mean by 'representative samples' (ITEM A)? (*2*)

(ii) How far do you agree that samples should always be representative? (*4*)

e) With reference to information from the ITEMS and elsewhere, assess the strengths and weaknesses of the two different types of interview identified in ITEM C. (*8*)

(*Total 25 marks*)

ANSWERS TO EXAMINATION QUESTIONS

OUTLINE ANSWERS

Question 3

Terms used in this passage (such as 'strategy' and 'technique') are not always defined in this way. However, you should accept the author's usage.

a) Choose two from questionnaires, participant observation, content analysis, use of secondary data, etc.

b) You should discuss, with examples, the ways in which data can either be processed or alternatively presented to the reader in an unprocessed form so that the researcher's interpretation and analysis do not interfere with the subject's experience. Link this with anti-positivist approaches.

Examples could be drawn from:

- Interactionist studies, such as Cohen and Taylor.
- Ethnomethodology, such as Sacks on conversations with potential suicides.
- Social anthropology studies where conversation is recorded.

c) A case study involves studying a single example. This could be an individual or family if the research was medical, psychological or conducted by social workers. This is not, however, the way in which the term is used in sociology.

Case studies could be on a gang (Whyte), a school (Ball), a factory (Beynon), a hospital (Goffman), a community (Goffman on the Shetland Isles) or a society (most social anthropology studies, e.g. Malinowski).

The problem of case studies is the extent to which they are representative of other cases. Uses include:

i) Testing a hypothesis by using an extreme case (Goldthorpe *et al.* chose Luton as the most suitable environment for embourgeoisement).

ii) Choosing a representative case (Ford's study criticising comprehensive schools).

iii) Letting the study stand alone as a complete work or using it for comparison (Malinowski or Mead's anthropological studies).

iv) As (iii), but as an ethnographic study from an interpretive viewpoint (Keddie).

The case study is often, but not exclusively, favoured by non-positivist sociologists.

d) i) Link structuralist and positivist sociology with quantitative, objective, large-scale techniques. Explain and illustrate.

ii) Give exceptional cases.

iii) Link interpretivist and micro-sociological approaches with qualitative, subjective, in-depth techniques. Explain and illustrate.

iv) Give exceptional cases.

v) Mention briefly other influences on choice of technique.

Question 4

Here the term 'method' is used in the sense that 'technique' is employed in Question 3.

In order to score high marks a variety of methods within each category must be considered in a critical fashion and comparisons made. Illustrations must help to explain a point and not just be listed. Crime and suicide provide useful examples to compare but should not exclude all others.

i) Link quantitative methods with positivist sociology. Explain and illustrate. Criticise by questioning the reliability, representativeness and validity.

ii) Give exceptional examples of positivist or structuralist sociology using qualitative methods.

iii) Link qualitative methods with interpretative and interactionist sociology. Explain and illustrate. Criticise as in i).

iv) Give exceptional examples of interpretive sociologists using quantitative methods.

v) Link qualitative methods with feminist sociology. Explain and illustrate.

vi) Criticise feminist use of qualitative methods.

Question 5

a) There are many possible answers, including: search for greater depth, check reliability or validity of original research, follow up new discoveries or interests, etc.

b) Substitute 'that person' or 'they' for 'he' (in which case 'someone' must be made plural, e.g. 'any persons').

c) This is straightforward but perhaps rather narrow for a 20-minute answer. There are strengths and weaknesses of questionnaires in general which can be addressed, but you must consider the special case of mailed (postal) questionnaires.

   You can examine the links between theory and methods, explaining why positivists may favour mailed questionnaires whereas interactionists and feminists may prefer methods that allow more involvement with subjects to discover meanings.

d) i)   Sampling involves studying only a small proportion of the population.

      Representative means the sample is typical of the whole population, therefore you can generalise your findings to the whole population.

   ii) Samples should be representative to allow generalisation. It may not be possible to get a representative sample of deviants, or where there is no suitable sampling frame. It may not be desirable to get a representative sample if you wish to study extreme or atypical cases. This is sometimes called a purposive sample. An example often cited is Goldthorpe and Lockwood's decision to select a sample of affluent workers who were most likely to have become middle class in order to show that this had not happened.

e) You must consider the strengths and weaknesses of the two types. You can use a comparative structure or a theoretical framework explaining why positivists prefer structured interviews whereas feminists prefer unstructured interviews. The aim of the research may influence the usefulness of the type of interview chosen. You could mention advantages and disadvantages of involvement, need for depth, empathy, etc.

TUTOR ANSWER

Question 1

a) What term is used to describe sociologists who model sociology on the natural sciences (line 2)?

Positivists advocate using the logic and methods of the natural sciences.

b) What are the differences between studying people and studying natural objects (lines 2–3)?

Natural objects have an objective existence; this means that they can be directly observed and measured. Like natural scientists, positivist sociologists and behaviourists in psychology restrict their subject matter to those phenomena which can be observed. Durkheim said that social facts should be treated like things.

People, unlike natural objects, have a consciousness and can reflect upon their own and others' behaviour. Because the mind is not directly observable and people attach meanings to behaviour, many social scientists are critical of the scientific approach. Weber saw the aim of sociology as the 'interpretive understanding of social action'.

Interpretive sociologists do not see social phenomena as having an objective existence, like natural objects. Social reality is constructed by interaction between individuals and groups.

Social behaviour does not follow universal laws, like natural phenomena, although much useful sociology depends on the view that behaviour is still predictable. Establishing correlations between phenomena allows the statement of probabilistic laws, not unlike those found in mathematics and theoretical physics.

Some scientists and sociologists see ethical issues as arising in the study of people which do not apply to other natural objects. However, the defence of animal rights indicates that this is not an undisputed view.

c) What do you understand by the term 'ethnographic methods' (line 8)?

These are methods employed by ethnomethodologists to discover and describe the ways in which people make sense of social situations. Generally this involves participant observation or listening to conversations. The aim is to share the experience of subjects without interfering with their everyday behaviour.

d)   Using research studies from any area of social life to illustrate your answer, outline the *practical* advantages *and* disadvantages of covert research (line 10).

The most common form of covert research is participant observation, although other undercover methods used include observation and experiments where subjects are either unaware of the real purpose of the research or unaware of being studied at all.

Covert methods allow access to groups who might exclude outsiders because their behaviour is illegal, shameful or secretive. Humphreys' 'Tea room trade' illustrates this although Polsky's studies of criminals and Barker's study of the 'Moonies' shows that access is not always restricted to those undercover.

However, the researcher may find himself restricted to studying groups where he (participant observation seems dominated by men) can pass as one of the subjects. Frequently young men have studied gangs, e.g. Williams on football hooligans. Pryce pointed out the necessity of being black for his study of Bristol, but Griffin was able to dye himself black for his research. Liebow made a virtue of his *difference* from his subjects, because, as an outsider, he was not seen as a threat.

The covert study of deviant groups may also entail a degree of danger. The researcher may risk discovery and reprisal during research or following publication. There is also the risk attached to joining in or witnessing deviant or secret behaviour. Wallis is convinced that Scientologists tried to discredit him through anonymous accusations. Rosenhan found it difficult to get out of a psychiatric hospital.

Covert research limits the means the observer can use to gather and record data without revealing one's identity. Being 'underground' limits the opportunities for asking questions, although Aggleton in a study of college students was able to get answers to a memorised set of key questions from all his subjects through informal conversation. Festinger used visits to the lavatory to make notes about an exclusive religious sect he had secretly joined.

Although there may be doubts about the reliability of covert participant observation, this criticism can be applied to all participant observation and other covert methods could be replicated. Zimbardo conducted an experiment which involved filming the vandalism of cars in various locations, and Daniel's experiments to test for racial discrimination have been subsequently repeated.

Finally, the major advantage must be the ability to minimise contamination of the research by influencing the behaviour of subjects. This problem was demonstrated in the work of Mayo and later Rosenthal and Jacobson. Rosenthal and Jacobson not only demonstrated the problem of the self-fulfilling prophecy, they also succeeded in doing so in an experiment using deception.

e)   What do you think might be the 'ethical or moral issues' referred to in line 13 above? How could you criticise this sociologist's approach on ethical grounds?

The researcher is invading the privacy of the group by observing them without their informed consent during what is likely to be an intensely personal activity. The presence of the observer in a non-religious capacity might be seen as offensive to their beliefs. Subsequent publication may cause embarrassment to individuals who could be identified (this can be overcome by disguising individuals, for example by scrambling different identities). The publication of research might expose the group to ridicule or threat.

Generally, covert participant observation involves the infiltration of relatively weak groups in terms of class or status, and although Becker talks of providing the view of the 'underdog' it is frequently the exotic lives of weak outsiders which are exposed to scrutiny.

There are no generally agreed professional ethics for sociologists, as there are for doctors, priests or lawyers. Polsky and Humphreys have debated the morality of covert research and come to opposite conclusions. This author does feel that such deception can be justified, although if the study could be shown to be significant and useful the case would be more convincing. Williams' research into hooliganism produced recommendations to help control threatening behaviour.

STUDENT'S ANSWER WITH EXAMINER COMMENTS

Question 2

a)   According to the passage, what advantage does the longitudinal survey have over the cross-sectional survey?

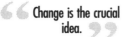 Change is the crucial idea.

> You can gain current information and insights into the way people change their attitudes and behaviour over a longer period of time.

b) Name *two* different types of question (line 13) which may be used in a questionnaire, and give an example of each.

Yes.

> 1 Closed questions, e.g. 'Did you vote Conservative?'
> 2 Open-ended questions, e.g. 'Why did you vote the way you did?'

c) '… the people being surveyed' (line 11) are chosen by different types of sampling. Discuss the advantages and disadvantages of different sampling techniques.

Should define and explain 'population', 'representative' and 'generalise'.

Good points, but no examples!.

How are random samples chosen?

Yes, but no examples.

Yes.

Not explained. Examples inappropriate.

> The different types of sampling are quota, random, stratified random, purposive and snowballing.
>
> A quota sample is chosen so that each unit is found in the same proportion that it is found in the population. This dispenses with the need for a complete sampling frame and allows any person meeting predetermined criteria to be chosen. In this technique you identify the relevant criteria, i.e. you have to anticipate the result. You could miss an important category and therefore your generalisation would be wrong. Also there is the temptation to choose amenable subjects. Errors are not calculable.
>
> In a random sample every unit has an equal chance of being chosen. This requires a complete sampling frame and you must use the people selected. Errors are calculable. But if it is small then it may not be representative. The US presidential elections were wrongly predicted in 1936 and 1948 as the samples were mainly middle class.
>
> Stratified random samples are taken at random from sub-divided populations. This ensures, even with small samples, that all relevant categories are represented.
>
> Purposive sampling is not representative because a specific type of sample is required, e.g. Gavron's 'Captive Wife' used the national housewives' register. Aggleton chose 'Spa Town' college because he knew the underachievers there. Goldthorpe and Lockwood chose Luton because it was 'ripe' for embourgeoisement.
>
> Snowballing is when one person leads to another to create a sample, e.g. D.J. West chose self-reporting delinquents. Hite chose those who responded. Daniel had no sampling frame available. Both snowballing and purposive sampling sacrifice representativeness to achieve their aim.

d) Examine the advantages and limitations of using questionnaires.

> Questionnaires are a comparatively cheap, fast and efficient method for obtaining large amounts of quantifiable data. Responses may be open or closed depending on the type of questions asked. Open-ended allow the respondent to compose their own answer and thus explain themselves fully, whereas closed questions may be an oversimplification. A problem with open questions is that the responses may be difficult to classify and quantify.
>
> Questionnaires may be administered in structured or unstructured interviews. Goldthorpe and Lockwood used structured interviews. This allowed any ambiguity to be clarified. But this type involves interviewer bias and is expensive. Standardised questions must be used to maintain consistency and reliability. Hyman showed the different results produced by using male and female interviewers.

Relevant points.

Unstructured interviews are unlikely to be used.

Relevant criticism.

Good points.

Wallis not used. Other examples better.

Relevant point.

Postal questionnaires are an inexpensive way of gathering data which is geographically dispersed. But the return rate is very low, therefore it is unrepresentative. Hite had only a 3% return rate. Only the literate, interested or those with time return a questionnaire.

Questionnaires avoid or limit interviewer bias or contamination. But some respondents may not be able to understand a question. There is no need for trained interviewers. But there is already prejudice in the selection and wording of questions. This imposes reality on the subjects.

Wallis used postal questionnaires to study Scientologists. Questions should avoid prejudgement, e.g. Oakley asked 'Do you feel dissatisfied with housework?' because she was looking for boredom. Variations in questions produce different answers. Kinsey rephrased 'How many times?' with 'Do you?' Sometimes respondents do not know the answers; Willmott and Young asked wives if their husbands had seen their families in the last 24 hours.

Subjects may fear officials and therefore avoid answering questions or answer wrongly, e.g. immigrants, criminals and religious sects.

Overall comments

Overall, a thorough answer with numerous good points. An equally good answer might make fewer points but develop and illustrate them more. The candidate does not examine theoretical issues, but nevertheless an A grade.

A Review Sheet for this chapter may be found on pp. 257–8.

SOCIOLOGICAL THEORIES

GETTING STARTED

The study of sociological theory is, for many students and teachers, the most daunting part of A-level courses. However good, responses to questions on any topic require the ability to apply and evaluate one or more theoretical approaches.

A basic command of theory is essential at an early stage in order to provide the framework for answering questions. Most of the answers in this book are organised on the basis of distinguishing different socio-logical perspectives. A more sophisticated understanding is necessary for answering questions which are specifically about theories and for produc-ing good answers to questions on substantive topics. For example, the ability to identify and apply a variety of Marxist or action approaches to topics such as deviance, education or power is likely to be expected by examiners for good answers.

The extent to which a detailed knowledge of theories is required depends on the syllabus. JMB asks more questions about theory than the other boards and requires a more detailed knowledge of the concepts used by the theories; this particularly applies to the different action theories.

The main themes of questions set on this topic are:

1 **Outline and critical evaluation of a specified theory.**
2 **Comparison of two particular theories.**
3 **Comparison of groups of theories such as structural and action theories or consensus and conflict theories.**
4 **Application of one or more theories to issues such as social change, social order or social control.**

Related material is found in the chapters on *Methods, Suicide and official statistics* and *The nature of sociology*. Most chapters benefit from the application of theory to topics and provide useful examples for theoretical discussion.

FUNCTIONALIST THEORY

ESSENTIAL PRINCIPLES

Functionalism is not a single easily defined theory. It is more a common perspective shared by many sociologists which comprises a coherent though varied approach to sociological problems. Many sociologists mentioned in textbooks as functionalists, most notably Durkheim, did not describe themselves in this way, and Radcliffe-Brown denied there was a functionalist school at all. Nevertheless, a common set of basic assumptions can be identified which are shared by most of the writers described as functionalists.

Functionalism is a structuralist perspective which emphasises the constraints imposed on individual behaviour by social forces. It is also a consensus perspective which explains social order in terms of shared values. The distinctive assumptions of functionalism include:

1   Society is seen as a system of interrelated parts. It is sometimes likened to a biological organism or a machine (see also the answer to Question 5 below).
2   The system has needs (functional prerequisites) which must be satisfied if it is to survive and remain stable, e.g. integration.
3   The parts can be studied and understood only by considering the relationships between individual parts and the part and the whole system. These relationships are based on functions, e.g. the relationship between education and the economy.
4   Functions are contributions that partial activities make to the working of the whole system. That is, the contribution the parts make to social stability by satisfying the needs of the system, e.g. the functions of the family which include reproducing culture through socialisation of the young.
5   The system is integrated by shared values, e.g. religious beliefs, and by interdependence based on the division of labour.
6   The precise form that social arrangements take depends on their functions. The whole system adapts so that the parts 'fit', e.g. the nuclear family developed to fit the needs of industrial society.
7   Inequality is seen as functional. Authority is given to those who can satisfy social needs and high rewards to those in functionally important positions.

CRITICISMS

These are general criticisms and may not apply to every functionalist writer or may apply to structuralist or consensus theories apart from functionalism.

1   Conflict theorists challenge the consensual view of human society. Harmony and integration are seen as overemphasised. It is the content of values, not the fact that they are shared, which unites societies, e.g. Western values of competitiveness and individualism can be seen as threats to integration. Conflict is seen as normal, not pathological. Consensus theories idealise institutions like the family and legitimise inequality.
2   Action theorists claim that structuralist theories offer an oversocialised view of individuals. The deterministic nature of structuralism concentrates on external social causes and ignores the importance of individual subjective experience. Human behaviour is purposive, not reactive. Individuals participate in the social construction of reality, they do not simply respond to a given objective reality.
3   Specific criticism of functionalism suggests:

■ Functionalism is teleological. That is, it tries to explain the origins of phenomena by identifying their effects (on the social system). This may be because some functionalism confuses the view that functions can be seen as effects or consequences with the idea that functions are purposes. Social arrangements do not exist because they meet functional needs, as the needs could go unsatisfied or be satisfied by other arrangements; e.g. children can be socialised outside the family and roles can be allocated without inequality of rewards.

■ Functionalism does not produce testable hypotheses and is thus unscientific.

■ Functionalism does not adequately explain social change. It tends to justify the status quo. The role of individuals who change society through conscious activities is ignored.

MARXIST THEORY

The term 'Marxism' is used for a variety of ideas developed from the writings of Karl Marx and his collaborators, particularly Engels. Marx was both an academic and political writer and a political activist. His work combines an ambitious analysis of history and capitalist society with a revolutionary programme.

Marxism began to influence sociology in a significant way only during the 1960s, so for most of this century sociology has ignored Marxism and Marxism has dismissed sociology. However, more recently Marxism has become an important strand in sociological thought and an invaluable source of critical material for A-level sociologists.

What is Marxism?

1   It is a theory explaining how society works which emphasises the importance of social class.
2   It is a theory of social change.
3   It is a political philosophy and programme for political action.

In A-level sociology we are concerned only with the first two aspects, but they are illuminated by an understanding of his revolutionary ideology and action.

Marxism is generally seen as a structuralist perspective which indicates how changes in society can change the consciousness and actions of individuals. However, it can also be seen as an action theory with individuals consciously pursuing goals and choosing the best means of achieving them. The constraints of the social (i.e. economic) structure restrict the rationality of the subject classes, who are kept falsely conscious by the dominant ruling-class ideology.

Marxism has become one of the dominant conflict theories in sociology and has influenced other conflict theories, e.g. Weber's work and modern feminism. The basis of conflict is the class struggle.

The key to understanding Marxism is the relationship between economic production (which is the central human activity) and other social phenomena, both ideas and institutions.

Marxist analysis is based on an examination of the relationship between the economic substructure of society and the superstructure of society.

The *substructure* comprises:

1   The forces of production, which is the term Marx gives to both the equipment and technological knowledge involved in producing goods.
2   The relations of production, which are the economic roles shaped by the forces of production, and crucially the relationships between these roles.

It is, thus, the relations of production which are the basis of social classes.

The *superstructure* comprises:

1   Social institutions such as the family, church, political system, education system, etc.
2   Ideas, beliefs and values including definitions of health and deviance, religious beliefs and the school curriculum.

The substructure shapes the superstructure, which in turn reproduces the substructure. Social change occurs when contradictions emerge in the economic substructure which prompt action by classes to challenge the domination of the ruling class. Thus feudalism fell when its ruling class could not meet the challenge presented by the rise of commerce and industry in towns. Marx similarly predicts the downfall of capitalism when contradictions will lead to the pauperisation of the proletariat, who will become class conscious and revolutionary.

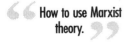 How to use Marxist theory.

The most usual application of Marxist theory to A-level sociology is to see various institutions as part of the superstructure of capitalist society and ask how they contribute to the preservation of ruling-class interests.

CRITICISM

1   Consensus theorists maintain that conflict is abnormal and undesirable. They share Marxist views on the process of cultural reproduction (by institutions such as the family, school, church and media) but dispute its purpose and the content of that which is transmitted. They see consensual values being passed on by socialisation for the common good, rather than ruling-class ideology being transmitted to maintain its hegemony.

Social problems are seen as related to industrialism rather than capitalism. Communism has been dismissed by Rostow (see Chapter 8 on *World sociology and development*) as a disease of transition, not a final goal of development.

2 Action theory since Weber has continually attacked the structuralism of Marxism, particularly the alleged economic determinism. This is exemplified by Weber's explanation of the rise of capitalism, which emphasises the role of ideas rather than technological development.

More modern interactionist theory puts increased emphasis on the consciousness of individuals. Rather than seeing this consciousness shaped by objective economic forces, it is suggested that if social situations are defined as 'real' by actors they are real in their effects. Thus, there need be no objective social reality, whether dominated by economic factors or not.

3 Conflict theories do not all accept Marxist analysis of phenomena such as the distribution of power (disputed by elite theorists) or family relationships (disputed by feminists). Above all, Marxist theories of class have been challenged, notably by Weber and followers.

FEMINIST PERSPECTIVES

There are a variety of feminist perspectives; they not only provide explanations of sociological phenomena but also suggest a suitable way of investigating society. (See Feminist methodology, p. 211.)

These perspectives have certain basic assumptions in common:

1 Sociology has operated within a patriarchal paradigm. Men have been the normal subjects of research and women, if considered at all, have been regarded as an afterthought or an unusual variation of men.
2 'Malestream' sociology has been perceived as ideologically neutral, whereas feminism is seen as biased.
3 Sociology needs to emphasise the importance of gender relationships in all topic areas.
4 Gender relationships are based on inequality of power.
5 Feminism condemns biological or functionalist explanations of gender roles which emphasise nature and tradition.

CRITICISMS

1 In addition to gender, sociologists must consider class, race, age, sexuality and disability as forms of inequality.
2 Feminism has focused on the experience of white middle-class women. H. Graham's work on servants reminds us that race and class are equally important in the analysis of domestic labour.
3 Feminism has neglected the experience of women in the Third World.
4 Feminism has neglected the study of masculinity and men. The motives of the oppressor (men) may be as useful as the experience of the oppressed (women).
5 Feminists' neglect of positivist methods has been criticised for overemphasising *action* at the expense of *structure*, and the subjective at the expense of the objective.

(These five criticisms fail to acknowledge the variety of feminist perspectives, e.g. Marxism–feminism does consider class in detail.)

6 Feminism is biased rather than value free.

The feminist answer to this is that value freedom preserves the (patriarchal) status quo.

VARIETIES OF FEMINISM

Liberal feminism

Gender inequality is the result of individual prejudice and ignorance which encourage unfair treatment or the institutionalisation of these prejudices into family life, education, media or the law.

Remedies lie in equal opportunity legislation and changing values through education.

Criticism

1 Overemphasises individual attitudes rather than systematic socially structured inequality.

2   Does not explain why these attitudes develop and persist.

Marxism–feminism

(Beechey, Bruegel, Barrett, Maynard.)

Women's oppression is the result of the class inequalities found in capitalist and other exploitative societies.
    This involves:

1   Within the family women reproduce labour power at no cost to the employer.
2   Women's experience within the family disadvantages them in the paid labour market.
3   Women constitute a reserve army of labour.
4   Marxist–feminists emphasise economic exploitation.
5   Feminist Marxists emphasise ideological control.

Criticism

1   Women are oppressed in socialist societies.
2   Why is it women, rather than men, or both men and women, who perform domestic labour?
3   The ideology of the family and gender, sex and sexuality applies to all women rather than only working-class women.
4   Capitalism has encouraged women into the paid labour market and given them more influence in the family.

Radical feminism

(Millett, Firestone.)

1   Male supremacy is the oldest and most universal form of domination.
2   All men have oppressed and exploited women.
3   The origins of patriarchal ideology lie in:

    Biological motherhood.
    Families based on marriage.
    Heterosexuality.

4   Sexuality, sexual violence and domestic violence are all forms of male oppression which are institutionalised into society, not individual forms of deviance. They are private and personal expressions of social inequality.

Combined perspectives

The account so far tries to impose a rather oversimplified view; many feminist theories and studies combine different approaches.

Delphy's *materialist feminism* uses Marxist analysis to explain the special position of women in the home. She distinguishes:

1   The industrial mode of production, where employers exploit workers.
2   The domestic mode of production, where men exploit women.

Barrett has suggested that feminists, and any other sociologist, might usefully incorporate some of the findings of modern biology. She is also prepared to consider sympathetically ideas from Freudian psychoanalytical approaches which had previously been rejected by feminists.

THE NEW RIGHT PERSPECTIVE

The importance of New Right thinking is the major influence it has had on political leaders and social policy in Britain and the USA. It has been less influential within the academic world of sociology, and at A-level has often become a pantomime villain to be attacked rather than considered.
    The New Right perspective has two main strands:

1   **The market liberal view** that the free market produces affluence and political freedom. Planned socialist economies produce poverty and political tyranny.
2   **The conservative view** that traditional values are threatened by trends in modern society. This conservative right promotes the conventional family, traditional education, narrow religious values and a degree of nationalism and ethnocentrism.

New Right ideology has been associated with Thatcherism in Britain and the Reagan–Bush administrations in the USA. Studying it may help our understanding of political actions such as reform of the Welfare State (changes in taxes and benefits), privatisation, educational reforms and reform of trade-union law.

THE ATTACK ON SOCIOLOGY

A more narrow concern has been the attack from the New Right on the subject of Sociology. Some would like it changed; some would like it removed from the curriculum. Sociology is seen as biased against capitalism, stressing poverty and inequality rather than wealth and freedom.

CRITICISMS: FOR

1   The case for a free market provides a useful criticism of Marxist analysis of capitalism. Both the economic failure and political consequences of Marxism can be assessed; thus the fall of communist states since 1989 can be examined.
2   It avoids the confusion caused by seeing functionalism as the sole alternative to conflict perspectives.
3   It encourages the examination of affluence rather than poverty. Even Marxists recognise the importance of an affluent (albeit for some only) consumerist society. The apparent success of the enterprise culture can be assessed.

CRITICISMS: AGAINST

1   The economic benefits of capitalism have been limited to some people in some societies.
2   Capitalism is not invariably associated with political freedom and human rights.
3   The attack on sociology is itself biased, with a very unrepresentative selection of books cited and limited evidence of biased teaching.
4   A small and unrepresentative group of academics have achieved undue attention because of their support for Conservative government.
5   For criticism of the application of New Right ideas, see Chapters 3, 7, 10, 11, 12 and 16.

APPLICATION OF THE NEW RIGHT PERSPECTIVE

Application of the New Right perspective to sociological topics can be found in appropriate chapters. Here is a reminder of some basic themes.

Stratification

Capitalism is seen as providing a framework for freedom of the individual. High rewards for the producers of wealth encourage economic growth, which will benefit all. The continued existence of an underclass may be explained by their behaviour and/or a misguided Welfare State.

Power and politics

Supporters of free-market economics follow Hayek and advocate the minimum of state interference in the lives of citizens. This will encourage economic efficiency and also increased freedom of choice for the individual.

The family

The conventional nuclear family is promoted.

Education

Where possible the benign hand of the market should be introduced. The virtues of traditional education are extolled, and many post-war reforms condemned.

The teaching of Sociology has been singled out for particular condemnation! (See below.)

Work

Trades unions are viewed with suspicion, as they interfere with the operation of free labour markets. Policies support an increasingly 'flexible' labour market.

Mass media

Governments should not broadcast or publish themselves and should minimise regulation of those who do.

However, elements of the New Right do favour control of 'immoral output'.

Welfare, poverty and social policy

There is a focus on the existence of a culture of dependency and a desire to reduce the Welfare State.

The nature of sociology

One of the main reasons that sociologists and Sociology teachers have taken notice of the development of the New Right is their attack on our subject.

ACTION PERSPECTIVES

These include:

1   Social action theories, which have developed from Weber (and Marx).
2   Symbolic interactionism, which has developed from Mead's social psychological approach.
3   Ethnomethodology, which was developed by Garfinkel as a sociological activity (rather than a theory) from the phenomenological philosophy of Schutz. Schutz himself criticised Weber's view of social action.

Despite the differences between these various action perspectives there are some generally shared basic assumptions:

1   Individuals or small groups are studied, not whole societies.
2   Roles are negotiated by individuals, not imposed by society or the ruling class, e.g. between doctors and patients or deviants and the police.
3   The social world exists in the minds of individuals, it has no objective reality; e.g. there is no real rate of suicide.
4   Social order emerges from shared meanings, so 'if men define situations as real they are real in their consequences' (Thomas).
5   Weber suggests that sociology should seek the 'interpretive understanding of social action'. This involves examining the meaning actors give to their own behaviour and the behaviour of others rather than seeking the causes of behaviour.
6   The general approach is anti-positivist and anti-scientific. The influences the choice of research methods which should seek insight into the actor's experience of the world. Language is seen as very important. 'Talk' is both a method and a source of data.

Social action theory

Even within this perspective there are variations, but the general model is one where 'actors' carry out actions to pursue goals. Their values and their perception of the situation influences their choice of goals and the selection of means to achieve them.

It is the meaning attributed to behaviour by the actor and others which distinguishes social action from biological behaviour.

Symbolic interactionism

The key concept is the 'self'. The self is how we see ourselves as objects in the social world. We can be self-conscious and act towards ourselves as well as others, e.g. we can get angry with ourselves. We see ourselves as we think others see us. Cooley called this 'the looking-glass self'.

Interaction, using symbols (particularly language), is possible because we can take the role of others. Others are either particular people, especially those who are important to us ('significant others', e.g. mothers, teachers and bosses), or 'generalised others' who represent the view that the wider society might have about us.

This ability to interact by taking the role of others is used by sociologists who use participant observation to step into the shoes of their subjects in order to see the social world as they do and share the meanings they give to symbols.

Deviant or abnormal individuals, groups or situations are often studied because the view deviants have of themselves is often different from the general or official view, e.g. those labelled delinquent or insane may see themselves as ordinary.

Ethnomethodology

The aim of ethnomethodology is to describe how people make sense of social situations using 'commonsense knowledge'. Commonsense knowledge is the shared meanings given to everyday encounters and provides the basis of social order. Particular events are seen as examples (called 'documents') of a broader set of events so people know what is expected of them. The general set of events provides the context which makes sense of the individual acts, e.g. coroners use their commonsense knowledge to reconstruct deaths to decide if they were suicides.

Garfinkel sees people as 'members' rather than 'actors', which is the term preferred by interactionists. Members assume that the social world has an objective reality which is seen and experienced by everyone in the same way. Others are believed to share our commonsense knowledge and do so sufficiently to allow for orderly encounters. If they do not appear to share our commonsense knowledge then we assume there is something different about them, e.g. they are mad, wicked, foreign or a child.

CRITICISM

1   Structuralist theories criticise action theories for their inability to explain or, in some cases, even recognise structural constraints on behaviour. Consensus-based theories question the absence of consideration of the way individuals are socialised into a pre-existing culture.

Conflict theories are more specific in their insistence that neither conflict nor the unequal distribution of power is given adequate consideration. Structural restraints are imposed on individuals whether they like it or not. The failure to recognise such limitations is seen, by Marxists, as false consciousness. The famous saying of the interactionist Thomas – 'if men define situations as real, they are real in their consequences' – could be inverted by Marxists to say that if situations are real, they are real in their consequences however they are defined by individuals.

Symbolic interactionism could be alleged to explain nothing as it suggests little more than that social situations are the product of action and that action is governed by the actors' perception of the situation.

2   There are internal debates within the action perspective. These may take the form of arguing that a theory goes too far in emphasising individual choice and the subjective nature of social reality. Or conversely, not far enough by still accepting the existence of an objective reality with which subjective meanings can be compared.

Touraine argues that it is necessary to recognise structural constraints and distinguishes 'action' which is creative or innovative behaviour from 'conduct' which is conforming to established norms.

Ethnomethodology, unlike other action theories, does not see the sociologist as a detached observer capable of finding the right answer and explaining behaviour with theories. Sociology is just another form of common sense shared by sociologists. This is why ethnomethodology often studies other sociology and sociologists, e.g. the suicide debate. However, sociology can differ from other forms of understanding if it is done in a 'self-conscious reflexive way' and is not based on unacknowledged commonsense assumptions.

CONCLUSION: MAKING SENSE OF THEORIES

The paragraph above suggests why ethnomethodology is seen by some as a waste of time. The possibility of sociologists studying sociologists studying sociologists, and so on, is not an enthralling prospect. Ethnomethodologists recognise this and choose not to do it. They have still been criticised for studying trivial issues and ignoring major social problems.

However, the action perspectives have made a significant impact on most sociology, which can no longer ignore the issues of meaning and the consciousness of actors.

The accounts of the various theories have naturally oversimplified them and tended to exaggerate the differences between them. The enduring problem for sociology is to find a way of locating individual action in the context of social structure. The founding fathers were aware of the problem even if they may not have resolved it.

Durkheim saw society as moral order which would contain the actions of individuals whether they were aware of it or not.

Weber saw social structure as based on the shared meanings given to social action but generally deals with action and structure separately.

Marx saw society as based on economic relations which influence the individual's consciousness and action.

POST-MODERNISM AND POST-MODERNITY

INTRODUCTION

Post-modernism has become increasingly popular as an approach explaining contemporary social life and as a critique of other sociological theories.

The main themes are:

The changing state of the world

Post-modernists claim that the contemporary world can no longer be described as 'modern'. The so-called 'project of modernity' (i.e. the goal of a progressive rational society) which has dominated Western societies since the Enlightenment is seen as discredited and over. Society can no longer be seen as progressing. Post-modernists have attacked modernity on ideological grounds. They criticise the products of modernity, such as modern architecture and assembly-line work. The modern state is seen as having the potential for totalitarian control and even the mass-produced killing found in Nazi camps.

The need to change sociological thinking

The ways in which sociology and other academic disciplines describe social life are no longer useful.

1   Post-modernism rejects the truth of so-called *metanarratives*. This is the term given to 'grand sociological theories' which claim to explain how society works. These 'grand theories', such as Marxism, offer explanations of many or all aspects of social life. Post-modernism argues that these theories are just 'big stories' which are no different to any of the other stories we employ to make sense of our lives.

2   Marx and Durkheim are also subjected to criticism for assuming that societies will progress to something better, and that rational scientific thinking can help to bring such progress about. Weber was rather less optimistic about the increasing rationalisation and bureaucratisation of society.

The main assumptions of post-modernism

1   **Contemporary society is leaving modernity behind.**
    Modern society, which succeeded pre-modern/medieval society, is being replaced by a post-modern society.

2   **The main features of 'modern society'** as described by post-modern writers are:

   ■ *Economic*: a capitalist industrial economy characterised by specialised workers, technological developments, mass production and mass consumption.

   ■ *Political*: the dominance of the nation-state as the major form of political organisation. The state is increasingly bureaucratic and centralised.

   ■ *Cultural*: the traditional and often religious thinking of pre-modern society has been replaced by rational scientific thinking.

3   **The main features of post-modern society**, in contrast, are:

   ■ *Economic*: some reversal of the trend towards a deskilled mass of unionised workers. The so-called 'flexible labour force' includes more female part-time workers, and new forms of employment and self-employment. Secure jobs for life, at least in some sectors of the economy, are no longer available.
     The economy is no longer dominated by mass-produced goods. There are more services and cultural products distributed through new media. Niche markets for specialised products have been developed. Images are sold as well as goods.
     Some writers have described these economic trends as post-Fordist.

   ■ *Political*: national governments exert less control. The New Right movement led by Thatcher and Reagan argued for the reduction of state activity. State-controlled industry was privatised. Globalisation has bypassed the power of some nation-states.

   ■ *Cultural*: it is the emphasis on cultural phenomena which has been perhaps the most attractive feature of post-modernism to students and teachers. Post-modern society is seen as concerned more with the image than with the object. In fact, one of the key concepts of Baudrillard's post-modernism is the *simulacrum*, which is an image (or a copy) of an image (or a copy) for which there is no original because it never existed or has been destroyed. This could be illustrated by nostalgic images of a past that never existed which are conjured up by TV fiction (such as 'Heartbeat' or 'The Darling Buds of May').

A CRITICAL REVIEW

Do we live in a post-modern society?

Critics question the assumption that the post-modern period is really distinct from the 'modernity' which preceded it. Instead, it is argued that the new features of contemporary society are simply further developments of capitalism. Capitalism has always encouraged technological development, and needed new products and new markets.

In *The McDonaldisation of Society* G. Ritzer recognises that some of the economic trends described by post-modernists are present in contemporary society, such as the globalisation of consumption and the importance of images. However, rather than seeing a complete break with the modernist past, Ritzer sees a continuation of the rationalisation of production described by Weber and F.W. Taylor. (See Chapter 13 on *Organisations*.)

Is modern society so bad?

The implied, or often explicit, disapproval of modern society can also be challenged:

- Modern methods of production have allowed the mass consumption of goods which were once the preserve of the rich, or not available at all.
- Modern political systems may be liberal and pluralist as well as totalitarian.
- Modern technological development has made available media products such as computers and VCRs which can be used to create images and other cultural products. This challenges the view that mass production always curtails rather than enhances freedom.

Is post-modern society just the next stage of capitalism?

Lash and Urry (1987) have suggested that Marxist theories can successfully incorporate some post-modernist ideas. Capitalism can be seen as having developed from an age of mass production and consumption. Contemporary consumer capitalism is disorganised, and is based increasingly on the production and consumption of information and other cultural forms rather than material goods. Some Marxist analysis can accept this if the profit motive remains paramount and exploitative economic relationships persist.

Indeed, the development of global markets and the shrinking of time and space through modern communications seem to sit quite happily with traditional Marxist views on imperialism as a form of capitalism.

Is post-modernism the ideology of patriarchy and consumer capitalism?

There have been some rare challenges to post-modernism on the basis that it has presented a series of unsupported attacks on feminism and is little more than an apology for the individualism and greed associated with the Thatcher–Reagan years. However, many feminists are incorporating post-modernism into their analyses of, for example, the media. In fact, the very diversity of feminist ideas can be seen as an illustration of post-modernism in sociology.

CONCLUSION

Post-modernism and its relationship with sociology can be seen in a variety of ways. My aim has been to simplify some ideas so that they can be consumed by A-level students. Ali Ratansi seems to have predicted this in 1995 when he wrote: 'No doubt A-level texts will soon incorporate "post-modernism" as a "perspective" in sociology.'

For some writers, however, a choice needs to be made between abandoning sociology in favour of post-modernist methods of analysis and rejecting post-modernism as largely irrelevant to sociological concerns.

In the 1970s many sociologists felt that the development of ethnomethodology was taking sociology nowhere. The same feeling that sociology should return to more empirical and less philosophical roots exists among those who remain more interested in explaining and changing society despite accepting the relativism of many post-modernists.

Do post-modern ideas mean the end of sociology?

Z. Bauman suggested that sociology could respond in three ways to the challenge presented by post-modernists:

1   Accept the post-modern arguments and abandon sociology. Sociology has assumed that society develops in a logical way, and that cultural phenomena can be explained rationally. If this is not the case, both the subject matter and the methodology of sociology should be replaced.
2   Sociologists could dismiss the claims of the post-modernists and even ignore the questions they have posed. Sociologists accustomed to evaluating empirical evidence are ready critics of post-modern prophets such as Baudrillard, who seem to have made unsupported assertions about pre-modern, modern and post-modern society.
3   Take the middle way between 1 and 2. Sociologists could rethink the subject, study the new social relations identified by post-modernism, and take on board some of the criticisms of a sociology based on scientific thinking.

THEORETICAL AND EMPIRICAL STUDIES

FUNCTIONALIST THEORIES

Durkheim

Although functionalism could be traced back before Durkheim, he can be seen as the major influence in establishing sociology as a distinct discipline studying social facts in a scientific manner. Certainly the influence of Comte's positivism and 'social engineering' and Spencer's biological analogy can be seen in his work. For Durkheim functional analysis involved finding both the causes and functions of social facts, i.e. how they maintain social order.

Durkheim saw society as a system based on a moral consensus. He distinguished simple societies, characterised by mechanical solidarity, from modern societies, characterised by organic solidarity. Integration in the former was based on common values, roles and practices. This solidarity was threatened by the division of labour which accompanied industrialisation but re-established through the interdependence of the differentiated parts.

Malinowski and Radcliffe-Brown

Malinowski used functional analysis to examine simple societies, thus bringing a sociological perspective to anthropology. He saw societies as social systems of interrelated parts which develop to meet common human needs.

Radcliffe-Brown was also a social anthropologist; he shared Durkheim's concern with social solidarity and confirmed his views on the integrating effects of religion.

Functionalism helped modern social anthropology to reject evolutionary views which dismissed unusual practices as primitive by identifying their current functions.

Parsons

Parsons produced the most complete modern version of functionalism and made it the dominant paradigm in post-war American sociology. His structural-functional analysis identified four functional prerequisites of social systems. These were:

1   *Adaptation* to the environment through economic activity.
2   *Goal attainment,* which is achieved through the allocation of resources by those given authority.
3   *Integration,* which is the need for social solidarity emphasised by Durkheim and Malinowski.
4   *Pattern maintenance,* which is the need to motivate members of society to play necessary roles and to conform to rules.

The first two are concerned with the demands made on the system from outside and the latter two are problems generated inside the social system. Social structure consists of the institutions which persist through time to satisfy these needs. The form they take depends on the value system of the society.

Merton

Merton developed a critique of functionalism and attempted to amend it to make it more appropriate for the analysis of modern industrial societies. He introduced new concepts which challenged the view of functions as universal, indispensable and positive.

Dysfunctions were the negative effects phenomena had on some people, e.g. Vogel and Bell's description of scapegoating the emotionally disturbed child to integrate the family.

Functional equivalents were alternative solutions to social needs. Thus we could question Davis and Moore's view that either social inequality or religion is 'necessary' if another social arrangement could be shown to have the same consequences for society.

MARXIST THEORIES

The Marxist contribution to modern sociology, primarily as a critique of consensus theories, can be found in most topics sociologists study. Rather than repeat accounts of research found above, e.g. the debates over the role of the state and the nature of schooling, it might be more useful to try and identify distinctive schools in Marxist sociology.

The Frankfurt School

There are common themes in the work of the founders (Marcuse, Adorno and Horkheimer) and followers (Habermas) of the Frankfurt School. They emphasise the obligation for sociologists to get involved in the critical analysis of capitalist society. This would reveal exploitation and constraints on freedom and then the potential for action to change the world. They are aiming at challenging false consciousness and encouraging class consciousness.

Marcuse became notorious in the 1960s for suggesting that students could be a 'detonator' of a revolutionary movement among, not the proletariat, but deprived groups such as ethnic minorities. He saw the relatively rich working class in the USA as enslaved by 'chains of gold' working to satisfy 'false needs'.

Althusserian structuralism

Althusser's attack on consensus-based positivist sociology is not based on a humanistic disapproval of alienation or the desire to encourage individual consciousness and action. He does reject crude economic determinism but still insists on structural explanations of behaviour (see also the Marxist approaches to education, Chapter 11). He argues that ideology and the institutions of the superstructure are largely independent of the economy (although ultimately the substructure is dominant). The superstructure supports the substructure through Ideological and Repressive State Apparatuses (ISAs and RSAs). The need ideologically to control the working class is reminiscent of Gramsci's account of hegemony.

Marxist–feminism

There are a range of feminist theories which have borrowed more or less from Marxism. Some have used Marxist concepts but in a feminist context, e.g. the argument that women who do not see their exploitation are falsely conscious. Women's labour is seen as expropriated by men rather than the ruling class. Delphy's work exemplifies this approach.

Others see the explanation of women's exploitation and subordination as lying in the capitalist system and insist that women are part of the working class. Sexism is seen as part of the superstructure of capitalism. Mitchell's pioneering writing on women's position in society follows this view.

ACTION THEORIES

Weber

Weber introduced the idea that sociology should study social action rather than social facts. He thus presented a challenge to the positivism of Durkheim and the alleged economic determinism of Marx.

He distinguished four ideal types of social action on the basis of their 'modes of orientation', i.e. the extent to which they were rational. He saw an action as rational if it involved the assumption that goals could be achieved by the use of particular means. The extreme types were:

1   Affective social action, which is spontaneous and stems from impulse and emotion.

2   Instrumental rationality, where the actor assesses the costs and benefits of pursuing a particular goal in a certain way.

Goffman

Goffman developed Mead's concept of the self, describing the presentation of self as like a dramatic production. He used the insights of symbolic interaction to describe the 'mortification of self' inflicted on psychiatric patients by the institution. He does not see the patient as a passive victim, however, and he also describes various strategies they use to fight back. He has employed participant observation to describe the meanings subjects give to behaviour and situations.

Becker

Becker has become familiar to A-level students because of his work on the labelling of deviants. This is consistent with the interactionist viewpoint. In addition we could mention earlier work which describes, like Goffman, the way in which roles are not just imposed on children through socialisation but actively and consciously acquired by adults. In a study of medical students he describes how they abandon the aim of learning to be doctors for the short-term role of being a successful student.

Cicourel

Cicourel is also a significant figure in the sociology of deviance, particularly in his criticism of crime statistics. His ethnomethodological account of the way police and probation officials define delinquency and delinquents using commonsense assumptions is a reminder that not all ethnomethodology can be dismissed as trivial, as he is obviously prepared to look at the 'tacit understandings' of the powerful and how they can be imposed on the weak. This is similar to the later work of Atkinson on suicide, where the commonsense assumptions of coroners play a major part in the definition of suicide.

EXAMINATION QUESTIONS

1   Comment on the assertion that there is not a unified interactionist perspective but several distinct intellectual strands.

(Question adapted by author)

2   Assess the contribution of different sociological perspectives to an understanding of social change.

(AEB)

3   Examine the similarities and differences between consensus and conflict perspectives in sociology.

(AEB)

4   Sociologists have often distinguished between theories of social structure and theories of social action. Outline and assess these two approaches to sociological theory.

(AEB)

5   Outline and assess the usefulness of the analogy between society and a biological organism.

(AEB)

ANSWERS TO EXAMINATION QUESTIONS

OUTLINE ANSWERS

Question 2

A good answer to this question will go beyond simply outlining the relevant arguments from Durkheim, Marx and Weber, although this would provide a suitable framework for an answer.

Perspectives must be critically assessed. Credit will be given for suitable illustrations. An awareness of variety within a perspective is always rewarded.

i) Functionalism presents an evolutionary model of change where social institutions adapt to 'fit' the changing needs of the social system.

    a)   Comte saw 'dynamics' (the scientific laws which explain social change) as one of the two main branches of sociology.

    b)   Durkheim on the effects of division of labour on social solidarity.

    c)   Parsons on the difference between traditional and modern society and the modernisation theory of development.

ii) Critics point out the tautological nature of such theories and the overemphasis on consensus.

iii) Marxism offers a revolutionary model of change which results from class conflict. Contradictions between the means and relations of production, e.g. competition between employers forcing down wages and concentration of capital encourage the development of class consciousness and revolution.

    One internal debate is on the extent of economic determinism or the influence of social action, e.g. the importance of Marxist ideas and revolutionary parties. The development chapter distinguishes between Marxist views which emphasise national development and those which are global theories.

iv) Critics have identified alternative causes of change, e.g. Weber, and also reject the alleged universalism or economic determinism of some Marxists. Mosca's explanation of the changes in ruling elites could be used.

v) Weber's *Protestant Ethic and the Spirit of Capitalism* emphasises the rejection of economic determinism and the significance of ideas in the development of capitalism.

vi) Criticism should come not just from those who reject Weber's specific concern with the Protestant ethic but from those Marxists who reject his ideas on the relationship between ideas and materialism.

Question 3

Good answers must deal adequately with both similarities and differences, though more emphasis on differences is acceptable and likely. Relevant illustration will aid comparison. As usual, diversity within the perspectives should be noted.

  i) Similarities:

    a)   Both structural perspectives.

    b)   Both study objective social phenomena.

    c)   Both usually adopt a positivist approach and related methods.

    d)   Note non-structural Marxism and Parsons' views on social action.

  ii) Differences; contrasting explanations of:

    a)   Social order, social control and deviance.

    b)   Social change.

    c)   Ideas and ideology (refer to education, religion and media).

    d)   The nature and distribution of power.

    e)   Roles.

Question 5

Rather than just outline various versions of the biological analogy, this question (and most similar ones) asks for a critical assessment of its usefulness to sociologists.

  i) Explain that analogies are models, not theories. They do not explain how society works, but compare it to a biological organism in order to simplify a complex abstract concept by portraying it in a simpler, more familiar and concrete form.

  ii) Identify the main principles of the biological analogy and show how they can be used as models of human society.

    a)   Structure: biological organisms are systems made up of interrelated parts. The structure is the relationship between the parts. Human society has structures which survive individuals and govern their behaviour.

    b)   Functions: biological organs perform activities that have functions, i.e. are related to the working of the system. Social arrangements have functions which contribute to the fulfilling of social needs.

    c)   Growth: biological organisms develop through a life cycle and evolve into more complex forms. Societies evolve into more complex forms (Durkheim), and the arrangements become more specialised (Parsons).

    d)   Equilibrium: Canon's concept of homoeostasis suggests that organisms are self-regulating. That is, they balance internal working with environmental conditions, e.g. sweating cools the body on hot days. This could be likened to Parsons' notion of 'fit' where social arrangements adapt to changing conditions.

    e) Normality and pathology: just as biological organisms have a normal balanced state so, too, do societies. Social order is seen as normal and deviance as pathological.

iii) Critics:

    a) Functionalists, including Spencer, who argued for the appropriateness of the analogy have pointed out discrepancies in the comparison, e.g. biological organisms have a specific form, societies do not.

    b) Marxists and other conflict theories point out the absence of consideration of power, the overemphasis on integration and the mistaken view of social order being based on equilibrium and normality.

    c) Interpretive sociology criticises the biological analogy for presenting an over-socialised view of man, who appears enslaved by social structures. Instead, they see order as socially constructed through interaction.

TUTOR ANSWER

Question 4

Sociologists have often distinguished between theories of social structure and theories of social action. Outline and assess these two approaches to sociological theory.

(**NB:** There is a great deal of material which could be included here and there is, therefore, the risk of producing an unbalanced or badly organised account. Good answers must include critical assessment.)

Structuralist theories are holistic and concerned with the influence of society on individuals as well as the relationships between different parts of society. They emphasise the ways in which individuals conform to social order. Functionalists see order as based on the acceptance of consensual values whereas Marxists see order imposed by the powerful. Individuals are seen as being born into particular social structures and learning the beliefs and values of their societies. Functionalists see this process as socialisation, whereas Marxists and feminists see it as indoctrination.

    Structuralist theories are conventionally divided into consensus and conflict perspectives. The dominant theories in the two perspectives are functionalism and Marxism. There are, however, not only divisions within each perspective (e.g. non-Marxist and anti-Marxist conflict theories such as radical feminism and elite theories) but also disputes and differences of emphasis between those sharing similar theoretical assumptions. There are varieties of both functionalism and Marxism. Some Marxists would not want their work categorised as exclusively structuralist (see Willis below).

    Functionalists see society as a system of interrelated parts. These parts are linked by their functions, i.e. the contribution that institutions make to satisfying the needs of the system, thus encouraging survival and stability. The emphasis on equilibrium has led critics to claim that functionalism is conservative and fails to explain change. This has led some anthropologists to turn their backs on Malinowski in favour of the structuralism of Lévi-Strauss or Marxist historical materialism. Where change is recognised it is seen as evolutionary as institutions adapt to 'fit' the needs of the system.

    Marxism emphasises revolutionary rather than evolutionary change. It is a dynamic theory which stresses the importance of one aspect of social structure, the economy, over all others. The methods and relations of production explain the development of other institutions and ideas which are seen as the superstructure, which is produced by and in turn reproduces the existing economic substructure. In a pre-communist society conflict, not stability, is seen as normal.

    Structuralist theories are frequently associated with a positivist approach to research and the use of the logic and procedures of the natural sciences. This is not inevitable but is encouraged by the view that individual behaviour is explicable in terms of external constraints. These external constraints are seen as having an objective existence like biological facts. Durkheim identified the causes of variations in suicide rates as being different degrees of integration or moral regulation. Marx saw both ideas and behaviour as explained by the group's relationship to production. Thus structuralist theories look for the causes of human behaviour in the structure of societies.

    Those theories which stress social action rather than structure tend to adopt anti-positivist methods. The interpretive critics of Durkheim's *Suicide* do not reject just his functionalist explanations but also his methodological approach. They deny the existence of social facts which exist independently of individuals. Instead they concentrate on trying to describe either the social meaning of suicide (Douglas) or the process by which such meanings arise (Sacks).

The assumptions of those non-structuralist theories which emphasise the importance of social action vary according to their origins and development. The two main strands of thought are symbolic interactionism and ethnomethodology. Both reject the view that individual behaviour can be explained by identifying objective social causes external to individuals.

Symbolic interactionism studies the ways in which individuals interact by responding to symbols, particularly language. (Talk also assumes great importance for ethnomethodologists both as a method and as a topic of research.) The individual is seen as having more freedom of action than is implied by structuralism. Individuals attribute meaning to the behaviour of self and others. The self is seen as developing from the actual or anticipated reaction of others (either significant or generalised others) to ourselves. Social reality is negotiated between active actors (teachers and pupils, police and 'offenders'), not imposed by outside forces.

Ethnomethodology is concerned with how individuals make sense of the world. Studies describe the 'commonsense assumptions', 'background expectancies' and 'tacit understandings' which are at the heart of social order. They reject the structuralist view that order can be imposed on individuals and instead see order as more fragile, constantly being created and re-created by everyday routine encounters. Whereas interactionists favour participant observation to share the experiences of subjects, ethnomethodology also uses experiments to identify how everyday routines develop (Garfinkel) or analyse conversation to identify commonsense assumptions (Sacks).

Those who support the individualist approaches stress the way they do not reduce people to the status of mindless puppets or take social reality for granted. Critics dismiss their findings as either trivial or incomplete, as they ignore the influence of power on individual behaviour.

So far this answer has suggested a crude juxtaposition between theories of structure and social action. However, this is not necessarily the case. Weber combined both in his work. He criticised Marxist economic determinism and the failure of Durkheim to consider social action as well as social facts. He advocates what he refers to as *verstehen* as the way to explain social meanings (like interactionists) but also sees social action as providing the basis of social structure. This view is echoed by the work of Parsons as well as those more obviously influenced by Weber such as Rex.

Marx himself discussed social action, and modern Marxists like Willis have used interactionist methods to examine the ways individuals can actively construct reality within the constraints of capitalism.

Perhaps the most influential recent attempt to unify the two apparently conflicting paradigms has come from Giddens. He has synthesised action and structural approaches. Like interactionists he sees men constructing their own social reality but not in isolation from the external influences resulting from the structures produced by the interaction of others.

STUDENT'S ANSWER WITH EXAMINER COMMENTS

Question 1

Comment on the assertion that there is not a unified interactionist perspective but several distinct intellectual strands.

> Interactionism is also known as interpretive sociology and it is concerned with the dynamics of individuals and how they experience the world around them. Interactionists see society as being a system and man as being a product of that system. He both creates and is created by the system. It would be true to say that there are several intellectual strands in the interactionist school of thought; however, it must be noted that there are several factors which unify them.
>
> Max Weber, in an attempt to analyse social action, developed 'ideal types' to which all action could be compared. These included emotional types, rational types, and traditional types. All of these types govern social action.

Interactionists criticise those who see society as a system.

Should define, explain, and perhaps illustrate, social action.

> Symbolic interactionism is a major type of interpretive sociology. Its founding father was George Herbert Mead, who was influenced by the writings and concepts of Cooley. Mead developed the concept of the self which is built up by an individual through continuous interaction with others through shared values and symbols. An individual goes through various stages in the building of the self concept - beginning with the play stage where roles of important others are taken on, through the game stage where there are 'generalised others' and then to a point where roles are internalised and interaction means that individuals have to analyse the roles of others and react accordingly. Symbolic interactionists have used a 'dramaturgical' analogy to describe how individuals take on roles to play to real or imagined 'audiences' or a narcissistic self. Herbert Blumer suggested that social reality therefore exists only so far as the individuals themselves perceive it.
>
> Ethnomethodology is the study of the methods individuals employ to explain their interactions and experiences. Harold Garfinkel developed the stage critic analogy where an individual stands back in a detached way and observes social action in the world around him.
>
> In his book *Stigma* Goffman showed how individuals, through social interaction, 'label' others in order to understand them. People still try to play a role in spite of these labels.
>
> All interactionists are non-positivists and criticise deterministic sociology such as functionalism and Marxism for failing to give credit to man as a controller of his own action. They also tend to use observation and participant observation in their research in order to see the world from the point of view of the actors. Interactionist theories are micro-theories which are concerned with individuals rather than social systems.

Language is the most important symbol.

First sentence good, but needs developing.

Should be linked to symbolic interactionism and explained.

Sound conclusion pointing out unifying factors. Should point out differences.

Overall comments

Overall, just a C grade answer which shows promise without sufficient development. The candidate does demonstrate an understanding of the main types of interactionist theory but should offer further explanation and illustration with research studies.

The differences, not just the similarities, within the overall perspective need bringing out explicitly.

A Review Sheet for this chapter may be found on p. 258.

THE NATURE OF SOCIOLOGY

SOCIOLOGY AS A SCIENCE

SOCIOLOGY AND VALUES

THEORETICAL AND EMPIRICAL STUDIES

GETTING STARTED

This chapter attempts to answer the question 'What is sociology?' It might appear to have been more logical to have begun the book here, but the examination questions which are answered below are possibly the most difficult to be found on the various syllabuses.

Under consideration are a collection of issues which are all concerned with the nature of sociology as a form of enquiry. The unifying theme of the chapter is the idea that there is a 'sociology of sociology and sociologists'. This means that there are sociological explanations of:

1 Relationships between sociologists and other people, particularly their employers and colleagues.
2 The way that people choose to do sociology.
3 Sociology as a form of knowledge produced by sociologists.

The main themes of questions set on this topic are:

1 **Assessing whether the logic and procedures of the natural sciences are appropriate for sociology.**
2 **The sociology of science.**
3 **Whether sociology can or should be value free.**
4 **The relationship between sociology and social policy.**
5 **Comparing sociology with other academic disciplines or non-academic forms of description.**

Definitions

The problematic nature of most of these definitions is often a central issue in examination questions.

■ *Sociology* is the study of human social behaviour. However, it is the distinctiveness of sociological approaches and methods, rather than the subject matter, which make it different from other behavioural and social sciences.

■ *Natural science* can also be defined in terms of its methods, although critics see it as more socially defined.

■ *Value freedom* implies detachment and impartiality at all possible stages of sociological research.

■ *Social problems* are issues of public concern.

■ *Sociological problems* are phenomena which await sociological explanations.

■ *Social policy* is the ideology which underlies the management of social, political and economic institutions in order to achieve a particular kind of society. Usually it is described in terms of areas of public policy, such as health, education and welfare.

Related topics include *sociological theory and methods, positivism* and the *suicide* debate.

SOCIOLOGY AS A SCIENCE

ESSENTIAL PRINCIPLES

The main issues in the discussion of the relationship between sociology and the natural sciences are:

1   Is it possible to do sociological research following the methods of natural sciences?
2   Is it desirable to do sociology scientifically?
3   What are the problems and difficulties of applying the logic and procedures of the natural sciences to sociology?
4   What is science?

The main positions in the debates over these issues can be summarised as follows:

a)   If the definition of science is uncritically taken for granted (i.e. as following particular procedures advocated by Medawar (1976) and Popper) then positivist sociologists argue that sociology could and should be scientific. This would produce the best data, which would be logical, generalisable and testable.
b)   Whilst still accepting this conventional view of the superiority of scientific methods for the study of natural phenomena there are those who question the reliability and validity of employing the same methods to do sociology.
       Practical, theoretical and ideological criticisms have been levelled against positivism in sociology. These are found below and in the chapters on *Methods* (21) and *Suicide and official statistics* (20).
c)   The conventional definition of science has been questioned by sociologists, philosophers and scientists themselves. Instead of accepting an objective definition, which sees science as involving particular procedures, some writers suggest that 'science' is socially defined and is thus culturally and historically specific.

If science is neither a special activity nor produces superior knowledge then the issue of its application to sociology seems far less important. It is, however, necessary when answering questions to assess the implications for sociology of the various conceptions of science.

SOCIOLOGY AND VALUES

The main issues in this discussion are:

1   Can or should sociology be value free?
2   Is sociology inevitably ideological?
3   What are the sociological causes of bias in sociological research?
4   What are the effects of bias on sociology itself and the wider society?

The case for objectivity has been made by positivists who, following Comte and Durkheim, see a scientific approach helping to find the truth which in turn will be beneficial to society. The sociologist should aim to be detached rather than involved with his subjects and morally neutral rather than committed to particular values. This freedom from social influence of context will produce objective and value-free sociology.

The case that sociology cannot be value free is frequently made by interpretive sociologists who see the very subject matter of sociology as socially constructed rather than having an objective existence. Gomm argues that the very idea of sociology, which is a social activity, being value free is unsociological.

The Marxist view that sociology is inevitably ideological and an apology for the existing system is not shared by lay critics of sociology in this country, who see sociology as biased in favour of the left.

The New Right have attacked contemporary sociology on a number of grounds.

Marsland (1987) wrote *Biased Against Business: Anti-Capitalist Inclinations in Modern Sociology.* He reviewed syllabuses and textbooks and alleged that Sociology was biased against capitalism. In particular, he argued that:

1   The benefits of the free market were ignored.
2   A Marxist critique of capitalism was uncritically accepted.

The first of these charges may have some substance, but the reader is unlikely to find that the second claim is supported by any of the popular textbooks they use.

P. Saunders (1990) supports Marsland's first criticism in a more convincing manner. He says that Sociology teachers are mistaken in using functionalism as the only right-wing alternative to Marxism. Functionalism has been simplified by critics into an easily criticised conservative approach, and dismissed as old-fashioned and ideological. Saunders sees Liberalism as the real alternative to Marxism, and promotes Hayek as a leading figure in New Right economics. Hayek is a liberal rather than a conservative; he is a critic of the economic failure and political tyranny of Eastern European state-planned economies. The communist regimes which maintained these systems have, of course, largely disappeared in Europe since 1989.

R. Scase (1991) criticises sociology for concentrating exclusively on the flaws of capitalism; this is particularly inappropriate following the collapse of Socialism in Eastern Europe. He says we should study not just poverty but also affluence and how it legitimises capitalism. The increase in the proportion of the workforce who are self-employed and their role in the class structure and the culture of enterprise are worthy of study. The pluralist defence of liberal democracy could be associated with the free-market economy to demonstrate that capitalism encourages the freedom of the citizen.

THE CAUSES OF BIAS IN SOCIOLOGY

Coercion

Bell and Newby mention libel laws, the Official Secrets Acts and intimidation by disgruntled subjects. Non-conforming academics have been denied employment or even imprisoned in many countries. (See 'Reasons for choosing methods', in Chapter 21.)

Finance

Research requires money. Financial support tends to come from government or business, either directly or indirectly. This can influence the topic of research chosen as well as the methods employed and ultimate publication of findings.

The profession

Sociologists belong to an academic community which can influence research. They work in institutions with career structures, ideologies and, as is increasingly recognised, markets for their work. This need not be seen as sinister, as the effect may be no more than the development of a distinctive school of sociology where particular topics are chosen and studied from a particular perspective using a particular set of methods. The influence of Chicago University and the London School of Economics could be used to illustrate this point.

Involvement

Sociologists have a variety of characteristics, e.g. gender, class, age and ethnicity. These will influence the way they interact with subjects. These characteristics and the influences listed above are at the centre of sociological research. This leads us to the next section.

THE EFFECTS OF BIAS

Effects on sociological research

" Refer to Chapter 21 on *Methods*. "
We can identify effects on the choice of topic (Who is paying? What is seen as a social problem?) as well as on approach and methods which can be influenced by the institution.

Bias in findings to conform to the sociologist's perspective has often been alleged. Marxists, functionalists and feminists seem to produce predictable findings. On a less political level we could note the problem of the self-fulfilling prophecy.

Effects on the wider society

It has been alleged that sociology can be used to control people in political, military and industrial contexts. Sociologists are employed to improve industrial relations and organisational effectiveness. Sociological research is used to explain and control social problems, and to create and evaluate social policy.

Sociology can also be seen as a form of ideology used to legitimate the existing order – for example, by blaming poverty on the poor or educational failure on families. Of course we could select examples with opposite effects.

THEORETICAL AND EMPIRICAL STUDIES

SOCIOLOGY AS A SCIENCE

Merton has written a sociological account of science as a profession. He saw scientists as both emotionally and rationally committed to certain ethics which ensured the purity of science and protected it from criticism. Science was described as universal, rational, public, detached and sceptical. No wonder sociologists wished to emulate this impressive way of doing research!

Popper claimed that the defining characteristic of a scientific theory is that it can be falsified. This means it states explicitly what evidence would be necessary to refute the relationship it asserts. Evidence can of course support a theory, but Popper sees all verification and thus all scientific theories as provisional. They are never finally proved and need constant re-examination. Thus, Popper defined science in terms of its logic as well as its procedures. He sees the controlled experiment as one of the most powerful tools available but it can only test a pre-existing hypothesis. The data gained depends on the initial purpose of the research. Hypotheses depend on preconceived theories. Thus, in a way he agrees with Kuhn, who sees experimentation as doing little more than support theories and not leading to discoveries. Popper is noted as a critic of Marxist theory on the grounds that it is irrefutable. Good theory is logical, general and can be refuted. Many sociologists, particularly positivists, approve of Popper's model and see it producing the best rational knowledge.

Kuhn denies the claim that scientists are open-minded. During periods of 'normal science' they operate within existing paradigms. These paradigms are sets of basic assumptions which are taken for granted. They set limits on the questions which are asked, the subject matter of the discipline and research methods. Evidence which is gathered and does not fit into the existing paradigm is either ignored or distorted, or increasingly complex explanations are sought. When the evidence against the paradigm is overwhelming then a scientific revolution occurs until the new paradigm is generally accepted.

Darwin established a new paradigm which dominated biology to such an extent that even his own reservations, about the possibility of the eye or cerebral cortex evolving by random mutation, were long ignored. The pioneers of the new paradigm in biology resulting from the identification of DNA have expressed their doubts about Darwin's model of evolution. The implication for sociology is that in the absence of generally accepted truths it remains pre-scientific.

Ziman is a physicist who emphasises the social dimension of scientific knowledge by insisting it must be public knowledge. This means that scientists cannot work in isolation but must have their work tried and tested by others. After considering and rejecting conventional definitions of science, which reduce it to a particular procedure, he defines science as:

a) An activity done by 'scientists', i.e. those accepted by the scientific community. (Nazi Germany excluded Jewish scientists and those who followed Einstein.)
b) A body of knowledge tested and agreed by scientists, i.e. a consensus of rational opinion.

Sociologists could be seen as comprising an academic community who examine each other's work.

Kaplan distinguished 'logics-in-use' from 're-constructed logics'. The former describes how research is actually done and what scientists actually think. (According to Watson's biography which describes the discovery of DNA, scientists are sometimes jealous, narrow-minded and they cheat.) The latter describes the published version of research which suggests that an open-minded and logical procedure was followed when, in fact, they were looking to confirm predetermined answers. Bell and Newby and also Hammond have described a similar discrepancy between published accounts of sociological research and what actually took place.

Broad and Wade show how deciding on the result before research has led some scientists to dispense with the research altogether and fake it. They describe Newton and Mendel as 'good cheats' and Burt as a bad one.

Sklair has described the development of 'big science' which, rather than being open-minded, serves the interests of business and government. If the sources of finance for sociology were investigated, similar claims could be made. The professionalisation of science and its later domination by government bureaucracy could be seen as challenging the idealised view of the open-minded individual and supporting Sklair's view.

SOCIOLOGY AND VALUES

Comte, in advocating a positivist scientific approach to sociology, might be seen as a champion of value freedom. However, he did argue that the point of sociology was to change society for the better, which is not the spirit of detachment we find in contemporary positivism. Comte felt that the revelation of sociological laws would lead to the developing of the best possible society.

Weber reminds us that knowledge is socially constructed and the sociologist employs his or her society's values when deciding what to study. He does recommend that when evaluating results the sociologist should be non-judgemental.

Gouldner described how American sociology drifted from a position of social criticism and reform to the professed neutrality of post-war positivism. The value-free collectors of facts enhanced their professional status and escaped criticism from a conservative establishment. Gouldner denies that this self-interest and ignoring of controversial social issues can be seen as value freedom, as the sociologists could be used by those in power. Following Gouldner's criticism the more open academic climate of the 1960s and 1970s saw the adopting of more critical positions by interactionists like Becker who advocate 'sympathising with the underdog', as the point of view of the 'overdog' (those with power) was already well known. Gouldner remained dissatisfied and claimed that Becker studied the underdog as a passive subject, not from the radical position of resisting those in power.

Shaw supported Gouldner's demand for commitment from a Marxist perspective. He analysed the history of sociology as both knowledge and activity produced by the economic substructure. He dismissed social criticism as a substitute for revolutionary action by those in safe professional employment.

Bohannan offered a much more personal justification for abandoning value freedom in an anthropological study. She defends human involvement rather than scientific detachment on two grounds. First, she had to challenge existing gender roles to gain access to the men's world of magic, religion and politics. Second, despite protests which were due to the tribe having no faith in modern medicine, she tried to get her sick friend to the modern hospital, suggesting that sociologists should not abandon their humanity to achieve value freedom by refusing to get involved.

Feminists, including Oakley, argue that value-free sociology supports the status quo. Feminists should try to change it and improve women's lives.

EXAMINATION QUESTIONS

1   'Whether we consider sociology to be scientific or not depends on which definition of science we choose.' Explain and discuss.

(AEB)

2   Examine the view that sociology can and should be value free.

(AEB)

3   Examine the relationship between sociology and social policy. Illustrate your answer with examples.

(AEB)

4   'Value judgements influence research both in the social sciences and the natural sciences.' Discuss.

(AEB)

5   ITEM A
    Simply choosing an explanation out of personal preference would not get us very far
    by itself. It is true that there are many occasions when human beings say they 'know'
    something to be true when what they really mean is that they 'think' it to be true. This
    would be the case if I were to say that I 'know' the Labour Party will win the next
5   election, for example. Science however aims at much greater certainty in its explana-
    tions than this. Having arrived at an hypothesis – a plausible or appealing story about

how something or other is caused – scientists do not then spend their time trying to persuade us of its truth by the logic of their argument, as philosophers do. Nor do they ask us to simply have faith in their belief, as theologians do. They try to *prove* its truth to us. This they do by *showing* it to be true.

10

Source: Adapted from *Theory and Methods in Sociology*,
P. JONES (Bell and Hyman)

ITEM B

So how common is cheating in science? Surveys show that both in Britain and America, only about one in four scientists is prepared to provide original data when requested. Unless there is something to hide, there is no reason for such refusal. One can only conclude that scientific fraud is extremely widespread. Moreover, it is not limited to minor figures: the verdict of history is that Ptolemy, Galileo, Newton, Dalton and Mendel all tampered with some of their data.

5

Why then do some scientists cheat? Not everyone, and perhaps not anyone, pursues science merely out of a quest for truth. At the best, people are heavily biased towards proving their own theories right, but they also want promotion, research grants and glory. Since all depend on publishing, the pressure to publish is enormous. It is obviously quicker to fake data than to run experiments and you can be sure of getting the desired result.

10

Another extremely common way of cheating is to run an experiment over and over again until the desired result is obtained and then publish it, quietly forgetting the negative instances. Other scientists get things wrong, not by cheating but by unconsciously seeing what they are looking for (even when it is not there) or failing to see what is there.

15

There is little risk of being caught. Except for the most important findings, little attempt is made to replicate; there is no prestige in redoing someone else's experiments.

Source: Adapted from *The Observer*, August 1989

ITEM C

Most of us rather hastily and thoughtlessly regard 'science' as a sort of collection of linear accelerators and space vehicles and organic chemistry models. In fact, it is not any of these things; it is only a systematic method of gathering and testing knowledge, involving certain formal procedures: gathering information, forming an hypothesis to explain the information, predicting certain consequences of the hypothesis and performing an experiment to test the prediction. If you investigate any area of knowledge by this method, you are doing science. If you use any other method, you are doing something else.

5

Source: Adapted from S.F. *The Game-Playing Literature in 'In the Problem Pit'*,
FREDERICK POHL (Corgi)

a) Briefly explain how scientists try to prove an hypothesis 'by showing it to be true' (line 10) ITEM A.   (*2 marks*)

b) ITEM B puts forward a number of reasons why science cannot be seen as objective. What are the implications of this for the belief that sociology is a science?
(*4 marks*)

c) Apart from the points raised in ITEM B, how far do you agree with the argument in ITEM C that science is a 'systematic method'?   (*6 marks*)

d) ITEM A suggests that human beings 'know' things to be true in ways other than the scientific method. On what other grounds do people claim that their beliefs or ideas are true?   (*4 marks*)

e) Using information from the ITEMS and from elsewhere, assess whether it is possible for sociology to be a science.   (*9 marks*)

(*Total 25 marks*)

ANSWERS TO EXAMINATION QUESTIONS

OUTLINE ANSWERS

Question 3

Answers must emphasise that there is no one simple relationship between sociology and social policy. Relevant material can be found in the debate on value freedom and reference made to the relationship between natural science and public policy. Examples of policy issues could include health, education, welfare, race relations, equal gender opportunities and crime.

i) The positivist view. Comte and Durkheim saw the potential of a scientific sociology explaining society and thus permitting prediction and control to improve it.

The modern view, where the role of the sociologist is seen as providing reliable data for social policy. Compare with medical research, which is scientific in procedure but committed to finding cures.

ii) Gouldner's critique of the claimed neutrality of post-war positivism.

iii) The role of sociology in defining social policy issues:

a) Pointing out that private problems have a social dimension, e.g. homelessness and feminist criticism of the family.

b) Making latent (hidden) problems manifest (public), e.g. the social and economic costs of educational inequality of opportunity or racism and sexism.

c) Identifying who has the power to define social problems and influence policy, e.g. Marxist or interactionist views on professionals. Becker on who defines social problems.

d) Encouraging reform, e.g. the influence of sociological research on educational reform and race relations policy.

iv) Point out that sociology can be divorced from social policy. Sociology can be concerned with the normal and acceptable as well as social pathology, e.g. the concern of ethnomethodology with everyday events or studies or ordinary, rather than deviant, youth.

Question 4

This question involves a consideration of some of the issues raised in questions 1 and 2. Good answers will show an awareness of debates about the influences of political, moral and academic beliefs on research in both the natural and social sciences.

i) Explain the positivist claim for the neutrality of the natural sciences and the justification of the application to sociology of the scientific method (Comte and Durkheim. Popper's view of science).

ii) Criticise the claim that either natural or social scientists are open-minded (Kuhn and Kaplan).

iii) The ethnomethodological critique of scientific and positivist sociological research as no more than 'common sense'.

iv) Causes of bias in both sociology and natural sciences:

a) Coercion.

b) Finance.

c) The academic institution and the professions.

v) Effects of bias in both on:

a) Research itself.

b) The wider society.

Question 5

a) By doing an experiment which can be replicated by others.

b) If scientists cheat, then the scientific method may seem less attractive to positivists. The scientific approach is less likely to produce valid findings; the status of knowledge may be challenged and other approaches seem equally reliable and valid. You could illustrate these and other points.

c) Here is your opportunity to evaluate the different conceptions of science discussed in this chapter and come to a conclusion. Six marks requires less than a page, so do not try to cover all views on science, as you must leave time to evaluate.

d) Any four from faith, religious commitment, tradition, authority, rely on experts, experience, etc., or other reasonable answers.

e) It's fine to use the positivist vs interpretive sociology debate as a framework. There are other relevant approaches, including feminist and 'realist' views. You must assess the arguments and come to a conclusion supported by your evidence from the items and elsewhere. It depends, of course, on how science is defined.

TUTOR ANSWER

Question 1

'Whether we consider sociology to be scientific or not depends on which definition of science we choose.' Explain and discuss.

The definition of science is problematic. If a conventional definition of science is adopted then arguably some sociology is scientific. However, if science is seen as socially not objectively defined, then some sociology may have similar characteristics to natural science but the attempts to emulate the scientific model seem less important.

Medawar claimed that science could be defined in terms of its method. He saw science as following a particular logic and procedure rather than being defined by its subject matter.

Popper refined and developed this view of science. He saw science as logical, useful and above all refutable. Scientific knowledge is built up by a continuing process of conjecture and refutation. It is not the final truth but the best provisional explanation. Popper criticised Marxism for being unscientific because it could not be falsified. (Popper means Marxism has not been expressed in a way which is capable of being disproved, not that it has been shown to be false.)

If we accept this definition of science then some sociology does indeed aspire to be scientific. The positivist tradition in sociology, pioneered by Comte and Durkheim, did try to emulate scientific methods because they were seen as superior ways of producing and testing knowledge. Durkheim advocated the use of the comparative method as an appropriate substitute for the experiment which is the favoured scientific method because of the possibility of control and its reliability.

Assuming the superiority of the scientific approach, positivists nevertheless encounter considerable difficulties in applying it to sociology. Involvement with subjects must be avoided because of the effects on their behaviour. This is illustrated by the Hawthorne studies and the self-fulfilling prophecy described by Rosenthal and Jacobson. Natural scientists encounter similar problems. The fact that the sociologist is part of the phenomena he studies may, however, exacerbate the problem.

Even if scientific knowledge is refuted and becomes obsolete scientists still assume that the phenomena they study follow universal and invariable natural laws. This is clearly not the case in sociology as patterns of social behaviour are culturally and historically specific. Indeed, sociological research itself may lead to changing patterns of behaviour, for example, teachers during training are made aware of sociological research which may influence subsequent behaviour.

Even if the idealised conception of natural science was accepted by anti-positivist sociologists they would not consider it a suitable model for studying social behaviour. In fact ethnomethodologists have dismissed science as being no different from other forms of common sense, with the scientific observer relying on subjective experience and interpreting his observations within a particular social context.

The main objection of interpretive sociologists to a scientific approach lies in their different view of the subject matter of sociology. They dismiss the existence of objective social facts and see social reality as socially constructed. Searle has argued that social scientists need explanations not of social facts but of 'intentionality and its effects'. He is emphasising the purposive nature of human behaviour and the meaning we attach to it. Winch has suggested that sociology should seek 'reasons for', not 'causes of' behaviour. This critique of positivism is exemplified by the debate over Durkheim's *Suicide*.

There is a wealth of material which can be used to criticise the idealised conventional definition of science. There is a sociology of science and scientists as well as a philosophical debate about the nature of science. Most of the following writers share the general assumption that science is socially rather than objectively defined. The implications for the scientific nature of sociology depend on the particular study.

Ziman follows Popper to the extent that he claims that science must be tested and agreed knowledge. Like Merton he sees the scientific community as openly testing ideas. He describes science as 'public knowledge'. The consensus of rational opinion he sees developing from this process is similar to Kuhn's notion of a paradigm.

However, Kuhn sees the scientist not as open-minded and rational but operating within limits which influence the questions asked, the subject matter and the research methods employed. Paradigms are the generally accepted foundations upon which subsequent theory is built. This applies during a period of normal science. Evidence which does not fit the paradigm is distorted or ignored. When the evidence against the existing paradigm is overwhelming then a scientific revolution occurs and a new paradigm emerges.

The implication of this view for sociology is that sociology, lacking the rational consensus described, is pre-paradigmic and therefore not (yet) a science. Although sociologists do work within academic communities and publish their research for criticism which conforms to the views on science of Merton and Ziman.

Kaplan has distinguished 'logics-in-use' (what scientists really do) from 'reconstructed logics' (the way in which their findings are presented in scientific papers). The presentation of research in conventional form suggests open-minded and rigorous procedures and legitimises science in the public's mind. Bell and Newby have described a similar distinction between the way sociological research is actually done (influenced by libel laws, institutional and financial pressures) from the way it appears in formal publications.

The approving view of the open-minded scientist is also questioned by Sklair, who looks at the way 'big science' is dominated by government and business interests. This, he claims, influences choice of subject matter and interpretation of findings. Broad and Wade have shown how this can lead to cheating by scientists, e.g. American scientists are alleged to have falsely claimed simultaneous and independent identification of the HIV as the cause of AIDS with French scientists.

Sociologists, as shown by Bell and Newby, also conform to outside pressures. This could be illustrated by the bias towards employer interests in some industrial sociology. More social research in the UK is directly or indirectly government sponsored. Gouldner sees the commitment to science itself, by sociologists, as an evasion of their responsibilities, as it allows them to be used by government and business.

STUDENT'S ANSWER WITH EXAMINER COMMENTS

Question 2
Examine the view that sociology can and should be value free.

Sounds like a 'science' essay.

Comte also talked about control which could be linked to value freedom.

Links positivism with value freedom.

Yes, but examples would help.

Consciousness rather than life distinguishes people from other subjects.

Yes, but de-humanise is an inappropriate term. Neutral is better.

Should include Gouldner's attack on positivism.

Comte believed that the application of the methods and assumptions of the natural sciences would produce a positive science of society. Sociology would show that society followed invariable laws and enable predictions to be made.

Supporters of this view were known as positivists. The most important was Durkheim, who agreed that scientific methods should be used and advocated the comparative method. One important aspect of this method was the concept of value freedom. Durkheim believed that by using the comparative method social facts could be studied as things. He believed that these social facts were external to the sociologist and therefore it was possible to study them objectively.

However, since sociologists are usually members of the society they study, they will already have a set of values which could overtly or inadvertently influence their study by introducing value judgements. Also if we knew before we were to study a topic that the research was done by a functionalist, Marxist or feminist we would ask ourselves whether preconceived ideas had influenced the study.

It is argued that value freedom is not a problem in the natural sciences since they are concerned with the objective study of usually inanimate objects. Sociology usually involves the subjective study of people and their actions and cannot be a scientific process.

Weber, who advocated social action theory, argued that sociologists' values did enter into their subject choice but that after that sociologists could be de-humanised by keeping their values separate from their analysis of the social world.

However, this point has been criticised by Gouldner in *Anti-Minotaur: The Myth of a Value-Free Sociology*. He argues that the separation of facts and values is as impossible as the separation of the man from the beast in the mythological creature the minotaur. Gouldner argues that they are integral parts of the same entity.

Becker gives other reasons for giving the underdog's view.

Good. Could be illustrated.

Avoid 'only natural'. This is the sociology of sociologists.

Example not explained.

Reasonable summary of Popper on science.

Good application of Kuhn to value freedom, but conclusion is unclear.

Not helpful. Talking about science not sociology.

Unhelpful. Science again.

Becker also agrees that values will enter sociological research and that objectivity can be achieved only by making clear one's values so they can easily be separated from the study. In *Whose Side Are We On?* he argues for a compassionate sociology sympathising with the underdog. He believes that since values are inevitable the sociologist will also be accused of bias.

Marxists share the view that any science of society would be ideologically biased according to its class position. Shaw explained changes in sociology as part of the superstructure deriving from and supporting class relationships. To gain objectivity Marxists believe that false consciousness must be overcome.

Therefore we can see that the possibility of sociology being value free is virtually an impossibility. Sociologists themselves are human and it is only natural that they could be influenced by money, coercion or their employers. Bohannan justifies involvement at the expense of detachment as otherwise she would not have been able to gain such insight as she did into a tribal society.

However, the problem of value freedom can also lead us to question the nature of the natural sciences. Many have criticised the natural science model from which Comte and Durkheim developed positivism. The general view of science is that hypotheses could either be verified or refuted by experimentation and that objectivity is possible by constantly trying to disprove previous theories.

However, Kuhn has argued that science is governed by paradigms which are accepted assumptions that all scientists have when entering a field of study. Thus natural scientists are not open-minded since they share prevailing assumptions about a topic. An enormous amount of evidence must be available for these assumptions to be replaced by new paradigms. Looking at sociology from this perspective the question of value freedom would not arise as there is no generally acceptable paradigm in sociology and is not then a science.

Also, the question of whether natural science is and should be value free is questionable. Many believe that scientists are detached from their area of study because studying chemicals, for example, is conceptually different from studying human behaviour. Winch believes social science is concerned with reasons for actions not their causes. However, can scientists be detached from their findings or the use to which research is put? For example, Einstein said he would rather have been a watchmaker had he known in advance the consequences of his theories.

This is more an ethical debate yet it proves that scientists have values which affect their studies. Therefore, the question of whether sociology should be value free is almost irrelevant owing to the many questions hanging over natural science.

Overall comments

Overall, a sound C grade answer which suffers from overemphasis on the science issue. It does address both parts of the question, i.e. 'can and should'. The answer would be improved by considering the sociology of sociologists and how values influence sociological research.

A Review Sheet for this chapter may be found on p. 258.

ADDITIONAL READING

INTRODUCTION

The reading I have suggested includes books, extracts from books and articles. It is neither an essential nor an exhaustive list but one based on material found useful by my students over a period of time. None of them read all or even most of the list.

Ask your teacher to guide you through this and any reading list recommended by examining boards, as the degree of difficulty varies considerably. At the beginning of your course you might find it useful to refer to textbooks written primarily for GCSE students. They will contain useful references to studies even if the overall approach is different to A-level. Abbreviations of the main journal references include: *The Social Science Review* (*SSR*); *Sociology Review* (*SR*); *The Social Science Teacher* (*SST*).

CHAPTER 1

The syllabus, examination papers, examiner reports, mark schemes and coursework guides from your board.

CHAPTER 2

Burgess, R 1988, Doing School Ethnography, *SSR* Vol. 3 No. 5
Gill, R 1988, Altered Images: Women in the Media, *SSR* Vol. 4 No. 1
Jorgensen, N 1987, *The Sociology Manual*, Framework Press
Morrison, M and J Pey 1987, *Writing Sociological Essays*, Longman
Burgess and Gill might give you some ideas on doing your own research. See also the references for Chapter 21.

CHAPTER 3

Banton, M 1987, The Davies and Moore Theory of Inequality, *SSR* Vol. 3 No. 2
Cuff, E and G Payne 1984, *Perspectives in Sociology*, Unwin Hyman
Devine, F 1994, Affluent Workers Revisited, *SR* Vol. 3 No. 3
Hughes, J The Concept of Class, *Teaching paper in Sociology*, Longman
Pilkington, A 1992, Is there a British Underclass?, *SR* Vol. 1 No. 3
Westergaard, J and H Resler 1976 *Class in a Capitalist Society: A Study of Contemporary Britain*, Penguin

CHAPTER 4

Miles, R 1982, *Racism and Migrant Labour*
Miles, R 1987, in P Trowler (ed.) *Active Sociology*, Bell and Hyman
Pilkington, A 1984, *Race Relations in Britain*, Unwin Hyman
Pryce, K 1979, *Endless Pressure*, Penguin
Pryce, K 1985, in M O'Donnell (ed.) *New Introductory Reader in Sociology*, Nelson
Pryce, K 1987, in P Trowler (ed.) *Active Sociology*, Bell and Hyman
Richardson, J and J Lambert 1985, *The Sociology of Race*, Causeway
Small, S 1994, Black People in Britain, *SR* Vol. 3 No. 4

CHAPTER 5

Abbott, P and C Wallace 1992, *An Introduction to Sociology: Feminist Perspectives*, Routledge
Buswell, C 1985, Gender and Sociology, *SSR* Vol. 4 No. 5
Lees, S 1983, How Boys Slag Off Girls, *New Society*, 13 October
Mayes, P 1986, *Gender*, Longman
Maynard, M 1987, Current Trends in Feminist Theory, *SSR* Vol. 2 No. 3
Oakley, A 1987, The Woman's Place, *New Society*, 6 March

CHAPTER 6

Field, D 1992, Elderly People in British Society, *SR* Vol. 4 No. 4
Wagg, S 1992, I Blame the Parents, *SR* Vol. 4 No. 2
O'Donnell, M 1985, *Age and Generation*, Tavistock

CHAPTER 7

Beynon, J 1987, A Prolonged Conservative Ascendancy in a Divided Britain, *SSR* Vol. 3 No. 1
Crewe, I 1985, Can Labour Rise Again? *SSR* Vol. 1 No. 1
Crewe, I 1987, in P Trowler (ed.), *Active Sociology*, Bell and Hyman
Crewe, I, Various post-election analyses, in *The Guardian*, 13 June 1983, 15 June 1987, 16 June 1987
Denver, D 1989, *Elections and Voting Behaviour in Britain*, Phillip Allan
Himmelweit, H *et al.* 1985, How Voters Decide, in M O'Donnell (ed.) *New Introductory Reader in Sociology*, Nelson
Riley, M 1989, Theories of Voting, *SSR* Vol. 5 No. 1
Riley, M 1992, Winner Takes All: 1992 General Election, *SR* Vol. 2 No. 1
Saunders, P 1985, The Sociology of the State, *SSR* preview
Scott, J 1986, Does Britain still have a Ruling Class?, *SSR* Vol. 2 No. 1

CHAPTER 8

Foster-Carter, A 1985, *The Sociology of Development*, Causeway
Foster-Carter, A 1991, Development Sociology: Whither now?, *SR* Vol. 1 No. 2

Sklair, L 1993, Going Global: Competing Models of Globalisation, *SR* Vol. 3 No. 2
Slattery, M 1985, *Urban Sociology*, Causeway
Webster, A 1984, Introduction to the Sociology of Development, Macmillan

CHAPTER 9

Harrison, P 1985, *Inside the Inner City*, Penguin
Jewson, N 1991, The Development of Cities in Capitalist Societies, *SR* Vol. 1 No. 2
Payne, G 1994, Community and Community Studies, *SR* Vol. 4 No. 1
Slattery, M 1985, *Urban Sociology*, Causeway

CHAPTER 10

Abbott, P and C Wallace 1992, *An Introduction to Sociology: Feminist Perspectives*, Routledge
Anderson, M 1983, How Much Has The Family Changed?, *New Society*, 27 October
Chandler, J 1993, Women Outside Marriage, *SR* Vol. 2 No. 4
Chester, K 1985, The Rise of the Neo-conventional Family, *New Society*, 9 May
Data base 1989, The Family, *New Society*, 6 March
Hood-Williams, J 1984, The Family: Demographic Trends, *SST* Vol. 14 No. 1 and Vol. 14 No. 2
Research round-up 1988, In Search of the New Man, *SSR* Vol. 3 No. 4
Timmins, N 1989, General Household Survey, *The Independent*, 6 December
Wilson, A 1985, *Family*, Tavistock

CHAPTER 11

Ball, S 1981, *Beachside Comprehensive*, Cambridge University Press
Ball, S 1987, in P Trowler (ed.), *Active Sociology*, Bell and Hyman
Ball, S 1986, *Education*, Longman
Chitty, C 1993, The Education System Transformed, *SR* Vol. 2 No. 4
Denscombe 1994, *Sociology Update 1994*, Olympus Books
Lees, S 1986, *Losing out: Sexuality and Adolescent Girls*, Hutchinson
Pilkington, A 1984, *Race Relations in Britain*, Unwin Hyman
Willis, P 1978, *Learning to Labour*, Saxon House
Willis, P 1985, in M O'Donnell (ed.), *New Introductory Reader in Sociology*, Nelson

CHAPTER 12

Ashton, D 1985, Unemployment: Why Pick on Youth, *SSR* Vol. 1 No. 1
Hyman, R 1987, in P Trowler (ed.), *Active Sociology*, Bell and Hyman
Hyman, R 1984, *Strikes*, Fontana
McCallagh, M 1985, Teaching the Sociology of Unemployment, *SST* Vol. 15 No. 1
McIntosh, S 1985, in M O'Donnell (ed.), *New Introductory Reader in Sociology*, Nelson
McIntosh, S 1981, Leisure Studies, in A Tomlinson (ed.) *Leisure and Social Control*, Brighton Polytechnic
Parker, S 1972, *The Sociology of Industry*, George Allen and Unwin
Parker, S 1985, in M O'Donnell (ed.), *New Introductory Reader in Sociology*, Nelson
Phizacklea, A 1990, *Unpacking the Fashion Industry*, Routledge
Taylor, L and P Walton 1971, Industrial Sabotage: Motives and Meanings, in S Cohen (ed.) *Images of Deviance*, Penguin

CHAPTER 13

Clegg, S 1992, Modern and Post Modern Organisations, *SR* Vol. 1 No. 4
Goffman, E 1970, *Asylums*, Penguin
Morgan, G 1992, The Sociology of Organisation, *SR* Vol. 3 No. 3
Salaman, G 1981, *Class and the Corporation*, Fontana
Salaman, G 1985, in M O'Donnell (ed.), *New Introductory Reader in Sociology*, Nelson

CHAPTER 14

Johnson, T 1972, *Professions and Power*, Macmillan
Johnson, T 1973, in G Hurd (ed.) *Human Societies*, RKP

CHAPTER 15

Bruce, S 1992, The Twilight of the Gods: Religion in Modern Britain, *SR* Vol. 2 No. 2
Butler, C 1995, Religion and Gender: Young Muslim Women in Britain, *SR* Vol. 4, No. 3
Glock, C and R Stark 1965, *Religion and Society in Tension*, Rand McNally
Glock, C and R Stark 1971, in K Thompson and J Tunstall, *Sociology Perspectives*, Penguin
Wallis, R 1985, The Sociology of the New Religions, *SSR* Vol. 1 No. 1
Wilson, B 1973, Secularisation and its Discontents, *The Times*, 13 October and 10 November

CHAPTER 16

Cohen, S and J Young 1981, *The Manufacture of News*, Constable
GUMG 1987, War and Peace News, in P Trowler (ed.), *Active Sociology*, Bell and Hyman
Palmer, G and C Littler 1979, The Invisible Heroes, *New Society*, 14 May
Research round-up 1986, GUMG, *SSR* Vol. 2 No. 1
Research round-up 1987, CCCS, *SSR* Vol. 2, No. 4
Wagg, S 1994, Politics and the Media in Post War Britain, *SR* Vol. 4 No. 2
Whannel, G and J Williams 1993, The Rise of Satellite Television, *SR* Vol. 2 No. 3

CHAPTER 17

Walker, C 1994, Managing Poverty, *SR* Vol. 3 No. 3
Pilkington, A 1992, Is there a British Underclass?, *SR* Vol. 1 No. 3
Westergaard, J and H Resler 1976, *Class in a Capitalist Society*, Penguin
Coates, K and R Silburn 1970, *Poverty the Forgotten Englishman*, Penguin

CHAPTER 18

Fahey, W 1985, The Social Aspects of Mental Illness, *SST* Vol. 15, No. 1
Gomm, R 1982, Unemployment and Health, *SST* Vol. 12 No. 1
Gomm, R 1985, Teaching the Sociology of Health and Underdevelopment, *SST* Vol. 14 No. 3
Gomm, R, A Howlett and J Ashley 1979, in R Meighan, I Shelton and T Marks (eds) *Perspectives on Society*, Nelson
Graham, H 1987, Women, Health and Illness, *SSR* Vol. 3 No. 1
Taylor, I 1994, Disabled by Society?, *SR* Vol. 3, No. 4
Taylor, S 1994, Beyond the Medical Model: The Sociology of Health and Illness, *SR* Vol. 4 No. 1
Waddington, I 1989, Inequalities in Health, *SSR* Vol. 4 No. 3

CHAPTER 19

Abbott, P and C Wallace 1992, *An Introduction to Sociology: Feminist Perspectives*, Routledge
Aggleton, P 1987, *Deviance*, Tavistock
Becker, H S 1966, *Outsiders*, Collier Macmillan
Becker, H S 1987, in P Trowler (ed.), *Active Sociology*, Bell and Hyman
Becker, H S 1985, in M O'Donnell (ed.), *New Introductory Reader in Sociology*, Nelson
Becker, H S 1987, Key Thinkers, *SSR* Vol. 3 No. 2
Hughes, G 1992, Taking Crime Seriously, *SR* Vol. 1, No. 2
Muncie, J 1987, Much Ado About Nothing? The Sociology of Moral Panics, *SSR* Vol. 3 No. 2
Williams, J 1986, Football Hooliganism, *SST* Vol. 15, No. 3
Williams, J 1988, England's Barmy Army, *SSR* Vol. 4, No. 1

CHAPTER 20

Jones, P 1985, *Theory and Methods in Sociology*, Unwin Hyman
Atkinson, J M 1977, in C Bell and H Newby (eds) *Doing Sociological Research*, Allen and Unwin
Atkinson, J M 1971, Societal Reactions to Suicide, in S Cohen (ed.) *Images of Deviance*, Penguin
Taylor, S 1988, *Suicide*, Longman
Slattery, M 1986, *Official Statistics*, Tavistock
Taylor, S 1990, Beyond Durkheim: Sociology and Suicide, *SSR* Vol. 6 No. 2
Jones, P 1993, *Studying Society: Sociological Theories and Research Practices*, Collins Educational

CHAPTER 21

Jones, P 1985, *Theory and Methods in Sociology*, Unwin Hyman
Jones, P 1993, *Studying Society: Sociological Theories and Research Practices*, Collins Educational
McNeill, P 1985, *Research Methods*, Tavistock
Meighan, R , I Shelton and T Marks (eds) 1979, *Perspectives on Society*, Nelson
Morrison, M 1986, *Methods in Sociology*, Longman
Pryce, K 1987, in P Trowler (ed.), *Active Sociology*, Bell and Hyman
Pryce, K 1985, Endless Pressure, in M O'Donnell (ed.), *New Introductory Reader in Sociology*, Nelson
Shipman, M 1981, *The Limitations of Social Research*, Longman

CHAPTER 22

Abbott, P and C Wallace 1992, *An Introduction to Sociology: Feminist Perspectives*, Routledge
Berry, D 1979, *Central Ideas in Sociology*, Constable
Brown, C 1979, *Understanding Society*, John Murray
Craig, I 1989, Structure and Action in Modern Social Theory, *SSR* Vol. 4 No. 5
Jones, P 1993, *Studying Society: Sociological Theories and Research Practices*, Collins Educational

CHAPTER 23

Gomm, R 1979, Neutrality and Commitment in Sociology, in R Meighan, I Shelton and T Marks (eds) *Perspectives on Society*, Nelson
Reeves, F 1979, Sociology: A World of Scarecrows and Supermen, in R Meighan, I Shelton and T Marks (eds) *Perspectives on Society*, Nelson
Coulson, M and C Riddell 1980, *Approaching Sociology*, Routledge
Trowler, P 1985, *Further Topics in Sociology* (especially material on science in chapter on Knowledge), UTP
Glover, D and S Strawbridge 1985, *The Sociology of Knowledge*, Causeway
Berry, D 1979, *Central Ideas in Sociology*, Constable
Burrage, H 1988, The Sociology of Science and the Science of Society, *SSR* Vol. 4 No. 2

REVIEW SHEETS

CHAPTER 3 SOCIAL CLASS

1 Outline two criticisms of Marx's view that there are only two social classes in capitalist societies.
2 Explain how changes in the pattern of ownership of business can be used to challenge Marx's theory of social class.
3 How did Weber explain social inequality? Identify two ways in which this differs from Marx's view.
4 List four criticisms of the functionalist theory of stratification.
5 The Registrar-General's classification has been criticised for not dealing adequately with women. Explain this criticism.
6 List arguments for and against the view that a 'new working class' has emerged in Britain.
7 Outline the divisions in the middle classes identified by:
   a) Wright.
   b) Goldthorpe.
8 List: Three possible *causes* of increased rates of social mobility.
   Three possible *consequences* of increased rates of social mobility.

CHAPTER 4 RACE AND ETHNICITY

1 Distinguish race from ethnicity.
2 What are the social characteristics which define an ethnic group?
3 List three effects of racist ideology which have been identified by Marxists.
4 Describe three characteristics of the underclass which Rex and Tomlinson identified in Sparkbrook (Birmingham).
5 Examine the explanations of racial inequality of Westergaard and Resler and Castle and Kosack, and identify:
   a) Two similarities in their views.
   b) Two differences in their views.
6 List different sources from which we acquire our views on the ethnic identity of ourselves and others.
7 List two differences between the New Right and Weberian concepts of an 'underclass'.
8 List two similarities between the New Right and Weberian concepts of an 'underclass'.

CHAPTER 5 GENDER

1 Define:
   Sex.
   Gender.
   Sexuality.
2 'The way in which we perceive women's sexuality is used to justify social control.'
   Explain and illustrate this statement.
   (You may wish to refer to the sections on gender in the chapters on *Religion* and *Deviance*.)
3 What is biological determinism?
   How have sociologists challenged biological determinism?
4 Explain what is meant by the claim that women are a 'reserve army of labour'.
5 Explain how the existence of a gendered labour market can be used to criticise the view that women are a reserve army of labour.
6 List criticisms of Oakley's view that housework is inevitably a negative experience.
   (You may wish to refer to the *Family* chapter.)
7 List criticisms of the view that housework is done exclusively by housewives.
8 How did Parsons explain the division of labour in the family?

CHAPTER 6 AGE

1 Identify the main age groups studied by sociologists.
   Explain why one is the least frequently written about.
2 Explain what is meant by the claim that childhood is a social construction.

3   List arguments for and against the view that children are no longer seen as an economic asset.
4   Explain what is meant by 'age patriarchy'.
5   Identify two sociological explanations of the development of a separate youth culture.
6   Which categories of youth are a) most likely and b) least likely to be studied?
7   Explain the relationship between economic development and the status of old people.
8   Examine the strengths and weaknesses of the view that the old are a disadvantaged minority.

CHAPTER 7 POWER AND POLITICS

1   Briefly explain four reasons why people might be 'deviant' voters.
2   Describe and explain the concepts of:
    a)   Class de-alignment.
    b)   Partisan de-alignment.
3   Outline two changes in the class structure of modern Britain which might affect voting behaviour.
4   Explain the pluralist view that power is dispersed rather than concentrated in the hands of a small minority.
5   Outline Weber's concepts of:
    a)   Power.
    b)   Authority.
6   Describe the 'three faces of power' (S. Lukes).
7   List arguments for and against the view that there is a dominant ideology in modern societies.
8   Contrast the New Right perspective on the state with one other perspective (Marxist, pluralist, elite theory).

CHAPTER 8 WORLD SOCIOLOGY AND DEVELOPMENT

1   Briefly distinguish sociological theories of development from theories of under-development.
2   Explain the following terms:
    Internalist.
    Global.
    Determinist.
    Voluntarist.
3   Outline Parsons' explanation of development.
4   Identify the similarities and differences between dependency theory (A. Gunder Frank) and world systems theory (Wallerstein).
5   a)   Explain two ways in which development can improve the health of a society.
    b)   Explain two ways in which international trade can damage the health of populations of poor countries.
6   List the three kinds of transnational practices described by Sklair.
7   Distinguish international relations from transnational relations.
8   Explain, using examples, what is meant by a global culture.

CHAPTER 9 LOCALITY, COMMUNITY AND URBANISATION

1   List some of the effects of urbanisation on Third World societies.
2   Briefly outline Jewson's stages of urbanisation.
3   Identify and illustrate three ways in which sociologists use the term community.
4   Outline sociological evidence which suggests that urban and rural ways of life are not distinct from each other.
5   According to Rex and Tomlinson, what were the three types of disadvantage experienced by ethnic minorities in the inner city?
6   What is environmentalism?
7   With reference to the inner city, outline two arguments which suggest that locality *does* influence social behaviour.
8   With reference to the inner city, outline two arguments which suggest that locality *does not* influence social behaviour.

CHAPTER 10 THE FAMILY

1   List the four main assumptions of functionalist approaches to the family.
2   Describe the two functions of the family identified by Parsons.
3   Explain the Marxist view that the family 'reproduces labour power'.
4   Outline the New Right view on single-parent families.
5   Give two examples each of:
   a)   How the state supports the family.
   b)   How the state undermines the family.
6   Give three reasons why ethnic groups may have distinctive patterns of family life.
7   According to Goldthorpe, how might British Asian families perceive Western family life?
8   Outline the strengths and weaknesses of feminist approaches to the family.

CHAPTER 11 EDUCATION

1   Outline Parsons' functionalist view of the role of education.
2   Give examples of the 'correspondence' between school and work (Bowles and Gintis).
3   Identify three similarities and three differences between Marxist and functionalist explanations of the role of education in society.
4   Distinguish the formal curriculum from the hidden curriculum.
5   Explain how the hidden curriculum might influence girls' experience of school.
6   List four reasons why sociological studies of the educational performance of ethnic minorities should be treated with caution.
7   Identify and explain two out-of-school factors which might influence educational achievement. (Choose one material factor and one cultural factor.)
8   How have pupil sub-cultures been used to explain success and failure in schools?

CHAPTER 12 WORK

1   How does Parker define:
   a)   Work?
   b)   Leisure?
2   Explain two feminist criticisms of Parker's account of leisure.
3   Explain two Marxist criticisms of Parker's account of leisure.
4   List four reasons why unemployment statistics might be inaccurate.
5   Outline how unemployment affects:
   a)   The unemployed.
   b)   Other members of society.
6   a)   Give one 'optimistic' view of the effects of new technology.
   b)   Give one 'pessimistic' view of the effects of new technology.
7   According to Marxists, what are the causes of alienation at work?
8   How have interactionists criticised the Marxist explanations of alienation?

CHAPTER 13 ORGANISATIONS

1   Briefly explain Michels' 'iron law of oligarchy'.
2   What are the main characteristics of Weber's ideal type of bureaucracy? List them under the two headings used by Littler.
3   Identify three advantages and three disadvantages of bureaucracy.
4   What were the main assumptions of Taylor's theory of scientific management?
5   Outline the main findings of the Hawthorne studies.
6   List three reasons why informal social processes might reduce the efficiency of organisations.
7   List three reasons why informal social processes might improve the efficiency of organisations.
8   Distinguish bureaucratic organisations from post-Fordist organisations.
   (You may wish to refer back to Chapter 12.)

CHAPTER 14 PROFESSIONS

1   Outline the functionalist view of the role of professions in society.
2   Outline the Marxist view of the role of professions in society.
3   How have functionalists explained the high status and rewards achieved by professionals?

4 How have Weberians (such as Parry and Parry) explained the high status and rewards achieved by professionals?

5 'Women are excluded from high-status and highly rewarded professions.' List evidence and arguments for and against this view.

6 Identify three similarities and three differences between professional associations and trades unions.

7 List some of the problems experienced by professionals who work in organisations.

8 Distinguish Marxist and Weberian views on the position of professionals in the class structure of modern societies.
(You may need to turn back to *Social class*, Chapter 3.)

CHAPTER 15 RELIGION

1 List three differences between sects and churches.

2 Briefly define secularisation.

3 How have sociologists tried to measure the extent of secularisation in society?

4 List four reasons for the growth of new religious movements.

5 Explain how the growth of sects can be used as evidence:
   a) *For* the secularisation of society.
   b) *Against* the secularisation of society.

6 Explain arguments which support the view that religion encourages social change.

7 Explain arguments which support the view that religion inhibits social change.

8 Identify the similarities and differences between Marxist and functionalist approaches to the role of religion in society.

CHAPTER 16 THE MASS MEDIA

1 Explain, using examples, how practical or technical considerations might influence the content of 'the news'.

2 List arguments:
   a) *For* the view that the output of the media depends on market forces.
   b) *Against* the view that the output of the media depends on market forces.

3 Distinguish the different Marxist approaches to the media associated with Poulantzas and Miliband.
(You may find it helpful to refer to *Power and politics*, Chapter 7.)

4 Explain the claim that 'the mass media promote a consumerist ideology'.

5 Identify examples of the different ways ethnic minorities are represented in the mass media.

6 Outline the role of the media in the process of deviance amplification.
(You will want to refer to *Deviance*, Chapter 19, before attempting this question.)

7 List the major criticisms of the 'hypodermic syringe' model.

8 Make a list of those theories and studies which portray audiences as homogeneous and passive.

CHAPTER 17 POVERTY, WELFARE AND SOCIAL POLICY

1 Define:
   a) Absolute poverty.
   b) Relative poverty.
   c) Subjective poverty.

2 Explain the concept of the culture of poverty.

3 Identify two weaknesses of the culture of poverty as an explanation of the persistence of poverty.

4 Outline the Marxist approach to the explanation of poverty in capitalist societies.

5 List those explanations which seem to blame poverty on the poor.

6 Outline three ways in which the Welfare State reduces inequality.

7 Outline Marxist criticisms of the role of the Welfare State.

8 Outline New Right criticisms of the role of the Welfare State.

CHAPTER 18 HEALTH

1 Explain briefly how the medical profession has been criticised by:
   a) Feminists.
   b) Marxists.

c) Ivan Illich.

2 List the various individuals and groups who may provide health care. Include both the paid and the unpaid.

3 Outline the evidence which supports the view that social class influences the effective use of health care.

4 Outline the evidence which supports the view that gender influences the effective use of health care.

5 What were the four main explanations of health inequalities examined by the Black Report?

6 Explain the argument that the sick may have contributed to their own ill health.

7 How have Marxists explained inequalities in health chances?

8 Assess the usefulness of the concept of the culture of poverty in explaining health inequalities.
(Refer to *Poverty, welfare and social policy*, Chapter 17.)

CHAPTER 19 DEVIANCE

1 Briefly explain what sociologists mean by 'sub-culture'.

2 How might the concept of sub-culture be used to explain the behaviour of football hooligans?

3 List the theories and studies which have employed the concept of sub-culture to explain deviance.

4 Explain why interactionists study the behaviour of the police and courts.

5 Compare two explanations of the low rate of convictions for 'white-collar' crime.

6 Outline Heidensohn's explanation of the low rates of female crime.

7 What, according to New Left Realism, are the three causes of crime?

8 Explain why New Left Realism has been criticised for supporting racism.

CHAPTER 20 SUICIDE AND OFFICIAL STATISTICS

1 Explain, with examples, Durkheim's four types of suicide.

2 Outline the method used by Durkheim to study suicide.
(Try to include the following terms in your answer:
hypothesis, comparative survey, statistics, suicide rate, secondary data, scientific.)

3 Give two reasons why sociologists are interested in coroners' decisions.

4 Why did Douglas study suicide notes?

5 Define:
   a) Reliability.
   b) Validity.
   c) Representative.
Illustrate each by referring to social statistics.

6 Why do interactionist sociologists study crime statistics?

7 Explain the value of surveys of victims of crime.

8 List reasons why crimes are:
   a) Not reported.
   b) Not recorded.

CHAPTER 21 METHODS

1 What are the main influences on a sociologist's choice of research methods?

2 Identify one method favoured by:
   a) Feminist sociologists.
   b) Interactionist sociologists.
   c) Positivist sociologists.

3 Give three reasons why sociologists use more than one method in a particular study. Illustrate your answer by reference to studies.

4 Distinguish qualitative from quantitative methods.

5 Identify sociological studies and the methods they employed which have been criticised on ethical (i.e. moral) grounds.

6 List the strengths and weaknesses of covert research methods.

7 What is an experiment? Describe the use of the experimental method in two sociological studies.

8   List and illustrate some of the problems experienced by sociologists when they ask questions.
    (You can refer to interviews, postal questionnaires, etc.)

CHAPTER 22 SOCIOLOGICAL THEORIES

1   Briefly explain the differences between structuralist and action perspectives.
2   Briefly explain the differences between consensus and conflict perspectives.
3   List three similarities and three differences between Marxist and functionalist theories.
4   What do symbolic interactionists mean by:
    a)   The self?
    b)   Significant other?
    c)   Generalised other?
5   List three main assumptions of Marxism–feminism.
6   Using examples outline two arguments for and two arguments against the usefulness of New Right perspectives.
7   Distinguish modern society from post-modern society under the following three headings:
    a)   Economic differences.
    b)   Political differences.
    c)   Cultural differences.
8   What are metanarratives?

CHAPTER 23 THE NATURE OF SOCIOLOGY

1   Outline two competing definitions of science.
2   List three practical problems which may arise when sociologists use scientific methods.
3   Why do interactionists reject the use of scientific methods?
4   Why do some sociologists use scientific thinking and methods?
5   Define ideology.
6   List three causes of the lack of objectivity in sociology.
7   With reference to Gouldner and Oakley, explain why value-free sociology may serve the interests of the powerful.
8   With reference to one area of social life, explain how sociology may influence social policy.

INDEX

USING THE INDEX

1   Sociological explanations based on Marxism, Functionalism, Interactionism and Feminism are to be found in nearly all the chapters and are usually identified by clear headings. They are not listed here.

2   The different types of social inequality are discussed in nearly all the chapters. They are listed here under class, gender, ethnicity and age. The list is not exhaustive.

3   Use your sociological understanding to study related concepts. For example you could follow up references to ideology by looking at: false consciousness, ideological state apparatus, legitimation, superstructure, patriarchy, Marxism, Feminism, Abercrombie, Althusser, Marcuse, etc.

book
shops

The Deutsche Nationalbibliothek lists this publication in the Deutsche Nationalbibliografie; detailed bibliographical data are available on the internet at http://dnb.dnb.de

ISBN 978-3-03768-122-0
© 2012 by Braun Publishing AG
www.braun-publishing.ch

1st edition 2012

Selection of projects: Markus S. Braun, Chris van Uffelen
Editorial staff: Antje Bertz, Manuela Roth, Stefanie Templin
Text editing and translation: Judith Vonberg
Translation preface: Geoffrey Steinherz
Art direction: Michaela Prinz

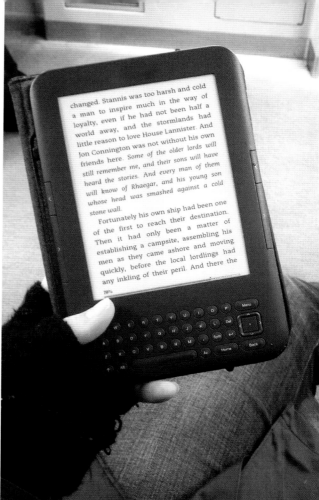

book clubs. Amazon, the American online bookshop founded in 1994, which is constantly creating new market segments and opening up markets, became the leading online shop in Germany in 2009 with 16.7 million customers. In Great Britain, where several large book trade chains filed for bankruptcy over the last few years, amazon already controls more than 30 % of the total book market. Another trend coming from the US is that popular bestsellers (like Harry Potter or fantasy novels) are becoming stock items in department stores and supermarket chains, while self-help literature is now also distributed by pharmacies and health food shops, gas stations or household goods chains.

A Glance into an Uncertain Future

The so-called digital revolution has been in full swing since the beginning of the new millennium. The "virtual book" or electronic book, available on the computer screen, as well as the alternative reading media like reading devices, tablet computers, smartphones and apps are being constantly expanded and improved. The e-book, first presented in 1988, is especially establishing itself in the category of royalty-free literature; in 2007 the Frankfurt Book Fair announced that 30 % of the reference books were also available as e-books.

These new media certainly represent a previously unknown competition for the traditional book market and reading behaviour. Whether one speaks in culturally pessimistic tones of the "death of the classical book trade" or whether and how books and the retail bookshops in conjunction with the new reading media and the online trade can survive remains to be seen.

However, the announcements from the book world in Great Britain from the fall of 2011 are certainly alarming. There, as in most other European countries, the bookshop is viewed as a synonym for culture and education: since 2005 almost 2,000 larger and smaller bookshops were forced to close on the island, with the total number dropping from 4,000 to 2,178 in July 2011. In the process 580 towns lost their bookshops. Many publishers and large book dealers are therefore currently attempting to pursue their traditional book sales in parallel with the new reading media. Another problem for the book trade is the discussion now taking place in many countries about lifting the price maintenance agreement (as was done in Great Britain in 1995). In this discussion the new media are also putting on pressure to ease and liberalize the rules currently in force.

»Every man who knows how to read has it in his power to magnify himself, to multiply the ways in which he exists, to make his life full, significant and interesting. «

Aldous Huxley

Academic Bookstore

Helsinki, Finland

Architect: Alvar Aalto
Owner: Stockmann plc
Year of opening: 1893
Year of opening in current location: 1969
Gross floor area: 5,000 m²
Books offered: extensive selection of non-fiction and fiction literature

The Helsinki flagship store of the Academic Bookstore, one of the oldest and best-known bookstores in Finland, is located in Kirjatalo ("Book Building") and was designed by the famous Finnish architect Alvar Aalto. The bright but stark interior lit by geometric glass skylights in the shape of open books creates a businesslike but attractive atmosphere, enhanced by the sober white marble staircases and balustrade. Inspired by the architecture of Italian piazzas, where people mingle in relaxed surroundings, the interior is not just a space for browsing and buying but a popular venue for cultural events – this is a hub, not just of knowledge, but of social interaction, laughter and friendship. Appearing white and hard at first glance, this is a bookstore that every visitor will quickly warm up to.

Alexis Bookshop & Café

Bratislava, Slovakia

Architect: Martin Jančok/
Plural, Aleš Šedivec/
Totalstudio
Graphic designer: Marcel
Benčik
Year of opening: 2010
Gross floor area: 170 m²
Materials: plywood, wooden
beams
Books offered: literature,
design, esoteric

In a network of firmly established booksellers, it's tough for a small, independent bookshop to stand out from the crowd. This ingeniously designed interior does just that. A flexible space perfect for hosting readings, projections, workshops and even minor concerts, the new Alexis Bookshop & Café in Bratislava is a triumph of imagination, functionality and aesthetic enjoyment. The store's two levels are connected with cascades that serve as auditorium space during public events and allow customers to sit, read, relax and chat in regular opening hours. New titles and bestsellers are prominently but not intrusively displayed at several mobile stands, and the store's two focal points – a checkout and a coffee bar – are placed simply at either end of the longitudinal space. The complex design has been realized with the utmost simplicity, enabling visitors to enjoy the multiple possibilities of this unique space.

Bücherbogen

Berlin, Germany

Owners: Ruthild and Wanda Spangenberg
Year of opening: 1980
Gross floor area: 500 m²
Books offered: architecture, art, photography, design, film, theater, fashion

More than thirty years ago, Bücherbogen am Savigny-platz GmbH was established in a former car repair shop in the massive brick viaduct underneath the Berlin S-Bahn. Renowned for its broad and in-depth selection of books on the arts, from architecture to fashion and film, the store was founded by Ruthild Spangenberg and became the nucleus of the continuing transformation of the Savignyplatz district into a premium location. The expansive and light-filled interior is a pleasant surprise for first time visitors, many of whom are artists or booklovers attracted from all over the world by the store's superb reputation. It is all too easy to get lost among the more than 25,000 titles on display, but it is hard to see how any visitor could regret an afternoon spent browsing these shelves.

Cook & Book

Brussels, Belgium

Owners: Déborah Drion, Cédric Legein & Albert Michiel
Year of opening: 2007
Gross floor area: 1,500 m²
Books offered: comics, travel, kids, fine art, music, lifestyle, literature, cooking, English books

At once a bookstore, a restaurant and a gastronomic shop, Cook & Book offers a fresh approach to books, mingling the cultural and the convivial in a single eclectic space. An array of colorful books dangles from the black ceiling and line the black bookshelves in the literature section, vibrant interventions on a dark canvas. Whimsical lightshades are juxtaposed with grand bookcases in red and black, creating a playful if slightly macabre atmosphere. According to its designers, the 1,500 square meter store offers 1,500 reasons to visit and be astounded – it is not hard to agree.

Diorama Bookshop

Rivoli, Italy

Architect: Andrea Bella
Year of opening: 2008
Gross floor area: 110 m²
Materials: wood, laminate floor
Focus of books offered: literature

Reading is an adventure, or so the architects of Diorama Bookshop in Rivoli, Italy believe. Accordingly, they designed the interior as a vast forest, the context of numerous fictional adventures in books throughout the ages. The pale wooden display stands furnishing the library were born out of the idea of books as leaves on the trees of the forest, harmonizing perfectly with the darker color of the outer walls to evoke the various shades of a forest setting. Positioned at the center of each exhibitor, chairs upholstered in red fabric invite visitors to take a seat at the center of their very own fantasy world. Imagination, innovation and functionality combine in radical new ways in this fantastical space, where the real world beyond its walls seems to simply disappear.

El Ateneo Grand Splendid

Buenos Aires, Argentina

Architect: Architect Fernando
Manzone
Collaborators: Daniel Brandi-
marte, Mara Fernandez
Year of opening: 2000
Gross floor area: 3,390 m²
Books offered: all types of
books available

Built as a theater in 1903, this bookstore in Buenos Aires represents a triumph of integration – old and new, luxury and simplicity, functionality and aesthetics are juxtaposed in perfect harmony. Major remodeling and restoration work was involved in the most recent redesign of the interior, which saw the magnificent main fresco in the dome restored, originally painted by the Italian painter Nazareno Orlandi. This grandiose celebra-

tion of the past is juxtaposed with the embrace of more contemporary features, including a modern coffee shop, a display of CDs and DVDs in the expansive central hall, and a basement dedicated to children's literature. Since its opening, El Ateneo Grand Splendid has become a meeting point for writers, artists and the general public and has attracted acclaim from around the globe – the story of this historic space is very far from finished.

E'Stile

Rome, Italy

Owners: Pino Vastarella/
Roberto Stermieri
Year of opening: 2007
Gross floor area: 160 m²
Books offered: fashion,
design, architecture,
photography, graphics

This new two-story concept store is a paradise for book and art lovers alike. The vast assortment of beautiful books and collectable items is housed in a stimulating wonderland that fuses a contemporary art gallery with a bookstore. Downstairs, the fashion room displays an array of trend books and magazines, indispensable for designers, students and lovers of fashion. Adjacent is a room used for a range of events, meetings and art exhibitions – a space where books, people, art and ideas can interact freely. Books on design, architecture and photography are displayed upstairs in a large space full of rich surprises for the curious visitor. An eclectic space, fusing cultures and traditions, this is a bookstore that cannot fail to delight, whatever your taste or interest.

» A room **without books** is like a body **without a soul.** «

Marcus Tullius Cicero

Foldaway Bookshop

London, United Kingdom

Architect: Campaign
Year of completion: 2010
Materials: cardboard
Books offered: latest high-quality publications and the most coveted architecture classics

As the digital revolution advances, the temporary Foldaway Bookshop was designed to celebrate the art form of the printed publication, welcoming visitors during the 2010 London Festival of Architecture. With a bespoke interior designed like a giant book and graphics created by design studio Campaign, the walls, shelving and sales counter were constructed entirely from cardboard and designed to be economical, recyclable and supremely flexible, allowing for a range of display options for a variety of events. Designed in three weeks and constructed in three days from just 58 sheets of cardboard, Foldaway Bookshop represents the ultimate in waste reduction and thriftiness. No compromises, however, were made on style – the Flexible Love Chair and Eurban's Carbon Cube provide modish, comfortable seating from which visitors can admire the remarkable interior.

Haymon Bookstore
Innsbruck, Austria

Owner: Markus Hatzer
Year of opening: 2000
Gross floor area: 120 m²
Materials: black floor-to-ceiling book shelves, mirror (ceiling)
Books offered: literature

Peering through the two large display windows, the curious passerby is treated to an astounding view of almost the entire store. A vast black canvas greets them, upon which books are displayed, perfectly lit and undoubtedly the celebrated central elements in this otherwise understated design. A glorious, almost hypnotic array of colorful books lines the floor-to-ceiling shelves and is reflected in the mirrored ceiling, generating a staggering illusion of vastness. Drawn to the vibrant products, the visitor is distracted only briefly by the uniqueness of this retail space before being overwhelmed once more by the books themselves which, unlike the sober interior design, refuse to be overlooked.

Heywood Hill

London, United Kingdom

Owner: the Duke of Devonshire
Year of opening: 1936
Gross floor area: 140 m²
Books offered: new, second-hand and antiquarian – classic English literature, travel, architecture

It was once declared in Vanity Fair that "For bibliophiles, heaven is a shop called Heywood Hill". An old-fashioned literary treasure trove, the shop is laid out on two floors of an elegant Mayfair townhouse. Part literary clubhouse offering luxury service, the shop boasts more than 3,000 loyal customers who use the renowned store to curate their reading and collecting. The design is modest, understated, allowing quality customer service to take center stage – from an exclusive first edition to a wall of beautiful books inviting an afternoon of browsing, Heywood Hill prides itself on its continued and well-deserved reputation as a paradise for book lovers. It is perhaps no surprise that The Spectator celebrated the shop as "a pilgrimage site for the well-read".

Hugendubel
Stuttgart, Germany

Architect: Matthias Franz
Innenarchitekten GmbH
Light Planning: Peter Andres
Year of opening: 2008
Gross floor area: 4,000 m²
Materials: fabric (floor),
perforated metal (ceiling),
luminous ceiling/ellipses,
printed glass banister, spe-
cially designed furniture
Books offered: general fiction
and non-fiction, audiobooks

With 4,000 square meters over three floors to play with, Matthias Franz architects were in their element in the design of this Hugendubel flagship store in Stutt-gart's city center. Color, shape and texture combine in ever new and unexpected combinations to surprise and captivate each and every visitor. Openings in the ceil-ings and floors offer glimpses onto other levels, inviting customers to explore. Highlights include the elliptical luminous ceilings, brought alive by a choreographed play of color and light dancing over the surface, the famed Hugendubel reader islands, and the oversized dice in the children's book section. The senses are stimulated, the mind engaged and human creativity inspired in this exhilarating interior.

Kid's Republic

Beijing, China

Architect: SAKO architects
Lighting design: Masahide Kakudate
Year of opening: 2005
Gross floor area: 166 m²
Materials: carpet, microcrystalline stone, MDF oil paint

This vast, eclectic space invites children to roam, play, read and sate their curious minds with vibrant colors, intriguing shapes and, of course, an array of books. Colored ribbon surrounds and encircles the space, capturing the young visitors' imaginations and encouraging exploration. The first floor houses an event room, where rainbow colors pulsate with energy, while 100-meter long strands of ribbon, twisting through the space in playful curving lines, invite children up to the picture bookstore on the second floor. There are no ordered bookshelves and seating areas here – instead, children are encouraged to use this paradise of play and learning entirely as they wish.

Korn & Berg

Nuremberg, Germany

Owners: Irene and Thomas Kistner
Year of opening: 1531
Year of opening in current location: 1844
Gross floor area: 110 m²
Books offered: literature, children, regional & local, academic titles, travel
Special features: exhibitions of contemporary artists in Nuremberg

Founded in 1531, this is Germany's oldest bookshop and a living tribute to the perseverance of those who have traded books within its walls over the last five centuries. Destroyed twice by flood and once during the Second World War, it has existed in numerous incarnations. In 1952, it was rebuilt completely, and a redesign in 2006 has restored the interior to a glorious, yet humble space, mindful of its past but yet ideally conceived for a contemporary clientele. Presented as a traditional library in nutwood and cliffstone, the ceiling bearing a Renaissance-style portrait in muted tones, the store entices visitors into the past, inviting them to browse in the quiet, leisured surroundings of this ancient house of wisdom.

Kubrick Bookshop & Café

Beijing, China

Architect: One Plus Partnership Ltd
Year of opening: 2010
Gross floor area: 320 m²
Materials: timber floor, stainless steel, metal, wallpaper, fabric, cement boards, Corian, ceramic tiles, green powder coating finished

Seeking to reconnect Beijing's history with the city's vibrant modernity, One Plus Partnership found inspiration in the ancient Chinese concept of "Five Elements" – wood, fire, earth, metal and water. The neutral gray concrete space is interrupted by eye-catching green joinery that functions as bookshelves, cashier counters and storage units, representing the element of wood. A curved strip of display cabinets suspended from the ceiling echoes Beijing's hanging walkways, while the wooden elements are designed like stacks of books, evoking knowledge accumulated through generations of this city's inhabitants. These appeals to a life beyond the bookshop's walls and beyond the here and now, encouraging visitors to communicate with each other and with their past, are complemented by the homely ambience of the cozy café area.

Libreria Palazzo Roberti

Bassano del Grappa, Italy

Owner: Manfrotto family
Year of opening: 1991
Year of opening in current location: 1998
Gross floor area: 830 m²
Books offered: all kinds except antiquarian and school books

Libreria Palazzo Roberti, one of Europe's most beautiful bookshops, is located in the prestigious Via Jacopo da Ponte, in the historic centre of Bassano del Grappa in the Venetian region. The palazzo, which today accommodates the bookshop, was built in 1663 and hosted artists and writers such as Antonio Canova and Giovanni Poleni. Grand frescoes by Giovanni Scajaro (a student of Gianbattista Tiepolo) decorate the main floor illustrating

events from the lives of Marco Antonio and Cleopatra. The vast assortment of books, the high-quality dark wooden furniture, the natural light pouring through the large majestic doors and windows, and the soft lighting provided by the beautiful Louis Poulsen lamps create a comfortable atmosphere where guests immediately feel at home.

Livraria Cultura

São Paulo, Brazil

Architect: Fernando Brandão
arquitetura + design
Visual artist: Carlos Matuk
Year of opening: 2007
Gross floor area: 4,200 m²
Materials: carpet tiles, wood,
steel structures
Books offered: all kinds

Seeking to revolutionize the concept of bookstore design, the designers of Livraria Cultura have fully integrated the vast interior with its urban surroundings, linking the fictional, often inward world of books with the real world beyond in a thrilling and innovative dialogue. Large open spaces allow visitors to wander and browse uninhibitedly, while quirky design aspects such as a sinuous wooden sculpture snaking through the air, a checkerboard floor and colorful beanbags ensure that no customer will ever be bored. Under the central ramp lies an open space with plasma-screen televisions showing daily information about the store – this is a place where contemporary technology and traditional books are launched into an exciting new and mutually enhancing relationship.

Livraria da Vila

São Paulo, Brazil

Architect: Isay Weinfeld
Year of opening: 2007
Gross floor area: 790 m²
Materials: concrete (floor), ceramics, stone, precast concrete panels, glass, stainless steel, acrylic wares

The Livraria da Vila is the result of the refurbishment of a two-story house, built on a very narrow, deep plot in São Paulo. Seeking design solutions that would enable customers to engage with the space and the products in the most enjoyable way, Isay Weinfeld chose an open plan layout, embracing the limitless possibilities for circulation and design that this allows. Revolving bookcases at the store's entrance welcome visitors into an intimate interior featuring low ceilings, dark tones and indirect lighting. Shelves of books cover the walls from floor to ceiling, while comfortable chairs and couches scattered through the store encourage visitors to sit and browse what seems like an infinite range of printed material.

Lukabuka

Riga, Latvia

Owners: Brigita Bula, Ieva Zibarte, Inguna Elere
Year of opening: 2009
Year of opening in current location: 2010 (Lukabuka Opera), 2011 (Lukabuka Riija)
Gross floor area: 20 m²
Books offered: architecture, design, fashion, urban studies, visual and performing arts, gastronomy

As the first specialized architecture and design-themed concept bookshop in Riga, Lukabuka has set a radical new agenda for Latvian design. Starting in 2009 with a small office shop at the home of the Latvian Artists Union, Lukabuka was soon invited to create a music, book and design store at the Latvian National Opera before unveiling a new interior one year later at the Latvian design and lifestyle concept store Riija. Designed as monochrome borderless spaces within existing structures, these stores offer a clean, uncluttered canvas for displaying high-quality books on design and architecture. The store itself embodies the very best in Latvian design, incorporating beautiful wooden birdcages, attractive concrete flowerpots and furniture made by local designers.

» Books are the ships which pass through the vast sea of time. «

Francis Bacon

Munro's Books

Victoria, Canada

Owner: James Munro
Year of opening: 1963
Year of opening in current location: 1984
Books offered: general books with an emphasis on literary fiction, history, current affairs, and children's books

Originating in 1963 as a modest paperback bookshop, Munro's Books now occupies a landmark location in the heart of Victoria's Old Town. This fine neo-classical building was designed by Thomas Hooper in 1909, the architect of many of the Royal Bank of Canada's finest commercial and public buildings. Its beautiful 7,3 meter coffered ceiling and magnificent Corinthian columns closely echo the great library of Ephesus built by the

Romans. When Jim Munro bought the building, which had been tastelessly modernized in the 1950s, he set to work restoring it to its former glory. In the space of just eight weeks, the store was refurbished and ready for business and has since received two heritage awards. Large fabric banners by artist Carole Sabiston depict the four seasons, while the smaller pieces are inspired by classic works of literature.

NGVI Bookshop

Melbourne, Australia

Architect: Tandem Design Studio with Meme Design
Year of opening: 2008
Gross floor area: 600 m²
Materials: lacquered plywood, Tasmanian oak, wool felts, bluestone
Books offered: adult's and children's art and design books

This striking new bookshop, embedded within one of Melbourne's most established institutions, the NGV International, offers an entirely unique retail experience. A porous shop front – a "sticky edge" – presents curated retail objects as if they were artworks, inviting customers to enter the shop along carefully managed runways and linger within the central reading room space. The main sales counter has been divided into five pods, break-

ing down the barrier between staff and customers. The neutral color palette is based on black and white overlaid with oak and a number of fabrics highlighting various merchandize zones. Felt cushions and multimedia touch screens mounted on the reading tables tempt visitors to linger and to browse the store's printed and electronic offerings.

Orell Füssli Bookshop

Bern, Switzerland

Architect: Roomplan
Owner: Orell Füssli Buchhandlungs AG
Year of opening: 2008
Gross floor area: 1,600 m²
Books offered: fiction, non-fiction, children and adolescents
Special features: audiobooks, DVDs, software, children's corner, French books, café

Located in the Westside shopping mall in Bern designed by Daniel Libeskind in 2008, this bookstore makes an architectural statement that equals that of its surroundings. Curved bookshelves – the key element in Roomplan's design of this three-story interior – draw the eye and guide the customer into the heart of the store. A spiral stair constructed from 50 tons of steel built elegantly around a glass elevator provides access to the upper floors where customers can enjoy a superb view of the shopping mall. Just one among several seating areas, a stunning 13 meter couch by deSede – the longest couch in Switzerland – invites visitors to linger, browse and relax in this highly functional, supremely sophisticated space.

Papasotiriou Bookstore

Athens, Greece

Architect: Emmanouil Kolokythas/Strange Attractors
Year of opening: 2005
Gross floor area: 869 m²
Materials: carpet tiles, wood, steel structures
Books offered: architecture, philosophy, literature, poetry, science

Conceived as a modern temple of knowledge and insight, the interior of the Papasotiriou Bookstore in Athens pays homage to the city's renowned literary heritage while welcoming modern visitors into a wholly contemporary space. Seeking to open a dialogue between the urban world outside the store and the playground of knowledge within, the designers chal-

lenged and redefined traditional concepts of interior and exterior. Illustrations of artworks from books adorn the walls, plunging the visitor into a glorious fictional world. Materials have been carefully selected to create a cozy, intimate atmosphere that invites daydreaming, before releasing the visitor back into the world of the real, filled with the refreshing inspiration of fiction.

Papercup Store

Beirut, Lebanon

Architect: FaR Architects in collaboration with Karim Chaya
Owner: Rania Naufal
Year of opening: 2009
Books offered: art, design, architecture, photography

Located in the Mar Mikhael neighborhood of Beirut, an area traditionally known for local craftsmanship, Papercupstore has a highly individualized approach to selling books that has attracted an army of devoted book lovers, from tourists to artists, journalists to librarians. The walls of the tiny space are covered with shelves, their contents neatly arranged into books on photography, architecture and contemporary art, as well as comics and stationary.

A sliding ladder and Victorian tiles lend an idiosyncratic touch to the otherwise neutral décor. As a regular venue for book or magazine launches and with a permanent coffee shop serving homemade cakes, it is no wonder that this store has become something of a local, even a national treasure.

Pro qm

Berlin, Germany

Owners: Jesko Fezer, Katja Reichard, Axel John Wieder
Year of opening: 1999
Year of opening in current location: 2007
Gross floor area: 120 m²
Books offered: art, architecture, urban studies, design, philosophy, fashion, film, music, theory
Special features: book presentations, lectures, exhibitions, concerts, etc. taking place on a regular basis

Founded in 1999 by Jesko Fezer, Katja Reichard and Axel J. Wieder, Pro qm Bookshop now resides in a late 1920s building originally designed by the office of modernist architect Hanz Poelzig and redesigned by the Berlin-based architects ifau and Jesko Fezer. Trading in books on art and architecture as well as politics and economics, the store itself is a testament to the sparse beauty and sophistication of contemporary design. With its clean white walls, slender gray display structures and subtle lighting, the interior represents a blank canvas, just waiting to be filled with the vibrant colors of the books themselves, the centerpiece of this simple, yet elegant interior. It comes as no surprise to hear that Pro qm was awarded the form Award for Best Design Bookstore in 2006.

Project Space

Vancouver, Canada

Owner: OCW Arts &
Publishing Foundation
Year of opening: 2011
Gross floor area: 42 m²
Books offered: art, design,
literature

As the possibilities inherent to digital space become increasingly infinite, the roles of physical and print spaces are being redefined. Project Space, an artist-run center operating as a project space, bookshop, publisher, programming space and studio, examines, challenges and supports this redefinition process. The bookshop/project space uses white to reflect a gallery setting, featuring accents of metal and raw wood to add warmth. Shelves constructed simply from wooden shipping pallets cover the main retail wall, while murals by alternating guest artists decorate the one by the front window, catching the eye of passersby and inviting them to enter. An antique table found in the building's basement sits in the center of the room – a quirky addition to this otherwise contemporary space.

{ prologue }

books-stationery

{ prologue } / prəʊ.lɒg / pronunciation [proh-lawg, -log] not

Prologue
Singapore, Singapore

Architect: Ministry of Design
Year of opening: 2009
Gross floor area: 1,550 m²
Materials: black tiles, cement screed, engineered timber strip, epoxy paint finish (floor), textured spray, timber laminate (walls)

Located in ION Orchard, Singapore's premier luxury mall, Ministry of Design's concept bookstore re-imagines and updates the conventional bookstore experience with the creation of the new-to-market brand Prologue. A central spine, curving sinuously through the bookstore, organizes the various zones and spaces, making navigation effortless and enjoyable. To enhance visual distinction, each book zone is crowned with a color-coded perforated metal canopy. Experienced as a collective, the eight canopies create a dynamic ceiling-scape that is both functional (guiding users between zones) and aesthetically stunning. A striking installation at the entrance starring a Godzilla-inspired creature unpacking books amongst a cityscape of packing boxes represents the store's enjoyable juxtaposition of ingenuity and eccentricity.

Rizzoli Bookstore

New York, USA

Year of opening: 1964
Year of opening in current location: 1985
Gross floor area: 409 m²
Books offered: art, architecture, photography, fashion, interior design, Italian, French, Spanish, and English literature

Designed in the French Classical style by Randolph Almiroty for Sohmer Piano & Co., Rizzoli Bookstore is housed in a six-story townhouse constructed in 1919 on West 57th Street just off Fifth Avenue in New York City. On the exterior, a massive stone archway frames a delicately patterned cast iron and glass entrance. The entire façade achieves a severe and refined classicism that continues in the interior, where cast iron chandeliers, ornately decorated vaulting, and a luminous Diocletian window create a tranquil oasis for booklovers amidst the hustle of Midtown Manhattan. The building's interior was restored for Rizzoli Bookstore in 1985 by the noted New York architectural firm of Hardy Holzman Pfeiffer Associates.

» So many books,
so little time. «

Frank Zappa

Selexyz Dominicanen

Maastricht, The Netherlands

Architect: Merkx & Girod
Owner: Procures Bussum
Year of opening: 2006
Gross floor area: 1,110 m²
Books offered: literature, art, science, law, children, cook, English books, etc.
Special features: reading spectacles, postcards, calenders, journals, (international) newspapers

This 13th-century Gothic church in the center of Maastricht lost its ecclesiastical function in 1796 and has since served variously as a stable for horses, a concert hall and the setting for Christmas markets. Now, with the installation of Selexyz Dominicanen bookstore in its cavernous space, the church has been restored to its full splendor. To maintain the spectacular view of the height of the church, the store's architects designed a steel a-centric "book tower" over two levels. The building's stunning ceiling frescoes dating from 1619 can be viewed and enjoyed from the second floor. It is not only the ancient architecture that astounds the store's visitors, however – with 40,000 books and 125 events held annually, this is an astonishing bookstore in a most remarkable setting.

Shakespeare and Company

Paris, France

Owner: Sylvia Whitman
Year of opening: 1951
Gross floor area: 120 m²
Books offered: literature, essays, history, poetry, graphic novels
Special features: new, second hand and rare books

Opened by George Whitman in 1951, Shakespeare and Company bookstore in Paris has become a home for writers and readers from all around the world, growing from its humble beginnings as a refuge for post-war expatriates into a world-renowned literary institution. Upon entering the store, you find a wishing well, where visitors throw coins as offerings to penniless Parisian writers. The floor is made of gravestones stolen from the Montparnasse cemetery, and tucked away in a romantic corner is the Poetry Cabinet. Everywhere are endless shelves and precarious piles of books. Climbing the red staircase to the first floor, you reach the children's section with the Mirror of Love, its glass covered with improvized notes containing tender messages.

Shibuya Booksellers

Tokyo, Japan

Architect: Hiroshi Nakamura & NAP Architects
Owner: Seita Fukui
Year of opening: 2008
Books offered: literature, design, lifestyle, entertainment, graphic novels
Special features: clothes, bags, stationeries and food

Established in Tokyo in 2008, Shibuya Publishing and Booksellers (SPBS) represents a radical departure from the traditional process of creating and selling books. Incorporating a publishing house and a bookstore, this independent enterprise both makes and sells books. Inspired by traditional bakeries where goods are dreamt up, produced and sold under the same roof, Nap Archi-

tects decided to apply the same successful model to the book industry. Finished books are displayed alongside half-conceived, half-written or half-printed volumes. The book production industry is revealed as a dynamic, organic business molded and influenced by the book lovers and intellectuals who gather in this cutting-edge space.

Strand Bookstore

New York, USA

Owners: Fred Bass and Nancy Bass Wyden
Year of opening: 1927
Year of opening in current location: late 1950s
Gross floor area: 315 m²
Books offered: used, new and rare books, literature, art, non-fiction

Until recently, Greenwich Village was the place where artists lived and congregated in cafés and bars discussing their latest accomplishments, ideas and creations. It was in this climate that the historical Book Row on lower Broadway was born. In 1927, Ben Bass began the legendary Strand Bookstore, which moved to its location at Broadway and 12th Street thirty years later. Still owned and run by the Bass family, the store has expanded to 5,110 square meters, holding an astonishing 29 kilometers of books on four levels. The Rare Books department now fills a whole level and is also a prime Manhattan location for book readings, screenings, receptions and gatherings. The Art department has become one of the largest in the world, and the store remains a haven of unexpected treasures and architectural curiosities.

Tanum Karl Johan

Oslo, Norway

Architect: Jarmund/Vigsnæs AS
Interior design: Riss AS
Lighting design: Linda Knoph Vigsnæs/Lysstoff
Year of opening: 2011
Gross floor area: 750 m²
Materials: plywood, Hi-Macs, epoxy based terrazzo with green glass, aluminum mirror, aluminum paint, green paint
Books offered: all kinds

Oslo's oldest bookstore has recently undergone a major and impressive renovation inspired by the slogan "bookstore for the future". Rather than sleek digital technology and installations, however, the architects chose to emphasize rough materials and the tactile presence of the printed books themselves in a bold endeavor to unite the building's glorious heritage with contemporary, even futuristic design elements. The dark green ceiling minimizes the visibility of the technical installations and generates a tranquil atmosphere, while silver painted columns and angular pine furniture add dashes of color and vibrancy. Inspired by concepts of stability and flexibility, calm and refreshment, JVA have created a store that will attract all generations of customers and readers, both now and in the years to come.

Taschen Store Beverly Hills

Beverly Hills, USA

Architect: Philippe Starck
Collages: Albert Oehlen
Year of opening: 2003
Books offered: art, architecture & aphrodisia

The elegant opulence and flamboyance that exudes from Philippe Starck's Taschen store in Beverly Hills has impressed designers and book lovers worldwide. Based around the design concept of a "Sistine Chapel", it represents a radical modernization of that historic building with its communal reading area, black leather banquette in the lounge area, purple mirrors, handmade glass walls and plasma TV screens. A luxury version of a traditional European wood-paneled library, the store's walls are lined in American walnut featuring artworks by Albert Oehlen and bronze-veneered fixtures. Warmth and sophistication combine in an orgy of extravagant luxury that is perfectly suited to the array of artistic and erotic tomes on display.

The Last Bookstore

Los Angeles, USA

Owners: Josh and Heidi Spencer
Year of opening: 2009
Year of opening in current location: 2011
Gross floor area: 1,486 m²
Books offered: all kinds (90% used, 10% new)
Special features: used LP shop, coffee shop, events venue

The starting point for The Last Bookstore's new design was the 1914 building that was to house the renovated shop. Pondering the giant columns and detailed ceiling, the designers were inspired to create an interior evocative of the late Victorian and early 20th-century period. The store's name and the declining state of the printed book industry further encouraged the owner to celebrate a past when bookshops thrived by absorbing century-old architectural influences. Juxtaposed with an apocalyptic theme inspired by the very same fears of the death of the printed book, these influences contribute to a spectacular interior that could be described as a retro-futurist steampunk aesthetic – a timeless fantasy world where visitors are taken on a journey beyond their everyday lives.

Van Alen Books

New York, USA

Architect: LOT-EK
Year of opening: 2011
Gross floor area: 33 m²
Materials: recycled wood doors, bolts, rods, cables, recycled wood planks, paint
Books offered: architecture and design

LOT-EK was commissioned by the Van Alen Institute to conceive and design Van Alen Books, a new architecture and design bookstore and public reading room located at the organization's headquarters in Manhattan's Flat-iron District. Inviting the public to linger and browse, the store features an imposing four-meter seating platform crafted from a stack of 70 recycled doors, which ascend to create a stunning amphitheater overlooking 22nd Street through glazed storefront windows. Sourced from Build It Green! NYC, a nonprofit supplier of salvaged building materials, the solid wood doors form a triangular installation evoking the steps of Times Square's TKTS booth. This highly visible and entirely unique storefront space is New York City's only book emporium and gathering place devoted entirely to architecture and design publications.